A pioneer, leading scholar, excellent mentor and colleague, and a good friend, Michael Leifer was one of the most important figures in the study of the international politics of Southeast Asia in the twentieth century. In this volume, several of his eminent students and colleagues critically engage Michael's key ideas and contributions, exploring their contemporary relevance to changing regional realities and ongoing scholarly work on Southeast Asia. In addition to being an excellent tribute, the essays in this volume are an important read for all scholars and students working on Southeast Asia.

Muthiah Alagappa; Director, East-West Center Washington

The book *Order and Security in Southeast Asia* is a worthy tribute to the intellectual achievements of the late Michael Leifer. Leifer brought to the study of Southeast Asian international relations the clear-eyed realism of the "English School" with its focus on order in a framework of a nuanced balance of power. In this volume edited by two of his last PhD students at the London School of Economics, other students, colleagues, and friends place his contributions to the analysis of the regional order in Southeast Asia in contemporary theoretical and policy settings. The result demonstrates the lasting relevance of Leifer's body of work to our understanding of the Southeast Asian regional international system.

Donald Weatherbee; Donald S. Russell Distinguished Professor Emeritus at the University of South Carolina, and author of *International Relations in Southeast Asia: The Struggle for Autonomy*

Michael Leifer's erudition and mentorship shaped a generation, not only of scholars who study Southeast Asia but of practitioners who craft policy for Southeast Asian nations. This reason alone is sufficient to warrant this handy and timely volume of essays that dissect Leifer's understanding and articulation of the international relations of Southeast Asia. In this the book succeeds brilliantly. I highly recommend it.

Tommy Koh; Chairman, Institute of Policy Studies (Singapore) and Ambassador-at-Large

Order and Security in Southeast Asia

Michael Leifer, who died in 2001, was one of the leading scholars of Southeast Asian international relations. He was hugely influential through his extensive writings and his contacts with people in academia, government and business in the region. He also inspired many students from Southeast Asia and beyond, an impressively large number of whom are now leading figures in their own right.

This book of essays, compiled by two of Michael Leifer's last PhD students, explores and reflects on the key themes of his work on Southeast Asia. In it Leifer's former students, colleagues and friends come together to discuss notions of order and the balance of power, security and regional institutions, maritime law and foreign policy-making processes, all of which preoccupied him during a career that spanned over 40 years. Leifer was one of the first scholars to consider the impact of maritime security and to realise that the interests of China potentially conflict with those of Southeast Asian states. In the area of foreign and security policy-making, Leifer emphasized the importance of balance of power calculations and the thirst for security expressed by small states.

A scholarly and personal volume devoted to Michael Leifer's vast contributions to the discipline of international relations, *Order and Security in Southeast Asia* is a must-read for students and scholars specializing in the region.

Joseph Chinyong Liow is Assistant Professor at the Institute of Defence and Strategic Studies, Nanyang Technological University, Singapore. His research interests include Muslim politics and international politics of the Southeast Asian region, and his publications include *Politics of Indonesia-Malaysia Relations; One Kin, Two Nations* (RoutledgeCurzon, 2004)

Ralf Emmers is Assistant Professor at the Institute of Defence and Strategic Studies, Nanyang Technological University, Singapore. His research interests lie in security studies, international institutions in the Asia-Pacific and the international relations of Southeast Asia. He is the author of *Cooperative Security and the Balance of Power in ASEAN and the ARF* (RoutledgeCurzon, 2003).

Routledge Politics in Asia series

Formerly edited by Michael Leifer

London School of Economics

ASEAN and the Security of Southeast Asia
Michael Leifer

China's Policy towards Territorial Disputes
The case of the South China Sea islands
Chi-kin Lo

India and Southeast Asia
Indian perceptions and policies
Mohammed Ayoob

Gorbachev and Southeast Asia
Leszek Buszynski

Indonesian Politics under Suharto
Order, development and pressure for change
Michael R.J. Vatikiotis

The State and Ethnic Politics in Southeast Asia
David Brown

The Politics of Nation Building and Citizenship in Singapore
Michael Hill and Lian Kwen Fee

Politics in Indonesia
Democracy, Islam and the ideology of tolerance
Douglas E. Ramage

Communitarian Ideology and Democracy in Singapore
Beng-Huat Chua

The Challenge of Democracy in Nepal
Louise Brown

Japan's Asia Policy
Wolf Mendl

The International Politics of the Asia-Pacific, 1945–1995
Michael Yahuda

Political Change in Southeast Asia
Trimming the banyan tree
Michael R.J. Vatikiotis

Hong Kong
China's challenge
Michael Yahuda

Korea versus Korea
A case of contested legitimacy
B.K. Gills

Taiwan and Chinese Nationalism
National identity and status in international society
Christopher Hughes

Managing Political Change in Singapore
The elected presidency
Kevin Y.L. Tan and Lam Peng Er

Islam in Malaysian Foreign Policy
Shanti Nair

Political Change in Thailand
Democracy and participation
Kevin Hewison

The Politics of NGOs in Southeast Asia
Participation and protest in the Philippines
Gerard Clarke

Malaysian Politics Under Mahathir
R.S. Milne and Diane K. Mauzy

Indonesia and China
The politics of a troubled relationship
Rizal Sukma

Arming the Two Koreas
State, capital and military power
Taik-young Hamm

Engaging China
The management of an emerging power
Edited by Alastair Iain Johnston and Robert S. Ross

Singapore's Foreign Policy
Coping with vulnerability
Michael Leifer

Philippine Politics and Society in the Twentieth Century
Colonial legacies, post-colonial trajectories
Eva-Lotta E. Hedman and John T. Sidel

Constructing a Security Community in Southeast Asia
ASEAN and the problem of regional order
Amitav Acharya

Monarchy in South East Asia
The faces of tradition in transition
Roger Kershaw

Korea After the Crash
The politics of economic recovery
Brian Bridges

The Future of North Korea
Edited by Tsuneo Akaha

The International Relations of Japan and South East Asia
Forging a new regionalism
Sueo Sudo

Power and Change in Central Asia
Edited by Sally N. Cummings

The Politics of Human Rights in Southeast Asia
Philip Eldridge

Political Business in East Asia
Edited by Edmund Terence Gomez

Singapore Politics under the People's Action Party
Diana K. Mauzy and R.S. Milne

Media and Politics in Pacific Asia
Duncan McCargo

Japanese Governance
Beyond Japan Inc
Edited by Jennifer Amyx and Peter Drysdale

China and the Internet
Politics of the digital leap forward
Edited by Christopher R. Hughes and Gudrun Wacker

Challenging Authoritarianism in Southeast Asia
Comparing Indonesia and Malaysia
Edited by Ariel Heryanto and Sumit K. Mandal

Cooperative Security and the Balance of Power in ASEAN and the ARF
Ralf Emmers

Islam in Indonesian Foreign Policy
Rizal Sukma

Media, War and Terrorism
Responses from the Middle East and Asia
Edited by Peter Van der Veer and Shoma Munshi

China, Arms Control and Nonproliferation
Wendy Frieman

Communitarian Politics in Asia
Edited by Chua Beng Huat

East Timor, Australia and Regional Order
Intervention and its aftermath in Southeast Asia
James Cotton

Domestic Politics, International Bargaining and China's Territorial Disputes
Chien-peng Chung

Democratic Development in East Asia
Becky Shelley

International Politics of the Asia-Pacific since 1945
Michael Yahuda

Asian States
Beyond the developmental perspective
Edited by Richard Boyd and Tak-Wing Ngo

Civil Life, Globalization, and Political Change in Asia
Organizing between family and state
Edited by Robert P. Weller

Realism and Interdependence in Singapore's Foreign Policy
Narayanan Ganesan

Party Politics in Taiwan
Party change and the democratic evolution of Taiwan, 1991–2004
Dafydd Fell

State Terrorism and Political Identity in Indonesia
Fatally belonging
Ariel Heryanto

China's Rise, Tawian's Dilemmas and International Peace
Edited by Edward Friedman

Japan and China in the World Political Economy
Edited by Saadia M. Pekkanen and Kellee S. Tsai

Order and Security in Southeast Asia
Essays in memory of Michael Leifer
Edited by Joseph Chinyong Liow and Ralf Emmers

Order and Security in Southeast Asia

Essays in memory of Michael Leifer

Edited by Joseph Chinyong Liow and Ralf Emmers

LONDON AND NEW YORK

First published 2006
by Routledge
2 Park Square, Milton Park, Abingdon, Oxon OX14 4RN

Simultaneously published in the USA and Canada
by Routledge
270 Madison Ave, New York, NY 10016

Routledge is an imprint of the Taylor & Francis Group

Typeset in Times by
Rosemount Typing Services, Auldgirth, Dumfriesshire

Printed and bound in Great Britain by
TJ International Ltd, Padstow, Cornwall

British Library Cataloguing in Publication Data
A catalogue record for this book is available from the British Library

Library of Congress Cataloging in Publication Data
Order and security in southeast Asia : essays in memory of Michael Leifer /
edited by Joseph Chinyong Liow and Ralf Emmers
p. cm – (Politics in Asia)
Includes bibliographical references and index.
1. Asia, Southeastern–Politics and government–1945- 2. National Security–Asia, Southeastern. 3. Leifer, Michael. I. Leifer, Michael. II. Liow, Joseph Chin Yong. III. Emmers, Ralf, 1974- IV. Series: Politics in Asia series.
DS526.7.O73 2005
327.59'009'045–dc22

2005005662

ISBN 0–415–36365–9 (hbk)
ISBN 0–415–36366–7 (pbk)

Contents

Contributors

Amitav Acharya is Professor and also Deputy Director and Head of Research in the Institute of Defence and Strategic Studies, Nanyang Technological University, Singapore.

Ang Cheng Guan is Associate Professor and Deputy Head (History) in the Humanities and Social Studies Education Academic Group of the National Institute of Education, Singapore.

Chin Kin Wah is Senior Fellow in the Regional Strategic and Political Studies Programme at the Institute of Southeast Asian Studies, Singapore.

Alan Chong is Assistant Professor in the Department of Political Science, National University of Singapore.

James Cotton is Professor in the School of Politics, Australian Defence Force Academy, University of New South Wales, Canberra.

Ralf Emmers is Assistant Professor in the Institute of Defence and Strategic Studies, Nanyang Technological University, Singapore.

Donald K. Emmerson is Professor at Stanford University, California, a Senior Fellow in the Stanford Institute for International Studies, and Head of the Asia/Pacific Research Center's Southeast Asia Forum.

Jürgen Haacke is Lecturer in the International Relations Department of the London School of Economics.

Christopher R. Hughes is Director of the Asia Research Centre and a Senior Lecturer in the International Relations Department of the London School of Economics.

Tim Huxley is Senior Fellow for Asia-Pacific Security, Editor of the Adelphi Paper series, and Corresponding Director of IISS-Asia at the International Institute for Strategic Studies, Singapore.

Yuen Foong Khong is Fellow of Nuffield College, Oxford University, and Senior Research Advisor at the Institute of Defence and Strategic Studies, Nanyang Technological University, Singapore.

Joseph Chinyong Liow is Assistant Professor in the Institute of Defence and Strategic Studies, Nanyang Technological University, Singapore.

Leonard C. Sebastian is Senior Fellow at the Institute of Defence and Strategic Studies, Nanyang Technological University, Singapore.

Sheldon Simon is Professor of Political Science and Faculty Associate of the Center for Asian Studies and Program in Southeast Asian Studies at Arizona State University.

See Seng Tan is Assistant Professor in the Institute of Defence and Strategic Studies, Nanyang Technological University, Singapore.

Michael Yahuda is Professor Emeritus of International Relations at the London School of Economics and a Visiting Scholar at the Sigur Center for Asian Studies, the Elliott School for International Affairs, George Washington University.

Foreword

This collection of essays has been prepared in memory of the late Michael Leifer, Professor of International Relations at the London School of Economics and Political Science (LSE) for thirty-two years. Michael was an astute observer of current affairs in Southeast Asia, while also having a firm grasp of the region's history. His numerous publications have touched on the balance of power, regionalism, maritime security, domestic politics, and foreign policy-making processes in Southeast Asia, and his writings inspired an entire generation of scholars interested in the region and beyond. As a Professor and PhD supervisor, Leifer had many students from the region who have since gone on to hold prominent positions in government, business, and academia. His interest in policy-making in various Southeast Asian countries has been exemplified in his close relationship with his former students, and the fact that his views on regional affairs had always been sought by the policy community in the region.

This volume had its genesis in a conference co-organized in his honor by the Institute of Defence and Strategic Studies (IDSS), the Asia Research Centre (ARC), and the Department of International Relations at the LSE. We were honored to have in attendance Frances Leifer and two of her sons, Jeremy and Richard. The chapters in this volume come out of the conference, and focus on Professor Leifer's work, building on aspects of his research and taking his observations as points of entry for further studies. In the spirit of sound academic research, chapter contributors have been encouraged to approach Leifer's scholarship with a critical edge, identifying both strengths and weaknesses as well as locating potential areas for further expansion for a new generation of scholars. This volume, therefore, will not only be a recollection of Leifer's ideas, but also provide provocative and stimulating reflections on how they may continue to be relevant for scholars and students of the international politics of Southeast Asia.

Barry Desker
Director, Institute of Defence and Strategic Studies, Nanyang Technological University, Singapore

Christopher R. Hughes
Director, Asia Research Centre, London School of Economics and Political Science

Preface

The backdrop to this book was a conference that, unexpectedly for Michael Leifer's family, was borne out of the desire of two of his ex-PhD students, Dr Ralf Emmers and Dr Joseph Liow, to organize an event that would focus on the key themes of his work as an academic; at the same time giving recognition to his achievements in the field of study of Southeast Asian politics. What resulted was a gathering of distinguished scholars at a conference held in Singapore, co-sponsored by the Institute of Defence and Strategic Studies and the London School of Economics, that took place over a day and a half on 13 and 14 May 2004, entitled "The Unending Search for Regional Order: Essays in Memory of Michael Leifer." Out of the essays that were written for that conference was borne this book, compiled and edited by Joseph and Ralf. This must have been no mean feat for them both when faced with such a distinguished list of contributors, at the same time finding time to continue with their own researches. What motivated these two young academics to engage in this overt act of homage? The exact reasons are probably best left for them to explain, but a good guess would be the very sudden departure of a mentor figure during a time of unique research and scholarship for each of them. In Ralf's case, my father died just two months before his thesis was to be completed. In Joseph's case, he was midway through the period of his thesis. The effect for both of them must have been catastrophic. My father bore his illness with great resilience and with typical good humor, and because of this, the end must have come even quicker for those not aware of his condition.

In June 2001, three months after he died, a celebration of my father's life was held at the LSE, organized by his long-time departmental colleague and friend Professor Michael Yahuda. The event was attended by friends, relatives, and colleagues who all gathered to celebrate the man who was now gone. For his family, the Singapore conference, almost three years on, proved this time to be a celebration of his work, reaching back in time as far away as the close of the 1950s. It was a comforting, and at the same time fascinating, re-opening of the door on that work which had inevitably closed abruptly with his untimely death. We were fortunate to be able to sit and listen to the discussions of those very subjects and themes that were central to his work, and there were moments when we even imagined how he might have participated in the conference had he too been there. We took away with us from this gathering, and the suggested idea of the pending book, the very great satisfaction that the work of a lifetime continued, and will continue, to form the subject of lively academic debate, and to act as a point of scholarly reference for those wishing to follow in his footsteps, picking up the thread where he finally left off. We were also indebted to Ch'ng Kim See, the Head of the Library of the Institute of Southeast Asian Studies, who went to very great lengths to compile a bibliography of my father's published works, drawn from the resources available to her at the Library. To me, there is something very fitting that a collection of his works should be housed in Singapore.

One of the markers that the conference highlighted was a particularly personal one—the dichotomy between work and home life, and the conference and the informal gatherings that took place around it, gave us an insight into the working side of my father's life that probably could only have been captured had we slavishly followed him around for a week at the LSE ("holding on to his coat tails" as he once put it when referring to his Director, at a time when he himself was Pro-Director at the LSE). The idea of drawing a sort of biographical sketch inevitably emerged during the course of the conference, and Professor Paul Evans especially, dangled some intriguing questions in front of us, such as why was it that my father chose Southeast Asia as his field of specialization, and what motivated him to pursue it in the way he did? The complete answers to these questions, if there can ever be such a thing, are probably lost in time, asking us to look back to a time over forty years ago. However, we know that while at the University of Adelaide from 1959 to 1963, his very first academic position where he lectured in politics, my father taught a Cambodian student who passed my father newspapers from Cambodia published in French (French having being one part of my father's undergraduate degree). We know that whatever he gleaned from these newspapers aroused his interest, and maybe caused him to turn his sights to Southeast Asia. The rest perhaps is history, but certainly his early writings as a young academic are testament to the path he had chosen to tread.

Turning to this book, a preface that leads off with one or two anecdotal asides and some very brief attempt at characterization, when juxtaposed with the academic essays that follow it, could perhaps be seen as a nice contrast between the themes of Michael Leifer, the man at home among his family, and the academic at work. While this might seem an over-optimistic idea, hopefully it might just help in some small way, to give the reader a different perspective on his outlook, and thus on the positions he took as a commentator on contemporary politics in Southeast Asia.

Not surprisingly as far as his work and his home life went, there was certainly no clear dividing line. At home growing up, there seemed to be a succession of all manner of people crossing the threshold, be they members of the foreign service of a Southeast Asian nation, academics from all corners of the globe, political consultants, members of the media, or of course students, all to be greeted warmly by their host. And home was not only a place of work and study, but also a place to follow world events, and he did this avidly, to the very end. The daily papers with the best foreign news coverage and favorite periodicals were ritually scanned and digested. As the BBC World Service was essential listening, so the evening television news was necessary viewing. Then there were the frequent telephone calls from sources and contacts, as well as the regular radio broadcasts conducted down the telephone in the hallway. These acts were all part of the daily ritual of harvesting and exchanging the fresh know-how that were the core of his trade, while we his family lived and breathed the experience from close quarters. So home and work were inseparable.

From a character perspective, it was always apparent to me that he was a very modest man. It's a fact of life that we don't always know or fully understand the extent of the work of those who are close to us, while it is going on. It was only after his death that I came to realize and to appreciate the scale of his achievement and the level of recognition that it was receiving. At home he didn't shout about what he was doing or make a point about where he was at, but his work and the subject just were, so to speak; they were like the bricks and the mortar. We could see what he was about but were not always able to gauge its significance. Hardly surprising when the events that he followed took place so far away from the world we knew.

The next point is one made at the conference, and which I feel is entirely right. He was at heart a very moral person, with a deep-rooted set of ethical values which he certainly derived from his Jewish roots and upbringing. This sense of morality seemed to have a knack of touching the lives of the people with whom he came into contact. A central theme of this morality and of his personality, was that he was a strong believer in doing right by people, and in doing the right thing. He always strove to be fair in his dealings with others and to be even-handed whenever he could. I suspect that he probably exemplified these character traits during his time as Pro-Director of the LSE, serving in that position at the School's request for an extra year before returning to his academic post.

There's an anecdote that comes to mind. The conference highlighted his established network of contacts throughout Southeast Asia that he was able to draw upon for source information and views on a confidential basis, passed on to him in the knowledge that he would not disclose his sources. And this would inevitably present him with something of a dilemma. I recall that on one occasion he had written a piece that was to be published in the *International Herald Tribune*, but its contents were sensitive and so the name of its author could not be revealed. He was looking for a pseudonym under which to write and after much brainstorming, he hit upon the name "Pierre Blanc." And I think that this is how he liked to be viewed and is also perhaps how he saw himself, as a "Pierre Blanc," rather than a "Pierre Noir" type of character. It reflected his true character and personality.

He also had a great sense of the value of things, and I mean both tangible and intangible things. This was something generational. Coming as he did from that part of London that was to the north of the East End, he was from a generation that I would call, to borrow a phrase from elsewhere, a “lost world,” that disappeared in the aftermath of the Second World War. It was a very different time and a very different experience, particularly growing up as a teenager in the shadow of the Holocaust, where some family members never made it to safety. There was, I suspect, an almost complete absence of materiality in his upbringing which was without privilege and without social advantage, and I believe that these formative years made a very deep if not total impression on much of his outlook on life. It was a time when families lived in close proximity and those ties and bonds were strong, something which at least in the country of his upbringing, England, appears now very largely to have been lost.

Against this backdrop, not surprisingly, he always warmed to the notion of a “community,” of people held together by common ties, be they ethnic, religious or national. He understood that smaller communities and groups had to stand together in order to maintain their identity and even just to survive. And because of this, and this is meant in a family sense, he was drawn naturally, to the notion of “order”; not an ordered household but one that provided a stable family life. It was this stability that percolated through the household, that gave him a place to write and to study. With this sense of community, he took immense pleasure from family occasions. He always enjoyed the conviviality of these gatherings, attaching as he did great value to them, always sharing his brand of humor with the rest of us with some fresh joke that he had saved up for the occasion.

When at home, he was always disciplined in his application to his work. During the first day of the conference, a thought crossed my mind triggered by something said. I thought long and hard, but I could not recall one instance in which he had ever announced that he thought he was going to miss a deadline or that he had in fact missed a deadline. He just seemed to have a remarkably steady discipline for whatever he happened to be working on at the time.

Looking back, there are the enduring snapshots framed in the memory. The picture of him in his study always working and writing or, to use a phrase that came up at the conference, scribbling. Always scribbling, making notes and taking notes. And when he was finished, the smoke clouds from a favorite pipe would signal to us that the day’s work was over. The pipe was one of his trademarks, and I don’t recall anyone ever complaining.

There were also the seemingly countless evenings, marked by lots of pacing up and down the carpet dictating his latest piece, while my mother listened and typed. And here I must pause for a moment to give credit where it is due, as it was my mother who devoted so much of her time for many years, typing up whatever he happened to have written, from short pieces to entire books, including his doctoral thesis so many years before. To understand the quantity of her labors and of her support for him, her efforts were put in for many, many years on a manual typewriter, a tool now long since retired thanks to the word processor and latterly the computer.

At the conference, there was some discussion of the importance of the right choice of words, and those discussions highlighted differences, that so easily arise, of individual interpretation and the meaning of particular words used. In the Leifer household, the most thumbed through book was the Thesaurus. While dictating, my father would often stop, not quite satisfied with his choice of word. That single word could change the entire nuance. If the book couldn't provide the answer, then there would not infrequently be lots of agonizing over a single word, and in these moments, the entire family was liable to be drawn into the agony as well, as he turned to us for some alternative assistance. Sometimes we hit upon the elusive word; other times we were left in thoughtful silence, not quite sure what the chosen word really meant!

He had an amazing capacity to consume books. He was blessed with the ability to speed read and to digest. When reading, he also had the ability to switch off to everybody and everything around him. More remarkably, he could do this while sitting in front of the television, as if doing so helped him to concentrate. Invariably, when he would come to visit in Hong Kong, where I was living, he would arrive and push a book into my hand saying "Here, have this. You'll like it. I read it on the plane!"

And in the Leifer household, how did these characteristics shape the lives of his three sons? My read is that his work ethic, his discipline, and his dedication to his subject inevitably percolated downwards as part of the fabric of the household. One of us, Richard, became a journalist, plying his trade with his writing. And the other two sons, Simon and I, both became lawyers. Did we all move in these directions because of a certain stability in our household, influenced by these unseen forces? I would like to think so. It was a huge unseen and unfelt presence. But it was there, and we all gained by it immensely.

So with these very few anecdotes and character features of Michael Leifer that I have thrown out, and having sat through two days of discussion and debate at the conference in Singapore, I could well make the connection between Michael Leifer the man at home and the man at work, and could well see how he touched so many of the people that he came into contact with at all levels.

And what of the stage he had reached in his work at the end? He had joined the LSE in 1969, with considerable personal surprise that he should be returning to the place where he gained his doctorate. And he remained there until the end. His academic career encompassed a first port of call in Asia, to Singapore in 1963, and a final port of call in 2001 ironically, or perhaps it was fated, also to Singapore, covering a sweep of many rich and full years. To take another phrase that was used in the conference a great deal, his glass was certainly not half empty; nor was it half full. I believe it was brimming over. He enjoyed his subject with a passion. Toward the end, after he had finished his final book, I had the sense that at that moment there was a kind of completeness to his work; a rounding off of the subjects he had set out to explore and to explain. Of course world events do not stand still, and had he lived, he would have continued to be an avid observer and commentator. Inevitably, the reins are handed down to the next generation, and I have little doubt that academics such as Ralf and Joseph will do as much for the study of the Southeast Asian nation states as did my father.

Jeremy Leifer

Acknowledgements

The editors would like to express their gratitude to the Institute of Defence and Strategic Studies, the Asia Research Center, and the Department of International Relations at the London School of Economics for funding this project. Special thanks to Yuen Foong Khong, Barry Desker, and Christopher Hughes for their support and advice on the conceptualization of this project. Nirupama Keshav provided valuable editorial assistance in the preparation of the final manuscript. The editors would also like to thank Frances Leifer and her sons who were supportive of this project from its initial stages. Needless to say, apart from the authors themselves, we the editors take responsibility for any shortcomings in the book.

Ralf Emmers
Joseph Chinyong Liow
Singapore
January 2005

1 Introduction

Joseph Chinyong Liow and Ralf Emmers

With the passing of the likes of O.W. Wolters, George McTurnan Kahin, Ralph Smith, Jeremy Davidson, Herbert Feith, and John Echols over the past few years, Southeast Asian Studies has lost some of its major personalities and most astute scholars of the region's history, culture, and politics. While these path-breakers for the academic study of Southeast Asia spanned the ideological spectrum from conservative historians to liberal and Marxist activists, they all held one thing in common aside from impressive publishing records – they all lived through the turbulent years of war, de-colonization, and nation-state formation as the region, and its constituent states and nations, came of age in international society. This compilation of essays celebrates the ideas and works of the late Michael Leifer, who ranks among these esteemed Southeast Asianists as a doyen of the study of international politics of the region.

The seminal works of Michael Leifer have contributed greatly to our study and understanding of the international relations of Southeast Asia. His intellectual journey across the region's complex history has been reflected in his published works, too numerous to be listed in this volume.[1] These have covered topics ranging from nationalism and the inception of new states into the regional security order through the formation and development of multilateral institutions to the domestic turmoil and regional uncertainty brought about by the 1997 regional financial crisis. Indeed, Michael Leifer was from a unique breed of scholars who not only wrote extensively about the trying and uncertain times of Southeast Asian history from a scholarly perspective, but also lived through them and in the process fostered close, personal relationships with Southeast Asian leaders who have been critical in moulding this very history. In so doing, he has left behind not only an impressive amount of scholarship, but also a rich intellectual legacy for students of Southeast Asia to build upon. The purpose of this volume thence is to capture the development of international politics in Southeast Asia through a careful study of Michael Leifer's writing on the region. There have been other attempts to recognize Leifer's contribution to the field, but this volume is the first that goes beyond a recapitulation of his seminal writings in order to dissect, investigate, and critique the ideas and subtexts behind his work.[2]

The theorist in Michael Leifer

As Southeast Asia moves into the twenty-first century, it has already been confronted with new security concerns such as the scourge of terrorism and the emergence of other sources of non-traditional security challenges that threaten the sovereignty and territorial integrity of regional states, as well as the cohesion of the region expressed through multilateral organizations such as the Association of Southeast Asian Nations (ASEAN) and the ASEAN Regional Forum (ARF). On closer inspection, it will be realized that the question of regional order lies at the heart of many of these issues, and the associated concerns over how the states of the region have attempted and should attempt to deal with them.

Michael Leifer, as many of the contributors to this volume recognize, was never explicit about his theoretical inclinations. Indeed, those who studied under him would be aware of his disdain for abstract theorizing that relegated solid empirical research to the peripheries of scholarship. In this light, one could suggest that, on the one hand, any attempt to tease out the theorist in Leifer is not only futile but goes against the grain of how Leifer should be 'read'. On the other hand, given his preoccupation with security, as pointed out by Donald Emmerson, Michael Leifer did in fact approach the topic (of security and insecurity) with a conceptual toolbox that included two well-known tools, rightly identified in Khong Yuen Foong's contribution, as 'order' and 'balance of power'. In this respect, the concepts of order (and the lack thereof) and balance of power form the conceptual point of entry into and key organizing theoretical principles behind Michael Leifer's empirically rich research on the international politics of Southeast Asia.

Regional order, balance of power, and the English School

Michael Leifer was never explicit regarding his theoretical inclinations, but contributors to this volume have uncovered glimpses of Elie Kedourie (who was his PhD supervisor at the LSE), Michael Oakeshott, Charles Manning, Martin Wight, and Hedley Bull in his thoughts and writings. In this regard, it is clear from his writings that Michael Leifer located himself within what is termed the 'English School' tradition of International Relations (IR), where the notion of international order has been an important conceptual and organizational theme. Hedley Bull, the predominant theorist of the English School, defined international order as 'a pattern of activity that sustains the elementary or primary goals of the society of states, or international society'.[3] Although not without its own limitations, we suggest that Bull's conceptual focus on the question of international order was a source of influence for Michael Leifer in his own work.

In several of his writings Leifer has laid plain his concern with the search for, and maintenance of, order in the security architecture of Southeast Asia. Be that as it may, it is also clear that Michael Leifer himself has never been overt in defining the concept of order as he applied it in his scholarship. Still, Leifer associated the quest for order with the workings of the balance of power, defined as an institution that sustains international order rather than as an overall structure in the international system, and the availability of countervailing power to react to a rising and threatening power. Balance of power was thus defined as policy rather than system. In contrast to the advocates of neo-realism who judge the balance of power in terms of adversarial relations and self-help, Leifer adhered to both a traditional realist and neo-Grotian interpretation of the balance of power concept. He often referred to the notion of an 'associative balance of power' in contrast to an entirely competitive one. In that respect, his intellectual framework was again strongly influenced by exponents of the English School of International Relations who saw in anarchy an impetus to cooperation rather than competition and conflict. Notwithstanding his emphasis on the balance of power as a cornerstone to his understanding of order, Leifer's reluctance to explicate the theoretical assumptions to his application has left more theoretically inclined connoisseurs of his scholarship somewhat disappointed. Khong Yuen Foong, for example, understandably laments Leifer's 'theoretically underdeveloped and methodologically imprecise' use of the concept, and suggests that 'if Michael Leifer had adopted ASEAN's preferred terms of the discourse to describe its aspirations (i.e. "peace and stability" as opposed to "order"), his assessment of ASEAN's achievements in international relations … would have come closer to the "half full" rather than "half empty" metaphoric glass'.[4] Chin Kin Wah, on the other hand, suggests that this methodological imprecision nevertheless had appeal for those among us 'not given to operating in tight theoretical frameworks'. In an interesting reading of Michael Leifer's methodology, Ang Cheng Guan further points to the fact that:

> Although Leifer is not considered a historian, his writings bore elements of the historian's reference – that the history of international relations should be understood and explained in terms of conduct rather than behavior; and the narrative/process-tracing is a more satisfactory approach to explain outcomes than covering laws.

Having said that, Khong's argument that Leifer's work could be further improved with greater conceptual clarification is well taken given the state of the discipline today, where scholars, both established and upcoming, face increasing demands for greater theoretical rigour in their analysis.

Because of this, Michael Leifer was not without his detractors. Some, in particular, have attempted to tease out the constructivist in him, suggesting for example that because culture was 'acknowledged, if not conspicuously privileged' by Leifer, he 'came close to being a constructivist'.[5] While there certainly were traces of constructivism in Leifer's work, as Amitav Acharya and Chin Kin Wah rightly point out, this would not necessarily make Leifer a constructivist, and sweeping statements such as that cited above betray a fundamental misreading and caricature of the ideas and work of Michael Leifer. To explicate that by highlighting and mentioning culture in his work Leifer 'conspicuously privileged' it as an explanatory factor is as unsound an argument as saying that Alexander Wendt privileges power simply because he concedes that 'the proposition that the nature of international politics is shaped by power relations … cannot be a *uniquely* Realist claim … since then every student of international politics would be a Realist'.[6] Mere reference to the term does not constitute abiding by its relevance, and it is the *context* of its usage that should be of importance. To be sure, in Michael Leifer's *Weltanschauung* international politics revolved around power, identity, and norms. On the one hand, it could be suggested, as Sorpong Peou does in an epistemologically straitjacketed fashion, that this makes Michael Leifer 'close to being a constructivist'. On the other hand, those working in the English School tradition, as Leifer did, would not necessarily see any tension in scholarship that addresses both material and ideational factors. As See Seng Tan highlights in his contribution to this volume:

> The progenitors of the English School were evidently drawn to 'a pluralistic methodology that aims to find ways of linking apparently disparate bodies of knowledge and understanding'. Indeed, they would insist, despite Bull's evident enthusiasm for the Grotian perspective, that a comprehensive understanding of international life is not possible without embracing all three interpretive traditions (realism, rationalism and revolutionism) originally staked out by Martin Wight.

More important, however, is to ask to what extent did Leifer privilege the ideational. Here, it is safe to say that even as he recognized the role of norms, culture, and identity, Leifer's essential focus in his preoccupation with order and security in Southeast Asia was, as Donald Emmerson, Chin Kin Wah, and Jürgen Haacke quickly remind us, the balance of power. Though Leifer conceded that the balance of power was not the only institution in international society through which order was brought about, it was, in Haacke's words, 'the most important'.

Institutions and multilateralism

In many ways, Michael Leifer's credentials as a 'sophisticated realist' are aptly demonstrated in his work on institutions, which has been fascinating for his reluctance to dismiss them outright as irrelevant, or even peripheral, to the international politics of Southeast Asia.[7] On the contrary, it appears in his writings on the ARF and ASEAN, for example, that Leifer laments these institutions' inability to reach their fullest potential. ASEAN was in Leifer's carefully chosen words an 'underdeveloped institution' because of its lack of commitment to more legalistic mechanisms that to his mind would restrain members more effectively.[8] As for the ARF, it was 'an imperfect diplomatic instrument for achieving regional security goals', and the main reason for this, as surmised by Leifer, was the fact that it was not premised on the balance of power, but rather on the leadership of ASEAN, a group of small states.[9] In fact, as

Amitav Acharya reminds us in his comparison of Leifer's work with those of constructivists working on Southeast Asia, 'the real difference . . . is not so much over whether regionalism matters, but under what conditions does it matter'. In this regard, the second section of the book in essence addresses one fundamental question: what role is there for formal regional institutions in the pursuit of order in Southeast Asia and the wider Asia-Pacific region? This conceptual question lies at the core of our discussion on regional institutions.

Michael Leifer was a student of regional institutions in Southeast Asia par excellence even before the formation of ASEAN. To Leifer, regional institutions were an important expression and indication of the existence or absence of order. Leifer often made plain his disagreement with the 'ASEAN Way' to regionalism, examined purely as a piece of political and diplomatic rhetoric rather than a distinctive model of regionalism. Nevertheless, to reduce Leifer's impressions of regionalism in the region to a prejudiced, euro-centric criticism of Asia would be a grave misreading of his core arguments. In point of fact, Leifer was far more sophisticated a critic of Southeast Asian regionalism. He often indicated his 'realism', if not outright pessimism, on the kind of security cooperation that had been achieved in Southeast Asia since the formation of ASEAN in 1967, writing for instance that 'it is as well to temper enthusiasm about the kind of security regime which has evolved among the ASEAN states'.[10] Leifer focused on the ongoing mistrust and disputes that existed among the member states and on how their inability to solve sources of tension undermined the quest for order in Southeast Asia. Nonetheless, despite his reservations, Leifer had on occasion also posited the ARF as a model of cooperative security for another region in the world; namely, the Middle East.[11]

His most conceptually driven work on the study of regional institutions was undeniably his 1996 Adelphi Paper on the ARF.[12] In his analysis, Leifer remained pragmatic about the potential role of the ARF and argued that it should be viewed 'as a modest contribution to a viable balance or distribution of power within the Asia-Pacific by other than traditional means'.[13] He further argued that the viability of the ARF was dependent 'on the prior existence of a stable balance, but it is not really in a position to create it'.[14] Leifer therefore linked the working of the balance of power to the operation of regional institutions, regarding the latter as dependent on the former. However, he did not perceive ASEAN and the ARF as cooperative security arrangements capable of moderating the regional balance of power. Not surprisingly, as Sheldon Simon reminds us, many analysts share Leifer's scepticism of the ARF on precisely the grounds that small states tend towards 'risk aversion' strategies that privilege sovereignty and non-interference, and to the extent that they continue to dictate the terms of multilateralism in the region, regional institutions are not likely to be able to manage security crises when the time comes.

At another level, Michael Leifer was a man who practised what he preached. He did not pontificate from an ivory tower, occasionally 'looking down' on these institutions to criticize their ineffectiveness and misplaced optimism. Instead,

Leifer was intimately involved in engaging multilateralism as a card-carrying member of the Council for Security and Cooperation in the Asia-Pacific (CSCAP), a Track II organization dedicated to promoting concepts of cooperative security to the inter-governmental ARF, and, as Jeremy Leifer acknowledges in his preface, was regularly consulted by media, government officials, political consultants, and members of foreign missions for his views on security developments in the region. Leifer was more than a distanced observer; he was interested in sharing his views and insights with a broader policy audience and making them as relevant as possible to the 'real world'.

Maritime security

Another dimension to Michael Leifer's study of the themes of order and security was the particular attention he gave to the management of maritime security in Southeast Asia. Leifer was particularly interested in the regional endorsement, application and interpretation of the United Nations Convention of the Law of the Sea (UNCLOS) and on the formation and maintenance of a peaceful maritime regime in the region.[15] While many commentators have only recently taken an interest in maritime security in the context of sea piracy and the threat of maritime terrorist attacks in Southeast Asia, Leifer had already developed by the late 1970s a tradition of scholarship on the security of sea-lanes and the politics behind maritime security management. This was demonstrated by his particular interest in the Straits of Malacca and Singapore, the study of which was the focus of a seminal volume published in 1978.[16]

Leifer's interest in maritime security was also demonstrated through his publications on the overlapping territorial claims over the Spratly Islands. He examined this complex case of disputes between China, Taiwan, Vietnam, the Philippines and Malaysia in terms of the balance of power and the absence of order in the South China Sea. Indeed, he argued that the Southeast Asian claimants did not enjoy access to an external source of countervailing power to resist China's rising hegemony in the South China Sea, and that ASEAN itself had 'no power to deploy because it is neither a defence community nor a party to a countervailing structure of alignments'.[17] As a result, Leifer perceived the absence of a source of countervailing force in the South China Sea as a direct threat to the Southeast Asian states involved in the territorial conflict, particularly Vietnam and the Philippines, and as indicative of the absence of order in the maritime regime. Moreover, Leifer was sceptical of the prospects that ASEAN might ever succeed in engaging China on this issue through the adoption of a binding code of conduct for the South China Sea.[18] Insofar as Michael Leifer's assessment of the South China Sea was concerned, his position was further instructive of his long-held belief that the usefulness of multilateral institutions was dependent on the prior existence of a balance of power.

Foreign and security policy-making

Given the importance of the balance of power to Leifer's study of the international politics of Southeast Asia, it was evident to his mind that, while he was not a neo-realist in the tradition of American IR theory, regional order was to a large part a structural phenomenon, and in Southeast Asia's case invariably dependent on the roles and interests of major powers. Be that as it may, Michael Leifer's vanguard understanding of the dynamics of Southeast Asian politics also led him to the study of the role of domestic politics and ideology in the making of foreign and security policies. It is from his studies of the foreign policies of selected Southeast Asian states that one realizes Leifer was far from being an advocate of the crass materialist realism that some have wrongly associated him with. Despite his propensity towards balance of power politics, and his sense that great powers had a key part to play in managing regional order, Leifer was also fully conscious of the fact that the states of Southeast Asia were, as James Cotton writes, themselves also 'active participants in the generation of order'.

Michael Leifer demonstrated an empathetic understanding of the problems of states establishing independence from colonial rule, recognized the fragility of the relatively new states of Southeast Asia, and was sensitive to their concerns. In other words, unlike many realists in the IR field today, Leifer was primarily interested in the security of small states and their involvement in balance of power politics.[19] Similarly he understood the difficulties of establishing effective governance in newly formed states made up of different and competing ethnic and religious groups and how these matters affected the making of foreign policy and accommodating regional partners despite competing territorial claims and differences of strategic perspectives. In short, Leifer was concerned with nationalism and state-building in Southeast Asia. As Tim Huxley argues, by suggesting that Singapore's foreign policy was driven not merely by 'geopolitical constriction', but also 'a national memory of being cast adrift to fend for itself against all expectations', it is clear that to Leifer's mind, Singapore's foreign policy was driven as much by distinctive ideologies (read 'nationalism') as by material factors.[20] It is further illuminating that even in his analysis of the rise of China and its potential repercussions for Southeast Asia, Leifer's primary concern was not for China's increasing military or economic power. Rather, as Chris Hughes highlights, it was 'nationalism' that would underpin Chinese hegemonic dispositions towards Southeast Asia. Leifer's seminal statement of foreign policy making however, must arguably be his study of Indonesia's foreign policy, which remains a key text for students of international politics in Southeast Asia. As highlighted by Leonard Sebastian's contribution to this volume, Leifer demonstrated an uncanny appreciation for the historical legacy behind the strategic outlook of Indonesian leaders and the intricate internal dynamics of the Indonesian political decision-making process.

While Michael Leifer wrote extensively on archipelagic Southeast Asia, his point of entry into the region was, however, Cambodia.[21] Moreover, his work on Indochina has been summarized and described by Ang Cheng Guan, an expert in the international history of Indochina, as 'to date one of the most, if not the most comprehensive and nuanced account of Cambodia's foreign policy in the early post-independence years'. In Ang's analysis, Leifer's writings had an element of 'objectivity or some may choose to call it his academic detachment'. It was this quality, and his vast and unmatched empirical knowledge of the region, that defined him as an area specialist who, as Michael Yahuda notes, nevertheless had no familial, personal or ideological ties to the region of his study.

Leifer and the study of Southeast Asia

Readers will note that this volume does not contain a concluding chapter. As editors, we have deliberately made this choice for two reasons. First, the narrative of Southeast Asia and its struggle with order and security has 'moved on' since Michael Leifer passed away. The scourge of terrorism has hit Southeast Asia, and threatens to intensify regional insecurities. As the ARF grapples with an uncertain security environment while being hamstrung by its own institutional incapacities that Leifer warned of, the crises in the Korean Peninsula and the Taiwan Straits are proving to fall further out of the reach of the organization's premonitions to regional order management. While Leifer's warnings in his 1995 Adelphi Paper that the fate of the ARF lies in the hands of the great powers and not of ASEAN, or his allusions to the weakness of ASEAN solidarity appear to be vindicated, the events are still unfolding, and only time will tell if Michael Leifer's reading of the international politics of Southeast Asia was correct.

Second, all the contributors to this volume agree that while Michael Leifer was an accomplished academic and scholar, he was equally well-regarded as a teacher, mentor, colleague, and person. Because of this, we thought it appropriate to end this volume with a reflective essay by Michael Yahuda, a colleague and close friend of Leifer's for more than thirty years.

Notes

1 A compilation of most of Michael Leifer's writings can be found in *Bibliography in Honour of Professor Michael Leifer 1933–2001*, Singapore: Institute of Southeast Asian Studies (ISEAS), 2004.

2 See Michael Leifer: *Selected Works on Southeast Asia*, compiled by Chin Kin Wah and Leo Suryadinata, Singapore: ISEAS 2004.

3 Hedley Bull, *The Anarchical Society: A Study of Order in World Politics*, London: Macmillan, 1995, p. 13.

4 See also Khong Yuen Foong, 'Making Bricks without Straw in the Asia Pacific?', *The Pacific Review*, vol. 10, no. 2, 1997, pp. 289–300.

5 Sorpong Peou, 'Realism and Constructivism in Southeast Asian Security Studies Today', *The Pacific Review*, vol. 15, no. 1, 2002, p. 130.

6 Alexander Wendt, *Social Theory of International Politics*, Cambridge: Cambridge University Press, 1999, p. 96–7.
7 Indeed, realists are often wrongly lambasted for dismissing institutions. Even so-called offensive realists of the tradition of American neo-realism do take into account institutions and their role in international politics. Such realists would not, surprisingly, be critical of the significant contributions that institutions may make, but this is markedly different from suggesting that realists do not account for institutions at all. See John Mearsheimer, 'The False Promise of Institutions', *International Security*, vol. 19, no. 3, Winter 1994/95, pp. 5–49.
8 Michael Leifer, *ASEAN and the Security of Southeast Asia*, London: Routledge, 1989, p. 150.
9 Michael Leifer, *The ASEAN Regional Forum: Extending ASEAN's Model of Regional Security*, Adelphi Paper No. 32, London: Oxford University Press, 1996, p. 53.
10 Michael Leifer, 'Debating Asian Security: Michael Leifer responds to Geoffrey Wiseman', *The Pacific Review*, vol. 5, no. 2, 1992, p. 169.
11 See Michael Leifer, *The ASEAN Regional Forum: A Model for Cooperative Security in the Middle East*. Working Paper 1998/1, Canberra: Australian National University, Department of International Relations, 1998.
12 See Khong Yuen Foong, 'Making Bricks without Straw in the Asia-Pacific?', *The Pacific Review*, vol. 10, no. 2, 1997, pp. 289–300.
13 Leifer, *The ASEAN Regional Forum: Extending ASEAN's Model of Regional Security*, p. 59.
14 Leifer, *The ASEAN Regional Forum: Extending ASEAN's Model of Regional Security*, p. 58.
15 See Michael Leifer, 'The Maritime Regime and Regional Security in East Asia', *The Pacific Review*, vol. 4, no. 2, 1991.
16 Michael Leifer, *Malacca, Singapore, and Indonesia*, Alphen aan den Rijn: Sijthoff & Noordhoff, 1978.
17 Michael Leifer, 'ASEAN as a Model of a Security Community?', in Hadi Soesastro (ed.) *ASEAN in a Changed Regional and International Political Economy*, Jakarta: Centre for Strategic and International Studies, 1995, p. 141.
18 ASEAN and China eventually reached agreement on a 'Declaration on the Conduct of Parties in the South China Sea' on the sidelines of the eighth ASEAN summit in Phnom Penh in early November 2002.
19 This would differentiate the 'realist' in Michael Leifer from realists such as Kenneth Waltz, John Mearsheimer, Henry Kissinger or Hans Morgenthau, who clearly had little regard for small states.
20 See Michael Leifer, *Indonesia's Foreign Policy*, London: Allen & Unwin, 1983, p. xiv; Michael Leifer, *Singapore's Foreign Policy: Coping with Vulnerability*, London: Routledge, 2000, pp. 13–15.
21 This initial foray was inspired by a Cambodian graduate student who had studied with Leifer in Australia during his time at Adelaide University.

2 Shocks of recognition

Leifer, realism, and regionalism in Southeast Asia

Donald K. Emmerson[1]

Michael Leifer was a prolific and wide-ranging scholar. The written record he left behind encompasses many sites and topics. Nevertheless, across Michael's four decades of publication, in the Southeast Asia-related books, monographs, chapters, articles, projects, and conferences that he wrote, edited, ran, or contributed to, the one concept whose frequency is unrivalled is *security*. In the titles of these works, from his first book in 1967 (*Cambodia: The Search for Security*) to his last conference paper in 2001 ("Promoting Security and Political Cooperation"), the word *security* occurs 20 times.[2]

Michael's focus on security reflected his understanding of its importance in the eyes of Southeast Asian states whose leaders were obliged time and again to deal with the *insecurity* of their region. Noteworthy, too, is the emphasis on vulnerability, a near-synonym of insecurity, in Michael's work on the foreign policies of Southeast Asian states. Not only did he make national vulnerability and regional entitlement the explanatory centerpiece of his insightful book on Indonesia's foreign policy. In the subtitles he chose for a chapter and a book on the foreign policies of Vietnam and Singapore, respectively, he pictured these states also "Coping with Vulnerability."[3]

The attention Michael paid to insecurity supports my intention here to offer and discuss a set of analytic themes that are available to anyone who would craft an account of regionalism in Southeast Asia. I have borrowed the first such theme from Michael's work: *insecurity*. He also wrote about the others: *identity*, *interests*, *institutions*, and *ideas*. I will argue that these five notions animate, respectively, these perspectives: realism, culturalism, rationalism, liberalism, and constructivism. I will then introduce and interpret the Asian financial crisis in 1997–99 and the war on terror since 2001 as systemic shocks with differentiating impacts on the relative plausibility of insecurity, identity, interests, institutions, and ideas as conceptual keys to Southeast Asian regionalism.

My conclusion may be summarized as follows: Taken together, these two shocks have differently affected the usefulness of the five outlooks as ways of understanding regionalism in Southeast Asia. In this context, the shocks have sharply increased the net analytic efficacy of *insecurity*-assuming realism and, to a lesser extent, *identity*-framing culturalism. At the same time, the crisis and the war have, again on balance, made *institution*-centered liberalist and *interest*-based rationalist assumptions somewhat less plausible, while considerably enhancing the utility of *idea*-featuring constructivism. Given the complexities and subjectivities involved, these judgments are meant to be read as mere estimates of rough magnitude relative to each other, not in relation to any absolute standard. Heuristic value, obviously, has no ratio scale.

Figure 2.1 visualizes this conclusion in crude form, without gradations to be added later. Pending these nuances, the *net* effect of the two shocks is summarized as having strengthened (+) or weakened (-), the adequacy of each approach for understanding regionalism in Southeast Asia.

The sequencing of the five clusters in Figure 2.1 is not random. It reflects approximately how much each approach assumes the givenness—the objective existence and resistance—of a putatively real world. Foundationalist epistemology thus defined *decreases*, if unevenly, *from right to left* in Figure 2.1, that is, from realism to constructivism. This same right-to-left dimension also roughly corresponds to the precedence of these perspectives in American political science since World War II, from realism as the earliest to constructivism as the latest approach.

Clusters of political science

Before addressing the top row in Figure 2.1—the impacts of events on perspectives—it will be helpful first to warrant the two rows lower down: the right-to-left sequence in which the approaches appear and the focus of each on a particular theme.

Ontology

Figure 2.1 runs leftward from portrayals of reality as basic and constraining to critiques of "reality" as constructed and contingent—from insecurity as a root condition to ideas as creative projections. The exact position assigned to any approach in between these extremes will depend on how it is construed.

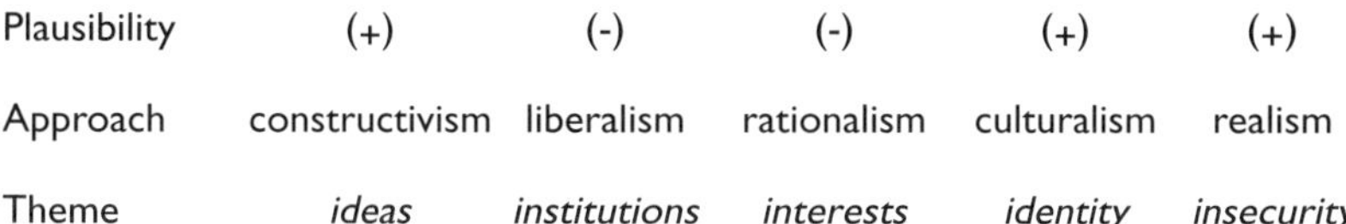

Figure 2.1 How have the Asian financial crisis and the war on terror affected the plausibility of different thematic approaches to regionalism in Southeast Asia? A summary of the argument.

Farthest right, at the foundationalist end of the spectrum, realism is deeply axiomatic about the presence and significance of insecurity among sovereign states that necessarily respond to international anarchy and temporal uncertainty by maximizing their power or balancing or bandwagoning the power of other states. At the opposite end of Figure 2.1, constructivists are least inclined to characterize absolutely, directly, and consistently the empirical world and how it works, given their preferred emphasis on the mediation of reality through perception and interpretation.

Compared with these extremes, the middle clusters in Figure 2.1 are more ambiguous and hence more arbitrarily ordered. Culturalism and rationalism advance no less confidently than realism does their respective core concepts—identity and interests. Yet culturalism and rationalism are less presumptive and more eclectic than realism when it comes to specifying prime actors, causal drivers, and the nature of the environment in which action occurs.

The realist emphasis on the state has no counterpart in culturalist and rationalist approaches. Culturalism encompasses multiple types and tiers of identity—personal or collective, ethnic or religious, original or diasporic, and subnational, national, regional, or civilizational in scale. Comparably, in rationalist discourse, self-interests, group interests, and national interests imply different units and levels of analysis.

Realism is not monolithic. There are classic and structural variants, and the prefix "neo-" has been used to distinguish newer from older work. Yet arguably realism has remained, over time, the most consistent and coherent—the most fully paradigmatic—of the five approaches. Scholarly faith in the centrality of the state and the primacy of conflict and uncertainty in a world of states has continued to underpin and stabilize realism as an enterprise. As focal themes, identities and interests have proven more protean and therefore less conducive to enduring consensus inside the respective approaches that feature these concepts.

Liberalism focused on institutions is a case in point. A conservative outlook on institutions would take them as given and caution reformers against tinkering with what might not be broke. Insofar as the state is itself an enduring institution, or a set of them, a conservative institutionalist approach would be located near realism. By linking institutions to liberalism, in contrast, I mean to characterize a perspective that focuses more on how democratic they are, and how they might be reformed to become more democratic. The malleability of institutions in this liberal view, its interest in democratic design, is closer to constructivism than it is to realism. Among other differences, democratic peace theory attributes to the accountability of domestic institutions a happy external effect that realism is inclined to deny.

The fifth and last approach, constructivism, asserts the power of ideas. Like realism, constructivism is diverse. Unlike realism, it features subjectivity and its projections. In the famous phrase of the pioneer constructivist Alexander Wendt, "Anarchy is what states make of it." Thus did he challenge the traditional realist conviction that the world beyond state borders really is anarchic. But just as

Wendt himself on this occasion was less of an anti-realist than his remark implies,[4] constructivism in the study of international affairs should not be confused with, say, deconstruction in the study of literary texts. Compared with its originally French cousin, constructivism in political science is less venturesome in style and epistemology. I prefer therefore to distinguish it from the other approaches in Figure 2.1 by its preoccupation with ideas, their projection and their effects. Constructivism remains, nevertheless, among all five perspectives, the least similar to realism.

Chronology

Figure 2.1 also, if not quite exactly, replays intellectual history. In the study of international relations in the United States,[5] the first school to emerge after World War II was realism, epitomized by Hans Morgenthau's *Politics among Nations* (1948) and, later, Kenneth Waltz's *Man, the State, and War* (1959). Next came rationalism (Downs 1957; Riker 1962) and, close on its heels, culturalism (Almond and Verba 1963; Pye and Verba 1965). The latter two streams flowed more in political economy (PE) and comparative politics (CP), respectively, than in international relations (IR). But the assumptions and concerns driving them also surfaced in IR, suitably adapted to fit that field's focus on foreign affairs. The liberalist critique of realism arrived later, beginning with Keohane and Nye (1977) and continuing through Keohane (1984; 1992). Only in the 1990s did constructivism fully challenge its predecessors, notably in Ruggie (1998) and Wendt (1999).[6]

Overall, in what I hope is a tolerable oversimplification, in post-World War II American political science one may periodize the arrival and rise of the each of the five approaches roughly as follows: IR realism in the 1940s and 1950s; CP culturalism and PE rationalism in the 1950s and 1960s; IR liberalism in the 1970 and 1980s; and IR constructivism in the 1990s.

And just as these approaches amounted to downstream variations of older—often far older—rivers of thought, so did the post-war versions develop revisions with currents strong enough to alter their own mainstreams. In the rationalist tradition, for example, theorists of "rational choice" refashioned the ancient notion of interest into a utility curve and matched it with other such curves in settings that were, if not game-theoretic, at least subject to quantification.

As for culturalism, in its structural-functionalist form as a search for congruence between attitudes and institutions, it took a beating from realists and rationalists in the 1970s and 80s, but staged a partial recovery in a different guise starting in the 1990s, thanks notably to Samuel Huntington (1996); Harrison and Huntington (eds 2000); and, most recently, Huntington (2004).[7] At the height of modernization theory in the 1950s and 60s, political culture had covered a variety of survey-researchable values and attitudes. In the 1990s, in effect, Huntington shrank the scope of culture to identity. And where earlier culturalists in political science had studied civic beliefs conducive to democracy, his concern for identity had more pessimistic roots in the specter of ethnoreligious or civilizational conflicts injurious to security.

Ideology?

Does the right-to-left sequence in Figure 2.1 also correspond to a series of political standpoints, from realism as a preference of the Right to constructivism as an outlook of the Left?

Possibly Michael Leifer was widely known for his realism. In a brief remark written in the wake of his passing, his London colleague John Sidel, while acknowledging Michael's stature and the loss to Southeast Asian studies, located him on the political Right.[8] As for Huntington, even a cursory scan of reviews of his culturalist scholarship would show that it is thought to belong on the Right. Comparably, one could argue for locating the liberal-institutionalist work of, say, Joseph Nye to the Left of Huntington's defenses of classically Western or Anglo-American identity but still to the Right of constructivism's suspicion of all ruling institutions.

But the correlation should not be overdrawn. Arranging internally diverse bodies of work by scholarly orientation is difficult enough. Imputing political differences to that same distribution risks making polemical what may already be Procrustean. Sidel classified Leifer merely in passing, without explanation. Nor is it even clear what it means to be Right or Left in these post-Cold War times.

In any case, students of ASEAN are not politically polarized into two camps: defenders of the Association at one end of the intellectual spectrum in Figure 2.1 versus critics at the other. Quite apart from increasing or reducing the analytic leverage of the five perspectives relative to one another, the impotence of ASEAN *qua* ASEAN in the face of financial turmoil and terrorist violence has weakened academic confidence in the Association across the political board. If realists are Right and constructivists are Left and the outlooks that separate them cluster in the political Middle—a controversial portrayal—these intellectually various observers would appear merely to have different reasons for questioning regionalism in Southeast Asia.

Realism reaffirmed

The Asian financial crisis (AFC) and the war on terror (WOT) have vindicated a realist view of regionalism in Southeast Asia by reaffirming the insecurity of that part of the world.

Insecurity has been and remains the core theme of realism and the core concern of ASEAN. Insecurity spurred the formation of ASEAN—Indonesian *Konfrontasi* against Malaysia, the perceived threat of communism from inside and outside the region, and the prospective vacuum evoked by the dismantling of a British presence "east of Suez" just as the Americans were losing their will to win the Vietnam War. Insecurity also motivated ASEAN's most notable diplomatic success—mobilizing global opposition to the Vietnamese occupation of Cambodia construed as a threat to ASEAN's Thai "frontline state." Meanwhile, following Indonesia's lead, the Association extended its definition of security beyond mere protection against military attack to include the socioeconomic and political "resilience" of its member states.

Arguably, when the AFC and later the WOT struck, the importance and breadth of ASEAN's commitment to regional security magnified the damage done to its reputation. For all its rhetoric, including pride in a uniquely consultative "ASEAN Way," the Association could neither prevent these crises nor move quickly to lessen the hurt they caused once underway.

It may be counter-argued that no reasonable person could have expected ASEAN to have foreseen and forestalled the AFC. The speculative attack on the Thai baht in 1997 came as a bolt from the blue. But there were signs of impending danger prior to that collapse. Over the first thirty years of its existence, ASEAN had made various efforts to improve the region's economy. By 1996, one might have thought, the organization would have had in place a warning mechanism that could have helped its members take steps, if not to prevent the crisis, at least to limit its scale and duration.

In pursuit of resilience, ASEAN might also have promoted economic and judicial reforms, including transparency, accountability, and probity, which could have reduced the extent to which "crony capitalism" had by 1997 weakened the immunity of local financial-legal systems to external shock. Instead, the first-ever meeting of ASEAN finance ministers was convened in March of that same year, nearly three decades after the organization's birth and merely four months before the baht's downfall in July.

Compared with the assault on the Thai currency, the terrorist attacks on the World Trade Center and the Pentagon in 2001 occurred far beyond ASEAN's purview. A clandestine planning meeting does appear to have taken place in Malaysia in January 2000. But the US government was made aware of that event. It makes no sense to fault ASEAN for Washington's failure to anticipate the catastrophe of September 11, 2001 and arrest the hijackers before they could strike. One must also note that transnational threats such as piracy, smuggling, and drugs, including terrorism, had been on ASEAN's agenda for discussion at least since December 1997, when the grouping instituted biennial meetings on these topics.

Nevertheless, what eventually galvanized ASEAN to move beyond talking about terrorism to acting against it came four years later in the form of foreign pressure and domestic experience. The pressure came from Washington in the wake of the 9/11 attacks in 2001, while the experience included a deadly series of bombings in Indonesia, first in October 2002 in Bali, and then in August 2003 and again in September 2004 in Jakarta, the city that hosts the ASEAN secretariat.

The AFC and the WOT did motivate ASEAN to take preventive steps against such threats. On the financial front these measures included an ASEAN Surveillance Process launched in October 1998 to promote early warning and peer review based on ostensibly full and candid exchanges of information among the member economies. The Process was originally to have been a Mechanism, but for the sake of member-state sovereignty that proposal was watered down.[9] Only in May 2000 did the finance ministers of ASEAN + 3 (China, Japan, and South Korea), gathered in Thailand, announce their Chiang Mai Initiative. And one could question the adequacy of even that first significant regional defense against disruptive capital flows and gyrating exchange rates.[10]

In any event, by then, the damage had been done. From 1997 to 1999, per capita income in the ASEAN region was thought to have lost a third of its value.[11] Indonesian GDP shrank 13 per cent in 1998. As for the WOT, its costs ran beyond the fatalities at bomb sites to include major losses of income from tourism, especially in Bali and southern Thailand. There were political consequences, too. The AFC precipitated or facilitated changes of regime in three of the hardest hit states—Indonesia, Malaysia, and Thailand. On a lesser scale, by targeting Islamist violence, the WOT stoked controversy and conflict in the more or less Muslim areas of Southeast Asia, including parts of Cambodia, Myanmar, and the Philippines.

Even if ASEAN itself is absolved of responsibility for these shocks, that judgment cannot flatten the spike in the insecurity of ASEAN's world to which the shocks gave rise. Nor does an analytic preference for extra-regional causes offer assurance that the region will not be hurt again by future turbulence along financial or terrorist lines. On the contrary, such an assessment highlights the ongoing vulnerability of Southeast Asia to struggles over power and wealth in a conflicted world over which ASEAN lacks control—a world that, for all the long-standing architecture of the international financial institutions and the United Nations, remains unpredictably volatile and insecure. The consonance with realist assumptions is obvious.

Admittedly, non-state actors were prominent in both the financial turbulence and the political violence that hit Southeast Asia. Traditionally, realism has featured the nature, behavior, and interactions of states—expansionary, counter-balancing, bandwagoning, and so on. Yet governments did not precipitate the AFC or the WOT. The financial crisis was triggered by individuals: hedge fund managers shorting the baht, the ringgit, or the rupiah while panicked borrowers and investors dumped these currencies for safer ones, accelerating the rout. The individuals who drove passenger jets into buildings in New York and Washington DC and into the Pennsylvania ground were not trained, armed, and set in motion by a state. Nor were the perpetrators of subsequent attacks, including those in Southeast Asia. When Osama bin Laden changed fields, from the construction business to the terrorist business, he did not leave the private sector.

Realism's core theme, however, is not the state. It is insecurity. In the Hobbesian view of the origin of the state, the condition—insecurity to the point of anarchy—precedes and justifies the existence of the actor—the state. Realists are not all Hobbesian. Yet there is rather more Hobbes than Locke in realism—more necessary force than social contract. When, in the interstices between states, private actors inadvertently or intentionally foment large-scale insecurity, as in the AFC and the WOT, their doings confirm the incipiently anarchic character of international relations. What realism claims to be realistic about is how hard it is for states to replace insecurity with comity in that larger world. As for states and the unequal relations between them, on which realism insists, they were acutely if differently relevant to understanding the repercussions of the financial crisis and the terror war in Southeast Asia.

Consider the AFC: While it would be unfair to blame the AFC on the US Treasury, the United States had favored open capital markets, whose vulnerability to manipulation in countries lacking regulatory safeguards allowed the crisis to occur. In this context, the pre-eminence of the world's sole superpower opened it to sharp rebukes from inside ASEAN. Washington was reproached for hostility, or indifference, or both—for torching the region's economies and then letting them burn.

The conspiracy charge came above all from then-Prime Minister of Malaysia Mahathir Mohamad. He did blame individuals, the investment-wizard-turned-political-philanthropist George Soros especially, and groups, including the Jews. But these charges were part of his broader indictment of the dominance of the West over the East in a world stacked in favor of the US and other already industrialized states.[12] Whatever its accuracy, Mahathir's rhetoric and its implied call for counterforce, echoing his earlier proposal for an East Asian economic community independent of the West, were in cognitive synch with a standard realist scenario whereby the concentration of power in some states triggers offsetting moves by other states.

More widely in Southeast Asia, Washington was accused of indifference as the AFC spiraled on. This charge came with particular intensity from Bangkok when the US chose not to extend direct bilateral help to the crisis' first victim, Thailand. Later in 1997 President Clinton himself dismissed the AFC, then ravaging Thai finances, as a mere "glitch in the road."[13] Yet when the crisis threatened Seoul, his administration quickly committed American resources to a major effort to rescue the South Korean economy.

The lesson to be drawn from this sequence upheld realist assumptions: In a time of crisis, it was balance-of-power logic more than humanitarian need—strategy more than sympathy—that explained how a big power, faced with several ailing lesser powers, decided which one to assist. The Cold War was over in Southeast Asia, but not, at least not fully, in Northeast Asia. Who knew what an economic collapse south of the Korean demilitarized zone would tempt the North to do? Who knew what the repercussions might be on strategically vital China and Japan? By this reasoning, what mattered most to Washington was not suffering but insecurity—realism's prime value. Measured by their respective potentials for insecurity, compared with the strategic risk in Korea, the shock to Thailand was not shocking enough to the United States.[14]

Thailand had the misfortune to have been hit before the extent of the storm was apparent. By the time Washington decided to aid South Korea, it was clearer that the AFC had the potential to wreak global havoc, and that US help would be needed to prevent that from happening. Nonetheless, the American decision to assist Seoul was signally influenced by the strategic stakes on the Korean peninsula, where the 38th parallel was a tripwire for US forces—stakes not present in the Thai case.[15] One may wonder, for example, whether Thailand's travail would have earned a higher priority in Washington if the AFC had downed the baht not in 1997 but in the early 1980s, when Thailand was still a strategically valuable "front-line state" against Vietnam's occupation of Cambodia—to use realist reasoning again.

The war on terror even more compellingly illustrates the importance of states—and their insecurity. I am not thinking of a causal line drawn backward from the jihadist hijackers of September 11, 2001 through Al Qaeda to the Taliban regime in Afghanistan that hosted Al Qaeda's leader, bin Laden. Osama was hardly a minion of Mullah Omar. Nor do I have in mind the sponsorship of terrorism by the "axis of evil"—Iraq, Iran, and North Korea—notwithstanding the evidence for such activity on the part of Teheran and Pyongyang. Nor is it necessary to recall how, in the 1980s, Washington backed the mujahidin against Moscow's occupation of Afghanistan in a hot war by proxy between states waging the Cold War, or how American sponsorship of anti-communist violence by extreme Islamists strengthened their ability later to turn against their benefactor.

It is enough, instead, to note how the size and vigor of the official American response to 9/11 dramatized realism's priority on the uses of state power in conditions of insecurity. Under President George W. Bush, the American state invaded Afghanistan, ousted the Taliban, invaded Iraq, toppled Saddam Hussein, chased Al Qaeda around the world, and selectively helped affected states track down local terrorists, including Jemaah Islamiyah in Indonesia and Abu Sayyaf in the Philippines. Inside the Beltway around Washington DC, experts warned of biological, chemical, and nuclear terrorism, including the chance of a "dirty bomb." The mixture of vulnerability and entitlement fueling American actions re-illustrated Leifer's insight about Indonesia on an extravagant scale. The mainly unilateral or bilateral character of these actions meanwhile fulfilled the realist expectation that in times of crisis a powerful state will tend to bypass multilateral institutions, except insofar as it can use them to ratify and thus amplify its chosen course.

By showing the limits of multilateralism, the war on terror supported a realist approach to regionalism. The threat of Islamist violence in Southeast Asia was not equally felt by all ASEAN member states. From state to state, the threat elicited different reactions with different implications. These differences depended in no small part on whether the country in question had a Muslim majority (Indonesia, Malaysia, Brunei); had a small Muslim minority some of whose leaders had taken up arms against the central government (Philippines, Thailand) or were actually or potentially estranged from it (Myanmar, Cambodia, Singapore); or had too few Muslims to make jihadism an issue (Vietnam, Laos).

Vietnam actually benefitted from the WOT insofar as inflows of tourism and investment were redirected toward it from less secure destinations. The state-by-state diversity of experiences of Islamist violence inhibited a fully or robustly regional answer to it.

This variety together with the fixation of the United States on counter-terrorism created unequal chances for states in Southeast Asia to gain from cooperating with Washington. The Philippines and Indonesia are cases in point. The presidents of these countries were the first heads of state or government in Southeast Asia to visit Washington after 9/11. They offered sympathy and support. Notwithstanding considerable ambivalence in the two Southeast Asian societies toward American intentions, Manila and Jakarta cooperated with the US on counter-terrorism, and were eventually rewarded with substantial packages of aid. American–Singaporean security relations grew especially close. The selectively bilateral character of the ensuing pattern—one (US) hub and a few chosen spokes—diluted incentives at the ASEAN level to move beyond rhetorical assurances to a concrete joint strategy for fighting the war on terror.

Compared with multilateral relations among states, bilateral ones are more readily kept confidential. That benefit became still more valuable following the widely unpopular American occupation of Iraq, which by September 2004 the UN secretary general agreed was "illegal" from the standpoint of the world body's charter.[16] Even the appearance of signing on to an American war on terror that justified the occupation of Iraq would have been toxic for ASEAN. And even without that anathema, the necessary reliance of counter-terrorist efforts on closely guarded intelligence, secret pursuit, and timely interdiction would have made multilateralism, let alone the "ASEAN Way," seem less a method than an impediment.

This is not to deny ASEAN's ability to express a consensus against anti-state violence in Southeast Asia. If the Chiang Mai Initiative was a regional response to the AFC, the declaration against terrorism adopted by the ASEAN Regional Forum at its meeting in Brunei in August 2002 was an adaptation to the WOT. Other declarations and steps could also be mentioned, including moves to set up counter-terrorism centers in Kuala Lumpur and Jakarta.

Yet if Michael Leifer were looking over my shoulder as I write, I think he would caution against treating these initiatives as signs of robust originality, autonomy, and proactivity on the part of ASEAN. I think he would resist this temptation toward institutionalist optimism. Certainly he did so in his essay on the ASEAN Regional Forum. The Forum in his eyes could not be understood except with reference to the major powers outside Southeast Asia. Their apparent tolerance of the grouping's existence was essential to its work. Without the involvement of the US, Japan, and China, the organization would surely lose momentum—or so he strongly implied. As a grouping of distinctly lesser states, ASEAN itself was subject to their "intrinsic limitations."[17]

Without the participation of Japan, China, and South Korea as partners with ASEAN's members in currency-swapping arrangements, the Chiang Mai

Initiative could not have been launched. US resources and incentives were comparably vital in encouraging the Southeast Asian states most affected by Islamist violence to bandwagon Washington's counter-terror campaign—more or less discreetly, within domestically set limits, and for their own policy reasons.

Realist calculation works both ways, however. If the wagon is not making headway, why climb on? In 2004, as the American war wagon in Iraq bogged down, the Philippines and Thailand climbed off, withdrawing their token non-combat contingents. Participation in that campaign by majority-Muslim Indonesia or Malaysia had been and remained out of the question. Among major ASEAN members, only Singapore continued, albeit with mounting worry, to support US policy in the Middle East. Yet advocates of regional unity in Southeast Asia were not about to treat the American state as a usefully common enemy. And their reluctance, too, had a realist—Leiferesque—reason: a desire to include the United States along with China and Japan in a stable balance of regional power.

Other approaches

The other four approaches in Figure 2.1 will be handled less thoroughly than realism, given Leifer's association with the latter approach and the focus of this book on his work.

Culturalism (+)

The Asian financial crisis had a slightly negative net effect on the plausibility of an identity-focused approach to Southeast Asian regionalism. Culturalist perceptions were, however, substantiated by the war on terror, which magnified the salience of identity both inside and outside the region. The overall increase in the relevance of culturalism did not match the comparable affirmation of realism or constructivism, but it was noticeable nonetheless.

The AFC did tempt some to make a culturalist distinction between the putatively market-worshiping West and the supposedly community-minded East when blaming the former for the latter's travail. The anti-Semitic overtones of Mahathir's vitriol against the West illustrated this choice. Unlike his critique of the US and the IMF, however, his racialist innuendo never really caught on. The financial crisis was never widely or convincingly accounted for in cultural terms. If anything, by abruptly ending Southeast Asia's "economic miracle," the crisis damaged the plausibility of "Asian values" as vital drivers of, and conceptual keys to, the success of the region.

The analytic impact of the WOT, on the other hand, was intensely culturalist. The muscular US responses to 9/11 and Saddam Hussein had a fiercely centrifugal effect on Islamist terrorism. By shattering Al Qaeda into more or less autonomous pieces while stoking anti-US sentiment across the Muslim world, Washington helped simultaneously to embed and arouse radical Islamism in local settings. A range of such contexts existed in culturally diverse Southeast Asia, where thwarted plots and violent acts linked to Jemaah Islamiyah (JI) made the ASEAN region a candidate for the title of WOT's "second front."

JI's apparent desire to attach Muslim-majority Indonesia, Malaysia, and Brunei to the relatively Muslim southern fringes of Buddhist-majority Thailand and Catholic-majority Philippines in a neo-caliphate that would leave ASEAN in pieces is, surely, an impossible dream. It is also impossible, however, to doubt the (positive or negative) impact on regional cooperation of a war on terror that so centrally implicates the overlapping of religion, politics, and violence and thus recommends attention to culture and identity as constructs affecting the nature and course of regionalism in Southeast Asia.

Rationalism (-)

The AFC and the WOT had, on balance, a negative effect on the plausibility of interest-focused rationalism as an approach to regionalism in Southeast Asia. The financial crisis did carry implications for economic regionalism that were amenable to rationalist explanation. Prior to the crisis, impatient at the pace of regional market liberalization, Singapore had begun to seek bilateral trade deals outside the region. The crisis confirmed Singapore's interest in making such deals. If regionalism meant developing closer economic ties with the neighbors, the AFC showed just how damaging over-reliance on the neighborhood could be. Negotiating bilateral agreements with economies outside the region could be seen, in game terms, as hedging one's bets for the sake of an interest in greater and more stable market access.

Yet rationalism works best when change takes place incrementally in a system whose rules are known. The approach is less useful in sudden whirlwinds of change that overthrow expectations, provoke emotions, and obscure the interests of the parties concerned. When a game gets "out of hand," it ceases to be a game at all.[18] In this respect, both the AFC and the WOT frustrated, at least temporarily, the rationalist preference for clear and measurable interests interacting to yield incremental change.

Even prior to the shocks, some aspects of ASEAN were ill-suited to rationalist assumptions. The Association's most notable accomplishment in the 1990s may have been its expansion to include all ten Southeast Asian states. The wisdom of that enlargement can be debated. But it cannot be explained without using the consummatory language of regional identity and security, quite apart from the late-joining members' instrumental interests in, say, economic gains.

Rationalism was neither entirely nor permanently disrupted by the force of the AFC and the WOT. On balance, however, these shocks showed the limits of a purely rationalist model of ASEAN. They did so not least by raising the possibility of future explosions that might again sideswipe both regionalism and the case for thinking of it as a stable interplay of negotiation, coalition, and interest—an ongoing game played in relative isolation from the larger, volatile, and impinging world.

Liberalism (-)

The two shocks were also moderately unkind to liberalism as an approach to regionalism. Especially at analytic risk was that perspective's tendency to place faith in institutions generally and democratic ones in particular.

ASEAN could hardly be blamed for the waves of hot money sloshing around the global economy in the run-up to the AFC. Yet in 1997, at the mature age of thirty, the group still could not monitor its members closely enough to warn them of their exposure to danger, including the glaring deficiencies in their financial practices to which, later, the crisis would in part be traced. Nor, in the months prior to the AFC, had ASEAN been able to prevent illegal and intentional fires set in Kalimantan and Sumatra from spreading a haze thick enough to clog lungs and close schools in neighboring Malaysia and Singapore—a disaster with origins entirely within the region.[19]

In liberalism's defense one could argue that democratic institutions might have made ASEAN surveillance and member compliance more likely. But this seems, at best, only partly correct. If democracy means reliance on voting, Indonesia might have been willing to submit to the will of the majority and end the haze, which by 1997 had become an almost perennial bane. That assumes, however, that enough members not affected by the smoke would have aligned themselves with those who were, rather than abstaining from deference to the region's largest country. And if private entreaties to Indonesia to do something were ineffective, would the threat of being shamed in a public vote have made Indonesia comply? As for democracy inside the member countries, could that not actually have strengthened the resistance of member states to intrusions by ASEAN, including monitoring local flows of footloose portfolio investment and leveraged foreign exchange?

As for the war on terror, the record of its prosecution in Southeast Asia did not clearly support liberalism's faith in the effectiveness of democratic institutions. The early stars of the WOT in Southeast Asia were two relatively illiberal countries, Singapore and Malaysia, each with its own Internal Security Act. In contrast, the more liberal climate prevailing in Indonesia led the government there to proceed less resolutely against suspected terrorists for fear of antagonizing Islamist opinion. In light of such evidence, one could wonder whether making ASEAN more democratic at either the national or the regional level would necessarily strengthen the war on terror in Southeast Asia.

None of this is to deny the ongoing pressures and incentives for ASEAN's members and the organization itself to become, in some sense, more liberal-democratic. Noteworthy, too, is the willingness of the already more democratic members to revise the sovereignty principle that inhibits timely intramural criticism. It is not coincidental that the foreign ministers of relatively democratic

Thailand and the Philippines were the first to make that case. Buoyed by the recent democratization of Indonesia, one could join Amitav Acharya in hoping for "participatory regionalism" in Southeast Asia.[20]

Yet the history of ASEAN does not inspire confidence in such an outcome. Consider, for example, how the action of reaching across intra-ASEAN borders with good intentions has been renamed over time: from "constructive intervention" to "constructive engagement" to "flexible engagement" to "enhanced interaction."

These concepts did not necessarily express a principled commitment to liberal institutions. At least as much, if not more so, they reflected a realist argument for national security: that only by insisting on each member's domestic vigilance—ecological, financial, even political—could all members protect themselves from the potentially disastrous consequences of allowing a preventable or manageable problem in any one member country to metastasize into a regional crisis. Liberalization, yes, but in security's name. The AFC and the WOT, by intensifying realist concerns, reinforced this tendency to downgrade liberal institutions to dispensers of due diligence and timely intelligence—a recipe for technocracy more than democracy.

Over time, consensus-seeking ASEAN diplomats edited and re-edited the clarity of "constructive intervention" into the timidity of "enhanced interaction"—a phrase so abstractly innocuous that one could no longer tell what it was a euphemism for. Acharya, while hoping for "participatory regionalism," was realistic about its prospects: Having strongly resisted "post-sovereign regional norms" and shown "no explicit commitment to democracy and human rights," ASEAN was not likely to become "a democratic community" anytime soon. The horrors of 9/11 and the Bali bombings had "diminished the space for civil society" in Southeast Asia. "Homeland security" had "assumed priority over human security"—the safety and dignity of individuals. In such conditions, ASEAN was more likely to reassert its traditional "official regionalism" than experiment with a more participatory kind.[21]

Constructivism (+)

As an approach to regionalism, idea-focused constructivism gained more credibility from the crisis and the war than any other approach save insecurity-featuring realism at the polar opposite end of Figure 2.1.

More than any of the other approaches, idea-centered constructivism accommodates contingency and change, precisely the features one associates with crisis. Relative to the other perspectives, the constructivist universe is in flux. Ideas come and go, rise and fall, as things happen and people come to think differently about them. Mindsets may outlast the conditions that gave rise to them. But underlying insecurity and collective identity, interests, and institutions are all less mutable than ideas. Insofar as the AFC and the WOT were intensely changeful and bypassed ASEAN as an institution while upstaging—outdating?—its norms, constructivist precepts gained plausibility.

Nor was any other approach more suited to acknowledging the sense in which these shocks themselves were driven by ideas: the AFC by free-market fundamentalism and the WOT by its Islamist counterpart. Admittedly, these attributions are at best incomplete. Prior to the economic crisis, "crony capitalism," the inverse of free-market thinking, had already weakened the capacity of local financial-legal systems to withstand external shock. As for "the war on terror" in Southeast Asia after 9/11, it involved a double response—not only to domestic Islamist "holy war," but also to secular American pressure to engage Al Qaeda on its presumed "second front."

Notice, however, how much these qualifications illustrate and thus reaffirm the utility of constructivist discourse. "Crony capitalism," "the war on terror," "holy war," a "second front"—these are all constructions. Almost as sudden as the AFC itself was the projection, in its wake, of "crony capitalism," previously limited to the Philippines, to describe Indonesia, Malaysia, and Thailand as well. "The war on terror" was, and in 2004 largely remained, a coinage of the Bush administration projected onto the larger world. Also subjective and self-serving were the "holy war" that the jihadists claimed to be waging and the "second front" label that war-metaphor-minded observers attached to Southeast Asia. What has mattered about these ideas is less their accuracy than their influence—precisely the constructivist point.

If the haze, the AFC, and the WOT had never occurred, the "ASEAN Way" might still be intact, or at any rate less challenged. The Association's hallmark pragmatism might have continued to keep second thoughts at bay. Instead, one crisis after another struck the region in clashes not of civilizations so much as of ideas. In such a strenuously symbolic context, the idea of regionalism ASEAN-style has been, in effect, upstaged and drowned out by other constructions. Regionalist policy intellectuals have been stimulated to come up with new ideas—"ideas that have the common aim of trying to revitalize and even reinvent ASEAN," to cite the impeccably constructivist ambition of a co-editor of, yes, *Reinventing ASEAN*.[22]

While the literal reinvention of ASEAN is, of course, a conceit, a constructivist perspective nevertheless opens a vista of relevant questions. The AFC in Southeast Asia left in its wake grave doubts about the "Washington consensus" in favor of deregulating markets and privatizing firms. Will it be replaced in Southeast Asia by an "ASEAN consensus" that is market-sensitive but allows a greater economic role for the state and more attention to the social character of economic relations? How, if at all, might such a regionalist discourse encompass, say, the economic populism of the Thai government—"Thaksinomics"—or Malaysia's relatively successful imposition of partial capital controls in response to the AFC? As bilateral agreements between ASEAN and non-ASEAN economies proliferate, will the ASEAN Free Trade Area also have to be "reinvented"? If so in what way, and based on what ideas for economic cooperation across such a diverse region? When Myanmar's brutal generals chose not to accept the rotating chair of ASEAN in 2006–07, they helped to save the Association's face in the eyes of liberals in Southeast Asia. But avoiding that showdown hardly settled, and may have intensified, the ideational struggle between opposing models of regional order: hands-off sovereignty to protect autocracy, or heads-up interaction to promote democracy.

Ideas are one thing; actual practices are quite another. The "reinvention" of ASEAN as an Economic, Socio-Cultural, and Security Community, for example, announced at the group's 2003 summit in Bali, may turn out to have been little more than a rhetorical flourish adopted to indulge the meeting's Indonesian host—the grouping's *primus inter pares*, a realist might say. But ASEAN will not run out of ideas. Indeed, from a cynically realist perspective, what else does the Association have?

Full circle

That ASEAN should want to call itself a security community brings me full circle back to Michael Leifer. At the beginning of this chapter, I illustrated his realist emphasis on insecurity by citing his interpretation of Indonesian foreign policy as a product of national vulnerability and regional entitlement. Vulnerability and entitlement are, of course, ideas. Had Leifer's argument in that book been made by a constructivist, the ideas would have been situated mainly in texts—and probably critiqued in counter-texts as well. Michael instead rooted them in physical, social, and historical conditions. Indonesia's strategic location and ample natural resources really did make it vulnerable to foreign intervention. But these same features combined with the archipelago's vast size to sustain in the minds of Indonesian leaders a sense of regional entitlement—"a proprietary attitude" toward Southeast Asia.[23]

That proprietary attitude—a mental construct—has suffered a series of debilitating shocks. Indonesia was hurt more by the AFC, and has been hurt more by the still unfolding WOT, than any other ASEAN country. Nor was Jakarta's sense of entitlement boosted by its inability, in 1999, to stop the tiny half-island of East Timor from exiting Indonesia. Yet for all the damage done to Indonesian national self-esteem, one can glimpse in the decision taken in Bali to launch an ASEAN Security Community a muted expression of the same proprietary outlook that Michael noted. For, in the long run, who but the largest—by far the largest—member of ASEAN will be, or at any rate feel itself to be, most entitled to influence how Southeast Asia protects itself in an insecure world? A security community in this sense creates a leading role that awaits the time when the actor already cast (or self-cast) to play it will be healthy enough to do so.

It may seem paradoxical to have argued in this chapter that the AFC and the WOT have especially valorized realism and constructivism, the two perspectives on regionalism in Southeast Asia that are the least alike, ontologically, chronologically, and, some might say, ideologically as well. But for all the differences that keep them apart, these perspectives are not mutually exclusive. They are more like the different axioms, preferences, and logics of inference used by different blind persons touching different parts of the regionalist elephant—each toucher fitting whatever is at hand into what she or he already "knows" is important, interesting, and necessary to comprehend the animal as a whole.

But not all approaches are equally productive. What actually happens to the elephant redistributes the significance of what is being touched—its aspects—and the heuristic leverage of the set of assumptions, priorities, and arguments favored by each toucher. In future, the identitarian aspect of regionalism could give way to the utilitarian use of ASEAN settings as games in which self-interested member states calculate and negotiate bargains on behalf of their material interests. In such an event, that instrumental aspect will become more salient, and a rationalist outlook on regionalism will become more insightful. Comparably, if ASEAN as an institution democratizes, that aspect will become more prominent while, correspondingly, liberalism gains analytic ground.

In the meantime, pending events (and shocks) still to come, realism, constructivism, and to a lesser extent culturalism, as approaches to Southeast Asian regionalism, remain the main net beneficiaries of the Asian financial crisis and the war on terror.

Notes

1 For conversations or correspondence that helped me in writing or revising this chapter I am grateful to—but, alas, cannot implicate—Jennifer Amyx, Ralf Emmers, Erik Kuhonta, Joseph Liow, and Danny Unger.

2 Security was also prominent in the connotations of the next most common conceptual references, to the balance of power (5) and order (4). These figures were calculated from a bibliography of 115 items kindly made available to me by Ralf Emmers and Joseph Liow. Excluded from the list were the many volumes written by others but selected by Leifer for the Routledge "Politics in Asia" series that he oversaw as general editor. References in the text are to Michael Leifer, *Cambodia: The Search for Security* (New York: Praeger, 1967); and Leifer with Daljit Singh, "Promoting Security and Political Cooperation," paper, 568th Wilton Park Conference, "Europe and Asia: Working towards a Partnership?" West Sussex, UK, 7–9 June 2001.

3 Michael Leifer, *Indonesia's Foreign Policy* (London: Allen & Unwin / Royal Institute of International Affairs, 1983), pp. xiv–xv, 111, 145, 155, 169–170, 173–174; "Vietnam's Foreign Policy in the Post-Soviet Era: Coping with Vulnerability," in Robert S. Ross, ed., *East Asia in Transition: Toward a New Regional Order* (Armonk, NY: M. E. Sharpe / Singapore: Institute of Southeast Asian Studies, 1995), pp. 267–292; and *Singapore's Foreign Policy: Coping with Vulnerability* (New York: Routledge, 2000).

4 See Alexander Wendt, "Anarchy Is What States Make of It: The Social Construction of Power Politics," *International Organization*, 46: 2 (Spring 1992), 424–425.

5 The United States is my own parochial intellectual "home." An effort to show how its American provenance has colored and limited the literature I cite lies beyond my present scope. On what a scholarly "home" implies, see my "Situating Southeast Asian Studies: Realm, Guild, and Home," in Anthony Reid, ed., *Southeast Asian Studies for a Globalized Age: Pacific Perspectives* (Tempe, AZ: Arizona State University PSEAS Monograph Series Press, 2004), pp. 1–29.

6 Hans J. Morgenthau, *Politics among Nations: The Struggle for Power and Peace* (New York: Knopf, 1948); Kenneth N. Waltz, *Man, the State, and War* (New York: Columbia University Press, 1959); Anthony Downs, *An Economic Theory of Democracy* (New York: Harper and Row, 1957); William H. Riker, *The Theory of Political Coalitions* (New Haven, CT: Yale University Press, 1962); Gabriel A. Almond and Sidney Verba, *The Civic Culture: Political Attitudes and Democracy in Five Nations* (Princeton, NJ: Princeton University Press, 1963); Lucien Pye and Sidney Verba, eds, *Political Culture and Political Development* (Princeton, NJ: Princeton University Press, 1965); Robert O. Keohane and Joseph S. Nye, *Power and Interdependence: World Politics in Transition* (Boston, MA: Little, Brown, 1977); Keohane, *After Hegemony: Cooperation and Discord in the World Political Economy* (Princeton, NJ: Princeton University Press, 1984); Keohane, *Institutionalist Theory and the Realist Challenge after the Cold War* (Cambridge, MA: Harvard University Center for International Affairs, 1992); John Ruggie, *Constructing the World Polity: Essays on International Institutionalization* (New York: Routledge, 1998); and Alexander Wendt, *Social Theory of International Politics* (Cambridge: Cambridge University Press, 1999).

7 Samuel P. Huntington, *The Clash of Civilizations and the Remaking of World Order* (New York: Simon & Schuster, 1996); Lawrence E. Harrison and Huntington, eds, *Culture Matters: How Values Shape Human Progress* (New York: Basic Books, 2000); and Huntington, *Who We Are: The Erosion and Renewal of American National Identity* (New York: Simon & Schuster, 2004).

8 John Sidel, [book review], *Survival*, 43: 4 (Winter 2001), p. 162.

9 Hadi Soesastro, "ASEAN in 2030: The Long View," in Simon S. C. Tay, Jesus P. Estanislao, and Soesastro, eds, *Reinventing ASEAN* (Singapore: Institute of Southeast Asian Studies, 2001), p. 304.

10 Twenty years before the AFC, in August 1977, an ASEAN Swap Arrangement (ASA) was established to help central banks cope with modest and temporary shortages in liquidity. At the Chiang Mai meeting in 2000, ASA's scope was expanded to allow a member central bank to swap its own currency for major international currencies for up to six months in amounts up to double that member bank's existing financial commitment to ASA. Even so, as of 2002, these commitments—a mere $150 million apiece from Brunei, Indonesia, Malaysia, Philippines, Singapore, and Thailand, and much less than that from the other four ASEAN members combined—were still negligible compared with the likely size of flows in a crisis. Even if Bilateral Swap Agreements are included, the total sum available to a suddenly needy member economy is "a drop in the ocean" that churns through global financial markets every day. (See Seok-Dong Wang and Lene Andersen, "Regional Financial Cooperation in East Asia: The Chiang Mai Initiative and Beyond," *Bulletin on Asia-Pacific Perspectives,* 2002–2003, pp. 90–91, 93 ["drop"].)

11 Mahathir Mohamad, "Asian Financial Crisis Not Over," speech accepting the "ASEAN Achievement Millennium Award," Singapore, 10 September [2001]; <http://www.southcentre.org/info/southbulletin/bulletin20/bulletin20.htm> as of 9 October 2004.

12 "We are pushed to become a backward, weak race which is recolonised and having to serve others," Mahathir told a Malaysian audience in 1998. "They [the West] are trying to destroy all we have built." Quoted by Peter Symonds, "Economic Crisis Fuels Tensions in Malaysian Government," 2 July 1998; <http:www.wsws.org/news/1998/july1998/mal-j02.shtml> as of 10 September 2004. See also Mahathir Mohamad, *A New Deal for Asia* (Kuala Lumpur: Pelanduk, 1999).

13 Quoted in Jane Skanderup, "The 1998 Asia Pacific Economic Cooperation Meeting: Opportunity for Relevance?", *PacNet Newsletter*, 43 (6 November 1998); <http://www.csis.org/pacfor/pac4398.html> as of 9 May 2004.

14 For evidence to this effect, see Robert E. Rubin with Jacob Weisberg, *In an Uncertain World: Tough Choices from Wall Street to Washington* (New York: Random House, 2003), pp. 212, 218, 228ff. Rubin was the US Treasury Secretary in 1997–99.

15 Looking back on the AFC, Rubin contrasted the fall of "an obscure currency, the Thai baht, in July 1997" (Rubin with Weisberg, *Uncertain World*, p. 212) with the severe risk to the world financial system posed by the AFC's arrival in South Korea in the following October (228 ff.; cf. 218). While stressing economic security, Rubin acknowledged the geostrategic concerns of officials from the State and Defense Departments and the National Security Council. They favored a bilateral American contribution to what became an IMF-led $17 billion package of support for Thailand. Rubin did not, and he won. But South Korea was "a crucially important military ally" with 37,000 US troops stationed near its border with North Korea (218), whose own troops reportedly had gone on a "heightened state of alert" (232). In this military-security league, Thailand could not compete. In December, with Rubin's approval, the IMF announced a $55 billion reform-and-rescue package for South Korea.

As for the AFC illustrating the (anti-realist) argument that states "matter less, in the sense that forceful imperatives of the world economy take power away from them," Rubin (215) flatly disagreed. "To me, the opposite is true. The potential impact of any one country's problems on others means that national governments matter more—an ineffective government in one country can have a damaging impact beyond that country's borders."

16 British Broadcasting Corporation, "Iraq War Illegal, Says Annan," *BBC News, World Edition*, 16 September 2004; <http://news.bbc.co.uk/2/hi/middle_east/3661134/stm> as of 20 September 2004.

17 This paragraph's last three sentences reflect Michael Leifer, *The ASEAN Regional Forum*, Adelphi Paper 302 (New York: Oxford University Press / International Institute for Strategic Studies, 1996), pp. 53, 59–60, and 58, respectively.

18 In this context it is not surprising that rational-choice theorizing should have been less popular among scholars in Southeast Asia than in the United States, a relatively orderly country unaccustomed to being overtaken by events it did not anticipate and could not control—at least prior to 9/11.

19 Simon S. C. Tay and Jesus Estanislao, "The Relevance of ASEAN: Crisis and Change," in Tay et al., eds, *Reinventing ASEAN*, p. 4.

20 Amitav Acharya, "Democratization and the Prospects for Participatory Regionalism in Southeast Asia," in Kanishka Jayasuriya, ed., *Asian Regional Governance: Crisis and Change* (London: RoutledgeCurzon, 2004), pp. 127–134.

21 Acharya, "Democratization," p. 140.

22 Simon S. C. Tay, "Preface," in Tay et al., eds, *Reinventing ASEAN*, p. xi.

23 Leifer, *Indonesia's Foreign Policy*, p. ix.

3 Michael Leifer and the pre-requisites of regional order in Southeast Asia

Yuen Foong Khong

Michael Leifer illuminated the international politics of Southeast Asia for all those who cared about the region. His scholarship was marked by a masterly and unrivaled feel for the pulse of the region. Unlike those of us who are "lumpers," that is those who write about "ASEAN" or the ASEAN states, Leifer was a "splitter."[1] He admitted that there might be such a thing as a corporate strategic perspective on occasion, but found the differing strategic visions of the ASEAN states more interesting and important. Thus he was more alert than most to divergences among the ASEAN states, as when he emphasized Indonesia's different interpretation of the Zone of Peace, Freedom and Neutrality (ZOPFAN), or the annoyance felt by Malaysia and Indonesia about the alacrity with which Singapore offered port privileges to the United States navy in the early 1990s. This eye for divergences was partly informed by Leifer's extensive fieldwork—where his former LSE students turned permanent secretaries and ministers would share confidences with their former teacher—but it was also actuated by a hard-nosed skepticism about ASEAN solidarity. His skeptical attitude allowed him to ask hard questions and protected him from accepting, at face value, the views and protestations of his Southeast Asian interlocutors. His approach may have annoyed a leader or two, but more often, it gained him the respect and trust of the more forward-looking leaders of the region. The result was that, time and again, Leifer produced the most incisive accounts of the international relations of Southeast Asia. It is unlikely that his mode of illuminating the international relations of the region can or will be replicated.

Unlike many lumpers (who are almost always political scientists), Leifer also eschewed unnecessary theoretical jargon in his work. But that did not mean that his work was devoid of theoretical or conceptual commitments. Those who follow it will quickly notice that it is informed by at least two central concepts: the balance of power and regional order. If one were to count the relative frequency with which these two concepts appear across all his work on Southeast Asia and the Asia Pacific, one would most likely find "the balance of power" to be his most important analytic workhorse, followed closely by "regional order." As we shall see later, the two concepts are intimately related in a causal way: the balance of power, for Leifer, is the necessary but not sufficient condition for regional order. Since Leifer's use of the balance of power concept will be discussed elsewhere in this volume, I will focus on his notion of regional order here.

"Regional order" was the outcome that Michael Leifer wanted for Southeast Asia; it was also his yardstick of choice to assess the international relations of Southeast Asia and the Asia Pacific. The recurrent theme in all of Leifer's writings on Southeast Asia was how elusive, and at times how illusory, regional order was. This chapter seeks to challenge this conclusion of Leifer's by arguing that his regional order yardstick is a misleading measure of Southeast Asia's (progress in) international relations. The concept is theoretically underdeveloped and methodologically imprecise, allowing the analyst to see disorder in every minor perturbation in the region. I propose replacing "regional order" with "peace and stability," the preferred terms of the discourse by ASEAN's policy elites. By the latter criteria, ASEAN and the Asia Pacific, contrary to the skeptics, have made impressive progress in the past forty years.

Leifer and regional order

"Order" and "regional order," it is worth noting at the outset, are concepts original to Michael Leifer in the way he employed them to evaluate the international politics of Southeast Asia. They do not appear in any of the ASEAN's foundational or milestone documents. The terms that recur repeatedly in these documents are "regional peace and stability." Peace and stability, not order, were ASEAN's terms of choice for its security discourse. Leifer did use the terms peace and stability frequently, but judging by the frequency of use and, more importantly, analytic context, his preferred concept for analyzing the international relations of Southeast Asia was regional order.

Although the term "regional order" appears frequently in Leifer's writings,[2] he did not elaborate on the concept at length. Perhaps he considered the meaning of the term to be obvious, or believed that it could be readily understood in the context in which it was used.[3] The concept was defined most explicitly in a lecture he gave at Chulalongkorn University in 1986, where regional order meant "the existence of a stable structure of regional inter-governmental relationships informed by common assumptions about the bases of inter-state conduct."[4] In another essay written at about the same time, Leifer saw regional order as "a structure of regional relationships that are widely accepted" by the relevant states.[5] Hence:

> It is possible to argue that the general pattern of the regional balance in East Asia in terms of distribution of power embodies a measure of stability from a sense of prudence. But it is not the same as a viable regional order which requires more than just a rudimentary code of inter-state conduct. It requires also the existence of a set of shared assumptions about the interrelationships among resident and external states.[6]

Prudence, a rudimentary code of inter-state conduct, gives a measure of stability, but such stability is not tantamount to a viable regional order. A viable regional order needs, in addition to prudence (and the balance of power), "a set of shared assumptions about the interrelationships among resident and external states." Elsewhere, Leifer has described these shared assumptions as "common goals" or "a common strategic perspective."[7] This emphasis on shared assumptions reflects Leifer's English School (of international relations) sensibilities.

As Liow and Emmers point out in the introduction to this volume, Leifer's choice of "order" as one of his major analytic concepts suggest that he was writing in the vein of the English School.[8] Secondary writings about the English School have not categorized Leifer as a member of it, even though he was a colleague of some of its major proponents at the LSE.[9] However, it is clear from Leifer's writings, and from his "recommended readings" for those who knew him, that he was influenced by Charles Manning, Martin Wight, and Hedley Bull.[10] Leaving aside the controversial Manning, it is not difficult to find important conceptual similarities in the work of Leifer and that of Wight and Bull, two of foremost writers of the English School.

A key claim of the English School is that even though the international system is anarchic, there are elements of society present to impart some sort of order to the system. And we know that these elements of society exist because of the common values (assumptions, for Leifer) that are at least shared by Western states. Consider Bull's elaboration of when international society comes into being:

> A society of states...exists when a group of states, conscious of certain common interests and common values, form a society in the sense that they conceive themselves to be bound by a common set of rules in their relations with one another, and share in the working of common institutions....they should *respect one another's claims to independence*...they should *honour agreements* into which they enter...they should be subject to certain *limitations in exercising force* against one another.[11]

Leifer's notion of the basis of a viable regional order is remarkably similar to Bull's notion of international society: it is concerned with the existence and acceptance of certain common values. The word society also appears in Leifer's writings about Southeast Asia occasionally.[12] The suggestion here is that his questions about regional order in Southeast Asia are also questions about the extent to which the Southeast Asian states form a regional "society of states." Is there such a society among the Southeast Asian states or the original ASEAN 5? Leifer was extremely ambivalent about the answer to this question, although he was more explicit about the prevalence of conflict in the region. In his *Conflict and Regional Order in South-east Asia*, Leifer argued that Southeast Asia had "not enjoyed a stable pattern of power" since World War II.[13] The sources of regional conflict and disorder included contestations over state identity, historical antagonisms, and problems associated with the transfer of sovereignty. These fissures lend themselves to intrusions by external states—read the great powers—who competed to "shape a regional balance,"[14] further complicating the prospects for regional order. The prevalence of such antagonisms, issues, and competition suggested to Leifer that although commonly shared assumptions or strategic perspectives existed, they tended to be dwarfed by divergent perspectives and assumptions, resulting in a situation where ASEAN's designs for regional order are often compromised by the prevalence of intra-mural differences.[15]

Although Leifer was not very explicit about the content of the assumptions that ought to be shared, it is possible to infer the latter from his analysis of the key events in ASEAN's history. The point to note is that the contents of those shared assumptions are again very similar to the shared values articulated by Bull: respecting one another's independence, exercising self-restraint in using force, and keeping promises. Leifer is more forthcoming on who should be doing the sharing. If ASEAN is the unit of analysis, there should be shared assumptions among (i) the ASEAN members about their relationships with each other and about the role of external states in the region; and (ii) ASEAN and the "external states" about the latter's relationships with ASEAN.

Among the developments that constituted major attempts on ASEAN's part to articulate "shared assumptions" (in the midst of a shifting strategic context) are the formation of ASEAN, ZOPFAN, the Treaty of Amity and Cooperation (TAC), and the ASEAN Regional Forum (ARF). I shall discuss the first three of these developments, focusing on Leifer's account of how important "shared assumptions" were to the creation and functioning of these institutions and the implications for regional order.[16] The general picture that emerges is that while Leifer acknowledges the presence of some common values behind each of these institutions, he remains skeptical about the extent to which those values were shared. His account focuses just as much, if not more, on the divergences in values and assumptions among the ASEAN states, and it is this emphasis on differences that allows him to question the existence of a Southeast Asian society of states. In the absence of a regional society, regional order remains an elusive goal.

ASEAN

One of the most important services that Leifer performed as the leading interpreter of the international politics of Southeast Asia was to remind his readers—especially those outside of Southeast Asia—that ASEAN was born out of the need for "regional reconciliation," not economic integration (as was the case with the European Union). The need for reconciliation arose out of the conflictual recent past among the young states of the region. And if one could speak of "formative events" for a region, Indonesia's military confrontation against Malaysia from 1963 through 1966 would be the one. It was also Leifer's example par excellence of the absence of shared assumptions and its consequences. Sukarno's refusal to recognize the legitimacy of the joining of Malaya, Singapore, and "British Borneo" (Sabah, and Sarawak) to form Malaysia, and his attempt to scuttle the project by military means, demonstrate how disagreements about the relationships among the states in the region can beget violence and disorder.

Sukarno's successor, Suharto, was more willing to countenance the existence of Malaysia and Singapore, and to consider them as legitimate players in the region. The formation of ASEAN in 1967 ushers in a period where the five members of the organization sought to articulate a set of shared assumptions about their relationships with each other, as well as with external states. Hence the Preamble to the ASEAN Declaration spoke of how mindful members of the new organization were about "the existence of *mutual interests* and *common problems*" and how, "in the spirit of equality and partnership," they sought to "contribute towards peace, progress and prosperity in the region." Moreover, they also agreed to (the Indonesian-inspired) view that Southeast Asia bore the "*primary responsibility* for strengthening the economic and social stability of the region," as well as ensuring "their *stability and security from external interference*."[17]

Leifer liked to remind his readers that it was at Indonesia's insistence that the paragraph about Southeast Asians being responsible for their region's order was inserted. His point was that Indonesia had a conception of regional order in which it, as the first among equals in the ASEAN entourage, would have a predominant role in shaping. Indonesia sought to ensure the latter by reserving to Southeast Asians, the "primary responsibility" for shaping their region's stability and security. In other words, outside states such as the United States, China, Japan, or the United Kingdom, were not to be given prominent roles in shaping regional order. Leifer was skeptical about this approach to regional order for two reasons. First, Indonesia's assumption that it was entitled to certain prerogatives as the largest and most populous state was not shared by its neighbors. Second, ASEAN was naïve to assume that it was capable of having a primary role in shaping regional order because its strength remained too far behind that of the great powers.

ZOPFAN

Four years after the advent of ASEAN, the five member states issued the Kuala Lumpur declaration, expressing ASEAN's hope "to secure the recognition of, and respect for, Southeast Asia as a Zone of Peace, Freedom and Neutrality [ZOPFAN], free from any form or manner of interference by outside Powers".[18] ZOPFAN, as Leifer points out, was a Malaysia-inspired response to the changing geopolitical situation in the region: the United States' impending withdrawal from Vietnam, and the US–China rapprochement. His analysis of the genesis of ZOPFAN is a tour de force of revelations about the intra-mural dissensions and how that resulted in a document "distinguished by resolutions rather than by resolve" where there was "much agreement in principle but little purposive action."[19]

No summary can do justice to Leifer's immaculately researched and nuanced account, but the thrust of his analysis was focused on how Malaysia's original proposal for ZOPFAN, which would involve the great powers (the United States, Russia, and China) "guaranteeing" Southeast Asia's neutrality, went against Indonesia's vision for regional order. Indonesia did not share Malaysia's assumption about the great powers in Southeast Asia, and it would prefer to keep them at arm's length, not offer them a policing role in the region. Indonesia was especially worried about China, which Malaysia seemed anxious to accommodate for domestic political reasons. Moreover, Indonesia was also annoyed by Malaysia's presumptuousness in attempting "to prescribe unilaterally for regional order", a role which it would prefer to reserve for itself as the *primus inter pares* within ASEAN.[20] Although the Philippines was publicly in favor of ZOPFAN, Singapore and Thailand preferred a continuing military role for the United States in the region, and in that sense they were skeptical about "neutralization" unless it could be defined as vaguely as possible. In the event, they went along with the Indonesian approach, in part because the latter, by being less explicit about the allowable role of outside powers (they are asked only not to "interfere"), permitted Thailand and Singapore to interpret ZOPFAN as being consistent with the balancing presence of the great powers. Leifer was unimpressed—rightly so—with such a lowest common denominator declaration, hence his conclusion that "the Kuala Lumpur Declaration of November 1971 did not constitute a true meeting of ASEAN minds.… Indeed in general provision the Declaration stood in direct lineal descent to Indonesia's visionary approach to regional order which had been incorporated in the preamble to ASEAN's founding document."[21]

TAC

In February 1976 the five ASEAN heads of state met in Bali, Indonesia, to concoct a response to the new geopolitics of the region. It was the first time that the heads of state had gathered under ASEAN's banner. Ten months earlier, the North Vietnamese military had marched into Saigon, and achieved their goal of national unification. Defeated in Vietnam and exhausted, the United States was likely to maintain a low profile in Southeast Asia for the foreseeable future. China and Russia, as backers of the victorious North Vietnamese, appeared to have the strategic momentum on their side. ASEAN's response to this new strategic context was to sign two documents: the Declaration of ASEAN Concord and the Treaty of Amity and Cooperation in Southeast Asia.

According to Leifer, the ASEAN Concord and the TAC, like ZOPFAN, represented ASEAN's approach to regional order.[22] The Concord made explicit ASEAN's interest in political stability and emphasized the intimate connection between the internal political stability of its members and regional stability and security. The Concord also reiterated the importance and relevance of ZOPFAN. The TAC, on the other hand, sought to provide a code of conduct for inter-state relations in the region. The most important and perhaps most obvious—given the circumstances—guiding principle was "mutual respect for the independence, sovereignty, equality, territorial integrity and national identity of all nations." Leifer's enumeration of the other guiding principles and the relationship between the overall package and regional order is best summarized in his own words:

> Although the totality of guiding principles—including settlement of differences or disputes by peaceful means and the renunciation of the threat or use of force – were unexceptional and unexceptionable, being drawn from the UN Charter, the strong sense of self-denying ordinance expressed was contemplated as a basis for regional order. To this end, the provision that made for the treaty to be "open to accession" by other states in Southeast Asia indicated an expectation that the socialist states of Indochina might be prepared to endorse the guiding principles.[23]

The assumptions, norms, and values shared by the ASEAN 5 were indeed unexceptional. These assumptions seemed to have functioned reasonably well for the ASEAN 5 in their first decade of "reconciliation" and in their dealings with one another. They have been conducive to mitigating bilateral disputes and bringing a modicum of civility in the conduct of inter-state relations among the ASEAN states. Hence it is not surprising that the states decided to present the principles as a code for regional inter-state conduct. Leifer is also perceptive to note that the provision for accession to the Treaty by other Southeast Asian states was an invitation to the states of Indochina, especially Vietnam, to accept the guiding principles enunciated by ASEAN.

Vietnam of course rejected this attempt by ASEAN—which it had seen as a Southeast Asian Treaty Organisation in a different guise—to stipulate its principles, however unexceptional, as the guide to regional relations. As Leifer puts it, "Vietnam steadfastly refused to acknowledge ASEAN as a corporate entity" and insisted on dealing with each of the ASEAN states on a bilateral basis.[24] In the August 1976 Non-Aligned Movement summit in Sri Lanka, for example, Vietnam and Laos objected to the inclusion of the ZOPFAN principles in the final communiqué on the grounds that there was no regional consensus for their inclusion. The reunification of Vietnam had concentrated ASEAN minds at the Bali summit and goaded ASEAN toward a more "collective approach to regional order," but as Vietnam's standoffish demeanor suggests, ASEAN's efforts came "not to any practical avail."[25] In December 1978, as Vietnamese–Kampuchean hostilities came to a head, Vietnam proceeded to invade and occupy Kampuchea, in open disregard of the TAC's first guiding principle for regional relations. Vietnam's rhetoric and policies indicated that it did not share the assumptions that ASEAN members claimed to hold in common, and had hoped that Vietnam would choose to share. ASEAN's attempt to shape regional order had suffered an enormous setback.

The thrust of Leifer's analysis seems to be this: events such as *konfrontasi* and Vietnam's invasion of Kampuchea suggest that the relevant resident and external players do not subscribe to a common set of assumptions about their interrelationships. In areas or issues where a set of common assumptions have been promulgated, such as the ASEAN Declaration, ZOPFAN, and TAC, what is striking are the differences deep below the surface commonalities, and the fragility of these common stances. Through overt actions and covert preferences, the states of Southeast Asia reveal that they share a set of assumptions only in the most superficial sense. In the vocabulary of the English School of international relations, the elements of "society" are weak to non-existent; that is why regional order remains elusive and illusory.

Order is in the eye of the beholder?

As the above analytic summary of Leifer's analysis of the region's epochal events suggests, it pays to be attuned to the underlying differences of interests and perspectives that inhere in each of the ASEAN states, and not to take ASEAN's public promulgations of solidarity and commonality at face value. The analyst who fails to probe beneath the surface expressions of commonality will miss some of the most crucial and interesting "movers" of Southeast Asia's security dynamics. These admonitions are well taken.

Insofar as Leifer took his own admonitions to heart in constructing his account of regional order in Southeast Asia, one might ask, how accurate and coherent is that portrait? Leifer's account—exemplified by his discussion of the ASEAN Declaration, ZOPFAN, and the TAC—emphasized the lack of genuinely shared assumptions, the fragility of a Southeast Asian society of states, and the elusiveness of regional order. It is this portrait of the ASEAN region as lacking in regional order that I wish to challenge. Leifer's portrait seems inconsistent with existing interpretations of how peaceful and stable Southeast Asia is. Depending on the regional space one has in mind—for the purposes of this article I distinguish between Southeast Asia (Indochina plus the ASEAN 5) and the original ASEAN 5—it is possible to argue that Southeast Asia has enjoyed substantial order in the past twenty or even forty years. Analysts who have compared the ASEAN 5 to other developing regions, for example, overwhelmingly conclude that the ASEAN region is the one oasis of peace and stability in a sea of chaos and violence.

In the early 1990s, Howard Wriggins and colleagues undertook a systematic, comparative examination of regional conflict in four regions—ASEAN, the Persian Gulf, South Asia, and the Horn of Africa—and found that "in Southeast Asia...a group of states [ASEAN] has moved remarkably far toward shaping a consultative regime that allows them to mute many of their differences and to deal collectively with states...outside their region."[26] ASEAN's performance was particularly impressive because "To expect that peaceful regional orders would promptly follow the dismantling of empires is to expect too much (although a sub region of Southeast Asia appears to have reached a close approximation)."[27] Similarly Ethel Solingen's analysis of the sources of "regional orders" in the Korean Peninsula, the Middle East, and the Southern Cone of Latin America repeatedly singles out ASEAN as an example of a sub-region where order and stability obtained. Being the methodological purist she is, Solingen decided not to include ASEAN as one of her full fledged cases because "[t]he choice of ASEAN for an in-depth analysis would have provided an easier case for confirming…the propositions I advance regarding strong internationalist coalitions and a highly cooperative cluster." [28] In other words, it was so obvious to Solingen that ASEAN was blessed with internationalist coalitions *and* regional order that to include it as a case study would have made her study vulnerable to charges of choosing the easiest confirmatory case. The contrast between Leifer's assessment and those of Wriggins, Solingen, and Alagappa (discussed below) as to whether regional order exists in Southeast Asia suggests that it is necessary to subject Leifer's notion of regional order to critical scrutiny.

Leifer, it must be said, is scrupulously fair in his description of "contending" and "common" assumptions among the ASEAN states. That is, where he sees commonality, he includes it in his account, and he does the same for divergences.[29]It is his "weighing" of these common and contending assumptions and the process by which he reaches his final assessment that are open to contestation. I suggest that the latter results from a conception of regional order that is vague and static; not explicitly identifying the assumptions that must be shared, and perhaps most importantly, not providing indicators for, or measures of, the degree to which those assumptions are shared. The result of these theoretical and methodological lapses is that the judgment as to whether regional order obtains is idiosyncratic.

Regional order: What is it and does it vary?

In Leifer's analytic scheme, the search for regional order is an "unending pursuit," to use Liow and Emmers' term. It is unending because since the 1950s, disorder—conflict and instability—has been the defining characteristic of Southeast Asia. Disorder, in other words, is a constant. This characterization of the region, I hope to show, is flawed. It is not easy to reconstruct how Leifer arrived at his assessment about the degree of order or disorder in Southeast Asia. In fact, to cast the issue in this way is already to misrepresent his approach. Leifer did not ask the "how much" (order) question; he asked the "whether or" (not there is order) question. And although he frequently linked his conclusions about the elusiveness of order to concrete events such as Vietnam's invasion of Kampuchea, more often than not his judgment seems to be informed by an assessment of whether the relevant players had common assumptions. That is why Leifer's analyses tend to dwell on the divergent assumptions of the Southeast Asian states.

The second problem with Leifer's notion of regional order is that it is not well defined. Regional order (the dependent variable) is defined in terms of what (supposedly) brings it about: common assumptions (the independent variable). If the latter exist, regional order obtains. If contending assumptions are the norm, as Leifer implies, regional order becomes elusive. The judgment about regional order can thus be made without reference to the amount of order or disorder on the ground (e.g. war or its absence), because the controlling indicator for the dependent variable (order) is the independent variable (common assumptions). If one detects divergent assumptions over a ten-year period, one is likely to conclude that there is no regional order even if military conflict and political instability were absent.

In contrast to Leifer, consider an approach that attempts to define regional order in terms of independent indicators (i.e. independent of what causes regional order). Order usually means the absence of military conflict and political instability. The meaning of military conflict is reasonably obvious. Any inter-state conflict that involves military clashes between two or more parties is an instance of regional disorder. The example par excellence of this is Indonesia's military confrontation with Malaysia and Singapore from 1963 through 1966. The meaning of political instability is more contentious, but those familiar with the region will probably agree that the kind of instability that was especially worrisome for ASEAN in the 1960s was any internal conflict or civil war that might draw in the great powers (as in Vietnam) or one's neighbors, as in the Corregidor incident, where the Philippines military was implicated in training Muslim insurgents for infiltrating the Malaysian state of Sabah.[30] Inter-state wars, military clashes, and civil conflicts that beget great power or (un)neighborly interference are thus reasonable indicators of disorder.

If these are the types of events that count against regional order, and if the relevant space is the region encompassing the ASEAN 5, then it would seem that the latter have been privy to some sort of regional order since the late 1960s. The ASEAN 5 managed to protect themselves from "another *konfrontasi*" (where a regional hegemon-would-be attempts to militarily intimidate its neighbors); "another Vietnam" (where civil war begets superpower intervention); and "another Corrigedor" (where a neighboring state provides military aid to one's insurgents). Using these "big ticket items" or major disorders—all of which ASEAN the organization was set up to prevent—as our criteria for regional order, it is possible to claim that there has been substantial regional order in peninsular Southeast Asia since the late 1960s.

The argument that regional order in the ASEAN region has not been so elusive also finds support in the work of others. In addition to the works mentioned above, Muthiah Alagappa's recent *Asian Security Order* provides further evidence for the "predictability and stability" of Asia since the early 1980s. Alagappa's introductory chapter contains an exhaustive list of the major conflicts in post-World War II Asia. Among the events that made Asia a region of conflict and instability are: the Korean War, the French (1946–54) and American (1964–75) wars in Indochina, the Indonesian confrontation against Malaysia and Singapore (1963–65), Chinese and Soviet-supported communist insurgencies in several Southeast Asian countries (1948–68), Vietnam's invasion of Cambodia (1978), the three Indo-Pakistani wars (1947, 1965, 1971), the Sino-Indian border war (1962), and the Sino-Soviet military clashes (1969) over contested boundaries.[31]

Based on Alagappa's list, it is possible to identify the periods of order and disorder in Southeast Asia (communist and non-communist) and in ASEAN (non-communist Southeast Asia). It is necessary to consider Southeast Asia and the ASEAN region (pre-1995) separately because some of Leifer's writings dealt with the former, while others focused on the latter. Going by Algappa's list, the years devoid of peace and stability in communist and non-communist Southeast Asia are 1946–54, (1948–68), 1963–65, 1964–75, and 1978–79. Hence if one considers the whole of Southeast Asia, the troubles of Indochina blot the region for the first thirty years after World War II.

If, however, one considers only non-communist Southeast Asia, or the geographical space covering the original ASEAN 5, only two events—neither a major war—blot the landscape: the communist insurgencies (1948–68) and Indonesia's confrontation with Malaysia and Singapore (1963–65). In other words, since the late 1960s, the ASEAN region seems to have experienced relative peace and stability. Hence Alagappa's overall claim for the volume: "Asia has now enjoyed relative peace for more than two decades."[32] In other words, the degree of disorder varied with time: by the early 1980s, Asia saw a qualitative change in the direction of greater regional order.

The point need not be labored. Leifer's conception of regional order, because it is not well defined and static, cannot capture the qualitative changes in the Southeast Asian security landscape. His facts were right (and probably more accurate than anyone else's) but the framework he used to assess them was flawed. Regional order, for Leifer, was a dependent variable that did not vary; such a research design, according to King, Keohane, and Verba, makes it difficult to "learn about causal effects."[33] It is possible to argue in Leifer's defense that regional order was a normative yardstick he used to assess the tenor and progress of Southeast Asia's international relations, and not a "dependent variable" to be explained. I address this point in the next section.

The basis of regional order: (What) common assumptions?

Like other writers of the English School of international relations, Leifer emphasized the importance of states sharing "common assumptions" if a viable regional order was to be realized. Common assumptions imply society, and society implies order. Leifer was not very explicit or systematic about what these assumptions are, but it is possible to infer them from his writings. For the states in a region to form a society, they should have common assumptions on the identities of the legitimate players; who are "resident" and who are "external", respecting one another's territorial integrity and political sovereignty, and exercising restraint in the use of military force. These assumptions were not shared—and were subject to military contestation—during Indonesia's confrontation with Malaysia and Singapore (1963–65). Indonesian president Sukarno considered the soon-to-be created Malaysia to be an illegitimate entity that threatened Indonesia's visions and prerogatives in the region. He saw Britain—a non-resident, ambitious neo-colonial has-been—behind the scheme in allowing Sabah, Sarawak, and Singapore to merge with Malaya, which was an affront to the dominant resident state, Indonesia. Consequently, Sukarno saw no political gains in holding off from confronting the newly formed Malaysia by military means.

There is nothing particularly complex or inscrutable about these common assumptions. I have used *konfrontasi* as the example to tease out the assumptions (that Leifer thinks states ought to have in common for the sake of regional order) because the incident is probably the crucial formative experience for the ASEAN 5, and it also informs Leifer's and many others' analysis of the region. The list of assumptions is by no means exhaustive, and if other examples, such as the principles articulated in ZOPFAN or the norms violated by Vietnam's invasion of Kampuchea, were used to flesh out the list, one might retrieve a few more, though the assumptions listed above are likely to remain prominent. But this does suggest that there is a weakness in Leifer's non-elaboration of so crucial a concept in his analytic scheme: proper and replicable use of the concept requires that the analyst come up with a list of the assumptions that matter, and if possible, some discussion of their ranking order. Without such an explicit listing and discussion, it would also be difficult to use as a normative yardstick because it is unclear how many of the assumptions must be present/absent and shared/unshared before one reaches a judgment about whether a society exists. However, I do not believe that this weakness invalidates Leifer's use of the concept as a positive (as opposed to normative) analytical construct because the assumptions that matter can to a large degree be inferred from his empirical examples. The problem is further mitigated by the fact that the assumptions that matter for Leifer (to qualify for regional society) are quite similar to Bull's (respect mutual independence, honor agreements, exercise restraint in the use of force). Perhaps Leifer would also consent to our equating the assumptions that must be shared (in his view) with those that have been enshrined in ASEAN's TAC.

Measuring commonality, society, and order

The more serious flaw in Leifer's analysis of regional order is his failure to provide indicators or measures of *the degree* to which these assumptions are shared. For, as I have argued, his determination of whether order existed relied almost exclusively on his analysis of whether assumptions were shared by the relevant states; the amount of actual conflict and instability on the ground was much less relevant. Without specifying measures for shared assumptions, two problems arise. First, the analysis of "how much sharing" is forced into an all-or-nothing mode. Put differently, the independent variable—"shared assumptions"—is a dichotomous, not continuous, variable in Leifer's formulation. This is a problem because the sharing of values and assumptions is always imperfect. Canada and Mexico constantly bristle at the unilateral assumptions and prerogatives of the United States; Britain is often the odd person out in a plethora of European Union initiatives. Do these departures from "common assumptions" of the United States or the European Union translate to a lack of society, and hence absence of regional order in North America or Europe? They do suggest that the order is imperfect, but that should not detract from the overall high degree of order.

The second problem is hinted at by the first. In the absence of explicit and defensible indicators of the degree of shared values, the task of adjudicating on the existence of society and regional order becomes an extremely subjective exercise. It also becomes difficult to adjudicate between interpretations that disagree on the extent of shared values and, by implication, the amount of regional order. Consider Leifer's treatment of ASEAN's policy of isolating Vietnam after the latter's invasion and occupation of Kampuchea. Leifer highlights Indonesia's and Malaysia's discomfort with ASEAN's corporate line because it was giving China dangerous and undeserved access into the region.[34] Given their recent histories, Indonesia and Malaysia saw China as the greater threat and feared that continued pressure against Vietnam would strengthened China's hand and influence in Southeast Asia, something they would prefer to avoid. Both came very close to defecting from the ASEAN line as they weighed their strategic interests against their "commitment" to the TAC norms of respecting the sovereignty and territorial integrity of others (Kampuchea in this case) and ASEAN's mode of consensual decision-making. What impressed Lefier was the fragility of ASEAN's corporate line, the tenuousness of their shared values, and the ease with which Indonesia and Malaysia may have defected from the corporate line. Highlighting these aspects reinforces the perspective that common assumptions are not genuinely shared among the ASEAN states and raises questions as to whether they form a genuine "society of states." In the event, Indonesian president Suharto tested a softer approach to Vietnam, the so-called "Kuantan principles" during his 1980 visit to the Malaysian town; this softer approach, however, was abandoned quite quickly, and Indonesia and Malaysia returned to the ASEAN fold.

For those who emphasize this return to the ASEAN corporate line, the events show that despite their avowed strategic unease with ASEAN's policy of pressuring Vietnam (and strengthening China), Indonesia and Malaysia shared enough common assumptions—about the principles enshrined in the TAC and the importance of consensus—with the other ASEAN members to allow these common values to trump their narrower strategic interests.[35] This interpretation of ASEAN's Vietnam/Kampuchean policy is not unassailable. In contrast to Leifer's interpretation which focuses on the pressures exerted by conflicting assumptions among the ASEAN states, this interpretation stresses the eventual triumph of common assumptions. In my view, Indonesia's and Malaysia's restraining themselves from defecting provides the best indicator of their sharing assumptions with the others, but this remains a very imperfect indicator. A truly rigorous appraisal of the two interpretations offered here is possible only if we have independent indicators or measures for how tightly, widely, and deeply shared those assumptions are. Admittedly, such indicators are not easy to design. But without these indicators, the existence or non-existence of common assumptions (and hence of regional order) is in the eyes of the beholder: even when outcomes seem consistent with the existence of common values, it is possible to deny their significance and imply that regional order remains elusive.

The above critique of Leifer has focused on his assumption of regional disorder as a constant, the inadequate specification of the contents of the shared assumptions conducive to regional order, and most importantly, the absence of indicators for the degree to which the order-enhancing assumptions are shared. These theoretical and methodological shortfalls, it is contended, give rise to an incomplete and idiosyncratic portrait of regional order in Southeast Asia.

Conclusion: In lieu of regional order

In his writings on ASEAN, Leifer liked to draw the reader's attention to the Preamble of the ASEAN Declaration, in which the signatories claim for themselves "primary responsibility" for ensuring the military, political, economic, and social stability of the region. Leifer wanted to remind his readers that the emphasis on regional autonomy (from external powers) was placed at Indonesia's insistence and that it reflected Indonesia's "prerogative approach" to regional order.[36]

It is interesting that the term "regional order" does not appear either in the Preamble or in the Declaration. It was Leifer's choice to replace the signatories' terms "stability and security" with "regional order." As I have tried to suggest, this substitution, whether conscious or not, has important analytical consequences. Stability and security, or peace and stability, are conceptually less complex than the notion of order. The referents of peace and stability are reasonably obvious. They imply the absence of wars ("no more Vietnams"), military crises/confrontations ("no more *konfrontasis*"), and unwanted military/political intrusions by neighbors or external states ("no more Corregidors"); insofar as these shocks are minor, temporary, or absent, one may conclude that a region experienced relative peace and stability.

The notion of order is more complicated, with stronger normative connotations. Many who use the term treat it as synonymous with peace and stability, which is acceptable insofar as they are explicit about what they mean by the latter terms. For Leifer, however, order is not synonymous with peace and stability, it connotes something more. For conventional deterrence or the existence of a power equilibrium can bring about peace and stability, but not, for Leifer, order. In Leifer's writings, for order to exist there must be something deeper, something more legitimate and widely accepted: shared assumptions about the relationships among the relevant states. Such as, for example, the ASEAN states' acceptance of Indonesia's *primus inter pares* role in regional matters (Leifer argues there is no such acceptance), or their acceptance of a balancing role for the United States in Southeast Asia (also no such consensus in Leifer's view). Absent the universal sharing of such assumptions, regional order, as Leifer understood it, did not exist. This is an exacting approach to understanding regional order, provided one is able to specify (i) the set of assumptions that matter, and (ii) explicit replicable criteria for assessing "how much sharing" of common assumptions is present; and (iii) the approximate tipping points for order and disorder. Without such criteria, one would not know which assumptions are to be assessed (for commonality) and the temptation to choose in ways consistent with one's received notions would be great; similarly, absent measures for the degree to which the (agreed set of) assumptions are "shared," our judgments about whether regional order exists will be idiosyncratic and arbitrary.

"Order," whether regional or global, seems like a concept or normative ideal that stems from the vantage point of the great or metropolitan powers. Whether it is the schoolmaster shouting "Order!" so as to bring his unruly pupils back behind their desks, or the great powers getting together to manage regional order, the notion (of order) is heavily tinged with managerial connotations. In that sense, ASEAN's avoidance of the term is telling. As small to middle powers, the states comprising ASEAN realized that regional order was not theirs to impose or manage; in fact, the very vocabulary of order might invite excessive interest from the great powers in ways not welcomed by ASEAN. Peace and stability, on the other hand, connote a less imposing and managerial approach. Through self-restraint, mutual cooperation, and economic exertion, each of the ASEAN states would have a role to play in moderating and minimizing conflict within the region.

If Michael Leifer had adopted ASEAN's preferred terms of the discourse to describe its aspirations for the region, his assessment of ASEAN's achievements in international relations, in my view, would have come closer to the "half full" rather than the "half empty" metaphoric glass. As the "half full/half empty" image suggests, Leifer was not far off: his descriptions of the international relations of the region will remain unsurpassed for years to come. If the argument of this chapter has merit, however, Leifer's assessments and judgments of what those developments mean can, and should, be queried. And that is for the better. As a senior colleague advised me early in my career: "In our line of work, it is better to be criticized than to be ignored." He is right in at least one sense: criticism implies that one's ideas are serious and substantive enough to warrant contestation and debate by others. As this volume indicates, Michael Leifer generated many such ideas in his illustrious career, and this chapter has attempted to interrogate only the one dealing with regional order.

Notes

1 John Lewis Gaddis, *Strategies of Containment: A Critical Appraisal of Postwar American National Security Policy* (New York: Oxford University Press, 1982), pp. vii–ix.
2 A rough count of how frequently the term "regional order" features in four of Leifer's writings used for this article reveals the following: 7 times in Leifer's 7-page "The Asean States: No Common Outlook," *International Affairs* (London: Royal Institute of International Affairs 1944–), Vol. 49, No. 4, October 1973, pp. 600–7(1973); 8 times in the 12-page chapter "The Balance of Power and Regional Order" in Michael Leifer, *The Balance of Power in East Asia* (London: Macmillan, 1986), pp. 143–54; 12 times in Chapter 1 of *ASEAN and the Security of Southeast Asia* (London: Routledge, 1989), and 8 times in Chapter 1 of *The ASEAN Regional Forum: Extending ASEAN's Model of Regional Security*, Adelphi Paper No. 302 (London: Oxford University Press for the International Institute of Strategic Studies, 1996).
3 See for example, Michael Leifer, *Conflict and Regional Order in South-east Asia*, (London: International Institute for Strategic Studies, 1980, Adelphi Paper No. 62), pp. 1–4; and Leifer, *ASEAN and the Security of South-East Asia*, pp. 1–15.
4 Michael Leifer, *ASEAN's Search for Regional Order* (Singapore: National University of Singapore, 1987), pp. 1–2.
5 Leifer, "The Balance of Power and Regional Order," p. 151.
6 Ibid., p. 152.
7 "The Asean States: No Common Outlook," p. 600; and "The Role and Paradox of ASEAN" in Leifer, *The Balance of Power in East Asia*, p. 125.
8 Joseph Liow and Ralf Emmers, "Introduction," this volume, pp. 2–3.
9 See Barry Buzan, "From International System to International Society: Structural Realism and Regime Theory Meet the English School," *International Organization*, Summer 1993, pp. 327–52; Timothy Dunne, *Inventing International Society: A History of the English School* (Basingstoke: Palgrave Macmillan, 1998); and B.A. Roberson (ed.), *International Society and the Development of International Relations Theory* (London: Pinter, 1998).
10 At the IDSS–LSE Conference in May 2004 in Singapore, James Cotton argued very convincingly that Elie Kedourie was a major influence on Leifer.
11 Hedley Bull, *The Anarchical Society: A Study of Order in World Politics* (New York: Columbia University Press, 1977), p. 13. Italics added.
12 Leifer, "The Role and Paradox of ASEAN," p. 126; Leifer, *ASEAN and the Security of South-East Asia*, p. 24.
13 "Conflict and Regional Order in South-east Asia," pp. 4–13.
14 Ibid., p. 1.
15 Leifer, "Some South-East Asian Attitudes," *International Affairs*, April 1966, pp. 219–29; "The Asean States: No Common Outlook," pp. 600–7; and *ASEAN and the Security of South-East Asia*, pp. 1–15, 73–77.
16 I will omit discussion of the ARF because space is limited here, and because I have discussed it in "Making bricks without straw in the Asia Pacific?" *The Pacific Review*, 10(2), 1997, pp. 289–300.
17 ASEAN Secretariat, *ASEAN Documents Series, 1967–1988* (Jakarta, 1988), p. 17. Italics added.
18 Ibid., p. 34.
19 "The Asean States: No Common Outlook," p. 607.

20 *ASEAN and the Security of South-East Asia*, p. 57.
21 Ibid., p. 59.
22 Ibid., pp. 64–86.
23 Ibid., p. 69.
24 Ibid., pp. 73–4.
25 Ibid., p. 73.
26 Howard Wriggins, "The Dynamics of Regional Politics: An Orientation," in Wriggins (ed.), *Dynamics of Regional Politics: Four Systems on the Indian Ocean Rim* (New York: Columbia University Press, 1992), p. 4.
27 Ibid., p. 15.
28 Ethel Solingen, *Regional Orders at Century's Dawn: Global and Domestic Influences on Grand Strategy* (Princeton, NJ: Princeton University Press, 1998), pp. 15–16.
29 See *ASEAN and the Security of South-East Asia*, Chapter 1.
30 For an excellent brief description of the incident, see Leifer, *Dictionary of the Modern Politics of South-East Asia* (London: Routledge, 1995), p. 82.
31 Muthiah Alagappa, "Introduction: Predictability and Stability Despite Challenges," in Alagappa (ed.), *Asian Security Order: Instrumental and Normative Features* (Stanford: Stanford University Press, 2003), pp. 1–32. I disagree with Alagappa on one minor point: he dated the communist insurgencies as lasting from 1948 to 1981, the latter being the date when China announced its termination of support for the Communist Parties of Southeast Asia. I believe a more accurate end date is the mid-1960s: the communist insurrection in Malaya ended in 1960, while the Communist Party of Indonesia had largely been exterminated by 1966.
32 Ibid., p. 3.
33 Gary King, Robert Keohane, and Sidney Verba, *Designing Social Inquiry* (Princeton, NJ: Princeton University Press, 1994), p. 130.
34 See Leifer, *ASEAN and the Security of South-East Asia*, Chapter 4.
35 Yuen Foong Khong, "ASEAN and the Southeast Asian Security Complex," in David Lake and Patrick Morgan (eds), *Regional Orders: Building Security in a New World* (University Park, PA: Pennsylvania State University Press, 1997), pp. 332–5.
36 Leifer, *ASEAN and the Security of South-East Asia*, pp. 5–6, 24.

4 Michael Leifer, the balance of power and international relations theory

Jürgen Haacke

The work of the late Professor Michael Leifer has been identified with a range of concepts, particularly those that he applied to the Association of Southeast Asian Nations (ASEAN), including diplomatic community[1] or internal collective security organization.[2] However, he is now arguably most often associated with the concept of the balance of power. The reason for this is two-fold. First, Leifer himself routinely used the concept throughout his illustrious career. Second, to the extent that Leifer's work has met with open criticism, such criticism has overwhelmingly focused on his invocation of the balance of power, particularly in terms of the concept's analytical power and related policy implications. Of particular importance in this regard have been two review essays respectively authored by Yuen Foong Khong and Sorpong Peou.[3] Khong's criticisms relate to Leifer's influential 1996 Adelphi Paper on the ASEAN Regional Forum (ARF).[4] In his review Khong argues that the analytical utility of the balance of power was far more limited than that of the concept of balance of threat to account for Southeast Asia's post-Cold War response to China. After all, he suggested, ASEAN was not in the business of engaging in a countervailing balance of power against the most powerful regional state, the United States, but instead was seeking protection against China. Khong also questioned the implicit policy advice that he understood Leifer to be giving. In particular he pointed to Leifer's argument that the prerequisite for a successful ARF might well be 'the prior existence of a stable balance of power'.[5] Khong believed that this prescription was fraught with danger if it was translated into policy practice. Significantly, he disagreed with Leifer not only on the need for a balance of power as a prerequisite for the ARF's functioning, but also in relation to the importance of the ARF in the absence of such a balance. As Khong formulated it, 'Thus in contrast to Leifer, I view the ARF not as "a valuable adjunct to the workings of the balance of power" but as a mechanism for defusing the conflictual by-products of power balancing practices.'[6]

More recently, Sorpong Peou has reinforced Leifer's association with the balance of power and realism by comparing and contrasting Leifer's work with that of the constructivist scholarship undertaken by Professor Amitav Acharya. However, in an interesting twist Peou contends that 'Leifer's thinking conforms to balance-of-threat logic' rather than to the conventional balance-of-power logic,[7] which he takes to be an inconsistency in Leifer's approach. While Khong and Peou agree that Leifer was a realist, they thus disagree about the logic that Leifer suggested was underpinning balance of power formation. Given this rather interesting disagreement, which is reinforced by Peou's additional comment that Leifer actually came close to being a constructivist, this chapter will look again at the way in which the balance of power has been used both in Leifer's empirical analyses and in his more explicit theoretical interventions. The aim of this dual approach, which involves examining many of Leifer's early as well as later works, is to provide a more rounded account in relation to the significance that the balance of power has played in Leifer's overall work. In particular, the chapter has the following three objectives: (1) to examine Leifer's basic understanding of the balance of power and how he applied the concept in relation to Southeast and East Asia; (2) to ascertain his preferred theoretical home in line with the significance he attached to the balance of power; and (3) to investigate the role of the balance of power as a factor in the foreign policies of individual regional states. These three objectives will be pursued sequentially in three sections dealing with the topics in turn.

Leifer and the balance of power

Although Professor Leifer consistently invoked the concept of the balance of power, he only rarely expressly differentiated its possible definitions.[8] Indeed, it was arguably only in the mid-1990s that he explicitly did so. Then, Leifer essentially distinguished between two key meanings of the balance of power.[9] First, he took the balance of power to denote a situation, or, more appropriately put, a description of a relationship between two or more states defined in terms of their respective capabilities. Second, he understood the balance of power in terms of a policy directed at preventing the establishment of undue dominance by one or more states that would be able to dictate the terms of regional order. Leifer saw these two meanings as being linked, and both are clearly integrated in his work. The former is evident not least in his analysis of political, economic and military developments at the global and regional level. In this context, Leifer distinguished between a global, regional and sub-regional or even local balance of power. He saw developments at the global and regional level as impacting on those at the sub-regional level, testified to not least by his use of the term 'balance of extra-regional influences',[10] and argued that these changes were factored into the foreign and security policies of individual states.

As regards the meaning attributed to individual components of the concept of balance of power, Leifer remained somewhat ambiguous. For instance, all that he would generally say on 'balance' was that he did not necessarily take this concept to imply a situation of equipoise or equal power, as is also illustrated by his frequent usage of the term 'balance or distribution of power'.[11] There is also some ambiguity in his writing on 'power'. Defining the concept, Leifer did suggest that power denoted capabilities.[12] However, when discussing either power or changes in the balance of power, he drew attention to a range of factors including quantitative and qualitative changes in military strength, present and future potential economic achievements, as well as developments in political-security relations, such as shifting political alignments and allegiances underpinned by fluid patterns of amity and enmity, particularly evolving ties with and among the major powers. In his own analyses of developments affecting the balance of power, then, Leifer took into account both material and non-material factors and examined power in the context of actors' interaction as well as the structures impinging on these interactions.

Leifer was not a dispassionate analyst of power transitions. Changes in the balance of power were central to his analysis and mattered to him, especially if they heralded potentially negative consequences for regional order. However, in reaching his own conclusions about changes in the balance of power as a situation, he relied not merely on relevant empirical developments, but also on the assessments of the leadership and other individuals within a region and their evolving perceptions on these matters. Not surprisingly, Leifer reached differentiated and different conclusions for seemingly similar circumstances about whether changes in the balance of power had occurred. Take for example his analysis of East Asia's regional balance of power after the enunciation of the Nixon Doctrine and US withdrawal from Vietnam, and his account of changes in the balance of power at the end of the Cold War.

The regional balance of power in East Asia: the early 1970s

It goes without saying that Leifer examined the international politics of East Asia in the context of the global balance of power that pitted the United States and the Soviet Union against one another. In the Cold War period, East Asian regional security against the expansion of communism rested above all on the network of bilateral alliances that the United States crafted and maintained with countries in the region in the form of a hub and spokes system. To many analysts, developments in the late 1960s and early 1970s seemed to bring about a change in the regional balance of power given the impending withdrawal from east of Suez by the British government, the enunciation of the Nixon Doctrine, and the coming relinquishment of Washington's position in Vietnam. Leifer took a more differentiated line, however. He agreed that Washington *believed* that 'proxies of the Soviet Union were attempting to revise the balance and distribution of power in East Asia to their global advantage.'[13] Yet he was cautious in the assessment that the impact of the developments at hand amounted to a change in the actual regional balance of power. Despite the Nixon Doctrine, he argued, Washington continued to be militarily involved in Asia (including in the form of secret wars waged in Laos and Cambodia). Moreover, China had entered into a strategic alignment with the United States. Not even when Communist forces won victories in Cambodia, South Vietnam and Laos did Leifer see a major change in the regional balance of power as having taken place. In his view, there was no monolithic Communist bloc given the tensions between China and Vietnam and the Khmer Rouge and Hanoi.[14] Yet he readily conceded that attempts to change the regional balance of power were still under way even in the 1980s, particularly as regards Indochina. As he spelled out the issue, 'the only change in the Indochina problem during the two phases of the Cold War was which particular major adversary required containing, not the stake involved – namely, the prospect of an adverse regional dominance with global consequences.'[15] Importantly, if in his view the balance of power ultimately did not undergo dramatic revision in the Cold War era, Leifer suggested that the same was not true for the post-Cold War period.

Changes in the regional balance of power after the Cold War

Examining the regional balance of power in the 1990s, Leifer argued in no uncertain terms that the end of Cold War had brought about 'the disturbing emergence of a new distribution of power to the apparent advantage of China'.[16] Indeed, for Leifer China was 'a rising and potentially dominant regional power'.[17] As he saw it, the change in the regional balance of power had a number of causes. One was that 'China is improving its military capabilities in an environment devoid of the constraints imposed by a Cold War balance of power'.[18] Another was the partial strategic withdrawal from Philippine bases by the United States. Still another was to him the effect in East Asia of the end of the Cold War, particularly the removal of direct threats to China formerly posed above all by the Soviet Union. Also relevant was the ending of the tacit China–ASEAN alliance over confronting Vietnam in Cambodia.

The revision of 'the balance or distribution of power… to the decided strategic advantage of China' mattered to Leifer because Beijing had 'long cast a political shadow over the region'.[19] Leifer was concerned above all about Beijing's 'steely assertiveness' in the prosecution of irredentist claims in the South China Sea. In his view, it was only the limitations in the sustained projection of military power that still constrained China's freedom 'to engage in a full-bloodied assertiveness'.[20] If these claims were realized, he noted, 'China would effectively encompass the maritime heart of South-east Asia, with disturbing implications for ASEAN.'[21]

Clearly, Leifer's analysis of the post-Cold War change in the regional balance of power is not attributable to a simple assessment of changes in material capabilities. This is underlined by his summary of the factors underlying regional strategic change in East Asia in the early 1990s.[22] According to Leifer, the United States had lost the will to uphold the regional balance of power, Russia no longer counted militarily, and Japan was viewed as a sleeping giant best left alone. The key factor, however, was the re-emergence of China as a major regional power. This assessment was based not least on the concerns about China communicated to him by decision-makers in Southeast Asia and perhaps elsewhere. Leifer was, of course, not alone in making this argument and emphasizing the attendant threat particularly as regards developments in the South China Sea.[23] However, as Emmers noted, the 'balance of power perspective ... exaggerates the potential danger resulting from emerging hegemons'.[24] It is noteworthy in this respect that Leifer never re-visited his position on China, notwithstanding writings on American unipolarity, studies on the massive socio-economic challenges afflicting China and the difficulties associated with military modernization, as well as research on China's grand strategy and its foreign policy outlook.[25] This diverse body of literature suggested that China would for the foreseeable future remain a country beset with enormous challenges relating to development and reform. Also, it suggested that Beijing's foreign policy and presence within Southeast Asia could be more benign than Leifer believed. It is not clear what Leifer would now make either of current analyses of China as a status quo power or of recent sea changes in China–Southeast Asia relations,[26] illustrated for example by China's accession to the Treaty of Amity and Cooperation in 2003.

It would appear that Leifer's assessment of the (potential) consequences of the posited change in the balance of power were accompanied by particular words of warning because ASEAN continued to embrace the same model of security in the post-Cold War period as it had done in the Cold War. That model of security addressed conflict avoidance and conflict management.[27] However, the model did not address the 'problem of power', and it failed to make practical provision for addressing 'the role of force in conflict and in its resolution'.[28] As Leifer pointed out time and again, there was no commitment within ASEAN ranks to common defence. Only at the level of individual states had ASEAN countries opted for balance-of-power arrangements, with four of the five original members at one stage relying on external countervailing power (as illustrated by the 1951 Mutual Security Pact between Manila and Washington, the 1954 Manila Pact, the Anglo-Malayan Defence Agreement and the revised Malaysian Defence Agreement from 1963, to which both Malaysia and Singapore were party). However, ASEAN itself did not come to share the need to develop countervailing power within the grouping. To Indonesia as ASEAN's *primus inter pares*, for instance, this was inimical given Jakarta's declared support for non-alignment and its repudiation of balance-of-power practices. In any case, as Leifer made clear throughout, ASEAN members have also tended to see their regional partners as potential adversaries. It was not least in view of bilateral tensions and divisions in strategic perspective that ASEAN had not reached agreement, 'specifically, over whether or not it should manage the regional balance or distribution of power on an exclusive basis'.[29] To be sure, Leifer did regard ASEAN as a security organization.[30] But, carefully qualifying his argument, he only ever described ASEAN as an intramural collective security organization in the limited sense of member states sharing a sense of indivisibility of their security as in a traditional collective security vehicle. What was also shared was the perception of the significance of internal threats to the survival of ruling governments. For

Leifer, however, this meant that 'ASEAN was not organized to deal with problems of power in an ungoverned world'.[31] Consequently, as Leifer added, ASEAN's operational security doctrine 'has depended on a supporting pattern of power in which the United States has played the critical balancing role'.[32]

Leifer's analysis of the balance or distribution of power treated as relevant a number of factors beyond the development and amassing of material capabilities. At the same time, his analysis of change to the existing distribution of power clearly reflected apprehensions concerning the political-security and military implications of China's rapid and successful economic modernization and renewal, which today might no longer be shared in full even within Southeast Asia. Leifer's cautionary words about the implications of a change in the balance of power are also tied to his analysis of ASEAN. To place these in perspective three questions will be addressed in the next section. First, given what he had to say on the balance of power, what is Michael Leifer's home within IR theory? Second, to what extent is his position on the balance of power a normative one? Third, what kind of practices does he associate with the balance of power?

Leifer, the balance of power and the English School

The context for the development of Michael Leifer's theoretical thoughts was in many ways provided by the London School of Economics. Leifer wrote his doctoral thesis with Elie Kedourie in the late 1950s on Zionism and Palestine in British opinion and policy and from the late 1960s onwards worked for more than three decades in the School's Department of International Relations. This is not the place to attempt tracing in detail in the form of a history of ideas how influential individual scholars such as Kedourie or Leifer's colleagues, including Hedley Bull, were for the development of his thought. It suffices to note that he seems to have shared with Kedourie an interest in whether after independence the new states would be able to rise above a romantic nationalism to focus on economic development for the benefit of their citizens. Equally, it is obvious from his work that he was able, and probably felt obliged, to engage with key figures of the English School. Indeed, for a while he himself taught Structure of International Society, the IR Department's introductory course to International Relations. From today's perspective, it is, of course, interesting that Professor Leifer was not explicit about his own theoretical approach, at least in the sense that he chose not to assume a specific label in his published work. But the very idea that he should have done so might not have appeared so obvious to him. After all, his theoretical interests were wide-ranging, and he was at least as much a political theorist as someone committed to International Relations. In many ways, he would also appear to have seen himself doing foreign policy analysis rather than adding to international theory (as discussed in the next section). Second, blunt theory-driven analysis, which would require 'theoretically coming out' and formulating hypotheses, so some of his former colleagues suggest, was for Leifer an exercise in 'intellectual masturbation', from which he preferred to abstain. Nevertheless, Leifer was sufficiently interested to take note of such efforts from whatever perspective. More often than not, however, he seems to have viewed with a measure of bemusement and suspicion, if not at times a sense of frustration, attempts to apply to the study of the international politics of Southeast Asia works building on what to him were trendy theoretical approaches. Such attempts all too often resulted only in what – to him – amounted at best to skewed analyses and inappropriate or flawed conclusions. Maybe it was in testament to his feelings about these matters that he considered it apposite, if not necessary, to intervene on at least three occasions in discussions on IR theory and Southeast Asia. For example, he took issue with the idea of applying functionalism to the study of ASEAN.[33] After the end of the Cold War, he sounded a cautionary note in response to the case outlined in writings on 'common security'.[34] And in the mid-1990s, he described as 'the height of intellectual naivety' the argument of those whom he saw as suggesting that the dialogical encounters at governmental level as part of the processes of the ASEAN Regional Forum justified notions of a new paradigm of international relations.[35]

A standard feature of these intermittent interventions in IR theory debates was the emphasis Leifer placed on the basic point that Southeast Asia's international relations were neither unique nor dissociable from the context of great power relations and realpolitik considerations of its resident states. Leifer considered it fully appropriate to draw on insights into international politics that emphasized the role of the major powers, the question of power and the significance of the balance of power. In other words, to make sense of the international, Leifer drew on ideas and concepts that we associate with the English School and perhaps most readily so with the pluralist perspective within this approach. However, if the international relations of Southeast Asia could in Leifer's opinion not be understood without reference to the great powers and the balance of power, the foreign policies of individual countries of the region could similarly in his view not be understood without reference to their history, their experiences with and reaction to colonialism, their geopolitical predicaments, and their domestic politics and civil–military relations. Notably, to understand the foreign policy of individual states Leifer also took an interest in the biographies of key political players, their thoughts, ambitions and idiosyncrasies. For Leifer's purposes, then, insights about international society in themselves were insufficient if the objective was to understand the international relations of Southeast Asia. Still, when it came to identifying the most important institution within international society, Leifer focused unswervingly on the balance of power.

The balance of power as the key institution of international society

Leifer would seem to have accepted the point of view that institutions other than the balance of power also serve to maintain international and regional order.

However, there is little doubt that for him the balance of power was the most important institution, more important than for instance international law or diplomacy. As he put it in the context of his analysis of Singapore's foreign policy, '[t]o the extent that International Law, with all of its shortcomings, is viewed as a supporting pillar of the independence of the Republic [of Singapore], then it serves as an instrument of the balance of power in its traditional function of upholding the independence of all states.'[36] From his perspective, therefore, international law was an auxiliary or dependent institution that was inadequate to uphold the independence of states. Not surprisingly, Leifer had little time for the advocates (as opposed to the analysts) of the so-called 'ASEAN way'.[37]

Leifer was similarly sceptical about the role of diplomacy in international society. Discussing the ASEAN Regional Forum (ARF), Leifer invoked the aphorism of 'bricks without straw' to highlight the uncertain effects of the dialogical–diplomatic encounters taking place. Nevertheless, for Leifer the ARF originally served two purposes. One was to promote co-operative security in the sense that the objective was to improve the climate in which relations among states in the Asia Pacific could develop. The other was to facilitate a stable balance of power. To the extent that the ARF built on diplomacy, however, Leifer did not see it as being able to ensure the maintenance of regional order. As Leifer argued: 'The ARF … can be seen as an imperfect diplomatic instrument for achieving regional security goals in that it seeks to address the problem of power which arises from the anarchical nature of international society without provision for either collective defense or conventional collective security.'[38]

This is not to say that Leifer did not recognize the importance of the balance of power factor in the context of the establishment of the ARF. But he did maintain that 'the prerequisite for a successful ARF may well be the prior existence of a stable balance of power'.[39] One could infer from his work that Leifer believed that the balance of power was ultimately left for the United States to uphold because only Washington would be able to deter a country such as China from disturbing regional order in Southeast and East Asia. However, as noted, Leifer seems to have thought that Washington's regional role could not necessarily be taken for granted. In such circumstances, diplomacy, unlike the balance of power, was insufficient to provide a stable order and maintain the independence of states.

A normative commitment to the balance of power

Bearing in mind the totality of his writings, few ideas probably mattered more to Leifer than the preservation of a system of independent states as well as freedom from malign forms of hegemony. This was for Leifer a normative position. Indeed, Leifer's normative commitment to international society is detectable throughout his work, including his post-Cold War writings. He was convinced that China had ambitions to become the region's primary or hegemonic power, and he intimated that in this capacity it might not behave like a good regional citizen but opt for military domination, with adverse consequences for the security and independence of regional states. In illustrating his argument, Leifer cited 'informed sources' who saw the decision to seize Mischief Reef as having been made at the highest levels of China's Communist Party.[40] Indeed, he regarded China's later concession in relation to the South China Sea as having been 'one of form only'.[41] Given his normative perspective, Leifer's verdict on the ARF was blunt. As he formulated it, '[a]ny expectation that the ARF itself might fulfil the role of balance of power by non-military means were dashed by China's rigid and adamant adherence to its irredentist agenda in the South China Sea.'[42] He even considered it to be a 'category mistake' to ask whether the ARF was capable of solving problems and conflicts such as those dividing China and ASEAN countries.[43]

For Leifer, the rise of China as a seemingly dissatisfied country probably evoked disturbing historical memories. He recognized that a balance of power factor permeated the establishment of the ARF, but regarded this diplomatic meeting place as inadequate to deal with China if the latter were to pursue its assumed military designs. Problems associated with a particular balance or distribution of power, which might give rise to the use of force, could not, he said, be altered through diplomacy alone. This, no doubt, was for Leifer a lesson that history had unambiguously taught. Given his normative commitment to the balance of power, it is not surprising that he disagreed fairly vehemently, especially in the mid-1990s, with the attempts by some scholars to discredit the concept as policy. He rejected point-blank, for instance, the argument that the balance of power was 'a mechanical contrivance of European provenance which is not suitable for regional circumstances'.[44] As he saw it, 'ASEAN's practice has contained an evident dimension of balance of power from the outset.'[45] This was a reference to the formation of ASEAN in *post-konfrontasi* Southeast Asia, as seen in particular from the perspective of Indonesia's closest neighbours. Leifer moreover rejected the view that 'indulgence in the balance of power would be a self-affliction best confined to the dust-bin of history along with colonialism because it would provoke confrontation and not facilitate reconciliation'.[46] There was no inevitability about this for Leifer, and he may have thought that overall the track record of the balance of power in hindering undue dominance and upholding the independence of states was fairly respectable. Although he was thus normatively committed to the balance of power as an institution to safeguard international society and the independence of states, it would be stretching the point if one said that he was, therefore, a sponsor of adversarial balance of power practices whenever a country exhibits hegemonic potential. His distinction between Hobbesian and Grotian forms of the balance of power testifies to this.

The balance of power: Hobbesian and (neo-) Grotian arrangements

Although the point has not always been noted, Leifer distinguished between a conventional or adversarial balance of power tradition associated with realism and an 'associative' or 'Grotian' balance of power tradition.[47] In other words, although it is the case that Leifer generally linked the balance of power with a countervailing political–military strategy to prevent undue dominance by any one state, he did not limit his understanding of balance of power practices to the formation of military alliances, collective security mechanism or unilateral defense force modernization. This is illustrated by his explicit mention of the Concert Arrangement in the early nineteenth century as one relevant example of a multilateral institution that would serve to engage and restrain a past and/or potential hegemon. Even though he was sceptical about its prospects in this regard, the establishment of the ASEAN Regional Forum was to him another attempt to promote a balance of power practice, in this case to prevent Chinese hegemony.

Consequently, it seems reasonable to argue that Leifer actually regarded it to be an empirical question whether Grotian-style or Hobbesian-style institutions meant to uphold the balance of power were most appropriate in dealing with hegemonic ambitions. Leifer clearly thought that where 'associative' balance of power arrangements could not necessarily be expected to prevent the rise of a hegemonic power, other countervailing balance of power arrangements might be required. In view of this, to assert or imply that Leifer a priori advocated countervailing balance of power practices in the event of changes in the balance of power seems unpersuasive. It was only in view of the absence of an alliance or collective security organization *in the context* of China's 'steely assertiveness' that he hinted at the importance of a sustained and viable American military presence, the alliance between the United States and Japan, and other bilateral security and defence arrangements between sub-regional states and Washington. Having discussed Leifer's intellectual and normative position according to which the balance of power is crucial for the independence of states, the chapter now moves on to explore how he employed the concept of balance of power in his capacity as an analyst of the foreign policies of individual Southeast Asian states.

The balance of power factor in foreign policy

Michael Leifer was an expert foreign policy analyst. This was well recognized in public even by senior government representatives from within Southeast Asia.[48] As a foreign policy analyst, it was one of Leifer's main achievements to demonstrate the significance of the balance of power factor (understood as a political motive) in the making of foreign policy in Southeast Asia, notwithstanding the widespread rhetorical attachment of many regional governments to ideas of neutrality and non-alignment and attendant political discourses. For Leifer, such official rhetoric was, of course, politically astute and understandable given Southeast Asia's colonial history, its relations with the great powers, and the many unresolved bilateral conflicts and fears about likely sub-regional or regional predators. But he refused to be taken in by attendant discourses. Indeed, as he saw it, the rhetoric clouded the actual key motivations underpinning foreign policy, and he firmly believed that in view of the challenges to survival and the independence of regional countries, balance of power considerations were a major motive informing the formulation of their foreign policy. Although he touched on the significance of balance of power considerations in the foreign policy of all Southeast Asian states, Leifer's main published foreign policy titles in this regard focused on three countries: Cambodia, Indonesia and Singapore. However, the remainder of this section will only briefly map out some of the arguments Leifer offered when highlighting the balance of power factor in relation to Cambodia and Singapore.

Cambodia

In his 1967 study of Cambodian foreign policy Leifer examines in great detail Prince Norodom Sihanouk's pursuit of 'neutrality' as a security strategy following independence. The main objective, as Leifer put it, was that 'Prince Sihanouk sought to use the opposing powers to establish a political equilibrium that would safeguard Cambodia's territorial and national integrity.'[49] Achieving a political balance among the Communist and the Western 'blocs' was considered necessary by Sihanouk due to perceived predatory ambitions on the part of Cambodia's two neighbours: Thailand and Vietnam (then conceived both as an independent South Vietnam and a possible reunified Vietnam at some point in the future). Sihanouk's strategy was to develop good relations with both the United States and China primarily with a view to making these powers keep their respective allies in check. A further rationale for pursuing this strategy of building good relations with Washington and Beijing was that Sihanouk was also keen to demonstrate that both the Western and the Communist camps threatened Cambodia so as to ensure that domestic divisions based on ideological attachments, which might conceivably be exploited by its neighbours and their backers (as happened in Laos), could be stunted before they would prove inimical to national consensus. As Leifer argued, Sihanouk was successful in pursuing this strategy in so far as he achieved at least for a while a position of 'carefully balanced non-alignment'.[50] In the event, however, maintaining the balance between West and East over time proved difficult, not least due to what Leifer argued amounted on Cambodia's part to hypersensitivity to shifts in the balance of power in Southeast Asia, as expressed above all in developments in Laos and South Vietnam in the early 1960s.[51]

As a consequence of these perceived shifts, so Leifer suggests, Sihanouk allowed diplomatic relations with the United States to rupture while he developed increasingly close ties with Beijing. The reason for the former was above all Sihanouk's conviction that 'the drift of events could not be controlled by the United States'.[52] Notwithstanding the events in South Vietnam, Sihanouk was more concerned about Hanoi than he was about Saigon, irrespective of the latter's much more threatening public rhetoric vis-à-vis Phnom Penh, as he believed that it was above all the Communist regime that embodied the territorial expansionism of Cambodia's neighbour. Relations with China thus assumed critical importance. As Leifer formulated it, 'Sihanouk viewed China as the only power capable of restraining the traditional expansion of the Vietnamese.'[53] Moving closer to China entailed balance of power considerations that were never explicitly articulated in formal policy, but preoccupied Sihanouk and shaped Cambodian foreign policy at the time. Moreover, adjusting Cambodia's policy of 'neutrality' in this way also constituted a further challenge. As Leifer carefully summarized the thinking underpinning Sihanouk's stance vis-à-vis China, '[i]f Cambodia was to survive, it had to demonstrate that it was more useful to the interests of China to seek the preservation of Cambodia than to promote its disintegration.'[54] At the same time, it also had to avoid Cambodia becoming a Chinese satellite state as a consequence of its balance of power strategy towards Vietnam.

Singapore

The balance of power factor is in many ways also at the heart of Leifer's analysis of Singapore's foreign policy.[55] This work is particularly interesting in the way it combines a perceptive analysis of Singapore's vulnerability with an incisive account of the multiplicity of avenues and methods its leaders have chosen to ensure the country's survival, security and prosperity. As regards its vulnerability, Leifer pointed to Singapore's geographical locus, historical ties of suspicion and enmity with its immediate neighbours, as well as its dependence on resources and social capital. As he also appreciated, Singapore's vulnerability has over time been further accentuated by actual and potential strategic changes. Recently, internal developments in neighbouring countries, such as the weakening of state capacity, have added to Singapore's continued apprehensions.

Leifer showed that Singapore's way of dealing with its vulnerability and the challenge and prospect of constant change that is potentially threatening its security and independence at both the sub-regional and wider regional level has involved finding and employing a variety of ways of compensating for and reshaping to advantage a regional distribution of power. As he put it: 'It naturally includes defence cooperation but does not exclude liberal internationalism in economic policy or engaging in multilateral forms of cooperative security arrangements which lack a military dimension.'[56] All-round development of the US–Singapore relationship has been a key platform of implementing Singapore's balance of power policy. Notwithstanding the deepening security partnership with Washington, Leifer's argument was that for Singapore the balance of power as a policy has not been about forging military alliances along the lines of nineteenth century European practice. Instead, the promotion of multilateral institutions has been a key aspect of Singapore's balance of power policy. Its sponsorship of the ARF is a key example in this regard, and similar arguments can be advanced for the roles of ASEAN and ASEM (Asia–Europe Meeting). According to Leifer, Singapore's 'ideal objective has been to encourage a regional pattern of multilateral power engagement capable of neutralizing potentially hostile forces, especially those geographically most proximate to the Republic, through the medium of institutional co-operation'.[57] In sum, then, this section has served to demonstrate how Leifer saw the foreign policies of Southeast Asian leaders as being both intimately tied to perceived changes in the wider regional balance of power and underpinned by balance of power considerations even though the latter have for the most part not been made very explicit.

Conclusion

In the light of existing interpretations of his underlying theoretical framework, it has been the objective of this chapter to review the status of the balance of power in the writings of the late Professor Michael Leifer. Leifer distinguished two basic meanings of the balance of power: (1) as a situation, and (2) as a policy. The chapter also examined how Leifer analysed changes in the regional balance of power and the balance of power factor in the foreign and security policies of Southeast Asian states. It has demonstrated that Leifer's commitment to the balance of power – as a foundation of regional order – was in many ways a normative one. It has also argued that it would be inappropriate to view Leifer as an advocate of blunt adversarial measures to oppose undue dominance in international society. In principle, he appreciated the value of both associative and countervailing forms of the balance of power, even though he seemed to lean more towards the latter. Pointing this out might well have appealed to Professor Leifer because it would have put the spotlight not so much on any one theoretical approach, but instead on only one of the basic conceptual building blocks for what he was really most concerned with: a refined analysis of the politics and international relations of Southeast Asia.

Notes

1 Michael Leifer, *ASEAN and the Security of Southeast Asia* (London: Routledge, 1989).
2 Michael Leifer, *ASEAN's Search for Regional Order* (Singapore : G. Brash for Faculty of Arts and Social Sciences, National University of Singapore, 1987).
3 See Khong Yuen Foong, 'Making Bricks without Straw in Asia-Pacific', *The Pacific Review* 10 (2) 1997: 289–300 and Sorpong Peou, 'Realism and Constructivism in Southeast Asian Security Studies Today', *The Pacific Review* 15 (1) 2002: 119–38.
4 See Michael Leifer, *The ASEAN Regional Forum: Extending ASEAN's Model of Regional Security* (Adelphi Paper No. 302, London: International Institute for Strategic Studies, 1996).
5 Khong, 'Making Bricks', p. 295, quoted from Leifer, *ASEAN Regional Forum*, p.57.
6 Khong, 'Making Bricks', p. 296.
7 Peou, 'Realism and Constructivism', p. 128.
8 For such differentiation see Ernst B. Haas, 'The Balance of Power: Prescription, Concept, or Propaganda', *World Politics* 5 (4) 1953: 442–77.

9 See Michael Leifer, 'Truth about the Balance of Power', in Derek da Cunha (ed.) *The Evolving Pacific Power Structure* (Singapore: ISEAS, 1996), p. 48.
10 See, for example, Michael Leifer, 'The ASEAN States: No Common Outlook', *International Affairs* 49 (4), October 1973: 600–7.
11 For nine possible meanings of 'balance', see Martin Wight, 'The Balance of Power', in Herbert Butterfield and Martin Wight (eds) *Diplomatic Investigations: Essays in the Theory of International Politics* (London: George Allen & Unwin, 1966), p. 151.
12 Leifer, 'Truth about the Balance of Power', p. 48. On the faces of power debate, see Colin Hay, *Political Analysis* (Basingstoke: Palgrave, 2002), chapter 5.
13 Leifer, *ASEAN Regional Forum*, p. 5.
14 See Michael Leifer, 'The International Dimensions of the Cambodian Conflict', *International Affairs* 51 (4), October 1975: 531–43.
15 Leifer, *ASEAN Regional Forum*, p. 6.
16 Michael Leifer, 'Indonesia and the Dilemmas of Engagement', in Alastair Iain Johnston and Robert S. Ross (eds) *Engaging China: The management of an emerging power* (London: Routledge, 1999), p.105.
17 Michael Leifer, 'China in Southeast Asia: Independence and Accommodation', in David S.G. Goodman and Gerald Segal (eds) *China Rising: Nationalism and Interdependence* (London: Routledge, 1997), p. 156.
18 Michael Leifer, 'Chinese Economic Reform and Security Policy: The South China Sea Connection', *Survival* 37 (2) 1995, p. 58.
19 Michael Leifer, 'International Dynamics of One Southeast Asia', in Hadi Soesastro (ed.) *One Southeast Asia in a New Regional and International Setting* (Jakarta: CSIS, 1997), p. 193.
20 Leifer, 'Chinese Economic Reform', p. 55).
21 Leifer, *ASEAN Regional Forum*, p. 17.
22 Leifer, 'Chinese Economic Reform', pp. 56–7.
23 See Denny Roy 'Hegemon on the Horizon? China's Threat to East Asian Security', *International Security* 19 (1) 1994: 149–68.
24 Ralf Emmers *Cooperative Security and the Balance of Power in ASEAN and the ARF* (London: RoutledgeCurzon, 2003), p. 44.
25 See William C. Wohlforth, 'The Stability of a Unipolar World', *International Security* 24 (1) 1999: 5–41; Greg Austin, *China's Ocean Frontier: International Law, Military Force and National Development* (St. Leonards, NSW: Allen & Unwin in association with the Department of International Relations, Australian National University, 1998). Also see Gerald Segal, 'Does China Matter?', *Foreign Affairs*, 78 (5) 1999: 24–36.
26 Alastair Iain Johnston, 'Is China a Status Quo Power?', *International Security* 27 (4) 2003: 5–56. For reviews of the China–ASEAN relationship, see Alice Ba, 'China and ASEAN: Renavigating Relations for a 21st-Century Asia', *Asian Survey* 43 (4) 2003: 622–47; and Jürgen Haacke, 'Seeking Influence: China's Diplomacy Toward ASEAN after the Asian Crisis', *Asian Perspective*, 26 (4) 2002: 13–52.
27 Michael Leifer, 'The ASEAN Peace Process: A Category Mistake', *The Pacific Review* 12 (1) 1999: 25–38.
28 Leifer, *ASEAN Regional Forum*, p. 12.
29 Leifer, *ASEAN Regional Forum*, p. 14.
30 Michael Leifer, 'Is ASEAN a Security Organization?' in K.S. Sandhu *et al.*, *The ASEAN Reader* (Singapore: Institute of Southeast Asian Studies, 1992), pp. 379–81.
31 Leifer, 'International Dynamics', p. 195.
32 Leifer, *ASEAN Regional Forum*, p. 15. Notably,although for Leifer ASEAN thus played no major role in *managing* the regional balance of power, he did not say that ASEAN would not be able to make any contribution at all to regional order.

33 Michael Leifer, 'The Limits of Functionalist Endeavour: The Experiences of Southeast Asia', in A.J.R. Groom and Paul Taylor (eds) *Functionalism: Theory and Practice in International Relations* (New York: Crane, Russak, 1975), pp. 278–83.
34 Michael Leifer 'A Reply', *The Pacific Review* 5 (2) 1992: 167–9.
35 Leifer, *ASEAN Regional Forum*, p. 59.
36 Michael Leifer, *Singapore's Foreign Policy: Coping with Vulnerability* (London: Routledge, 2000), p. 99.
37 Leifer repeatedly used the term 'security culture' which he glossed as 'distinctive security culture of conflict avoidance and conflict management'. See Leifer, *ASEAN Regional Forum*, pp. 9, 12, 19, 41. He did not embrace the concept of the 'ASEAN way', even as shorthand for a wider set of practices and norms that would have included the principles that he seemed to endorse from the vantage point of someone committed to international society. On this point, see Amitav Acharya, *Constructing a Security Community in Southeast Asia: ASEAN and the Problem of Regional Order* (London: Routledge, 2001) and Jürgen Haacke, *ASEAN's Diplomatic and Security Culture: Origins, Development and Prospects* (London: RoutledgeCurzon, 2003).
38 Leifer, *ASEAN Regional Forum*, p. 53.
39 Ibid., p. 57.
40 Ibid., pp. 37–8.
41 Ibid., p. 43.
42 Ibid., p. 51.
43 Ibid., p. 59.
44 Leifer, 'Truth about the Balance of Power', p. 47.
45 Ibid., p. 49.
46 Ibid., p. 47.
47 For a fuller discussion of these two conceptions of the balance of power, see Richard Little, 'Deconstructing the Balance of Power: Two Traditions of Thought', *Review of International Studies* 15 (2) 1989: 87–100. As Little also put it, the balance of power metaphor has from its origins 'been Janus–faced, looking in one direction at the competing interests between states and in the other at their common interests'. See Richard Little, 'A Balance of Power', in Greg Fry and Jacinta O'Hagan (eds) *Contending Images of World Politics* (Basingstoke: Macmillan, 2000), p. 60.
48 S. Jayakumar, 'Opening Statement', Thirty-third ASEAN Ministerial Meeting, Bangkok, 24 July 2000, at http://www.aseansec.org
49 Michael Leifer *Cambodia: The Search for Security* (London: Pall Mall Press, 1967), p. 18.
50 Leifer, *Cambodia*, p. 63.
51 Ibid., p. 18.
52 Ibid., p. 103.
53 Ibid., p. 134.
54 Ibid., p. 134.
55 Michael Leifer, *Singapore's Foreign Policy: Coping with Vulnerability* (London: Routledge, 2000).
56 Leifer, *Singapore's Foreign Policy*, p. 26.
57 Ibid., p. 25.

5 Untying Leifer's discourse on order and power

See Seng Tan

Introduction

Political realism is often understood as a relatively homogeneous and internally harmonious tradition predicated upon certain essential suppositions and concepts.[1] This, of course, is not to imply that its proponents do not allow for differences and variations within their "tradition."[2] Be that as it may, those nuances for the most part do not resist the associated Hobbesian visions of pervasive insecurity, recurrent conflict, and universal expectations of war and violence. Nor do such nuances detract from the widespread tendency among apologists of political *neo*-realism to represent their tradition as a positivist monologue shorn of ambiguities and tensions that could potentially undermine its presumed unity and harmony. In so doing they conveniently ignore the more ambivalent aspects of contributions by those operating in a somewhat different cultural time and space, but who likewise claim allegiance to the realist tradition.[3] Hence they elide awkward elements of history and practice, such as inconsistencies and paradoxes, and enforce logical closure upon discourse. In so doing they ensure that the conditions on which they rely to explain continuity and change in global life, usually understood in terms of some "deep structure" that is at once autonomous, objective, extra-historical, and extra-political, are hence upheld.[4]

Against that backdrop, the writings of Michael Leifer on order and power serve as a compelling reminder that antinomies animate the realist tradition in ways that many realists either downplay or simply ignore. This is particularly, though not exclusively, true of neo-realists who, in the name of theoretical parsimony and methodological rigor, valorize logical closure and defer or exclude questions which interrogate the very limits that affirm the tradition as settled and unified. When listening to Leifer through positivistic ears, one encounters a discomforting dissonance born of the fact that his arguments tend to strain neo-realist arguments. Consider, for example, his annotations of ASEAN (Association of Southeast Asian Nations) variously as an aspirant security community, a balance-of-power institution, and an expression of cooperative security.[5] Resolution of the apparent tension in these statements can come about in either of two ways. On the one hand, one may deny Leifer the status of a true realist, or simply write him off as a dubious analyst lacking in conceptual rigor, whose gratuitous blend of three distinct theoretical concepts to elucidate ASEAN dynamics strains credibility. His perspective is thereby considered too vague, ambiguous, and contradictory to warrant serious theoretical attention. After all, Leifer is not a formal theorist nor did he ever pretend to be one.

On the other hand, in granting Leifer's arguments "breathing space," so to speak, we find in them a basis for reflective examination of our presuppositions of realism as a tradition. If anything, the domain of International Relations (IR) is one in which ambiguity "is not to be imputed to the inadequacy of our concepts," as Aron once remarked, "it is an integral part of reality itself."[6] In that respect, Leifer would probably not want us to make too much of his ideas of regional order and balance-of-power, especially not in rendering those into unifying labels for things too complex and ambiguous to be reduced to singular concepts. In like fashion, Hedley Bull intimated that "it is always erroneous to interpret events as if international society were the sole dominant element"[7]—a startling statement, considering that it was made in reference to a conceptual linchpin of the English School, of which Bull was a prominent representative.

In contrast, neo-realist monologues seem to resist the notion that ambiguity in international life cannot simply be resolved by attempting to reduce the "essential contestability" of one's constructs and concepts. For example, neo-realist constructions of post-Cold War Asian security reduced the ambiguity and complexity of the region to alarmist caricatures, most of them uncalled for.[8] A deeper reflection on realist scholarship, however, would suggest that the tradition contains antinomies that render realism, at least potentially, an open-ended dialogue. Such openness likely emulates the uncertainty and disarray of historicized reality in better ways than do the simulated hyper-real figurations inscribed by neo-realist discourse, whose archetypes precede and produce the very reality that they purport to typify. And it is due precisely to neo-realist efforts to supplant the classicists who have spawned provincial renditions of the tradition, which, if you will, "dutifully perform in accordance with the required stereotypes".[9]

Not so for Leifer's ruminations on order and power, one may argue, thanks to the open-ended "nature" of his discourse, which is properly understood only in the context of its making. Such a context involves, namely, a dialogue among students of the region, but also within the wider community of IR theorists. Like all contributions to those conversations, Leifer's *oeuvre* is marked by ambivalences, contradictions, and lacunae. Unlike many contributions to those conversations, however, his writings may be construed as attempts, not just to report on the world of Asian security, but, if only indirectly, to bring that world to bear, in a reflective way, upon the tradition—on its cherished concepts and revered knowledge claims. It involves, if you will, an effort to speak not only *of* an "other" but also *to* it; it demonstrates a commitment to dialoguing with the world even as it contributes to its objectification. Against the mimetic models of positivist social science, Leifer's work provides us with a better sense of why the positivists-rationalists can speak of but cannot reply to reality. Given its interpretive approach, it "retains a certain humility in the face of the final authority of the text" of the social world with which Leifer's texts seek to commune.[10]

The purpose of this chapter is two-fold: to theoretically deconstruct and dialogically imagine Leifer's ideas of regional order and balance-of-power.[11] Our knowledge of the world of Asian security owes as much to Leifer's contributions as to those of any other analyst, and it is in that sense that devotees (and detractors) of his *oeuvre* are bound by a shared indebtedness and intertextuality. In reading his discourse as an effort to grapple, at times successfully and at other times not, with a world-text that is open and ambiguous, we see that the realist tradition does not have to be (indeed it is not) the suffocating straitjacket that many neo-realists, thanks to their one-dimensional positivistic readings, have made it. Less so a plea for fidelity to classical or traditional realist texts, the concern here has to do with restoring a respect for practice in history. If anything, Leifer's texts are an invitation to reflect historically and dialogically on the ambiguous world-text of Asian security.

Two qualifications are in order. First, nowhere does the foregoing suggestion of Leifer's discourse as "dialogical" rely on my assignation of intention on his part. Rather, the claim is rendered out of recognition for the *consequentiality* rather than intentionality, if not of Leifer the scholar, then certainly of his texts.[12] A text, according to Roland Barthes, "is not a line of words releasing a single 'theological' meaning (the 'message' of the Author-God) but a multi-dimensional space in which a variety of meanings, none of them original, blend and clash."[13] A dialogical reading is made possible by the philosophical openness of Leifer's texts, a contested and contestable space that potentially permits a wealth of interpretive possibilities. Nor am I implying, second, that his *oeuvre* has succeeded in liberating political realism from the positivistic "fetters" imposed by neo-realists, whose *re*visions of realism seem oriented toward a technical interest in control more than in the desire (usually self-professed, no less) for reflection. If positivism is essentially the disavowal of reflection, as Habermas contends, then the continued reliance by the dominant paradigms of IR on positivist-rationalist foundations makes the possibility of imminent change unlikely.[14]

Theoretical deconstruction

Recent scholarship on Machiavelli suggests that this venerated thinker often amounts to little more than a caricature in the hands of realists.[15] Importantly, such critiques neither dispute the view that Machiavelli's ideas demonstrate congruence with aspects of the realist tradition nor purport to expose Machiavelli as un-Machiavellian. What they challenge is the claim, widely held, of an unproblematic link between Machiavelli and contemporary neo-realist thought. It is a link that more properly reflects modern concerns with tradition-making—where pride of place is given to stories of origins, reified teleologies, and grand narratives of continuity and discontinuity—than with what this or that classical thinker actually said or wrote. No deep structure or meaning, already given and settled, exists within the contested site named "Machiavelli" waiting to be uncovered by some intrepid scholar, that would permit the sketching of uncomplicated trajectories from that to another equally contested site, political realism. No such structure exists, that is, other than iterated assertions of its existence, usually by the makers and guardians of tradition.

Even a perfunctory review of Leifer's writings would reveal an abiding concern with order and power.[16] Leifer has been described, at least on one occasion, as a political realist.[17] Whether that amounts to a caricature of Leifer in the way neo-realist constructions of Machiavelli are has not, if at all, engendered the antagonistic reactions that the latter situation clearly provoked. If anything, there is a widely shared consensus that the realist tradition has enjoyed an inordinate influence in Southeast Asian IR, and still does to a commanding extent.[18]According to one view, Southeast Asian security studies have long eschewed the appeal of theory and normative reasoning because "they primarily involve recognition of prevailing reality not in terms of what a particular situation should be but instead what it actually is."[19] In other words, so pervasive has epistemic realism been to the formation and conservation of knowledge about Southeast Asia that the contributions made by the Leifer *oeuvre* to a realist impression of the region cannot be overstated. Sorpong Peou makes the following observation: "Of all the realists who have studied Southeast Asian security, however, Michael Leifer was no doubt the most influential. Known as the 'dean' of Southeast Asian security studies, he wrote extensively on this region and painted a realist picture."[20]

But precisely what or which "realism" does the Leifer corpus present to us? A careful reading of Peou's evidence implies that Leifer, "disciple of traditional realism" that he was, would nevertheless find common cause with his neo-realist brethren, whose discourses pivot on "material power" considerations and power-balancing logics.[21] Yet Leifer's writings betray a discomfort with the certitude of positivist-rationalist arguments in their insistence in locating explanation in deep structures. Suspicious of attempts to uncover a reified teleology in Southeast Asian security, he would take issue, say, with those who sought to construct narratives of grand purpose, vision, and effort that could conceivably explain present-day felicities.[22] Take, for example, his resistance to the notion that there is a notably "distinctive ASEAN peace process" which shaped the course of regional peacemaking in Southeast Asia:

> ASEAN relates to peace through a general influence exercised on member governments to observe standard international norms and not through applying any distinctive process to a particular conflict which may be transformed as a consequence.[23]

Nor would neo-realist explanations that privilege system-level causes and the primacy of material factors do—not all the time at least. Questions of ideology and identity vie alongside power distributions and power-balancing practices for analytical attention.[24] This, assuredly, is not quite the same as neo-realism. Indeed, many of the key restatements of neo-realism in the 1990s emerged as a consequence of its engagement with (or, for others, its cooptation of) constructivism.[25] Even then, their efforts in addressing questions on "identity" or the "balance-of-threat" work hard at locating themselves, in quite self-conscious ways, within the exacting parameters established by Waltz and other leading neo-realist figures who continue to obsess in the endless search for deep structure and natural teleology.[26]

Not so for Leifer, whose realism approximates that of E.H. Carr and other classicists who understand social relations as ordered and predictable but not always reducible to certain eternal or self-evident laws. Rather, to the extent that regularities in international life can be ascertained, those classicists would just as likely regard them as the effects of a usually arduous and protracted effort, at times calculated and at other times accidental, to form and preserve a consensus—an historically established *tradition*—that is at best fragile, implicit, and normative. Hence, while neo-realists see the balance-of-power as an enduring feature and fixed property of the international system, which accounts for the continuous reproduction of international anarchy, classicists in general would treat that formulation as, to use Bull's words, "quite inadequate."[27] In contrast to the neo-realist intimation that there is an inevitable tendency for power balances to arise, they argue instead that balances emerge as a consequence either of conscious effort on the part of members of the system, or "fortuitously" because states do not always seek to maximize their relative power position.[28] Clearly, that interfacing between cunning and caprice, between agency and structure, is more Machiavellian than neo-realist renditions, with their insistent privileging of instrumental control over objectified realities, can ever hope to be. For instance, we may recall that the Renaissance humanists, among other things, were responsible for the motif that "it was always open to men to exercise their *virtù* in such a way as to overcome the power of *Fortuna*."[29] Yet classical *virtù* is always accompanied by the recognition that all-encompassing control (both as abstract ideal and practical reality) is forever beyond one's grasp—a humility that evades the neo-realist, or, for that matter, Hobbes, who placed his faith in the power of Leviathan. It is for this reason that Inis Claude once conceded that, "in accepting the balance-of-power system one refuses to become so preoccupied with order so as to subordinate all other values to it, and acquiesces in some lack of order as incidental to the desiderata of cultural pluralism, political freedom, and administrative decentralization."[30]

Finally, what connections, if any, are there between the English School and Leifer's discourse? As with political realism, we are hard-pressed to locate instances wherein Leifer may have openly displayed his English School credentials, if indeed he regarded himself as an adherent of that tradition. In any case, the purpose of this investigation, as with any deconstruction, is not to discover deep structures but to highlight various effects made possible by a particular text as it dialogues with other texts. One such encounter, in a discussion on the ASEAN Regional Forum, is as follows:

> The ARF, however, can be seen as an imperfect diplomatic instrument for achieving regional security goals in that it seeks to address the problem of power which arises from *the anarchical nature of international society* without provision for either collective defense or conventional collective security.[31]

In the same text we also find this comment on ASEAN: "the cardinal rule of international society—the sanctity of national sovereignty—violated by Vietnam's invasion, was at the heart of ASEAN's Treaty of Amity and Cooperation. Indeed, it was ASEAN's effective *raison d'être* as a regional organisation."[32] Consistent references to "international society" in Leifer's writings suggest that whatever his intellectual proclivities, the *effect* of his discourse often privileges conceptual categories and linguistic conventions associated with the English School.[33] Positivist-rationalists have long dismissed that genre as "speculative, unconfirmed or 'pre-operational'."[34] Yet a comprehensive assessment of English School scholarship makes clear that its adherents have variously relied on interpretive, positivist, and critical assumptions,[35] drawn as they are to "a pluralistic methodology that aims to find ways of linking apparently disparate bodies of knowledge and understanding."[36] Indeed, they would insist, despite Bull's evident enthusiasm for the Grotian perspective,[37] that a comprehensive understanding of international life is not possible without embracing all three interpretive traditions (realism, rationalism, and revolutionism) originally staked out by Martin Wight.[38] Hence, without endorsing Wight's categories, it may be said of Leifer's work, linked dialogically and intersubjectively to traditional realism and the English School (but not necessarily bounded by those), that it reflects openness when subjected to a deconstructive reading.

Dialogical imagination

Leifer's reflections on regional order and the balance-of-power acknowledge, if only implicitly, the importance of language in Southeast Asian security studies as a way of coming to terms with the intersubjective understandings of the traditional community of statesmen.[39] Over a decade ago Ken Booth opined: "Our work is our words, but our words do not work anymore."[40] However, Booth's prescient observation was preceded by that of Wight, who insisted that, "the stuff of international theory…is constantly bursting the bounds of the language which we try to handle it."[41] This notion of the centrality of language in security studies—alien to most neo-realist renditions—is also apparent in

Leifer's discourse, particularly its commitment to trace the thinking of statesmen already embodied in their practices. His work therefore is not without the various critical tensions considered in the previous section. Indeed, as the following analysis demonstrates, it is precisely this sort of antinomy that animates his writings, where ambiguity and contradiction "out there" in the "real world" is captured, via reflective reason, in the "right here" of the realist tradition as it grapples with certain real and protean conditions still not fully understood. In order for one to be a realist, Leifer's *oeuvre* seems to be saying, one has to be a critical non-realist at the same time.[42] Only through such "self-critique"—which involves inviting reality to confront us, at times brusquely so—can we avoid, where possible, the unreflective objectification and reification of our claims.

Order where none exists

In Leifer's classic statements on regional order in Southeast Asia, there is acknowledgement that the collective aspiration within ASEAN for regional order appears undeniable, not least where formal Association documents are concerned. "And yet," it is noted of the Bangkok Declaration, "if that Declaration is read as a whole, including its preamble, it should be evident that inherent in the document is also an expression of greater ambition. That ambition is the establishment of a system of regional order."[43] Elsewhere, it is observed that the Treaty of Amity and Cooperation "was the means adopted to try to create a wider structure of ordered interstate relations."[44] What regional order entails is "the existence of a stable structure of regional inter-governmental relationships informed by common assumptions about the bases of interstate conduct."[45] The relationship between "bases of interstate conduct" and assumptions about such is clarified in a similar argument rendered in the wider context of East Asia:

> It is possible to argue that the general pattern of the regional balance in East Asia in terms of distribution of power embodies a measure of stability from a sense of prudence. But it is not the same as a viable regional order which requires more than just a rudimentary code of inter-state conduct. It requires also the existence of a set of shared assumptions about the interrelationships among resident and external states.[46]

But there are problems, not least where ASEAN and regional order are concerned. That regional order remains an elusive dream, always beyond our grasp no matter the wealth of resources and force of will brought to bear in attempts at fulfilling it, is apparent: "Regional order in a full sense has always been beyond the corporate capacity of ASEAN."[47] Beyond also, it might be added, the corporate capacity of positivist-rationalist analysts to order the world of Asian security as they see fit. More fundamentally, it is the dearth of "shared assumptions"—intersubjective understandings—about international life that denotes the absence of regional order;[4] "ASEAN has not been able to promote security to the extent of forging a region-wide structure of relations based on common values and interests."[49] Such a view also informs Leifer's thinking regarding the long-held Indonesian mantra of regional solutions to regional problems: "Implicit in the idea of regional solutions to regional problems is an assumption that not only are there 'natural' regions, but also that their resident states will share the same view of the nature of regional problems and how to address them."[50] How indeed, when Association members continue to treat one another with mistrust and suspicion?

> The regional enterprise was embarked upon in the full knowledge that certain underlying facts of political life could not be changed at will, including the sense of vulnerability of some member states. In other words, foreign policy would always be a problem among member states; some partners in reconciliation would remain potential enemies.[51]

In another comment, it is noted that regional security dynamics "are beset by a competitive edge which makes the notion of regional order an inappropriate point of reference."[52] That said, regional order "of a kind" *still* obtains, presumably when statesmen exercise their *virtù* and succeed occasionally in taming, if only for a moment, the capricious power of *Fortuna*, or when *Fortuna* smiles on the region quite apart from the concerted efforts of practitioners:

> If regional order in the grand sense has been beyond the capacity of ASEAN, order of a kind has been realized on an intramural scale. The management of interstate tensions within ASEAN, underpinned by an established habit of cooperation, has given rise to a sense of security community… Regional order in the grand sense lies beyond the current capacity of ASEAN but its more limited version is of considerable importance, certainly in comparison with the condition of relationships among its members before August 1967.[53]

Significantly, in paradoxically contending that order of a kind obtains where none exists, this statement continues to resist the easy slide toward an ideological conclusion. In contrast to claims that ASEAN has arrived as a security community, or that it constitutes a nascent or incipient security community on its way to becoming a mature one, the temptation to reify teleology is refused in favor of a deliberate ambivalence that records only desire with no hint whatsoever of any commensurate design or destiny:

> An evolving practice of political co-operation expressed in bureaucratic and ministerial consultation has served also in ASEAN's case to create a subregional security community. *The sense of community is still embryonic*, however, exemplified in recurrent expressions of bilateral tension which place a strain on intramural relations.[54]

A final illustration to conclude this treatment on regional order comes in the form of an intriguing comment: "the pressing problem of regional order for ASEAN is one of conservation, not innovation."[55] In other words, no idealistic dream of regional renovation or neo-liberal institutional project of organizational transformation need apply; the aim, simply put, is to maintain the status quo. Here the realist in Leifer surfaces starkly—a realist accent which neo-realists may likewise recognize, possibly even claim, as one of their own. But that is not all. Oddly enough, a critical non-realist inflection seems also to "emerge" from the text:

> It is well understood that conservation cannot be achieved by standing still... Nonetheless, regional order in the practical sense for ASEAN will depend on adequate attention being paid to the commonplace, which requires special attention because it is commonplace and, therefore, in danger of being taken for granted.[56]

Regional order, the text seems to hint, is ultimately about instantiating and hence reconstituting boundaries and borders—the "commonplace" elements which shore up the purported ontological integrity and primacy of states and, by extension, the state system. It is a delicate acknowledgement that articulations of anarchy, danger, and fear are necessary in order that the limits of state-centric discourse can be affirmed and sustained. It is the fragile admission that "sovereign states" and "ASEAN" are never more than effects of representational practices that can be made to work only so long as alternative or rival voices can be excluded or silenced.[57] Nevertheless, it is also thoroughly modern in that it is a mobilization to arms; it is a clarion call for constant vigilance among the troops against potential dangers which threaten life "as we know it"—including, one surmises, imprudent neo-liberal and/or constructivist endeavors at erecting edifices using "bricks without straw."[58] Here Leifer no longer plays analyst but statesman.

Power-balancing as paradox

IR debates in the 1980s demonstrated just how one-dimensional the balance-of-power idea could be in the hands of some neo-realists.[59] Combined with the supposition that power can only be defined exclusively in coercive terms, balance-of-power came to be understood as adversarial, hostile, and competitive.[60] This neo-realist propensity to read power-balancing in so monological a fashion elided alternative conceptions of balancing in communal or cooperative terms.[61] Furthermore, it is treated as an enduring feature and fixed property of the international system, which, according to social constructivists, accounts for the continuous reproduction of the "institutions" of international anarchy and self-help.[62] The understanding of balance-of-power as both coercive *and* communal, and as both cause *and* effect can be found in Leifer's discourse.

As with his writings on regional order, his observations on balance-of-power are equally a site open to contestation and double readings. Indeed, at times it is unclear whether regional security management in ASEAN operates via power-balancing or cooperative security, and even then the text is ambiguous on whether those practices constitute the very things for which they are named. As noted earlier, it is unlikely that Leifer would want us to treat his concepts with the sort of absolutism with which neo-realists often treat theirs. After all, the essential contestability of concepts is but a function of the social world. The aim of this discussion is not to survey his entire corpus on power-balancing, which comprises a formidable collection, but to select a few examples that best illustrate those antinomies and ambivalences. Three areas are particularly noteworthy.

We begin with power-balancing as comprising both coercive and communal elements. The former is apparent in the following description of East Asian security dynamics, but even then it is evident Leifer is already widening the parameters of the idea or appropriating it in a more flexible way so that reality does not end up "bursting the bounds of the language"[63]:

> The balance-of-power that exists in terms of a condition is reflected in a competitive pattern of regional alignments… Accordingly its revision or managed confirmation constitute contending alternatives but to be confronted primarily in political terms because prudence constrains the use of military means traditionally associated with the practice of the balance-of-power as a policy of states.[64]

Consider as well this thought: "Balance-of-power as an actual policy of states has been clearer in terms of a common goal which has been to deny the emergence of any undue dominance or hegemony."[65] This statement is sufficiently ambiguous to connote both competitive and cooperative senses in power-balancing. Again, we see this in a careful exegesis of the purported "origins" of balance-of-power logic behind the formation of ASEAN:

> The Concert of Europe had been predicated on the concept of the balance-of-power, but in the second half of the twentieth century this notion was anathema to a non-aligned Indonesia whose participation in ASEAN was critical to the Association's existence and viability. Yet without identifying it with European practice, ASEAN was established with balance-of-power clearly in mind.[66]

Repudiation of an established regional security practice for its European roots makes good sense for a region that has just been decolonized. Establishing a regional institution predicated on the balance-of-power would seem impossible, even ludicrous, especially with the undisputed regional leader, Indonesia, openly embracing a policy of nonalignment. Evidently, the New World of America was not the only post-colonial outpost fending off "undesirable" Old World practices, not least the balance-of-power.[67] Yet the creation of ASEAN, we are told, is based, if only informally, on power-balancing. The regional power to be balanced, of course, was Indonesia, whose "hegemonic aspiration" had to be restrained:

> A regionally autonomous structure of order under Indonesia's guidance was an abiding aspiration but not one shared by its fellow member governments. Indonesia's regional vision challenged the logic of the balance-of-power which in Southeast Asia has always been influenced by extra-regional forces. Such a perspective separated Indonesia from its regional partners, which still valued access to extra-regional sources of countervailing power.[68]

Elsewhere we find a supporting argument in reference to the Indonesian proposal for a "regional solution" to regional order: "A 'regional solution' may thus be both a formula for regional order, and a euphemism for regional hegemony."[69] That the balancing which other ASEAN members sought to erect against Jakarta had a coercive or competitive cast to it is not in doubt, in view of the troubled history especially among Indonesia, Malaysia and Singapore. That Jakarta could be "coaxed" into such a joint regional venture, however, must also be attributed to its *willingness to cooperate* with neighboring states seeking to impose institutional constraints on it:

> President Suharto well understood that one way to restore regional confidence and stability would be to lock Indonesia into a structure of multilateral partnership and constraint that would be seen as a rejection of hegemonic pretensions… [Indonesia] assumed responsibilities for regional order as the effective *primus inter pares* of [ASEAN]. The extent to which Indonesia's example of political self-denial in the interest of regional order may be emulated within the wider Asia-Pacific is central to any parallel between ASEAN and the ASEAN Regional Forum.[70]

The notion of a preponderant power's volitional exercise of what Ikenberry calls "strategic restraint" vis-à-vis smaller or less powerful states is by no means a recent insight.[71] Writing about the balance-of-power, Bull describes a similar situation involving the United States—a view preceding neo-liberal institutional attempts in the 1980s to explain similar phenomena:

> Is it the case that a state which finds itself in a position of preponderant power will always use it to "lay down the law to others"? Will a locally preponderant state always be a menace to the independence of its neighbors, and a generally preponderant state to the survival of the system of states? The proposition is implicitly denied by the leaders of powerful states, who see sufficient safeguard of the rights of others in their own virtue and good

> intentions. Franklin Roosevelt saw the safeguard of Latin America's rights in United States adherence to the "good-neighbour policy."[72]

That a communal notion of balance-of-power requires, among other things, a commitment by preponderant powers to strategic restraint underscores a second antinomy discernable in Leifer's writings. Do power balances promote moderation and thereby produce stability, or are they themselves the *outcomes* of moderation? In Claude's reflections on the Concert of Europe, his contention flies in the face of contemporary wisdom:

> That this moderation is viewed as the essential foundation for the functioning of the balance-of-power system rather than as a consequence of its functioning is evidenced by the fact that the fading and ultimate collapse of the efficacy of that system is customarily attributed to the decline of those factors that sustained moderation.[73]

In a discussion by Leifer on the ARF we find the following argument:

> Indeed, the prerequisite for a successful ARF may well be the prior existence of a stable balance-of-power. The central issue in the case of the ARF is whether, in addition to diplomatic encouragement for a culture of cooperation driven partly by economic interdependence, the region shows the makings of a stable, supporting balance or distribution of power that would allow the multilateral venture to proceed in circumstances of some predictability. The ARF's structural problem is that its viability seems to depend on the prior existence of a stable balance, but it is not really in a position to create it.[74]

On the one hand, it is claimed that the success of multilateral security institutionalism depends on the prior existence of a stable balance-of-power, hence attributing a measure of causality to the latter. On the other, the preceding illustrations of moderation on the part of Indonesia (and, for Bull, the United States) in ensuring a viable balance in their respective circumstances imply that power-balancing can be a *consequence* as much as a cause. Indeed, Leifer's attribution of ontological priority to a "stable balance" (in the above quotation) does not automatically preclude the probability of the prior existence of moderation and restraint on the part of members of a multilateral security regime. Hence in contradistinction to the common argument that the balance-of-power promotes moderation, his texts reflect both instances: moderation as consequence of, as well as prerequisite for, a successful balance.

A third antinomy resides in Leifer's later writings on ASEAN in which balance-of-power shares pride of place with another idea. Power-balancing, we are told, does not adequately explain the "nature" of institutional dynamics in ASEAN even though its leaders had balancing "clearly in mind": "ASEAN is best understood as an institutionalized, albeit relatively informal, expression of 'cooperative security' which may serve as both a complement and as an alternative to balance-of-power practice."[75] Here we get a sense of Leifer's efforts in responding to ideas promoted by Track 2 communities in the post-Cold War expansion of intellectual activities throughout the Asia-Pacific oriented toward influencing the policy process. For Leifer, cooperative security is to be contrasted with the classical notion of collective security, which, as embodied in the League of Nations, is principally about the institutionalization of balance-of-power. However, cooperative security is distinct because it forgoes the idea of sanctions, which constitutes the trademark of a collective approach. By its very nature it eschews problem solving "because its working premise is that the ideal conditions for finding regional solutions should be sought with others, as opposed to against them." Rather, the main vehicle of cooperative security is "dialogue and suasion."[76]

Any notion that Leifer may have finally found in cooperative security his conceptual muse would be sorely mistaken, however. The balance-of-power is neither relegated nor abandoned in his later works. As with regional order and balance-of-power, the ambiguous world-text of Southeast Asian security continues to evade capture by idealized concepts, including one favored more or less by the Track 2 communities in a region that has long resisted the lure of "Western theory." In Leifer's discourse ASEAN "is best understood" as an expression of cooperative security, but with a significant qualifier—"institutionalised, albeit relatively informal."[77] As an idea that competes with as well as complements the balance-of-power, it is unlikely that the grip which the latter idea, contested though it be, has had on Leifer's works would be relaxed any time soon. Indeed, others elsewhere have argued that cooperative security in some respects can be accommodated within the balance-of-power idea, particularly its communal side.

In a sense, that possibility has already, if only subtly, been "anticipated" by Leifer's discourse; for instance, ASEAN has been described as "an aspirant intramural *security regime* based, in principle, on respect for those international norms set out in the TAC [Treaty of Amity and Cooperation]."[78] The employment of the term "security regime" in this statement to depict the Association is no accidental move, or so it would seem. But why particularly that term and not "security community," the idiom of choice in at least several of his works? Popularized by Robert Jervis, the concept, among other things, is of interest to this discussion because of the historical case study Jervis selects for his research as emblematic of a security regime—the Concert of Europe.[79] With the invocation of the Concert we return, full circle, to the balance-of-power. This is not to imply that Leifer had it in mind to exploit these interconnections. Again, it bears repeating that no attribution to intentions is warranted in this exercise in deconstruction. Rather, we are concerned with the consequence or effect of discourse.

And it is in that same spirit that another reading becomes possible, a reading occasioned by Leifer's regime notion as well as the comment (referenced earlier) on conservation as ASEAN's most pressing problem in regional order, where it is argued that "regional order…will depend on adequate attention being paid to the commonplace, which requires special attention because it is commonplace and, therefore, in danger of being taken for granted."[80] On his part, Ashley has referred to "a tradition of regime anchored in the balance-of-power scheme and constitutive of the modern state system":

> The regime should not be construed to organize and regulate behaviors among states-as-actors. It instead *produces* sovereign states who, as condition of their sovereignty, embody the regime. So deeply bound is this regime within the identities of the participant states that their observations of its rules and expectations become acts not of conscious obedience to something external but of self-realization, of survival as what they have become.[81]

Thus understood, quite possibly the most important accomplishment of Leifer's discourse on order, power, and community is its continued production, empowerment, and legitimization of political subjectivity, whether as sovereign states or specific regional institutions. In helping to frame the domain of Southeast Asian security studies, in privileging certain political identities while excluding others, it is Leifer's writings, more than many self-professed constructivist works on Southeast Asian security, which have facilitated the constitution and instantiation of identity in that part of the world—in quite circumscribed ways, doubtless, but also in a fashion that ascribes critical respect for the paradoxes and tensions of international life much more than neo-realists, or for that matter some neo-liberals and constructivists, have done.

Conclusion

By way of Michael Leifer's open-ended texts on regional order and the balance-of-power, this chapter has sought to reclaim some of the tensions that animate the realist tradition in ways neo-realists have either downplayed or simply ignored. In contrast to positivist-rationalist scholars who attempt to impose a singular foundational reality on the heterogeneous world-text of international life, Leifer's discourse, linked intertextually with other interpretive traditions, draws critical attention to some of the metaphysical conceits of IR theory. With their shrill pontificating about parsimony and rigor, scholars who pursue a purely instrumentalist control over an objectified reality—without pausing to hear what the "real world" has to say in return—hide the fact that IR "is a language that enables us to shift and maneuver, outflank and charge, turn tail and run, retreat into historical ambiguity, commandeer resources where we can find them, shed one uniform and don another, and return to fight another day".[82] As we have seen, Leifer's *oeuvre* is not without its own shifts, flanking maneuvers, retreats, and uniform changes. But it commits these moves without any hint of hypocrisy or prevarication. With the untimely passing of Michael Leifer, Southeast Asian security studies has lost a choice interlocutor. Nevertheless, his texts live on, variously instructing, disciplining, constructing, excluding, empowering, demolishing. They "return to fight another day." They always do.

Notes

1 R.B.J. Walker, "History and Structure in the Theory of International Relations," *Millennium*, Vol. 18, No. 2 (1989), pp.163–83.
2 J.W. Taliaferro, "Security Seeking under Anarchy: Defensive Realism Revisited," *International Security*, Vol. 25, No. 3 (2000), pp.128–61; Robert Gilpin, "The Richness of the Tradition of Political Realism," in Robert O. Keohane (ed.), *Neorealism and Its Critics* (New York: Columbia University Press, 1986), pp.301–21.
3 Richard Little, "Deconstructing the Balance-of-power: Two Traditions of Thought," *Review of International Studies*, Vol. 15, No. 2 (1989), pp. 87–100.
4 Richard K. Ashley, "Untying the Sovereign State: A Double Reading of the Anarchy Problematique," *Millennium*, Vol. 17, No. 2 (1988), pp.227–62.
5 Michael Leifer, *The ASEAN Regional Forum*, Adelphi Paper 302 (London: IISS/Oxford University Press, 1996); *idem*, "The ASEAN Peace Process: A Category Mistake," *The Pacific Review*, Vol. 12, No. 1 (1999), pp. 25–38; and *idem*, "Regional Solutions to Regional Problems?" in G. Segal and D.S.G. Goodman (eds), *Towards Recovery in Pacific Asia* (London: Routledge, 2000), pp. 108–18.
6 Raymond Aron, *Peace and War* (London: Weidenfield and Nicholson, 1962), p. 7.
7 Hedley Bull, *The Anarchical Society* (London: Macmillan, 1977), p 55.
8 Barry Buzan and Gerald Segal, "Rethinking East Asian Security," *Survival*, Vol. 36, No. 2 (1994), pp. 3–21; Aaron L. Friedberg, "Ripe for Rivalry: Prospects for Peace in a Multipolar Asia," *International Security*, Vol. 18, No. 3 (1993/4), pp. 5–33.
9 R.B.J. Walker, "The Hierarchicalization of Political Community," *Review of International Studies*, Vol. 15 (1999), p. 152.
10 Richard K. Ashley, "Political Realism and Human Interests," *International Studies Quarterly*, Vol. 25 (1981), p. 212.
11 As inspired by James Der Derian, who sought to read Hedley Bull's writings on diplomatic culture as an open-ended text, which invites, to itself, new interpretations ("Hedley Bull and the Idea of Diplomatic Culture," in Rick Fawn and Jeremy Larkins (eds), *International Society After the Cold War* (London: Macmillan 1996), pp. 84–100).
12 Here I am again indebted to Der Derian.
13 Roland Barthes, *Image–Music–Text* (New York: Hill and Wang, 1977), p. 146.
14 Jürgen Habermas, *Knowledge and Human Interests*, trans. J.J. Shapiro (Boston, MA: Beacon Press, 1971), p. vii.
15 Hayward R. Alker, *Rediscoveries and Reformulations* (Cambridge: Cambridge University Press, 1996); Timothy J. Lukes, "Lionizing Machiavelli," *American Political Science Review*, Vol. 95, No. 3 (2001), pp. 561–75. On Machiavelli's commitment to civic humanist republican goals, see Isaiah Berlin, *Concepts and Categories* (New York: Viking, 1982) and Quentin Skinner, *The Foundations of Modern Political Thought*, 1 (Cambridge: Cambridge University Press, 1978).
16 Besides those listed in n. 5 above, Leifer's works examined here include: *Conflict and Regional Order in South-east Asia*, Adelphi Paper 162 (London: IISS, 1980); "The Balance-of-power and Regional Order," in *idem* (ed.), *The Balance-of-Power in East*

Asia (London: Macmillan, 1986), pp. 143–54; *ASEAN's Search for Regional Order* (Singapore: Faculty of Arts and Social Sciences, National University of Singapore, 1987); *ASEAN and the Security of South-East Asia* (London: Routledge, 1989).

17 Sorpong Peou, "Realism and Constructivism in Southeast Asian Security Studies Today: A Review Essay," *The Pacific Review*, Vol. 15, No. 1 (2002), pp. 119–38.

18 Tim Huxley, "Southeast Asia in the Study of International Relations: The Rise and Decline of a Region," *The Pacific Review*, Vol. 9, No. 2 (1996), pp. 199–228; Sheldon W. Simon, "Realism and Neoliberalism: International Relations Theory and Southeast Asian Security," *The Pacific Review*, Vol. 8, No. 1 (1995), pp. 5–24.

19 K.S. Sandhu, "Strategic Studies in the Region," in Desmond Ball and David Horner (eds), *Strategic Studies in a Changing World* (Canberra: Australian National University, 1992), p. 299. Leifer seldom, if ever, displayed his credentials as a political realist.

20 Peou, "Realism and Constructivism", p. 121.

21 Peou, "Realism and Constructivism", pp. 127, 128.

22 Amitav Acharya, *The Quest for Identity* (Singapore: Oxford University Press, 2000), and *Constructing a Security Community in Southeast Asia* (London: Routledge, 2001).

23 "The ASEAN Peace Process," p. 26.

24 *ASEAN and the Security of South-East Asia*, and "Regional Solutions to Regional Problems?".

25 Steve Smith, "Foreign Policy Is What States Make of It: Social Construction and International Relations Theory," in V. Kubálková (ed.), *Foreign Policy in a Constructed World* (Armonk, NY: M.E. Sharpe, 2001).

26 See Ashley, "Untying the Sovereign State."

27 Cited in Andrew Hurrell, "Society and Anarchy in the 1990s," in B.A. Roberson (ed.), *International Society and the Development of International Relations Theory* (London: Pinter, 1998), p. 20.

28 Bull, *The Anarchical Society.*

29 Skinner, *The Foundations of Modern Political Thought*, p. 98.

30 Inis L. Claude, "The Balance-of-Power Revisited," *Review of International Studies*, Vol. 15, No. 2 (1989), pp. 84–5.

31 *The ASEAN Regional Forum*, p. 53, emphasis added.

32 *The ASEAN Regional Forum*, p. 16.

33 This is not to imply that the English School is to be treated as synonymous with the study of international society (Little, "The English School's Contribution," p. 398).

34 Alker, *Rediscoveries and Reformulations*, p. 187.

35 Andrew Linklater, *Beyond Realism and Marxism* (London: Macmillan, 1990).

36 Little, "The English School's Contribution," p. 397.

37 Bull, *The Anarchical Society*, pp. 24–7.

38 Martin Wight, *International Theory: The Three Traditions* (London: Leicester University Press, 1991).

39 Leifer was one who, in his writings, would choose his words with extra care (author's communication in January 2004 with this volume's editors, both of whom studied with Leifer).

40 Ken Booth, "Security and Emancipation," *Review of International Studies*, Vol. 17 (1991), p. 313.

41 Martin Wight, "Where is There no International Theory," in Hebert Butterfield and *idem* (eds), *Diplomatic Investigations* (London: Allen and Unwin, 1966), p. 33.

42 Ashley, "Political Realism and Human Interests," pp. 227–8; also see R.N. Berki, *On Political Realism* (London: Dent, 1981).

43 *ASEAN's Search for Regional Order*, p. 1.

44 *Conflict and Regional Order in South-east Asia*, p. 34.

45 *ASEAN's Search for Regional Order*, p. 1.

46 "The Balance-of-Power and Regional Order," pp. 151–2.
47 *ASEAN and the Security of South-East Asia*, p. 143.
48 Note the similarities between Leifer's notion of regional order and that of international order (Hedley Bull and Adam Watson, "Introduction," in Bull and Watson (eds), *Expansion of International Society* (Oxford: Oxford University Press 1984), p. 1).
49 *ASEAN and the Security of South-East Asia*, p. 157.
50 "Regional Solutions to Regional Problems?", p. 115.
51 *ASEAN's Search for Regional Order*, p. 18.
52 "The Balance-of-Power and Regional Order," p. 154.
53 *ASEAN's Search for Regional Order*, pp. 13, 15.
54 *ASEAN and the Security of South-East Asia*, p. 157, emphasis added.
55 *ASEAN's Search for Regional Order*, p. 21.
56 *ASEAN's Search for Regional Order*, p. 21.
57 Ashley, "Untying the Sovereign State," p. 252.
58 In the same essay Leifer warns: "To interpret [the ARF's] role in terms of a new paradigm in international relations would be the height of intellectual naivety" (*The ASEAN Regional Forum*, p. 59).
59 Little, "Deconstructing the Balance-of-Power."
60 David A. Baldwin, "Power and Social Exchange," *American Political Science Review*, Vol. 72 (1978), p. 1224.
61 Ralf Emmers, *Cooperative Security and the Balance-of-Power in ASEAN and the ARF* (London: Routledge, 2003); See Seng Tan with Ralph A. Cossa, "Rescuing Realism From the Realists," in S.W. Simon (ed.), *The Many Faces of Asian Security* (Lanham, MD: Rowman and Littlefield, 2001), pp. 15–34.
62 Alexander Wendt, "Anarchy is What States Make of It: The Social Construction of Power Politics," *International Organization*, Vol. 46, No. 2 (1992) pp. 391–425.
63 Wight, "Where is There no International Theory," p. 33.
64 "The Balance-of-Power and Regional Order", p. 154.
65 "The Balance-of-Power and Regional Order", p. 145.
66 *The ASEAN Regional Forum*, p. 13.
67 Barbara Tuchman, "If Mao Had Come to Washington: An Essay in Alternatives," *Foreign Affairs*, Vol. 51 (1972), pp. 44–64.
68 *ASEAN and the Security of South-East Asia*, pp. 5–6.
69 "Regional Solutions to Regional Problems?" p. 109.
70 *The ASEAN Regional Forum*, p. 13.
71 G. John Ikenberry, *After Victory* (Princeton, NJ: Princeton University Press, 2001).
72 Bull, *The Anarchical Society*, p. 110.
73 Claude, "The Balance-of-Power Revisited," p. 80.
74 *The ASEAN Regional Forum*, pp. 57–8.
75 "The ASEAN Peace Process", p. 27.
76 "Regional Solutions to Regional Problems?" p. 109.
77 "The ASEAN Peace Process," p. 27.
78 "Regional Solutions to Regional Problems?" p. 110, emphasis added.
79 Robert Jervis, "Security Regimes," in Stephen D. Krasner (ed.), *International Regimes* (Ithaca, NY: Cornell University Press, 1983).
80 *ASEAN's Search for Regional Order*, p. 21.
81 Richard K. Ashley, "The Poverty of Neorealism," in *Neorealism and Its Critics*, p. 294.
82 Richard K. Ashley, "The Achievements of Post-Structuralism," in Ken Booth, Steve Smith and Marysia Zalewski (eds), *International Theory: Positivism and Beyond* (Cambridge: Cambridge University Press, 1996), p. 240.

6 Do norms and identity matter?

Community and power in Southeast Asia's regional order

Amitav Acharya

Introduction

Among the principal contributions of Michael Leifer to the study of regional order in Southeast Asia was the investigation of Southeast Asian regionalism, particularly the role of ASEAN and the ASEAN Regional Forum. In some recent literature, Leifer has been portrayed as a realist or a neorealist who dismissed the role of regional institutions. This chapter argues that the real difference between Leifer's and the newer constructivist understanding of Southeast Asia is not so much over whether regionalism matters, but under what conditions does it matter. Leifer viewed material forces, such as the prior existence of a great power balance, as a precondition for effective regionalism. He paid less attention to norm dynamics and the politics of regional identity formation and did not consider them as having an independent effect on regional order. This chapter argues that taking account of the role of regional norms and identity formation offers a more complete explanation of Southeast Asian regionalism, including its achievements and failures, than Leifer's strategic and diplomatic investigations focusing on the regional balance of power.

Leifer was never self-consciously theoretical. He was firmly in the tradition of an area specialist. His style was interpretative, grounded in history and backed by a first-hand knowledge of contemporary developments acquired through extensive and frequent visits to the region. Moreover, his realism was implicit and was non-dogmatic.[2] Leifer stressed the balance of power as the key factor shaping order and stability in Asia. He considered the US strategic umbrella to be the crucial factor in ensuring the security and stability of Asia Pacific. He regarded the ASEAN Regional Forum as an "adjunct" to great power balances. After recognizing its achievements for much of the 1990s, Leifer became increasingly critical of ASEAN, especially post-1997, thus taking note of ASEAN's failure to respond effectively and unitedly to the Asian economic crisis and the increased intra-mural discord that marked Singapore–Malaysia relations.

But even without the benefit of a body of writing couched in theoretical jargon, what seems fair to say is that Leifer's perspective was closer to Hedley Bull's than to John Mearsheimer's. The very fact that Leifer devoted a considerable amount of his intellectual energy to the study of regionalism—his book on ASEAN and the monograph on the ARF remain among his most important works—suggests that he took regionalism seriously. His criticisms of ASEAN were more nuanced and qualified than what a neorealist like Mearsheimer would think of international institutions. Like Bull, Leifer recognized that international institutions are an integral part of the ordering mechanisms of world politics. His work took cognizance of ASEAN's accomplishments as well as its failures. (Hence in his preface to my book *Constructing a Security Community in Southeast Asia* (xi), Leifer mentioned ASEAN's "mixed institutional experience.")

Perhaps the real difference between his work and the work of those like myself who take a more sociological view of regionalism was not in considering whether regionalism mattered, but in discussing what made it matter. Here, Leifer stressed the role of structural and material determinants. The sociological and ideational investigation of regionalism, on the other hand, begs attention to norms, identity, and community. Such approaches focused "on discursive and social practices that define the identity of actors and the normative order within which they make their moves" and "insist on the importance of social processes that generate changes in normative beliefs."

Despite, or perhaps because of, his grounding in the English School, Leifer viewed Southeast Asian regionalism in essentially diplomatic terms. He was especially attentive to inter-governmental conflict and cooperation within ASEAN, the security dependency of its members, and the nature of great power interactions as key determinants of regionalism. Changes to these, especially the balance of power, made for stronger or weaker regionalism. In contrast, despite being cognizant of norms, identity, and socialization in Southeast Asian regionalism, Leifer did not consider ideational forces and regional institutions as regulative and transformative.

This distinguished his work from that of others, especially my own. In my approach, the success or failure of Southeast Asian regionalism is explained not just by the great power balance, but also by ideational forces, including norms and the politics of identity building. Norms and identity matter; while they are not the only determinants of regionalism in Southeast Asia, they are a central determinant. Moreover, regional institutions are not mere adjuncts to balance of power politics. They also help shape balance of power politics. The language and notion of community, rather than that of regime or balance of power, is relevant in analyzing security order in Southeast Asia. Regionalism in Southeast Asia is not a sideshow to power politics, but a potentially transformative dynamic. In the following sections, I develop these arguments in four parts, looking at norms, identity, community, and power respectively.

Norms

Unlike neorealists, Leifer was not oblivious of the role of norms; nor was he averse to the language of community. In 1987, he observed that ASEAN had progressed to become "a working diplomatic community" and "assume a prerogative role of a kind in an intermittent process of negotiations about establishing regional rules of the game." Elsewhere, he identified these norms as "respect for national sovereignty, non-interference in another state's domestic affairs and renouncing the threat or use of force in settling disputes." He also noted the exclusion of defense cooperation from ASEAN's "corporate agenda, although it was sanctioned on an inter-governmental basis outside the Association primarily as a confidence-building measure."

Leifer's writings on ASEAN recognized not just its legal-rational norms but also its socio-cultural norms (the distinction, derived from Peter Katzenstein's work, is more fully developed in my book, *Constructing a Security Community in Southeast Asia)*. These included "consultation and cooperation" and "consensus." Although Leifer avoided the term "ASEAN Way," preferring to use "ASEAN model," his recognition of the above meant he was basically speaking of the same thing. Furthermore, Leifer recognized ASEAN's preference for informalism, another aspect of the so-called "ASEAN Way," as a factor behind its success.

Leifer did not specify to what extent these norms mattered. He would characterize non-interference as "a cardinal as well as self-serving principle shared by all ASEAN members." But whether he would credit this norm with the maintenance of regional order in ASEAN remains unclear. In his view, bilateral tensions in ASEAN had never been "serious enough…to constitute a *casus bellum*." Yet, didn't the fact that there was no serious *casus bellum* have something to do with ASEAN and its norms? It is noteworthy that the acknowledgement of the role of the non-interference norm in war-avoidance has come from countries such as Singapore, whose realist foreign policy outlook Leifer so clearly recognized and perhaps endorsed. As Singapore's former Foreign Minister, S. Jayakumar, once put it, adherence to non-interference "is one reason why no military conflict has broken out between any two ASEAN countries since the founding of ASEAN."

In an essay published after the 1997 Asian economic crisis, Leifer disparaged ASEAN's capacity to provide "regional solutions to regional problems," because "ASEAN's provision for dispute-settlement, incorporated in its Treaty of Amity and Co-Operation of 1976 has never been invoked." Yet, the dismissal of this norm was not true to Leifer's own interpretation of the behavioral meaning of the norm itself. To equate regional solutions with legalistic approaches such as the dispute-settlement procedures of the Treaty of Amity would go against Leifer's own interpretation of the "ASEAN model." As he wrote in the same monograph: "Over time, it became clear that ASEAN was not about formal dispute settlement or conflict resolution *per se* but rather about creating a regional milieu in which such problems either did not arise or could be readily managed and contained." One can pursue regional problem-solving by creating the right political atmosphere in the region, rather than developing legalistic approaches to conflict resolution. Leifer's critique conflates regional solutions to regional problems with self-reliance. What "regional solution" really meant to ASEAN's founding fathers was not autarchy, but minimizing outside intervention in Southeast Asia, at a time when such intervention was a persistent and worldwide aspect of the Cold War milieu, and when the credibility of outside security guarantees was declining (thereby making them less necessary and perhaps dangerous to rely on). Leifer himself recognized this when he noted that "ASEAN...was established by Southeast Asian states alone without the intervention or support of a major external power." He also observed that while ASEAN's founders sought a "proprietary role in managing regional order" through ZOPFAN, this role reflected a "conviction that close cooperation among regional states would have an insulating political effect, thereby overcoming the need for any demeaning policing function being accorded to external powers."

In *Constructing a Security Community in Southeast Asia*, I analyze the impact of norms on ASEAN. Some of these norms are foundational to the grouping, meaning that they existed before ASEAN was established; others were constructed through a process of interaction among ASEAN elites.[3] My list is almost identical to Leifer's norms. But I hold that norms mattered much in shaping the regional order of Southeast Asia, citing (among others) cases such as Indonesia's opposition to the Vietnamese invasion of Cambodia, on the ground that a violation of the norm of non-use of force had occurred, despite the fact that Jakarta had sought friendly relations with Hanoi and, unlike Thailand, perceived little threat to its security from the communist regime there. Another major example would be Thailand's return to the non-interference principle after some debate in 1998, even though the Chuan Leekpai government had strongly favored a dilution of the principle in favor of "flexible engagement" for reasons of domestic politics and national interest. In these cases, norms shaped the response of ASEAN members in a certain direction, even when national concerns and positions would have dictated otherwise.

As my book argues, not all of the ASEAN norms have been adhered to by its members all the time. Consensus-seeking, consultations and avoidance of legal approaches have been diluted since the formative years of ASEAN. But no dramatic violation of the core norm of a pluralistic security community, non-use of force to settle disputes, occurred during the period covered by the book: 1967-97. Indeed, the minimalist claim for an ASEAN security community rests on this simple empirical fact: the original members of ASEAN had not fought a war against each other during the period (the fact remains that they have not done so to date, despite sharp tensions in Singapore–Malaysia relations). The debate over whether ASEAN is a security community or not should be grounded in empirical evidence, rather than depend on one's liking or dislike for ASEAN.

To say that norms have shaped ASEAN's functional approach to regional order is not to say that they have always ensured ASEAN's effectiveness or given it the moral high ground. The moral importance and functional value of norms are not static, and they can be context- and issue-dependent. Norms that were initially conceived as moral and functional could become immoral and dysfunctional with the passage of time and with the advent of new challenges. *Constructing a Security Community in Southeast Asia* argues that security communities may decline as a result of such changes. Non-interference once exerted a moral appeal against the threat of neo-colonialism and superpower interventionism. But later it came to be discredited for sanctioning state repression in Burma. And while non-interference and regional autonomy were, and continue to be, important in avoiding inter-state war in Southeast Asia, they have become functionally deficient in coping with transnational dangers such as financial volatility or terrorism. Hence while norms do matter, they do not necessarily matter in a positive, progressive manner. They can matter negatively, by creating barriers to obstacles to change. The same stickiness that makes them important can also render them morally unappealing and functionally outdated. Yet, to say that norms arrest progress is not to dismiss their relevance; they are important in shaping both positive and negative outcomes. The discussion of non-interference in *Constructing a Security Community in Southeast Asia* amply testifies to this.

Identity

At one level, Leifer appeared to be highly skeptical of Southeast Asia's claim to any regional identity. Speaking of "regional identity and coherence," he argued that "even if shaped by geography, such an identity is governed by political considerations." Moreover, regional identity could be undermined by "the likely prospect of regional differences over strategic perspective, or the definition of the prime external threat." Hence, Leifer disagreed with my perspective, developed in *The Quest for Identity: International Relations of Southeast Asia,* that puts identity-formation at the center of its explanatory framework. Unlike Leifer, I take regional identity developed through socialization and "governed by political considerations" seriously. *The Quest for Identity* argues that regions are not geographically given or culturally pre-ordained. Region-building is a social and political act; like nationalism and nation-states, regions may be "imagined" and constructed. An identity-based perspective looks beyond physical or structural constraints on regional identity. *The Quest for Identity* investigates the international relations of Southeast Asia by looking not just at what is common between and among its constituent units (the unity in diversity approach), but at how the countries of the region, especially the elite, engaged in a process of socialization within an institutional context (ASEAN) and in that process "imagined" themselves to be part of a distinctive region.

Although he viewed unsympathetically my attempt to present ASEAN as an imagined community, Leifer would not ignore ASEAN's contribution to the social construction of a regional identity. "The measure of coherence enjoyed by the notion of Southeast Asia," he argued in a 1997 chapter, "is a direct result of the imaginative initiative taken in August 1967 by the five founding governments of Association of South-east Asian Nations (ASEAN)." In this sense, regional interactions and imaginations had created greater coherence in a region whose original claim to "region-ness" was questionable. This is precisely my argument in *The Quest for Identity*, which holds that ASEAN's self-conscious attempt to imagine and build a regional order despite intra-regional physical and political differences was an important factor which must be taken into account in any consideration of regional order in Southeast Asia.

The Quest for Identity investigates, rather than assumes, identity-building in Southeast Asian regionalism. It recognizes the distinction between regional identity as an accomplished fact and regional identity as a quest, or "identity in being" and "identity in the making."[4] Southeast Asia has not achieved the kind of regional identity that would last forever, but there has been a significant and self-conscious effort at regional identity-building, especially since the formation of ASEAN. More importantly, I argue that it is the relative success and limitations of this effort, rather than just material forces and circumstances facing the region, such as shifting patterns of great power rivalry, that explain many significant aspects of regional order in Southeast Asia, which traditional approaches to Southeast Asian security could not explain.

The history of the international politics of Southeast Asia prior to 1997 provides considerable evidence of this "identity-in-the-making." These efforts range from the 1947 Asian Relations Conference in New Delhi, when delegates from Southeast Asia rejected associating themselves too closely with the Indian and Chinese regional frameworks, to the deliberate inclusion of "identity" in ASEAN's founding document. ASEAN rejected requests for membership by countries such as Sri Lanka, and the possibility of membership by India and Australia on the ground that they did not form part of the Southeast Asia region.

It is also important to note how the definition of "Southeast Asia" has changed over time due to ASEAN's region-building project. In 1955, there was little distinction between South Asia and Southeast Asia. The "Conference of South-East Asian Prime Ministers" which acted as official sponsor to the historic Bandung Conference of Asian and African states includes the Prime Ministers of India, Ceylon, Pakistan, Burma, and Indonesia (also known as the Colombo Powers). British deference to this entity in the face of Dullesian disdain undermined the foundation of the Southeast Asian Treaty Organization (SEATO). But as ASEAN started the process of regional identity-building, it left out India, Pakistan, and even Ceylon, from its conception of what constituted Southeast Asia.

Some of Leifer's writings come fairly close to recognizing ASEAN's efforts at "registering a corporate political identity." Leifer also recognizes that ASEAN members "avoided any explicitly Western notions of how to organize groups of states in cooperative security" and instead "drew on a common cultural heritage in which the effective management of political problems should be emphasized." Constructivists would have little problem in accepting this claim about a common cultural heritage as a basis for identity-formation. Finally, Leifer recognized that some aspects of ASEAN's approach to regional order bore a stamp of distinctiveness, including their attempt to "develop a practice of close consultation and cooperation…[which] gave rise to a distinctive security culture of conflict avoidance and conflict management." Commenting on Singapore's ties with China, Leifer writes that "Singapore began a guarded encounter with China at the official level without compromising its attempt to register a South-East Asian identity." This suggests that the identity-building effort did matter in Singapore's foreign policy, even though the logic of normalizing relations with China might have seemed a compelling security need.

Leifer argues that to use regional identity even as an analytic tool is limiting and misleading, because it leads one to concentrate "on the wood of the region to the neglect of the trees of the foreign policies of the resident states." But this was precisely what makes the study of regional identity important. Most studies of Southeast Asian history share what Legge called a "tendency…to focus on the constituent parts of Southeast Asia [rather] than to develop a perception of the region as a whole as a suitable subject of study." But this approach overstates intra-regional differences and tensions, lending false support to the *realpolitik* view of the region as an area of rivalry and revolt. On the other hand, looking at the woods offers insights not available from a country-specific approach favored by realist scholars for whom the nation-state remains the basic unit of international politics. It also leads to the neglect of the normative and ideational environment within which policy-makers interact.

Ignoring identity as an analytic tool also leads to the undue neglect of long-term historical processes that go into the making of international and regional orders. Scholarship on Southeast Asian international relations has tended to be a-historical, or "event-driven," rather than based on a careful appraisal of long-term trends. It is then hardly surprising that the most powerful support for an identity-based approach to Southeast Asia, including its international relations, comes from historians. In contrast, realist scholars of Southeast Asia have spent little time with pre-colonial events, even when they tend to present, implicitly or explicitly, some of the region's rivalries as primordial and intractable. If political scientists are to take note of Southeast Asian historiography, they become more sympathetic to an identity-based approach to the regional order of Southeast Asia, granting more recognition to the "wood of the region."

Community

As noted earlier, Leifer termed ASEAN a "diplomatic community." He distinguished it from a "political community," which could be defined as a "grouping of states which are committed ultimately to overcoming the sovereign divisions between them," or a "defense community" in the manner of a fully integrated military alliance. Yet, his understanding of ASEAN's achievements is not really very far from a minimalist notion of a pluralistic security community, or what Adler and Barnett would call a "nascent security community."

A major problem with the security community debate is the absence of a commonly accepted definition of what constitutes a security community.

Members of a pluralistic security community do not require "overcoming the sovereign divisions between them", as Leifer seems to assume wrongly. Their main obligation is to manage intra-mural conflicts without resort to force. Critics of ASEAN as a security community often cite the existence of intra-mural tensions within it. But the security community theory does not claim that tensions and disputes would not arise within the grouping; it only expects that they are resolved without resort to force.

In an essay published in 1995, two years before the collapse of the Thai currency that signaled the onset of the Asian economic crisis, Leifer could "claim quite categorically that ASEAN has become an institutionalized vehicle for intra-mural conflict avoidance and management...ASEAN has been able to prevent disputes from escalating and getting out of hand through containing and managing contentious issues." Indeed, this seems to have been the consensus view of most observers of ASEAN before the economic crisis, including many of its latter-day critics. Among scholars and analysts who had recognized ASEAN as a security community in the above sense are Noordin Sopiee (1986) and Soedjati Djiwandono (1991) from Southeast Asia, and Richard Mansbach (1997), Donald Weatherbee (1984), Sheldon Simon (1992) and David Martin Jones (the latter as late as 1997) among others in the West.[5]

While accepting ASEAN as a diplomatic community, Leifer would insist that this could not have been independent of power realities. Hence, ASEAN's "political heyday as a diplomatic community" was the by-product of "a unique pattern of international alignments, distinguished, above all, by a strategic partnership between the United States and China." *Constructing a Security Community in Southeast Asia* shows that a community-building project can indeed go against power realities. ASEAN was established, as Leifer himself concedes, without assistance from major powers, and was intended to manage regional order at a time of US and British strategic retrenchment. In many ways, the very formation of ASEAN posed a challenge to the approach to regional order that the US, the most powerful Western nation, had advocated, this being through regional alliances such as SEATO. In the 1990s, ASEAN was able to steer discussion over multilateral security toward the creation of the ASEAN Regional Forum despite US and Chinese objections. It did so not through material power, but through the prestige and persuasive force of its normative arguments.

Instead of participating in SEATO-type alliances, members of ASEAN were able to enhance their security by adhering to one of the core diplomatic norms enshrined in its constitutional documents, the non-use of force in intra-mural relations, during a 30-year period: 1967–97. This is the main basis for using the framework of security community to investigate ASEAN. While the security community building project faced several limitations and challenges, which include, among other things, persistent intra-mural tensions, (especially in Singapore–Malaysia relations) failure to cope with the burdens of membership expansion, and above all, failure to tackle conflict-causing transnational threats which would necessitate a dilution of the non-interference norm, the failure to recognize the absence of military conflict among ASEAN countries would be a serious omission.

Constructing a Security Community in Southeast Asia concludes by positing whether ASEAN would be able to move to the next stage in the security community-building project (which Adler and Barnett would call an "ascendant" security community), or whether it would decay into anarchy and disorder (which I termed in my book a "decadent" security community). Indeed, the view that security communities are not linear constructs and that they can rise and decline is a theme more fully developed in my book than in the Adler and Barnett volume. But these limitations and challenges facing ASEAN need not, and should not, justify the outright dismissal of norms and identity from one's analytic framework that may be used to assess its contribution to regional order in Southeast Asia. On the contrary, inclusion of these ideational variables offers a richer and ultimately more satisfying explanation of ASEAN—both its achievements as well as its limitations.[6]

The analytic richness of the security community concept derives from the fact that it allows consideration of both material and ideational forces in the making and unmaking of regional order. Other factors that contribute to war-avoidance, such as deterrence (which rests on rational calculations of hard military power) and security regime (which is also rationalistic), permit no space to ideational forces. Thus, my difference with Leifer primarily concerns the scope of our respective analytic frameworks. Leifer's remained ultimately power-centric. I consider realist explanations of ASEAN's fortunes (focusing on fluctuations in the regional balance of power which in turn depended on the US military presence) to be parsimonious but partial.

Power

In his critique of the ARF Leifer noted that "The ARF's structural problem is that its validity seems to depend on the prior existence of a stable balance, but it is not really in a position to create it." In making this claim, Leifer was closer to the English School than to American neorealism. In his *Anarchical Society,* Bull contended that "both general and local balances of power, where they have existed, have provided the conditions in which other institutions on which international order depends (diplomacy, war, international law, great power management) have been able to operate." One could presumably include regional diplomacy and institutions in the category of "other institutions on which international order depends." But this does not mean one can dismiss the question of whether regional norms and institutions themselves contribute to a stable balance of power, and should not be seen purely as having a secondary importance. Ralf Emmers has developed this theme in relation to the ARF in his book *Cooperative Security and the Balance of Power*, which grew out of a Leifer-supervised dissertation.

To some extent, Leifer accepted that a balance of power order can be pursued by means other than military force: through diplomacy and "institutional-locking." ASEAN had practised such diplomatic balance of power by entangling Indonesia into ASEAN when Suharto "understood that one practical way of restoring both regional confidence and stability would be to lock Indonesia into a structure of regional partnership which would be seen to disavow hegemonial pretensions." This notion of balance of power is similar to John Ikenberry's concept of "institutional self-binding" (Ikenberry: 2001). Similarly, Leifer viewed the ARF as a device to "lock China into a network of constraining multilateral arrangements underpinned hopefully by a sustained and viable American military presence" which would in turn "serve the purpose of the balance of power by means other than alliance." This acceptance that multilateral arrangements can be "constraining" has much in common with institutionalist scholars like Keohane and Martin.

My perspective argues that the effect of international norms and institutions includes, but can go beyond, constraint, binding and locking. They can be transformative in the sense that norms and institutions can affect the legitimacy of alliances, the chief instrument of power politics. Collective norms can delegitimize alliances; the displacement of SEATO by ASEAN offers an example of how this might happen. They can socialize, as opposed to constrain, a hegemon and turn its coercive structural power into a legitimate public good. Hence, American military presence and its bilateral alliances in the post-Vietnam era have not worked purely as instruments of exclusionary and competitive power politics. This latter tendency, inherent in any classic alliance posture, has been moderated by regional institutions like ASEAN and turned into a collective public good for the region. Hence regionalism, instead of being an adjunct to power politics, has actually rendered it softer and cooperative.

Moreover, regionalism has given weaker actors a voice which they would otherwise lack if they pursued security unilaterally or through unequal military alliances with the great powers. Regional norms and institutions assume a crucial role when great powers retrench, as in the 1960s and 1970s, when ASEAN members, including those who maintained alliance relations with great powers, realized that the British and US withdrawal from the region rendered their external security guarantees questionable. Hence, they turned to ASEAN regionalism. They also realized that associating too closely with the US militarily would aggravate tensions with the communist powers, Vietnam and China. Against this backdrop, seeking help from external powers was hardly a practical way of addressing the security threats they faced, which were primarily internal in nature. To do so would have undermined their domestic legitimacy even further.

Regionalism in Southeast Asia proved important in the early 1990s, another moment of flux in the regional balance of power caused by the Soviet withdrawal from Vietnam and by rising Chinese military power. Then, as Leifer pointed out, the discourses and dialogues of multilateralism culminating in the ARF helped to engage the US. I agree with this assertion. What is perhaps more important, I would add, is that ASEAN-based multilateral diplomacy delegitimized and discouraged extreme balancing behavior (such as the US temptation to contain China). Instead, regional diplomacy helped to secure China's engagement in regional affairs.

It may thus seem that regional norms and institutions have made their impact only when great powers retrench, or are distracted or defeated. This would be consistent with a neorealist understanding of power and institutions. But great power retrenchments are a recurring and persistent feature of international politics; hence regional diplomacy that promotes the socialization and engagement of major powers at such junctures is an important factor shaping international order. This is a point recognized by both Leifer and myself. In Asia, multilateralism in the post-Cold War era has helped stability at a time of great power retrenchment by discouraging extreme balancing behavior of the kind identified by realists (such as Aaron Friedberg), such as containment (of China) bandwagoning (with China).

Conclusion

Leifer's work on regionalism in Southeast Asia left room for some ambiguity. In general, he considered institutions to be subject to balance of power. This was clear in his critique of the ARF and his explanation of why ASEAN succeeded as a diplomatic community. Yet, his work is replete with references to ASEAN norms and corporate culture. One cannot be entirely certain whether Leifer considered these ideational forces to be irrelevant or simply of secondary importance relative to power politics. He provided hardly any conceptual analysis of how these ideational elements related to, and interacted with, the material balance of power. But if norms and identity are so inconsequential, why make so many references to them? If the balance of power can be shaped by regional cooperation, then can one justifiably view institutions as pure adjuncts to power politics? If institutions did not matter, then how could one speak of ASEAN as a "diplomatic community" and "categorically" recognize ASEAN's role as "an institutionalized vehicle for intra-mural conflict avoidance and management" which had enabled it "to prevent disputes from escalating and getting out of hand through containing and managing contentious issues"?

For Leifer, the agency role of weaker states in norm-setting, norm-compliance and the politics of regional identity-formation, could not determine regional order against the dictates of the balance of power. His definition of regional order focused on the primacy of the US military presence. Yet, by drawing on empirical evidence and theoretical arguments in my own writings as well as those of others, an alternative view of Southeast Asian and Asian regional order is possible. ASEAN's success then as now depends on defending its norms, increasing socialization, and pursuing a regional identity, especially when the balance of power was in flux and outside power security guarantees least credible (as in the wake of the British withdrawal from east of Suez and the US withdrawal from Vietnam). While Leifer would argue that the limitations of AESAN or the ARF resulted from the structural fact that they depended on the regional balance of power which could only be manipulated by the powers themselves, I would explain the limitations of ASEAN in terms of intra-mural sociological and ideational forces, such as failure to comply with norms, and the increased difficulties of socialization and identity-formation created by membership expansion. My earlier work on ASEAN followed Leifer closely by stressing security dependency and the balance of power, but I became increasingly convinced that, while important, these provided only partial explanations. Instead of accepting merely that a favorable balance of power is an essential precondition for the success of regionalism, I gave more play to the view that regionalism itself can have a role in the making and working of the balance of power.

The role of norms and identity-building is especially important for the study of Southeast Asian regionalism because its material resources are few and its bureaucratic organization is not developed. ASEAN regionalism has been primarily a normative regionalism. Hence, no serious investigation of ASEAN can be complete without consideration of the role of norms and the issue of identity-formation. For the same reason, the concept of community is an important analytic tool for investigating Southeast Asian regionalism and regional order. This is because the notion of security community allows the use of norms and identity as analytic tools to investigate international relations, while neorealism or neoliberalism would ignore such variables.

Realism remains the dominant approach to the study of regional order in Southeast Asia (and in Asia more generally). There is little question that Leifer's intellectual perspective will outlive his untimely death. His writings helped shape an influential approach to Asian security that assumed the centrality of the balance of power, especially the US role as a regional balancer. Leifer's analysis of Southeast Asian regionalism served as the single most important source of inspiration and guidance for my own work on the subject. But simply replicating his approach would not have sufficed for my own intellectual quest. One could make a more meaningful contribution to scholarship on the subject by bringing to center-stage the ideational variables which were left implicit and underdeveloped in his scholarship. This may not imply a rejection of his approach, or a rejection of power variables in the making of regional order. It means giving ideational forces more play as determinants of regional order and recognizing their transformative potential. Unlike a powerful if increasingly "questioned approach"[7] in American social scientific literature on international relations, I do not see material and ideational explanations as alternatives. It is not necessary to establish the superiority of one approach by casting other approaches as "alternative explanations" and then rejecting them. Leifer's ability to rise above a cynical, patronizing, and orientalist[8] attitude (one that totally dismisses the ability of local actors to do anything positive or good cooperatively without depending on Western powers) towards Southeast Asia's efforts to build a cooperative regional order cleared the way for alternative scholarship that focused on the role of regional norms and identity.[9] His encouragement of scholars who took such an approach helped to ensure that the study of regional order in Southeast Asia would not be dominated by a single approach or methodology, but would accommodate a growing and healthy measure of diversity, featuring arguments and accommodation between power-based, materialist perspectives on the one hand and those that accord an important place to ideational forces (norms and identity) and socialization on the other. This may have been his most important intellectual legacy.

Notes

1 I include myself in this group, although I think it blurs the important divergence between cultural and sociological approaches, or those who stress the relative importance of traditional culture versus those who emphasize actor socialization based on modern principles of international relations, as determinants of regionalism.

2 I can attest to Leifer's tolerance and even encouragement of divergent perspectives. Although I was not one of his students, my book, *Constructing a Security Community in Southeast Asia* was written substantially under his guidance—as a result of continuous interaction with him between 1997 and 2000. He was a hands-on editor, meticulous in his attention to detail and quick and forthright in his critique of any (mis)interpretations in my study of ASEAN. His criticisms ensured that the book's constructivist claims did not stray too far from empirical evidence. We disagreed over the initial title of the book. My preference, *Avoiding War in Southeast Asia*, did not evoke much enthusiasm in him, on the ground that it smacked of a "worst-case" assumption, since there had been no serious prospect for war in Southeast Asia since ASEAN's creation in 1967. The fact that he attributed this state of affairs to the US-led balance of power order in Asia, whereas I credited a good deal of it to ASEAN regionalism, was one important aspect of our intellectual disagreement. But this never prevented us from discussing the book, eventually published in his "Politics in Asia" series, over countless meetings during his visits to the region or on the margins of international conferences and in numerous e-mail exchanges over a four-year period. Without his constant encouragement and timely reminders, the book would not have been conceived, much less completed.

3 My selection of the first set of norms (legal-rational) was determined by the fact that they were enshrined in ASEAN's constitutional documents, including the Bangkok Declaration of 1967, the Kuala Lumpur Declaration of 1971, and the two core documents to emerge from ASEAN's inaugural summit in 1976: the Treaty of Amity and Cooperation and the Declaration of ASEAN Concord. Indeed, non-interference and non-use of force are also the core norms of the UN which regional institutions all over the world self-consciously emulated. As such, the prominence of these norms could be established independently of intra-ASEAN interactions during the critical periods of the Cambodia crisis. In so far as the second set of norms (socio-cultural) are concerned, after examining how they evolved through intra-ASEAN elite interactions, I analyze the impact of these norms on subsequent intra-ASEAN relations, thereby avoiding tautology.

4 Other reviewers of the book recognized this distinction, Diane Mauzy refers to my approach as "centring on the efforts to construct a regional 'identity'." (Mauzy 2000: 613).

5 For a discussion of some of these perspectives, see Acharya (2001: 128, 203). In a 1997 book, David Martin Jones commented on ASEAN: "It might at best be considered a security community" (Jones 1997: 185). Donald Weatherbee has also argued that "[ASEAN already is] a 'security community,' in which expectations about warlike behaviour by members of the community toward each other have been virtually eliminated" (1984: 264). Noordin Sopiee has asserted that: "[ASEAN contribution] has been to bring the ASEAN area to the brink of what Karl Keutsch has termed a pluralistic security community. Such a system is one at peace, where no nation continues to accept war or violence as an instrument of policy against another community member and where no actor seriously prepares for war or violence against another. There is no guarantee that such a situation will be sustained in the future. Peace is always a constant struggle. But to come close to being a security community from a starting point so distant within a time span so comparatively short is no mean achievement. Admittedly the ASEAN security community has in part been the result of other factors, not the least of which was the perception of extra-ASEAN threats. But without the existence of ASEAN there would today be no such quasi-security community. And history tells us that common external threat can lead to division as well as unity" (1986: 229).

6 In *Constructing a Security Community in Southeast Asia,* I use the concept of security community primarily as an analytic tool to permit a broader investigation of ASEAN that was not available in the existing literature. As stated in the Introduction (6), the book "does not assume, a priori, that ASEAN has become a security community in Deutsch's terms—or perhaps become a full-fledged security community. Rather, the purpose of this exercise is to use the idea of security community as a framework within which to examine the evolution and nature of ASEAN's political and security role and identify the constraints it faces in developing a viable regional security community."

7 As Fearon and Wendt, and others, have acknowledged, the earlier academic debate between rationalism (and materialism) and constructivism as mutually exclusive paradigms falsely obscured the significant common ground that obtains between them. The recent move toward "synthetic" or "eclectic" theorizing is thus a step in the right direction (Katzenstein and Shiraisu 1996).

8 I use the term "orientalism" to denote imagery about Asian and Southeast Asian regionalism similar to that which Said applied to a particular kind of Western knowledge about the orient. Broadly stated, orientalism is a "set of stereotypical images according to which the West is seen as being essentially rational, developed, humane, superior, authentic, active, creative, and masculine, while the orient is seen as being irrational, aberrant, backward, crude, despotic, inferior, inauthentic, passive…" (Macfie, 2000: 4). Looking at some, but by no means all, commentaries on Asian and Southeast Asian regionalism in recent years, one cannot but be struck by the manner of contrasting European and Asian regionalism or critiquing Asian regionalism as an impossible, failed and even laughably decadent project. While the European regionalism (both modern such as EU, NATO and classical such as the Concert of Powers) is viewed as "rational" and "developed," Asian regionalism is viewed as "underdeveloped," "backward"; while European regionalism is seen as an "authentic" model, Asian regionalism, even with its own claims about culture and identity, is seen as "crude" and "aberrant," and while European regionalism is seen as "active" and "creative," able to adapt to new security challenges and developments, Asian regionalism is seen as "passive" and "reactionary." These stereotypes are sometimes left implicit in the writings of scholars, conforming to what Said called "latent" orientalism, while for some, they are presented in cynical voices in a way Said would characterize as "manifest" orientalism (Said, 110–114). Interestingly, the critics of Asian regionalism have been branded as "realist." While I acknowledge that not all realists are orientalists, the intellectual link between orientalism and realism is stressed

by Macfie, who notes that critics of Said's formulations on orientalism often include scholars "firmly wedded to a traditional (realist) approach" (Macfie, 2000: 5).

9 I am not the only scholar in such a situation; Jürgen Haacke is another example of a constructivist whom Leifer nurtured at LSE.

Bibliography

Acharya, Amitav, *Constructing a Security Community in Southeast Asia: ASEAN and the Problem of Regional Order*, London: Routledge, 2001.

Djiwandono, J. Soedjati, *ASEAN: An Emerging Regional Security Community?*, Jakarta, CSIS: Occasional Paper, May 1991.

Fearon, James, and Wendt, Alexander, 'Rationalism v. Constructivism: A Skeptical View,' in Walter Carlsnaes, Thomas Risse and Beth A. Simmons, eds., *Handbook of International Relations*, London: Sage, 2002.

Ikenberry, John, *After Victory: Institutions, Strategic Restraints, and the Rebuilding of Orders after Major Wars*, Princeton, NJ: Princeton University Press, 2001.

Jones, David Martin, *Political Development in Pacific Asia*, Cambridge: Polity Press, 1997.

Katzenstein, Peter, and Shiraishi, Takashi, *Network Power: Japan and Asia*, Ithaca, NY: Cornell University Press, 1996.

Macfie, A. L., ed., *Orientalism: A Reader*, Edinburgh:Edinburgh University Press.

Mansbach, Richard W., 'Southeast Asia in the Global Political System', in Jae Kyu Park and Melvin Gurtov, eds., *Southeast Asia in Transition: Regional and International Politics*, Seoul: The Institute for Far Eastern Studies, Kyung Nam University, 1977.

Mauzy, Diane, 'Review of *The Quest for Identity: International Relations of Southeast Asia*, by Amitav Acharya,' *Contemporary Southeast Asia*, 22/(3) 2000: 613–5.

Said, Edward, Orientalism, London: Routledge, 1978.

Simon, Sheldon, 'The Regionalization of Defense in Southeast Asia,' *Pacific Review*, Vol. 5, No. 2, 1992.

Sopiee, Noordin, 'ASEAN and Regional Security,' in Mohammed Ayoob, ed., *Regional Security in the Third World*, London: Croom Helm, 1986.

Weatherbee, Donald E., 'ASEAN Regionalism: The Salient Dimension', in Karl D. Jackson and M. Hadi Soesastro, eds., *ASEAN Security and Economic Development*, Berkeley, CA: Institute of East Asian Studies, University of California, 1984.

7 Realism and regionalism in Southeast Asia

The ARF and the war on terror

Sheldon Simon

Introduction

Analysts of security institutions in the Asia-Pacific have employed contending theoretical frameworks for decades. For Europeanists security multilateralism had been embedded in NATO since the 1950s within a remarkably stable balance of power, but the situation in the Asia-Pacific seemed more ephemeral. From the 1950s onward regional security arrangements were created and dissolved with disturbing rapidity. For the most part, only US-led bilateral arrangements persisted. This record of weak security multilateralism was persuasively documented by one of Asian realism's most prominent analysts, Michael Leifer. More recently, however, a new security regionalism has emerged in the Asia-Pacific embodied in the ASEAN Regional Forum (ARF). The ARF incorporates both outsiders such as the United States and the European Union and most of the members of the Asia-Pacific littoral. Its stated purpose is *liberal*, that is, to ameliorate security tensions among its members through confidence-building, transparency, preventive diplomacy, and conflict management. *Realists* insist, however, that the ARF's real utility is to help institutionalize a stable Asia-Pacific balance of power by committing the major powers – the United States, China, and Japan – to regional processes in their security policies. The current war on terror is a test of these alternative views.

A hallmark of Michael Leifer's distinguished career was his skepticism about the utility of multilateral regional security institutions in Asia for resolving core security concerns of the region's members. Instead, he saw a classical balance of power centered on significant states as the basis for regional order. As with the exponents of the English School of International Relations – represented by Hedley Bull – anarchy could be an impetus to cooperation as well as a setting for conflict.[1] Although doubting the efficacy of the "ASEAN Way" for regional security based on consensus, Leifer acknowledged that the ARF contributed in a modest way to a balance of power in the Asia-Pacific. However, that contribution was based on the prior existence of a stable balance brought about by the actions of states rather than the ARF as its creator.[2]

Professor Leifer, then, could be described as a *realist* who devoted much of his professional life to explicating cooperative security in Southeast Asia. As

Ralf Emmers points out, *security regimes* neither make the use of force unthinkable nor resolve disputes among states. Rather, a security regime effects a code of conduct – formal or informal – among its members that reduces mutual threat perceptions. While realists – including Michael Leifer – acknowledge the utility of security regimes, they are seen as instruments employed by states to enhance their separate statures.[3] Nor do security regimes create a shared strategic perspective; each member maintains its own security policy. Some may be in alliances, others not. Members may even balance against each other, as is certainly true in the ARF. At most, a security regime creates agreements among member states designed to restrain great power ambitions by promoting norms and principles, which insure that more powerful members do not threaten smaller cooperative partners.[4] Thus, both cooperative security and alliances continue to characterize East Asian international politics while collective defense does not.[5] Put another way, the US "hub-and-spokes" alliance system and ARF multilateral security discussions run along parallel tracks in East Asia.

Cooperative security emphasizes dialogue, confidence building, reassurance, and transparency among members rather than the resolution of specific problems. At its best, cooperative security may offer alternatives to the strategy of deterrence through preventive diplomacy by which issues are addressed *before* they become security problems among states. An example might be ways of effecting maritime cargo security before it becomes an international trade problem in an era of transnational terrorists.

In the early twenty-first century, alongside traditional security concerns involving territorial disputes and a striving for international prominence, a panoply of new challenges has arisen, including the spread of weapons of mass destruction (WMD), illegal migration, drug and human trafficking, AIDs, illegal small arms transfers and money laundering, as well as the rise of transnational Islamist terrorism. Not only do these challenges best lend themselves to cooperative security but they also fit the definition of *comprehensive security*, that is, issues that are neither territorial disputes nor military confrontations but rather challenges to social stability and, therefore, to the political legitimacy of governments. Moreover, almost all of these challenges require multilateral cooperation. However, solutions are not necessarily cooperative-sum as neoliberals prefer.[6] For example, illegal Indonesian labor migration to Malaysia may alleviate unemployment in Indonesia, but during an economic downturn, illegal migrants exacerbate Malaysia's own employment problems as well as social tensions through increased crime. Thus, forced repatriation may reduce Malaysia's social problems while they increase political tension between Kuala Lumpur and Jakarta.

Nevertheless, as we shall see, cooperative security through the ARF has at least made some politically and militarily weak states feel more comfortable through discussions of regional security with larger powers. Talk has been frank; and mutually beneficial processes unrelated to specific conflicts have been created, including Search and Rescue procedures, Peacekeeping, and Disaster Relief measures.[7]

The origins of the ARF[8]

The ARF emerged from ASEAN in the 1990s. The end of the Cold War left the Asia-Pacific searching for a new organizing principle for security.[9] While traditional alliances remained, including bilateral treaties with the United States and the Five-Power Defense Arrangement—a multilateral agreement among Great Britain, Australia, New Zealand, Malaysia, and Singapore—these seemed inadequate to deal with security matters of a nonmilitary nature such as transnational crime, environmental hazards, and illegal population movements.[10] Moreover, "traditional" security issues persisted in the form of unresolved territorial disputes, divided states, nuclear weapons proliferation, and conflicting maritime jurisdictions resulting from the 1982 UN Law of the Sea.

Some kind of cooperative security enterprise linking the region to its major partners in Northeast Asia and North America was needed to fill the gap. Through the 1976 Treaty of Amity and Cooperation, ASEAN members had already pledged among themselves to resolve intra-ASEAN disputes peacefully (or postpone their resolution). Underlying the vision of a larger security order was the hope that the treaty's peaceful resolution commitment could be extended to other states. This practice would constitute a kind of minimal diffuse reciprocity. That is, while ASEAN would not expect outsiders automatically to come to members' aid in times of crisis or leap to their defense if attacked, at least outside countries could be asked to renounce the use of force in settling any conflicts they might have with the Association's members. The unstated object of these concerns is, of course, China—the only "extraregional" state with territorial claims in Southeast Asia.[11] This is essentially a realist vision of the ARF. If successful, it would encourage the People's Republic of China (PRC) to explain and clarify its security policy and planning. China's neighbors, through the ARF, could then respond with their concerns about the PRC's policy in hopes of modifying it and thus enhancing regional stability. In exchange for PRC transparency, other ARF members would reciprocate.

Liberal theorists hope that the ARF can go beyond realism to shape cooperation. If the ARF can devise joint cooperative military actions such as multinational maritime patrols, search and rescue operations, anti-piracy activities, and oceanic environmental monitoring, then cooperative security will be launched. To date, however, these hopes remain for the most part embryonic. Nevertheless, the transparency measures that have begun are a first step in the liberal direction insofar as they help to create mutual confidence.

The ARF's origins can be traced to a realization in the early 1990s that ASEAN by itself would be unable to dominate political-security discussions across the entire Asia-Pacific rim. The region's two indigenous great powers—Japan and China—are in Northeast Asia. The two remaining potential conflict flashpoints—Korea and Taiwan—are also outside ASEAN's spatial realm. Moreover, the United States, as the sole remaining superpower, concentrates its forward-deployed Asian forces in Northeast Asia. In the post-Cold War era, therefore, Southeast Asia feared that it would once again become marginalized in Asia-Pacific regional security.

Fortunately for ASEAN, however, no exclusive Northeast Asian efforts were made to create a subregional counterpart to ASEAN, though the 2003-04 Six Party talks on North Korea's nuclear weapons potential could evolve in that direction. Early on, China remained wary of security multilateralism as a device to constrain its regional ambitions. Japan was still viewed with suspicion by the rest of Northeast Asia as unrepentant for its World War II brutalities, and the Koreas were understandably focused on their forty-year military stalemate at the 38th parallel. In effect, ASEAN was able to fill this vacuum by offering to create a new region-wide entity modeled on the Association's process of consultation and dialogue. Because this approach fell well short of collective defense, it was not threatening to any potential adherent. Nor would a new regional forum interfere with individual states' security links to outsiders.

Purposefully imitative of the ASEAN Post-Ministerial Conference (PMC), the ARF objective was to develop a predictable and constructive pattern of relationships in the Asia-Pacific. In sum, the ARF would be a transparency and reassurance mechanism for the Asia-Pacific, providing the whole region with opportunities for ASEAN-style dialogue. By themselves, the PMCs were viewed by Northeast Asians as insufficient for broad discussion of their subregion's concerns on such region-wide issues as competitive arming, maritime exclusive economic zone rules, and the roles of China and Japan. Although ASEAN understood that these issues needed to be addressed along with the exclusively Northeast Asian concerns mentioned above, the Association also desired to create a body that would acknowledge ASEAN's institutional status as *primus inter pares*. The ARF achieved this goal by ensuring that ASEAN states would be the venue for the ARF's annual meetings; that ASEAN would dominate the agenda; that intersession study groups, each composed of two states, would always include an ASEAN member, and that the ASEAN consensus principle would prevail in ARF decisions.

Still, Washington, Tokyo, and Beijing had to be persuaded that such security multilateralism was in their interests. The first Bush administration opposed the idea, fearing that a multilateral security body would somehow weaken traditional bilateral US ties to the region. President Bill Clinton had no such qualms, however. Indeed, the Clinton administration's early foreign policy viewed multilateral diplomacy as a device for spreading the costs of common security among friends—a neoliberal position. Nor was Clinton concerned that a Pacific security forum would undermine traditional US alliances, which would be sustained as bedrock guarantees, while a new body discussed post-Cold War security. For Japan, the ARF provided an opportunity gradually to legitimize its voice in regional security affairs independent of the United States. The ARF also provided a venue for South Korean–Japanese security dialogue in the same setting offered to the United States and China. That is, a generally sensitive bilateral security relationship could be ameliorated within a larger multinational setting.

Convincing China of the ARF's utility was more complicated. The PRC is suspicious of any institutionalized multilateral security organization. The People's Liberation Army (PLA) particularly resists attempts to probe its doctrine and order of battle, while the Chinese leadership generally is apprehensive that an Asian international security organization might become involved in the Taiwan issue. Nevertheless, if an Asia-Pacific security organization was inevitable, then the ASEAN concept was acceptable, mainly because it ensured that neither Tokyo nor Washington could dominate. Moreover, China could not afford to be excluded from such a group for fear of isolation in regional security affairs.

The process of regular regional security discussions only began with the 1992 ASEAN summit, which decided to extend the annual post-ministerial discussions with dialogue partners to cover security. The motivating factor was the strategic uncertainty created by the end of the Cold War. By 1994, the PMC talks had led to the ARF's creation. In fact, the ARF is the most comprehensive security forum in the world with 23 members including the 10 ASEAN states, ASEAN's dialogue partners (Australia, Canada, the United States, Japan, New Zealand, South and North Korea, the European Union, Mongolia, China, Russia, and India), and an ASEAN observer—as of 1997—Papua New Guinea. (East Timor joined the ARF in 2005.)

Concerned that international security discussions unduly pressure states to change their policies, the members agreed that there would be no ARF secretariat or formal report of its annual meetings. Only the Chairman's Record of the Proceedings was accepted. As in ASEAN, decisions are based on consensus, and any ARF agreements are implemented on a voluntary basis. No sanctions can be imposed on members, nor are there provisions for suspending or expelling members whose actions may be deemed to be in violation of ARF decisions.[12]

By its second meeting, the ARF agreed on a three-stage progression toward comprehensive security for Asia, which would move from confidence-building to preventive diplomacy, and finally on to the development of mechanisms for conflict resolution. The development of these mechanisms was subsequently renamed "elaboration of approaches to conflict" out of deference to China's concern that conflict resolution could be interpreted as justifying the ARF's interference in members' internal affairs.[13]

By 1997, the ARF had formed three working groups (known as intersessional groups or ISGs), which met between the annual meetings. These groups address the issues of confidence building, peacekeeping operations, and maritime search and rescue. A subsequent ISG on transnational crime was added by the end of the decade. All of these could be called confidence-building measures, and they are useful in generating a degree of trust among countries that have a history of mutual suspicion. The basic question, however, is whether the ARF will develop the capacity to go beyond confidence building to preventive diplomacy.

At the initiative of Thailand's Foreign Ministry, and with UN support, three ASEAN–UN workshops in preventive diplomacy were held in Bangkok in 1993 and 1994. The most interesting outcomes of these meetings were an examination of ASEAN's Treaty of Amity and Cooperation (TAC) as a model for conflict resolution and the possibility of a peacekeeping training center for Southeast Asia. Although the Bangkok workshops and their Indonesian counterparts on the South China Sea disputes are useful gatherings to give all sides an opportunity to air their views or perhaps create sufficient synergy to come up with innovative proposals, such as a regional peacekeeping center, there are stringent limits on ASEAN and ARF accomplishments. Neither body has dealt with the ubiquitous bilateral border and territorial disputes among all ASEAN members. Nor have they arrived at solutions to persistent problems of smuggling, piracy, and the illegal movements of people across borders. These issues are all still handled, for the most part, bilaterally.

Nevertheless, ASEAN PMCs, senior officers' meetings (SOMs) and ARF workshops have generated a cornucopia of transparency possibilities—that is the discussion of security intentions. Both ASEAN and the ARF agree that security transparency is a prerequisite for more sophisticated preventive diplomacy and conflict resolution. Thus, in 1993, Malaysia hosted a defense dialogue forum for ASEAN and several of its dialogue partners to discuss threat assessment, doctrine, and arms acquisitions. Other confidence-building measures (CBMs) that have been raised in ASEAN-related gatherings include advance notification of military exercises, hot lines among political and military leaders, extension of the Russian–US incidents-at-sea agreement to the entire Asia-Pacific, and a regional maritime, air surveillance, and safety regime. These all fall within the trust and confidence-building category as defined by the ARF.[14]

A reexamination of the ARF's early years reveals a division on security issues comparable to APEC's split on economic issues. ASEAN and China prefer to keep discussions general to avoid disagreements, while the United States, Australia, Canada, and Japan seek to devise practical CBMs capable of early implementation. Although the 1995 ARF meeting succeeded in raising the Spratlys issue and eliciting a vague Chinese agreement to future ministerial discussions, there has been no change in Beijing's insistence that it will only discuss the disposition of the Spratlys with other claimants bilaterally, will not accept third-party mediation, and will consider joint development activities only when its sovereignty is acknowledged. In March 2005 Roweva, Beijing agreed to postpone sovereignty disputes and entered into an understanding with Vietnam and the Philippines for trilateral petroleum exploration in their overlapping zones. Beijing's growing naval activities in Southeast Asia forms the basis for the perception of a "China threat." The ARF's efforts to convince its members to publish and exchange information on strategic doctrines, orders of battle, and arms acquisition plans comprise the region's attempt to engage China in collaborative security transparency. So far, such efforts have been unavailing, although China's three Defense White Papers have increasingly discussed the PLA's military doctrine.

The realist challenge[15]

For Michael Leifer, the ARF presented an analytical challenge. On the one hand, it embodied the neo-liberal concept of expanded cooperative security, by the year 2000 encompassing all Asia-Pacific states, including even North Korea—though excluding Taiwan at China's insistence. India was also inside, though not Pakistan; and beyond the Asia-Pacific, the European Union had obtained membership—stretching the meaning of what was identified as a "regional" security organization. Yet even as the ARF engaged in confidence-building seminars and intersessional meetings, its impact on traditional security concerns such as the disposition of the South China Sea islands was minimal. National military might remained determinative as contending countries occupied various islets in the Spratly archipelago and prepared to defend their claims with gunboats if necessary. Indeed, the ARF was not created to address specific concerns. This was one of the main considerations in convincing China to join and, at the same time, one of the greatest frustrations for the United States. Even before the rise of terrorism to its global agenda, Washington had pressed the ARF to ask its members for more transparency in military doctrine and orders of battle and hoped to see the Forum develop a robust human rights agenda.

While the ARF's record in coping with traditional security concerns is modest at best, a new security agenda that may be more amenable to multinational approaches emerged in the second half of the 1990s. This new agenda covers a plethora of concerns, all of which impact several countries simultaneously. They include the regional haze caused by forest fires in Indonesia, narcotics trafficking and the illegal trade in small arms, the smuggling of people across national borders, maritime piracy, and the aftermath of the Asian financial crisis. These concerns have been highlighted in recent ARF Chairman's Statements beginning in 2000. Moreover, unlike core security issues that reflect realist visions of international politics where one country's gain is frequently obtained at another's expense, the new security agenda provides neo-liberal solutions. That is, resolving the issues enumerated above benefits virtually all of the countries involved. For example, collaborative measures to reduce piracy foster greater maritime trade, reduce ship and cargo insurance rates, and lower the risk of ocean pollution caused by the hijacking of oil tankers.

Unfortunately, an examination of core security issues does not reveal this kind of success. The 1997–98 financial crisis could have provided an opportunity for Asian states to rationalize the purchase of conventional weapons via the ARF. Instead, leaders preferred to focus on transparency in arms acquisitions as a CBM. The opportunity to mutually reduce arms purchases as an economic recovery measure was also missed. As John Garfano put it: "Because there are several very different reasons for weapons acquisition, including government prestige, concern with long-term Chinese capabilities, and professionalizing the military, it is unlikely that mere transparency will get to the heart of the problem." Garfano pointedly concludes: "CBMs have not yet accomplished anything that would prevent or even deter such acquisitions."[16]

Critics of the ARF also point to its weak institutionalization. There is no Secretariat and no central depository for information on ARF reports and decisions. (The ASEAN Secretariat provides some minimal support.) Therefore, it is extremely difficult for the ARF to be proactive, that is, to gather the information needed for early warning about a conflict—crucial for preventive diplomacy (PD) or terrorist monitoring—without a secretariat or information depository.[17] Moreover, as in ASEAN, there is no power to impose sanctions if ARF resolutions are not implemented. These weaknesses with respect to preventive diplomacy exist to alleviate country concerns that PD is a precursor to the ARF becoming involved in states' internal affairs. Yet, effective collaboration to counter transnational terror undoubtedly entails exactly that.

Nevertheless, there are some encouraging signs. Over the past few years, the ARF has placed non-traditional security issues on its agenda, including illegal migration, piracy, and small arms trafficking. All of these can be tied to terrorist movements within the region, their funding, and lethal capabilities. Still, Malaysia and Indonesia within ASEAN and the ARF are reluctant to link non-traditional security concerns with counter-terror. For domestic political reasons—large Muslim populations—they underplay multilateral counter-terror agreements, while displaying a greater willingness to collaborate bilaterally for specific operations, for example, apprehending particular terrorists.[18]

Can the war on terror advance ARF cooperative security?

In tandem with ASEAN's November 2001 Counter Terrorism Declaration in Brunei, the ARF in late July 2002 also issued a Statement on Measures against Terrorist Financing and agreed to establish an Intersessional meeting on counter-terrorism and transnational crime. The latter has been meeting annually, though whether its deliberations have created new member counter-terror cooperation is unclear.[19] The July 2002 ARF Statement mandated several actions that could strengthen anti-terror cooperation, including the creation of national Financial Intelligence units which would share information on public lists of terrorists whose assets have been frozen as well as members' implementation of several UN resolutions designed to halt terrorist financial transfers.

There is no doubt that Southeast Asian terrorist actions are transnational and, therefore, a *regional* as distinct from an exclusively *national* security challenge. *Jemah Islamiyah* (JI), by far the most important terrorist organization in Southeast Asia since 2000, has been involved in bombings in Jakarta, Batam, Manila, Bali, and in aborted plans to attack diplomatic missions, US navy personnel, and US commercial firms in Singapore. Moreover, with the August

2003 capture of JI's operations chief, Hambali, in Thailand, interrogation revealed a direct financial link to *Al Qaeda*.[20] Indonesia's Police Chief, subsequent to the Bali and Jakarta Marriott bombings, stated that "it is vital for Indonesia...to receive information or funding from other countries for counter-terror efforts." In turn, Indonesia is prepared to provide access to data requested by other countries.[21]

Southeast Asian anti-terror cooperation has been "weak and inconsistent."[22] Only three ASEAN states have ratified the 1999 International Convention for the Suppression of the Financing of Terrorism. Because terrorists operate both *within* and *among* states, effective counter-terror cooperation must begin with strong domestic legislation and enforcement capacity. Yet only Singapore meets both these criteria in Southeast Asia. The original ASEAN Five have all created some form of financial monitoring units that can be employed against terrorists; however, lack of well-trained staff, minimal integration with law enforcement, and loopholes in the enabling legislation render it difficult to find and freeze these assets except in Singapore. Moreover, Southeast Asian governments have not taken the initiative to publicize companies suspected of supporting terrorism.

These hesitant and half-hearted cooperative efforts by ASEAN members fit Michael Leifer's assessment of Southeast Asian security: that states will resist sharing sensitive information on domestic matters that could embarrass or challenge the political positions of ruling elites. How does this weak national base affect the ARF? Rhetorically, the Forum is committed to an anti-terror agenda. ARF Chairmen's Statements from July 2002 onward have emphasized the need to combat terror; and the ARF has created workshops on Financial Measures against Terrorism and an Intersessional Meeting on Transnational Crime and Terrorism. So, the ARF has proposed that security against terror is a cooperative matter, not a case of states balancing with or against one another. In June 2003, ARF members adopted two statements that linked new measures to fight piracy with anti-terrorism. Singapore's foreign minister noted that the JI network captured in Singapore had plans to carry out attacks on US vessels in the Strait of Malacca.[23]

At its Phnom Penh Tenth Annual Meeting, the ARF announced that member state experts were developing a legal framework that all countries could adopt as a uniform base to address transnational terrorism and crime in the Pacific. However, given the varying levels of law enforcement transparency as well as political controls of judicial authorities, the efficacy of such a framework is problematic at best. Optimistically, the 2003 ARF Statement concluded that the Forum's work on "common security threats, including transnational terrorism, transnational crime, [and] piracy" had advanced the ARF to preventive diplomacy. At the same time, however, "the Ministers acknowledge ASEAN's continued leading role in the ARF and the need to proceed at a pace comfortable to all."[24]

The ARF Statement on Cooperation Against Piracy pleaded for "regional cooperation to ensure that maritime criminals and pirates do not evade prosecution" and underlined the fact that "effective response to maritime crime requires regional maritime security strategies and multilateral cooperation in their implementation."[25] The ARF countries account for over 80 percent of global maritime trade; and most of the piracy that occurs in Southeast Asia takes place in coastal and archipelagic waters. Interdiction and arrest, therefore, require cooperation among navies and coast guards, law enforcement, shipping companies, and port authorities. The ARF Statement proposes combined anti-piracy exercises, the training of naval and merchant marine personnel in anti-piracy, and the designation of prescribed traffic lanes for supertankers with coast guard and naval escorts in areas with a high level of piracy incidents. Nevertheless, the ARF also reiterated its traditional mantra that cooperation must respect all members' territorial integrity, sovereignty, and jurisdiction, and insisted on voluntary participation.[26] In practice, it has been difficult to elicit effective maritime cooperation in Southeast Asia. ASEAN members generally refuse the right of "hot pursuit" to their neighbors bent on apprehending maritime criminals. Moreover, prosecuting pirates has not been a high priority even when they are apprehended. Whether this will change as terrorist groups engage in maritime attacks remains to be seen.[27]

Proceeding at a pace comfortable to all is essentially a restatement of the ASEAN consensus norm—in effect a unit veto arrangement—that reinforces the traditional ASEAN/ARF prohibition against interference in members' internal affairs. While the ARF acknowledges that "terrorism [and] its links with trans-national organized crime…as well as illegal movements of nuclear, chemical, biological and other potentially deadly materials forms…a complex set of new security challenges," the Forum itself is unable to establish common criteria to deal with them, legislation to stop them, or collaborative enforcement mechanisms.[28] Individual state assessments of how well they can cope with terrorism by themselves probably determine their willingness both to share information and to permit other states to become involved in apprehending terrorists in their territories.

The ARF and China

A realist/constructivist case could be made that the ARF was created by ASEAN to "entrap" China—a potentially rising hegemon—into a new set of international norms that would reduce the possible use of force among members, enhance security transparency, and promote cooperative solutions to conflicts. The challenge of terrorism lends itself to these hopes because terrorism is not sponsored by any ARF state and is a threat to all. Counter-terror, therefore, should promote the ARF agenda of cooperative security while incorporating China into these plans.

In fact, China's "New Security Concept" reiterated at the July 2002 ARF meeting—although originally proposed as a counter to the persistence of US bilateral alliances—emphasizes that comprehensive security could be a basis for

China's anti-terror cooperation. In its discussions with ASEAN members on counter terrorism, PRC officials have conflated Beijing's actions to suppress Islamic separatists in its western provinces with ASEAN member policies in Southeast Asia.[29] This theme was elaborated at the June 2003 ARF meeting when China proposed a new ARF "Security Policy Conference" consisting of military officers and defense officials. The idea would be to promote security through united action rather than seeking "absolute security for oneself and threaten[ing] other parties' security."[30] While this initiative was also part of a Chinese effort to present an alternative to American-dominated counter-terror arrangements in Southeast Asia, it might also be an indicator that China has a role to play in regional counter-terror cooperation.

China's courtship of the Southeast Asian states has continued with the PRC's accession to ASEAN's Treaty of Amity and Cooperation (TAC)—in effect a non-aggression pact requiring that all signatories resolve disputes peacefully. China's signature constitutes a form of assurance that it will not use force to resolve its claims to the South China Sea islands. Nevertheless, there is still no Code of Conduct for that dispute.[31] While China's signature on the Joint Statement on Cooperation in the Field of Non-Traditional Security Issues suggests that a formal base for counter-terror cooperation has been laid, nevertheless, there is still no indication that the PRC has, or plans to, become involved in Southeast Asian efforts to defeat Islamist terrorism. For example, there is no published evidence that Chinese law enforcement or intelligence agencies are working with their Southeast Asian counterparts on these concerns.[32]

Is the ARF losing its stature to APEC in counter-terrorism?

When the ARF was created in the mid-1990s, the ASEAN states devised a parallel institution to the Asia-Pacific Economic Cooperation (APEC) forum. The latter was formed in 1989 to promote regional trade and investment liberalization and to insure that the Asia-Pacific did not fall behind other regional trade organizations such as the North American Free Trade Agreement (NAFTA). Because APEC is an intergovernmental economic body, Beijing reluctantly agreed to Taiwan's participation as an *economic entity*, not as a state. It was understood that APEC would not deal with security matters, particularly those involving militaries and territorial claims. ARF dialogues would address these; and because only states deal with security, Taiwan was excluded from membership in the ARF. Thus, through the 1990s, a division of labor existed between the ARF and APEC whose dialogues ran along parallel tracks. Both followed ASEAN procedures, that is, consensus. Both also required individual country follow-through to implement international agreements.

There is, however, one significant distinction between the two organizations. The ARF operates at the foreign minister level, while APEC is a venue for heads of government. Thus, the prospect for workable international understandings is greater in the latter than in the former. In the post-September 11 era, APEC's agenda has expanded to include security. In fact, as early as the 1990s, national leaders' meetings took place on the sidelines at APEC to discuss the important concerns of the day. For example, meetings between Chinese and US leaders during that decade helped to relieve strained relations; and, in 1999, the two forged a common approach to the North Korean problem at the APEC summit. A follow-on meeting to the 1999 APEC summit also prepared the way for securing ASEAN's acquiescence to the dispatch of UN peacekeepers to East Timor.[33]

At APEC's 2001 Leaders Meeting, the forum issued its first formal statement on security matters—a "Supplementary Statement" on counter-terrorism. From that point on, security matters have come to dominate APEC's agenda. From a realist perspective, one could explain the rise of security concerns within APEC by referencing the dominant US role. However, more is involved. The anti-terrorist agenda met the needs of a number of states forging a commonality of interests that had frequently been absent on purely economic matters. Anti-terrorism has led to a significant improvement in Sino–US and Malaysia–US relations.[34]

Nor was it difficult for APEC members to agree that terrorist activities imposed economic costs. Among the most notable of these in Southeast Asia was the devastating impact on tourism as a result of the Bali bombing. Depressed business and consumer confidence could also lead to lower levels of investment. Moreover, protecting vulnerable production sites, refitting ships, and higher insurance premiums all underlined the economic price of counter-terror. By 2003, APEC, through its Transportation Working Group, had devised measures for port and ship security and had created a Counter-terrorism Task Force. In effect, the overlay between APEC and the ARF on security matters was now complete.

There was some resistance within APEC to this conflation of security and economics. Malaysia, Indonesia, and Vietnam—though surprisingly not China—expressed concern about the new agenda but ultimately acquiesced. All ultimately agreed that stopping terror went hand in hand with APEC's goal of promoting economic prosperity. Unlike the ARF which tended to issue statements of general principles, at its 2003 Bangkok meeting, APEC agreed on specific measures to place controls on the trade of shoulder-fired missiles, specific enhancements of port security, and a coordinated approach to fighting bio-terrorism—among other measures. APEC also agreed to a US proposal for setting up a new Asian Development Bank terrorism fund to help developing countries strengthen port security and combat money laundering.[35] The fact that the APEC summit was attended by heads of government meant that obligations could be made with some assurance of national follow-through.

Other forms of anti-terror multilateral cooperation

Anti-terror collaboration in the Asia-Pacific has gone beyond the ARF and APEC. As a cooperative security venture ASEAN+3 is also involved. In January 2004, they agreed to set up a joint task force on transnational crime, the proceeds of which have often funded terrorist activities. Responsibilities were divided among several countries with Thailand taking the lead in drug trafficking, Singapore in economic and cyber-crime, Indonesia in counter-terrorism, and with Malaysia and Brunei focusing on piracy and people trafficking. ASEAN and China signed a separate memorandum on terrorism and cyber-crime cooperation.[36]

Southeast Asia's Regional Center for Counter-Terrorism, inaugurated in July 2003 with US funding, houses researchers and holds training seminars. The Center has been sensitive about any US connection because of the concerns of Southeast Asian Muslims that its focus will be exclusively anti-Islamist. Therefore, it has not yet become a clearing house for regional intelligence or a coordinating mechanism for joint operations. Moreover, although the United States provided start-up financing, its operations are now funded locally.[37]

Indicative of Indonesia's effort to reclaim regional leadership after the devastation to its economy and political position by the 1997-98 financial crisis, the 1999 secession of East Timor, and the 2002 and 2003 Bali and Jakarta Marriott bombings has been Jakarta's new initiative as ASEAN chair for 2003-04 to create an ASEAN Security Community (ASC). The proposal is designed to restore Jakarta to ASEAN leadership by acknowledging the importance of fighting terrorism transnationally to the Association's future. The ASC would include centers for combating terrorism, peacekeeping training, and regular meetings of ASEAN police and defense officials. At its October 2003 summit in Bali, the Concord II declaration promoted the security community concept and for the first time in the Association's history pointed to "democracy" as one of ASEAN's goals. Nevertheless, the Bali Concord II declaration stressed that the security community was not a defense pact but rather a mechanism to tie together existing policies and agreements. This rather deflated description of the Indonesian vision does not bode well for any brave new ASEAN actions.[38]

Confirming Indonesia's efforts to assume a leading role in Southeast Asia's counter-terror activities, although not a formal component of the ASEAN Security Community, was a meeting of 22 Asia-Pacific states' police forces hosted by Jakarta in Bali. The purpose of the January 2004 gathering was to boost coordination and information-sharing. Particular emphasis was given to the use of high-tech equipment in investigating and preventing terror attacks. Moreover, Indonesia's National Police Chief promised that his country would establish a 24/7 anti-terrorism office and hotlines for global requests about suspected terrorists. A joint secretariat on terrorism would be established in Jakarta involving Indonesian National Police and Australian Federal Police. This center would be equipped with a forensics laboratory. As Indonesian President Megawati Sukarnoputri put it in her opening remarks to a follow-on Bali conference in February 2004: "This solid coordination mechanism is necessary, for only in this way we would be able to penetrate into the terrorist networks and cells…that are tightly and closely built. I am of the high expectation that, in this

Conference, you will be able to agree on such a crucial coordination mechanism."[39]

Conclusion

Many analysts share Michael Leifer's realist skepticism about the effectiveness of regional security organizations in the Asia-Pacific. In Southeast Asia particularly, small weak states are defensive realists, concerned with protecting what they have rather than expanding their control of other territories and populations. Their risk aversion helps to explain why ASEAN, the ARF, and APEC all privilege national sovereignty and non-interference in domestic affairs over the kind of openness needed for transnational counter-terror activity. Nevertheless, collaboration against regional terror groups, such as JI, is a cooperative sum venture. All states benefit when terrorist cells are exposed and shut down. ASEAN, the ARF, and APEC have taken measures to exchange sensitive information about national financial matters through measures designed to disrupt terrorist finances. Bank records, for example, are being made more available for law enforcement scrutiny by other countries. Some national intelligence sources and methods are shared—a prospect virtually unheard of prior to the Bali bombing—particularly in the ARF with respect to transnational crime.[40]

Counter-terror activities, then, are adding a problem-solving mindset to the ARF's less intrusive concentration on confidence-building. Moreover, ARF members are developing "coalitions of the willing" to advance counter-terror cooperation as seen in the 2003 meetings among law enforcement agencies from Malaysia, Indonesia, Thailand, the Philippines, and Cambodia.[41]

The United States is hopeful that the ARF will become a more important security player, particularly as the security concerns of Northeast Asia affect the entire Asia-Pacific littoral. In February 2004, Assistant Secretary of State James Kelly stated that Washington might be willing to provide additional resources to the ARF to address the crucial concerns of North Korea's nuclear weapons as well as terrorism.[42] Within hegemonic stability theory, this may be a way for the United States to encourage the ARF to adopt the American security agenda in the post-September 11 world. It could also be a sign that the Bush penchant for security unilateralism is being modified in East Asia if one takes into account the increasingly active US roles in the ARF, APEC, and the six-party talks on nuclear weapons in North Korea.

In sum, though Michael Leifer's realist explanation for the ARF's modest achievements is still valid, Asia's post-September 11 international context has significantly changed. At the top of the agenda now are the need to combat terrorism and nuclear weapons proliferation—concerns that virtually all Asian states share and which require multilateral cooperation. This agenda is tailored for the kind of regional multilateral cooperation for which the ARF was created. Moreover, for reasons cited earlier in this chapter, APEC and *ad hoc* more limited regional groups are also grappling with the same challenges. The early twenty-first century may witness, therefore, the incorporation of multilateral security cooperation into realist national thinking as a way of dealing with core security issues. This has become possible because states for the time being may be less concerned about balancing against each other than with working together to defeat common threats: transnational religious terrorism and WMD proliferation.

Notes

1 See the Introduction to this volume by Ralf Emmers and Joseph Liow.
2 Michael Leifer, *The ASEAN Regional Forum: Expanding ASEAN's Model of Regional Security* (London: International Institute of Strategic Studies, Adelphi Paper No. 302, 1996), pp. 58–59.
3 Ralf Emmers, *Cooperative Security and the Balance of Power in ASEAN and the ARF* (New York: RoutledgeCurzon, 2003), p. 2.
4 Ibid., pp. 52–53. Also see Emmers, "Security Cooperation in the Asia-Pacific" in See Seng Tan and Amitav Acharya, eds, *Asia-Pacific Security Cooperation: National Interests and Regional Order* (Armonk, NY: M.E. Sharpe, 2004).
5 For a discussion of the coexistence of alliances and cooperative security in East Asia, see Sheldon W. Simon, "Realism and Neoliberalism: International Relations Theory and Southeast Asian Security," *The Pacific Review*, (8,1) January 1995, pp. 5–24.
6 John Garfano, "Can Security Communities Be Constructed? Would They Help? The ARF as a Test Case," unpublished paper presented to the Belfer Center's Council on Emerging National Security Affairs, Harvard University, June 2001.
7 Ibid., p. 7.
8 This section is drawn from Sheldon W. Simon, "Managing Security Challenges in Southeast Asia," *NBR Analysis* (13,4) July 2002, pp. 6–11.
9 Maria Consuelo C. Ortuoste, "The Establishment of the ASEAN Regional Forum," paper presented to the Multilateral Institutions in Asia Seminar, Asia-Pacific Center for Security Studies, Honolulu, July 14, 2000.
10 This new security agenda is explored in Sheldon W. Simon, ed., *The Many Faces of Asian Security* (Lanham, MD: Rowman and Littlefield, 2001).
11 Curiously, Southeast Asian states do not mention Taiwan in their concerns about China's claims to the Spratly islands, even though China's and Taiwan's claims are exactly the same.
12 This description of the ARF's circumscribed nature is found in M.D. Abad, Jr., "Confidence Building in the Asia-Pacific: The Role of the ASEAN and the ARF," paper presented to the Indonesian Air Force Command and Staff College, Bandung, February 2, 2000.
13 See the discussion in William T. Tow and Richard Gray, "Asia-Pacific Security Regimes: Conditions and Constraints," *Australian Journal of Political Science*, no. 33 (1995), p. 446.
14 Trevor Findlay, "The Regional Security Outlook," in Gary Klintworth, ed., *Asia-Pacific Security: Less Uncertainty, New Opportunities* (New York: St. Martin's Press, 1998), pp. 275–292.
15 Some of the discussion in this section of Michael Leifer's assessment of the ARF is drawn from his IISS monograph, *The ASEAN Regional Forum*.
16 Garfano, *op. cit.*, p. 7. See also Sheldon W. Simon, "The Economic Crisis and Southeast Asian Security," *NBR Analysis* (9,5) December 1998; and Carlyle Thayer, "Multilateral Institutions in Asia: The ASEAN Regional Forum" (Honolulu, HI: Asia-Pacific Center for Security Studies, Seminar Series, October 2000).

17 Thayer, *op.cit*., p. 20.
18 Shawn Crispin, “Safety First,” *Far Eastern Economic Review*, October 30, 2003, p. 17.
19 See the U.S. Council for Security Cooperation in the Asia-Pacific (CSCAP) Special Report #10, November 7, 2003 published by Pacific Forum in Honolulu.
20 Remarks by Dr Kumar Ramakrishna of Singapore’s Institute of Defense and Strategic Studies in the CSCAP Roundtable: “Terrorism in Southeast Asia: Perspectives from the Region,” *Issues and Insights* (3,2) February 2004 (Honolulu, HI: Pacific Forum), pp. 5–6.
21 *Suara Pembaruan* (Internet Version) January 19, 2004, in FBIS, *Daily Report—East Asia*, January 21, 2004.
22 Zachary Abuza, “Funding Terrorism in Southeast Asia: The Financial Network of Al Qaeda and Jemah Islamiya,” *NBR Analysis* (14,5), December 2003, especially pp. 60–66.
23 *Agence France Presse (AFP)* Hong Kong, June 18, 2003 in FBIS, *Daily Report—East Asia*, June 19, 2003.
24 *Chairman’s Statement: Tenth Annual ASEAN Regional Forum*, Phnom Penh, June 18, 2003 as published by The ASEAN Secretariat. www.aseansec.org/14845.htm.
25 *ARF June 2003 Statement on Cooperation Against Piracy And Other Threats to Maritime Security* published by The ASEAN Secretariat. www.aseansec.org/14837.htm.
26 Mushahid Ali, “Maritime Security Cooperation the ARF Way,” *IDSS Commentaries* (Singapore: Institute of Defence and Strategic Studies, July 2003).
27 Ibid., p.2.
28 *ARF June 2003 Statement on Cooperative Counter-Terrorist Action on Border Security* published by The ASEAN Secretariat. www.aseansec.org/14835.htm.
29 Lyall Breckon “Beijing Pushes ‘Asia for the Asians’,” *Comparative Connections—An E-Journal of East Asian Bilateral Relations*, July–September 2002, p. 2.
30 Cited in Lyall Breckon, “SARS and a New Security Initiative From China,” *Comparative Connections*, April–June 2003, p. 3.
31 ASEAN+3 Summit Statement, October 8, 2003.
32 *Joint Declaration of the PRC and ASEAN State Leaders*, Bali, October 8, 2003, carried by *Xinhua* (Beijing) in FBIS, *Daily Report—East Asia*, October 10, 2003.
33 For an excellent account of how APEC has evolved to include security matters, see John Ravenhill, “Mission Creep or Mission Impossible? APEC and Security” (a paper presented to the Reassessing Security Cooperation in the Asia-Pacific conference, cosponsored by the Institute for Defence and Strategic Studies, Singapore, and the Mortara Center for International Studies, Georgetown University, Washington, DC, November 20–21, 2003.
34 Ibid., pp. 10–11.
35 Arabinda Acharya, “APEC Summit: Regionalizing the War on Terror,” *IDSS Commentaries*, November 2003; also see Sheldon W. Simon, “President Bush Presses Anti-Terror Agenda in Southeast Asia,” *Comparative Connections*, October–December 2003, pp. 1–2.
36 AFP (Hong Kong) January 10, 2004 and *The Nation* (Bangkok) (Internet Version) January 11, 2004, both in FBIS, *Daily Report—East Asia*, January 12, 2004.
37 Simon Montlake, “Southeast Asia Cooperation Emerges Out Of Bali Attack,” *Christian Science Monitor*, July 14, 2003; Sheldon W. Simon, “Terrorism Perpetrated and Terrorists Apprehended,” *Comparative Connections*, July–September 2003. pp. 7–8; and *Bernama* (Kuala Lumpur) (Internet Version) February 5, 2004 in FBIS, *Daily Report—East Asia*, February 9, 2004.
38 *AFP* (Hong Kong) June 16, 2003 in FBIS, *Daily Report—East Asia*, June 17, 2003; and John McBeth, “ASEAN Summit: Taking the Helm,” *Far Eastern Economic Review*, October 16, 2003, p. 39.

39 *The Jakarta Post* (Internet Version) January 20, 2004, in FBIS, *Daily Report—East Asia*, January 20, 2004; and *Antara* (Jakarta) February 4, 2004, in FBIS, *Daily Report—East Asia*, February 5, 2004.

40 Comments by a former high level Australian transnational crime official, John McFarland, at the "Reassessing Security Cooperation in the Asia-Pacific" meeting, Georgetown University, November 20, 2003.

41 See the discussion in Sheldon W. Simon, "Theater Security Cooperation in the U.S. Pacific Command: An Assessment and Projection," *NBR Analysis*, August 2003.

42 "U.S. Diplomat's Security-Forum Vision," *Far Eastern Economic Review*, February 12, 2004, p. 10.

8 Nationalism and multilateralism in Chinese foreign policy

Implications for Southeast Asia[1]

Christopher R. Hughes

Michael Leifer observed in 1996 that ASEAN would be preoccupied in future years by external security threats as it faces the 'disturbing geopolitical fusion'[2] of the extension of its would-be security community from its Southeast Asian origins to Northeast Asia. Many of these problems are driven partly by the dynamics of the domestic politics of ASEAN's neighbours, whether it be the territorial disputes in the South China Sea, the divided nation issues of Taiwan and the Korean peninsula, or the changing balance of power between the established major states and rising powers such as India and China.

Highest among Leifer's concerns in this respect was the impact of Chinese nationalism on Beijing's regional policy. As Leifer himself puts it:

> The rising power in Asia-Pacific as the twenty-first century approaches is China, whose leaders harbour a historical resentment of national humiliations inflicted on their weakened state by a rapacious West. China's successful post-Cold War economic reforms have provided it with a historic opportunity to realize a sense of national destiny, which many regional states view with apprehension.[3]

It is beyond the competence of this chapter to add anything to what Leifer and others have already said about ASEAN's policy towards China, other than to note that he described this in terms of a wary acceptance of the need to accommodate a rising China, while not taking its leaders' assurances of peaceful and good regional intent at face value.[4] Since 1996, however, there have been some significant developments in Beijing's policy towards ASEAN that deserve further exploration in order to assess whether Leifer was right to be so wary about the impact of Chinese nationalism.

Of particular significance is China's gradual acceptance of a multilateral approach towards Southeast Asia. This has now developed to a degree where Beijing is beginning to set the regional agenda, most recently reflected in the plan for a China–ASEAN Free Trade Area and its accession to the ASEAN Treaty of Amity and Cooperation. With the view of China as an anti-status quo power also being challenged by some outstanding new work on Chinese foreign policy,[5] now is a good time to ask whether Leifer's assumptions about the link between Chinese nationalism and Beijing's foreign policy need to be moderated or developed further.

Nationalism and Chinese foreign policy

For the sake of analytical clarity, this chapter will treat nationalism as an ideology of mass mobilization that is distinct from the much broader policy-related activities of nation building or state building. In this sense nationalism constitutes one of the main dynamics of modern Chinese political culture, 'a kind of thought, a kind of faith, and a kind of power'[6] (to borrow from Sun Yatsen's definition) that is deployed by elites to mobilize the population. Beyond making the specific claim to statehood on behalf of a putative nation that is common to all nationalisms, it can be deployed as a political resource in many forms and for many different purposes. Its constituent themes and aims thus vary considerably over time and place, depending on who is making them and in pursuit of what political strategy.[7]

In assessing the impact of nationalism on China's policy towards Southeast Asia, however, it is important to note that the resurgence that has occurred since 1989 has been accompanied by a growing multilateralism that is not normally associated with a revisionist kind of foreign policy. In the economic field, the origins of this regional multilateralism can be traced as far back as China's 1986 membership of the Asian Development Bank (ADB), followed by its role as a founding member of APEC in 1989. Rather than being set back by the nationalist fervor of the 1990s, it was extended to regional security through China's role in the 1994 establishment of the Asian Regional Forum (ARF). As the division between traditional security and economic stability has become blurred after the Asian Financial Crisis and with the increasing international concern over 'non-traditional security' threats, the trend towards multilateralism has continued with China's active role in the ASEAN+3 since 1997[8] and ASEAN+1.[9] Most recently, Beijing's proposal to develop an ASEAN–China Free Trade Area by 2015 was enshrined in the November 2002 Framework Agreement on Comprehensive Economic Cooperation, and the following year the PRC signed up to the ASEAN Treaty of Amity and Cooperation.[10]

It might be possible to explain this parallel development of nationalism and multipolarity by proposing that the former now has a relatively weak impact on China's foreign policy making. The long historical perspective seems to go against such a conclusion, however, given that the country's leaders have frequently resorted to nationalistic foreign policy issues to promote their domestic agendas. From Sun Yatsen and Chiang Kaishek through Mao Zedong, Deng Xiaoping and Jiang Zemin, all of China's leaders have mobilized the population at times by stressing their nation's glorious cultural tradition, large population and territory as reasons for the country to play a special international role. Within the Chinese Communist Party (CCP) tradition, Mao used the 1958

Taiwan Strait Crisis and the 1959 Sino-Indian border conflict to mobilize the population behind the Great Leap Forward and then divert attention away from its failure. Mao also believed that tension over the former should be maintained indefinitely as 'a means of educating all the peoples of the world, first of all the Chinese people'.[11] When Deng Xiaoping faced a crisis of legitimacy after the 1979 'Beijing Spring', he attempted to delegitimate dissidents by linking them with the evil machinations of external powers and then focused attention on the Taiwan problem by elevating national unification to the status of one of the three main tasks to be completed in the 1980s.[12] The post-1989 leadership also attempted to rebuild the legitimacy of the CCP as the party of national salvation through a patriotic education campaign that stimulated anti-American and anti-Japanese sentiments and accused the democracy movement of being supported by external powers. Deng himself linked international affairs with domestic nationalism at this time when he called on the country to prepare to resist invaders,[13] portraying a post-Cold War order in which China would be the victim of aggression as the prospect of war between the superpowers was replaced by conflicts between the North and the South and a war against socialism.[14]

Events in the 1990s also show that China's political elite is not always able to control the mass movements that are stimulated by their deployment of nationalism, which is why it is often referred to as a 'double-edged sword' in Chinese texts. From the 1919 May 4 Movement, through the civil war and up to 1989, revolutionaries and dissidents alike have been able to use nationalism to delegitimate the ruling elite. Under the policy of 'reform and opening' since the late 1970s, this dynamic has been increasingly hard to manipulate as society has become more pluralistic and aware of international affairs. At times of heightened tension, such as the 1995-96 Taiwan crisis and the 1999 Belgrade incident, the Cox Report and the growing use of military intervention by the United States and some of its allies in Iraq and the Balkans, the leadership appears to have faced a real crisis of legitimacy.

The same elite–popular dynamic of nationalist politics can be seen occurring with respect to Southeast Asia. When news of atrocities against the ethnic Chinese community in Indonesia during the fall of the Suharto regime spread via the Internet, the government eventually gave in to demands for Beijing to take strong measures and departed from its policy of non-interference by voicing its concern.[15] Although it is true that the South China Sea disputes have not been used either by the elite or popular nationalists to mobilize the crowds in Chinese cities, even those who take an optimistic view of Beijing's tentative movement towards acceptance of a code of conduct do not rule out that this could mask the postponement of a revisionist agenda to threaten the international status quo once China has the military capability to do so.[16] Similarly, given that acceptance of the 'one-China principle' by ASEAN was made the condition for the deepening of China's multilateralism in Southeast Asia, the Taiwan issue is certainly the rule that governs Beijing's behaviour in the region rather than the exception that it might appear to be when viewed from a broader perspective.

Given the enduring nature of the problems of the South China Sea and Taiwan, the sensitive position of the ethnic Chinese communities in Southeast Asia, and the continuing uncertainty of China's domestic politics, it is hard to sustain the view that Beijing's multilateralism in Southeast Asia can be entirely separated from the politics of Chinese nationalism. Indeed, some of these problems may become even more complex for the Beijing leadership to handle as multilateralism develops. Economic integration under the China–ASEAN Free Trade area, for example, is creating a different kind of pressure to depart from its established policy of non-interference in the internal affairs of Southeast Asian states, as the possibility is now raised of using the ethnic Chinese in the region as an economic, political and cultural interface between China and ASEAN.[17] A more detailed exploration of the relationship between multilateralism and nationalism thus seems to be required before Leifer's scepticism can be allayed.

Nationalism and multipolarity

An alternative way of interpreting the relationship between Chinese nationalism and Beijing's multilateralism in Southeast Asia is to view the latter as effectively strengthening China's presence in the region in the face of competition from the United States and Japan. Such a view is proposed by Haacke, who interprets Beijing's policy as a way of promoting the Chinese ideal of a post-Cold War multipolar international order.[18] This is also problematic, however, given that there has been a significant decline in Chinese discussions of multipolarity of late,[19] just when Beijing's multilateralism has been accelerating and deepening.

China's multipolarity discourse, moreover, actually appears somewhat later than Beijing's practice of regional multilateralism. Although Chinese analysts trace the origins of multipolarity to Mao Zedong's Theory of the Three Worlds, given that the term 'multipolarity' (*duojihua*) took on its current post-Cold War meaning only after Deng Xiaoping advocated it in a speech of March 1990,[20] this view should be treated as a retrospective imposition on the past. It was only after Deng deployed the term in 1990 that it was able to become a formal element of the Party line, included in the work report presented by General Secretary Jiang Zemin to the 14th CCP Congress in October 1992. The inclusion of Deng's speech in the third volume of his *Selected Works*, published in 1993, also made it the key reference point for policy-makers and academics concerned with analysing the foreign policy crises of the late 1990s. Given that China joined the ADB in 1986 and APEC in 1989 and that Jiang Zemin pointed out in his 1992 work report that it had already established close relationships with 77 groups of states (*qishiqi guo jituan*), it is doubtful whether multilateralism can be seen as merely a product of multipolarity.

The vital clue to the relationship of multilateralism with nationalism lies in the way that the traditional form of power balancing though alliances is entirely absent from Chinese discussions of multipolarity. This can be seen when Chinese commentators claim that poles are centres of international power that are not necessarily alliances and do not need to have 'subsidiary' states or engage in adversarial power politics in order to influence the world.[21] The closest that academics and official policy statements have come to recommending anything like an alliance system since the end of the Cold War is to call for the formation of 'strategic partnerships', the paradigm for which was developed with the 'strategic partnership of equality, mutual confidence and mutual co-ordination toward the 21st century'[22] established with Moscow and extended to various states and organizations since then, including ASEAN in October 2003.[23] These, however, explicitly state that such partnerships are not to be directed against any third-party state. Moreover, the formula has even been extended to China's relations with the United States. Multipolarity, therefore, cannot be seen as power balancing in the sense of China's history of statecraft stretching from *Sun Zi* to Mao's 'leaning to one side' and playing the strategic triangle, the European tradition from Renaissance Italy to the post-Westphalian settlement in Europe, or contemporary American neo-realism. Chinese academics are fully aware of this crucial distinction of the post-Cold War version of multipolarity, when they distinguish it from older versions of multipolarity that are based on the balance of power.[24]

One way to explain this lack of power balancing in China's current version of multipolarity is to point out that nearly all its allies happen to be weak and failing states, such as North Korea, Myanmar and Pakistan. Even those commentators who want to present China as trying to balance US power have to admit that none of these states can really be considered to be 'allies' operating in a balance against the United States.[25] Moreover, such a view is supported by Chinese analysts of the international situation, who point out that even a 'united front' with India and Russia would be woefully insufficient to balance US power.[26] Yet this realization of the limitations for China to engage in power balancing does not explain why multipolarity should play such a prominent role in Chinese discussions of foreign policy and why it should have been articulated so extensively since 1990.

To understand this, it is necessary to view multipolarity as an essentially domestic discourse that is designed primarily to soothe nationalist pressures, rather than as a foreign policy prescription. In this respect Johnston rightly points out how multipolarity discourse has been used for a whole range of political strategies, ranging from fear-mongering by 'conservatives' to its deployment by moderate voices trying to head off 'hard liners who believe that the unipolar moment requires more vigorous balancing against the United States'.[27] Even Deng Xiaoping was more concerned about maintaining the domestic reform programme than about providing positive advice for foreign policy making when he made his March 1990 speech, two-thirds of which is concerned with explaining that China has to have more rapid domestic economic development if it is to become a pole in the new world order. This promise that economic development would make China a pole in the new world order can be understood as subsidiary to his more pressing concern of keeping the reform process on track. It is an argument that reached its full form and final political victory when Deng made his Southern Tour speeches in the winter of 1992. When Jiang Zemin presented multipolarity to the 14th Party Congress the following year, it was thus part of a much larger work report that enshrined the consolidation of Deng's market-orientated reforms.

In the context of China's domestic debates, therefore, the discusson of multipolarity in the 1990s can be seen as an attempt to maintain Deng's line of not taking a leading role in international affairs. This is why it is defined in the essentially negative terms of anything that is opposed to the unipolarity ascribed to the United States, while China itself is said to be able to do little in terms of balancing other than developing its economy and upholding Deng's line of 'not taking the lead' (bu dang tou). In the meantime historical forces will push the world towards an increasing number of poles of power, expanding to include not just China, the United States and Russia but also the Third World, Western Europe, Canada, Australia, Japan, India and the EU. Beijing will not need to do much while such states and blocs oppose the attempt of the US to consolidate its economic and technological superiority. Comfort can also be taken from the observation that the limits of American power have been revealed by the crumbling of sanctions on China and the over-extension of its forces in the Balkans and Iraq.[28]

Multilateralism as power balancing

Given the primary domestic purpose of multipolarity discourse, it is quite feasible to dismiss its relevance to Beijing's multilateralism, let alone any kind of challenge to the international status quo. This is especially true for Southeast Asia, where Deng never listed ASEAN as a pole. It could certainly qualify as one, given that his original list of the United States, China and the Soviet Union has since been expanded to include not only large states such as India and Brazil but also a bloc (*jituan*) such as the EU.[29] It is not hard to fathom the reason for this exclusion of ASEAN from multipolarity discourse, because treating it as a pole would detract from the possibility of using regionalism as an alternative method for projecting China's international influence when faced by the rise of post-Cold War US supremacy.

Johnston's remark that 'moderate' commentators on international relations in China advocate the use of multilateralism to constrain US behaviour thus deserves more attention than he gives it. This is because even those figures who argue for caution in standing up to the United States, and counsel against the formation of alliances and 'united fronts', are still very clear that war cannot be avoided if there is a threat to core national interests, such as an invasion of Chinese territory or the movement of Taiwan towards independence.[30] Moreover, they cannot ignore the concerns of more hard-line nationalists over the possibility that the development of the US doctrine of humanitarian intervention, or 'human rights above state rights', poses a direct threat to China's national national unity by encouraging independence movements in Tibet and Xinjiang.

Even Lee Teng'hui's 'two states theory' has been portrayed as an attempt to use the 'Kosovo effect' to Taiwan's advantage. This encouragement of secessionist sentiment is also seen as having important implications for China's regional policy, as Pakistan is perceived to have been encouraged by the new US doctrine to try to gain Nato support for the Kashmir Muslims as part of its conflict with India, and the maritime clash between North and South Korea had been caused by the increased confidence of the latter. Meanwhile the return of the US military presence in Southeast Asia, accompanied by the strengthening of Washington's alliance with Japan and its intervention in Central Asia, is seen as part of an attempt to build a firewall around China.[31]

To understand why multilateralism is used to defend China against such threats, it is necessary to go back to the way in which it developed out of Deng Xiaoping's failure to play the balance of power. This began just as he was consolidating his leadership position in December 1978, when Washington failed to support the Chinese attack on Vietnam and then went on to continue to guarantee the security of Taiwan by passing the Taiwan Relations Act. It was following this that the PRC formally announced that it had renounced alliances in favour of a policy of diplomatic self-reliance in 1982. When Mikhail Gorbachev came to power in Moscow in 1985, Deng continued to express his aversion to alliances when he warned that China was sufficiently aware of its own limits not to try to play the strategic triangle.[32] It was in the following year that the PRC began to move down its path towards regional multilateralism by joining the ADB. It was also during the 1980s that Deng began to voice his belief that the developing states of the South were emerging as an international force for peace and stability that would work on China's behalf, without China having to take a leading role.

During the 1980s, regional multilateralism was thus gradually replacing alliances and alignments as a way to enhance China's regional influence and promote its national interests without confronting the superpowers, and China's natural support was to come from the developing world. With the foreign policy crises of the 1990s, this movement began to be expressed in a dilemma presented by the task of protecting China's core national interests in somewhat nebulous descriptions of policy towards the United States, such as 'some struggle, some peace; struggle but do not break' (*you dou you he, dou er by po*). What this means is that a balance has to be struck between facilitating a stable and peaceful relationship with the United States on the one hand, to ensure that US policy continues to serve China's domestic and foreign policies of modernization and national unification, while Washington also needs to be warned against deploying the methods it used to destroy the Soviet Union at the same time. Central to this policy is the strategic art of 'making people yield without fighting' (*bu zhan er qu ren zhi bing*), which can foil the US and Western plans to contain China, while still maintaining the strategic partnership for the twenty-first century with the United States so long as this serves the national interest.[33]

Because Beijing's use of alliances as part of this formula for protecting the national interest would only lead to a new Cold War, and possibly even a hot war, the only alternative for balancing US power is to reduce bilateral frictions and raise China's status in the international mainstream by winning the support of the majority of states for the international norms that it advocates. In this way Beijing can manage China's relations with the superpower and work towards building the rules of a 'new international order' through multilateral security dialogue and with the cooperation of organizations such as the ARF.[34] This policy orientation has direct implications for regional policy because it is premised not only on the acknowledgement that China is an economically and technologically backward country that is unable to confront the United States and has a natural alignment with the South, but also on the realization that many of China's neighbouring states are suspicious of its intentions.[35] The search for a way to protect core national interests thus provides a strong impetus for Beijing to accelerate its regional multilateralism.

It is within this context that the movement that had already been advanced by membership of the ARF in 1994 was accelerated with the establishment of the ARF+3 in 1997 and premier Zhu Rongji's first proposal for an ASEAN–China free trade agreement at the ASEAN+China meeting in November 2000. The immediate impetus for these developments was to respond to the Asian Financial Crisis and to allay regional concerns over the impact of China's imminent WTO membership. Yet they also arose out of an acute sensitivity towards the need to maintain relations with as many states as possible in order to constrain US power under a global system defined by the struggle between 'one superpower, many great powers'.

Multilateralism after 9/11

While multipolarity is an essentially empty concept for the making of foreign policy, then, regional multilateralism presents an effective way to protect China's core national interests. This trend has been strengthened by developments since the terrorist attacks of September 11, 2001 on the United States (the '9/11 Incident'). Since then China has continued to shy away from directly confronting the United States over issues outside its immediate vicinity, such as the US-led invasion of Iraq. Moreover, ASEAN is still not defined as a 'pole' of international power, and its commentators continue to hope that the EU will be able to stand up to an American hegemony that has not gone into the decline that was expected in the early 1990s.[36] Meanwhile, the use of regional policy as a way to protect China's core national interests from the expansion of US power has continued to take an increasingly prominent position in Beijing's diplomacy. Knowing that cooperation with Japan remains tightly constrained and that regional cooperation in Northeast Asia has stalled, Southeast Asia is presented as the region where political breakthroughs are most likely to be made on the back of economic integration. The economic slowdown in the US, combined with the continuing post-1997 malaise of the Southeast Asian economies, has also provided the conditions for ASEAN to adopt a more positive attitude towards the proposal for a free trade agreement with China that had been coolly received in the region only the previous year.[37]

In some respects the conditions for China's multilateralism in Southeast Asia have also been partly put in place by the shift in Washington's priorities away from normative issues of human rights and trade in favour of the War on Terror. In this climate, Beijing's attempt to shape the rules of international behaviour appear to be somewhat less of an open challenge to US power than did the coalition of Southern states that formed around a communitarian interpretation of human rights standards under the Bangkok Declaration in 1993,[38] or the debate on 'Asian values' triggered by some of the ASEAN leaders. In Chinese foreign policy thinking, this shifting in the ranking of international norms is reflected in the way in which concerns that once arose over the Clinton administration's increasing tendency towards humanitarian intervention have now largely been suppressed in favour of the argument that a new international ethics and culture of 'peace and righteousness' has developed. Even comparatively weak states are able to increase their power by upholding such standards because they are based on opposition to invasion, racism and terrorism. Meanwhile, a 'democratization' of international politics is said to be taking place as the states of the South find their voice, a trend to which the PRC is urged to pay great attention as the biggest developing state.[39]

That the move towards multilateralism in Southeast Asia is designed to protect China's core national interests can also be seen in the way in which Beijing deploys what it calls the 'New Security Concept' in the region. The genesis of this idea is held to have had close links with the region as Chinese scholars trace its key elements back to the principles contained in the report delivered by China to the 1996 ARF Inter-Sessional Support Group on Confidence-Building Measures in Tokyo, when the PRC is said to have begun to accept that engaging with multilateral security organizations, formal dialogues and track-two dialogues are all ways to protect national security. Such is the origin of the formula that was presented in full as the New Security Concept to the ARF Foreign Minister's conference at Bandar Seri Bagawan on 31 July 2002.[40]

Although the meaning of the New Security Concept remains nebulous, like the ambivalent foreign policy formulae that were floated at the end of the 1990s, it is not hard to see that the intention behind it is to protect China's core national interests from the hegemonic power of any other state, be it the United States, Japan or India.[41] In evaluating the nature of China's multilateralism in Southeast Asia, it is important to emphasize how the New Security Concept also manages to encapsulate a fairly realist, state-centric understanding of multilateralism. Drifte, for example, summarizes the main themes of the 1996 document as being resistance against the external imposition of values and ideologies, the splitting of China, indiscriminate sanctions against China on international issues, conflicts and wars in some countries in the region, encroachments on China's sovereignty, and defense of maritime rights and interests.[42] There are also a number of essentially neo-realist elements in Alagappa's distillation of the document, which include pursuit of a balance among the major powers in Asia, building up military strength, along with a good-neighbour policy with all Asian neighbours, the mobilization of international support for economic modernization, and the projection of China as an indispensable and responsible regional player.[43]

In the post-9/11 climate of non-traditional security threats, Chinese commentators also stress that the inclusion of the principle of 'equality' in the New Security Concept amounts to ruling out the use of such threats by 'powerful states' as an excuse to interfere in the domestic affairs of weaker states. It is further added that the formula pays little attention to the role of non-state actors. Underlying the concept there is thus said to be a fundamental difference between developed and developing states over the nature of the new security agenda: while the developed more readily emphasize the impact of 'non-traditional security' threats such as environmental problems or non-state referent objects, such as human health and welfare and the global ecology, such issues are seen by the developing to be more of a threat to their own survival as states.[44]

It is, of course, no coincidence that this emphasis on state sovereignty in the New Security Concept is fully in harmony with ASEAN's principles, as enshrined in the Treaty of Amity and Cooperation to which China has now signed up. While it has been argued that the New Security Concept has little appeal in the Asia Pacific region,[45] this is somewhat beside the point given that it has been devised in a way that makes it compatible with the state-centric principles so dear to ASEAN. In this respect, China and the ASEAN states share the view that there need be no direct clash between multilateralism, maintaining statehood, and dealing with transnational threats such as terrorism. This is just as true of Beijing's other regional initiatives as it is of its policy towards Southeast Asia. The participating states of the Shanghai Five/SCO have thus signed numerous agreements on reducing the military presence in the border areas, and combating terrorism, splittism and extremism. These have allowed the SCO to defend the national interests of its members by joining the regional and global struggle against terrorism, and to promote regional economic cooperation, while not antagonizing the United States by appearing to be the formation of an alliance or opposition to any third-party state.

It would be a mistake, however, to assume that this tactical unwillingness to engage in alliance politics is the same as the absence of a strategic goal to establish regional or even global hegemony, as Johnston infers.[46] It is true that we do not find Chinese policy makers or academics talking directly about China playing an active role in balancing US power in a way that can be remotely compared with the behaviour of the Soviet Union in the Cold War, and neither is China building bilateral alliances with regional powers. However, to equate this lack of alliance systems with the absence of a desire to enhance China's international influence can only be sustained in isolation from the larger picture of Beijing's foreign policy thinking, where the hole left in multipolarity by the absence of power balancing is filled by the convergence of developing states around a state-centric version of multilateralism that serves its own national interests well.

China and ASEAN in the extra-regional context

At the global level it is already possible to see some inklings of the ways in which China is using its relationship with ASEAN to develop a counterweight to US power. Witness, for example, the 2004 agreement for their respective representatives to the UN to engage in regular consultations, their joint position that the UN should play a leading role in the reconstruction of Iraq, and the statement of support for China's role in working towards a resolution of the North Korean nuclear weapons issue.[47] Moreover, while the furthest that multipolarity discourse has been able to impinge on the China–ASEAN relationship has been in the form of the joint declaration on a strategic partnership for peace and prosperity, both sides have expressed the hope that the ASEAN+3 mechanism can lead to the development of an 'East Asian community'.[48]

Such balancing of US power remains light so long as China is unable to treat ASEAN or the ASEAN+3 explicitly as a 'pole' of global power. This needs to be judged in light of the fact that Beijing has taken all the most recent significant initiatives leading to regional integration, however, with ASEAN sometimes grudgingly accepting this as its relative economic power has declined since 1997. If Beijing expressed this development in terms of multipolarity, this would of course set alarm bells ringing in Washington about its policy in Southeast Asia, which is already being described as 'aggressive'.[49] Moreover, if China projected its economic power too far and too fast, it would do little to allay the fears that it acknowledges exist in the the capitals of the region, where the US presence is still valued as a force for external security.[50] China has thus gone to great lengths to reassure ASEAN that it will be the major driving force behind the regional project. In this respect, Leifer is still correct in concluding that the corporate identity of ASEAN within the wider changing international dispensation in Asia endures primarily 'because it is in the interest of China, in particular with Russian and Indian support, to support the sustained diplomatic centrality of ASEAN within the ARF as a way of promoting greater multi-polarity, defined with reference to the post-Cold War standing of the United States'.[51]

While China's use of multilateralism to expand its international influence thus faces the constraints of the extra-ASEAN balance of power, its recent initiatives show how its leaders have already departed substantially from Deng's principle of not taking a lead in relations with the developing world. Multilateralism is a much safer way to do this than traditional power balancing through alliances against a far more powerful United States. While the changing priorities of international society since the 9/11 Incident have provided new opportunities for a convergence with the ASEAN states, the same can be said of the broader processes of globalization which feature so much in the agreements between ASEAN and China.

From this perspective, rather than seeing globalization as displacing a declining multipolarity discourse,[52] it is probably more accurate to understand it as being brought into Chinese foreign policy rhetoric to complement multilateralism in articulating the kind of power balancing that multipolarity has never been able to provide. When President Jiang Zemin described the world situation as characterized by 'political multipolarity, economic globalization' in his work report to the 16th Party Congress in November 2002, he was thus juxtaposing the two discourses in a way that makes them compatible with the pursuit of China's national interest.[53] From Jiang's point of view, the transnational problems of economic integration, the environment, international terrorism and arms proliferation that are addressed jointly by ASEAN and China might be forcing relations between states to be characterized by 'constructiveness' 'cooperation' and 'partnership', but neither side confuses this with the idea that globalization weakens the power of authoritarian states that is so popular in American foreign policy thinking. Instead, the Chinese attitude to globalization is encapsulated in Jiang's theory of the 'Three Represents', a kind of developmental techno-nationalism that offers the prospect of 'leap-frogging' the advanced industrial economies and balancing the danger that the United States might use its economic power to gain political control over the world. In fact, if Mao's Three Worlds Theory is relevant in the global era, so far as China's Ministry of Information Industry (MII) and the CCP's Central Policy Research Office are concerned it is in the sense of a struggle against the 'information hegemony state' to assert its control over the 'information sovereign states' of Japan and Europe and the 'information colonial and semi-colonial states' of the South.[54]

This challenge to the view of globalization promoted by much American foreign policy rhetoric and academic literature of a 'hyperglobalist' inclination is very much in sympathy with views of state sovereignty that are dominant in the ASEAN model of regionalism. It is a version of globalization that has arisen out of a reaction to events such as the decision of the G7 to reduce the debts of the world's poorest states on condition that they should meet Western human rights standards, the establishment of the International Criminal Court and the arrest of General Pinochet in London, and the promotion of a doctrine of 'human rights before sovereignty' as a way to justify military intervention around the world that has not been legitimated by the UN Security Council.[55] On closer analysis, then, globalization supports multilateralism in playing the power-balancing role that China's version of multipolarity is unable to perform.

Conclusion

Leifer's scepticism towards the ARF and his concerns over the rise of Chinese power derive from his English School belief that it is folly to ignore the realities of power balancing in international relations. There is no need to indulge in hawkish visions of China as a revisionist power in pursuit of a new-sinocentric order in order to do justice to the diplomatic realities and political context which determine how Beijing uses multilateralism to protect and promote interests that are defined in the context of a highly nationalistic political culture. An increasingly wealthy China already represents the reality that the balance of power has changed, and that it makes little sense to talk of challenging a 'status quo' that has already ceased to exist (if it ever did exist). From this perspective, rather than being an anti-status quo power, China has been socialized into the realism of international society all too well insofar as its leaders accept that working through multilateral regional organizations is a good way to engage in the power balancing that makes diplomacy possible.

Maintaining a stable balance of power, however, is inevitably complicated by the realities of China's economic growth. Chinese observers who believe that China's GDP could overtake that of the US around 2017 continue to make reassuring noises that can engage those calling for more defiance against the United States by restating Deng Xiaoping's optimistic view that their country's rise to power will lead not only to multipolarity, but also to the eradication of war when accompanied by the development of the EU and the Third World. But they are also aware that economic strength alone is not enough to guarantee that a state becomes a pole. What is important is comprehensive national power, as shown by the ability of the Soviet Union to balance the much wealthier US in the Cold War and the continuing inability of an economically powerful Japan to play a political role.[56] Russia also stands out as an example of the limits of power balancing through the formation of peaceful alliances, given Moscow's failure to halt the Nato campaign against Yugoslavia and the eastward expansion of Nato and its acceptance of Washington's renunciation of the ABM (Anti-Ballistic Missile) Treaty. The roots of this weakness are attributed to the failure to develop national power, the overestimation of one's own importance, weakening oneself through domestic political disunity and daring to take a lead. In short, China has to avoid becoming another Russia by not over-estimating the extent of its comprehensive national power when using multipolarity to promote its own interests.[57]

The Asian Financial Crisis and the War on Terror have, however, strengthened the argument that China has the opportunity to avoid Russia's fate by extending its influence through a multilateralism that does not directly challenge the United States or ruffle the feathers of its neighbours. Similarly, the increasing deployment of the concept of globalization indicates not so much a movement away from the state-centric focus of Chinese foreign policy thinking, as a rearticulation of power balancing that is derived from an essentially nationalistic discourse.

The resulting deployment of regional multilateralism to expand Chinese influence in the context of US global preponderance has particularly important implications for China's relations with ASEAN. In relation to China's claims in the South China Sea, the need to reassure the Southeast Asian states with which it hopes to work to increase its regional influence mitigates against deploying such an issue to enhance the CCP's claims to be the party of national salvation, in the way that relations with Taiwan, Japan and the United States are used in domestic politics. In this respect, maintaining Deng Xiaoping's principle of shelving the issue of sovereignty over such disputes is seen not only as a way to avoid international conflict but also as a method for soothing the heated popular emotions over historical issues that exist in China and its neighbours.[58] Yet, so long as China's political culture remains highly nationalistic, it will continue to constrain the country's leaders from taking multilateralism so far that it might appear to be offering a compromise to other states on an issue that can be defined as a core national interest. This is even more so in the case of Taiwan.

The South China Sea disputes thus remain unresolved, while ASEAN's acceptance that Taiwan is a part of China is the fundamental principle on which China's relationship with ASEAN has been established. Moreover, economic integration can add a new complexity to old nationalistic problems. Maintaining a hands-off policy towards the ethnic Chinese populations of Southeast Asia, for example, is already becoming more complex as their economic role offers a tempting resource for expanding China's influence in the region under multilateralism, which could resurrect questions over their loyalty and protection both inside China itself and in their countries of residence.

In conclusion it could be said that Michael Leifer was right to be highly critical of the proposal that the extension of the ASEAN model of peace-making beyond Southeast Asia could address core issues of regional security.[59] Moreover, as China's growing economic power enables Beijing to take more of a lead in setting the agenda in Southeast Asia, the limits of its influence will continue to be defined more by the external balance of power than by the states of the region themselves, bearing out Leifer's observation that the structural problem of the ARF 'is that its viability seems to depend on the prior existence of a stable balance, but it is not really in a position to create it'.[60] As for the impact of Chinese nationalism, it has been argued above that Beijing's multilateral turn does not represent a departure from its state-centric understanding of international relations or a dilution of the nationalistic issues that are so vital to the legitimacy of its leaders. The question remains, therefore, as to what China's political culture will make of the logic of international anarchy in Southeast Asia as its economic power continues to grow.

Notes

1 Paper delivered to conference on 'The Unending Search for Regional Order: Essays in Memory of Michael Leifer', hosted by the Asia Research Centre of the LSE and IDSS, 13–14 May 2004, Singapore.

2 Michael Leifer, *The ASEAN Regional Forum* (Adelphi Paper, IISS, London, 1996) pp. 17, 48; 'The ASEAN Peace Process: A Category Mistake', *The Pacific Review*, 12:1, 1999, p. 34.

3 Leifer (1996), p. 54.

4 Leifer (1996), p. 54.

5 The most outstanding example of this is Alastair Iain Johnston's thoroughly researched article, 'Is China a Status Quo Power?' *International Security*, 27:4 (Spring 2003), pp. 5–56.
6 Sun Yatsen, *Sanmin zhuyi* (*Three Principles of the People*), (Taibei: Da Zhongguo tushu youxian gongci, 1969), p. 1.
7 For a general overview see Yongnian Zheng, *Discovering Chinese Nationalism in China: Modernization, Identity and International Relations* (Cambridge: Cambridge University Press, 1999); Suisheng Zhao, 'Chinese Intellectuals' Quest for National Greatness and Nationalistic Writing in the 1990s', *China Quarterly*, 152 (December 1997), 725–45; Joseph Fewsmith, *China Since Tiananmen: The Politics of Transition*, Cambridge: Cambridge University Press, 2001, esp. pp. 132–220. For the range of debate see the texts covered by Johnston, and also Christopher R. Hughes, 'Interpreting Chinese Nationalist Texts: A Poststructuralist Approach', *Journal of Contemporary China*, 2005:14(3), May, pp. 57–77.
8 ASEAN+China, Japan, ROK.
9 ASEAN+China.
10 For an overview of these developments see Jürgen Haacke, 'Seeking Influence: China's Diplomacy Toward ASEAN After the Asian Crisis', *Asian Perspective*, 26:4, 2002, pp. 13–52.
11 'Record of Conversation of Com. Mao on 2 October at the Meeting with the Six Delegations of Socialist Countries', Vladislav M. Zubok, Constantin Pleshakov, *Inside the Kremlin's Cold War. From Stalin to Khrushchev* (Cambridge, MA: Harvard University Press, 1996), p. 226, and in Zubok, 'The Khrushchev–Mao Conversations, 31 July–3 August 1958 and 2 October 1959'.
12 See Deng Xiaoping's March 1979 speech, 'Uphold the Four Cardinal Principles', *Selected Works of Deng Xiaoping (1975–1982)*, (Beijing: Foreign Languages Press, 1984), pp. 166–191, and 'The Present Situation and the Tasks Before Us', *Selected Works*, pp. 224–258.
13 Deng Xiaoping, 'Gaige kaifang zhengce winding, zhongguo da you xiwang' ('The Policy of Reform and Opening is Stable, China Has Great Hope', *Deng Xiaoping wenxuan* (*Selected Works of Deng Xiaoping*), Vol. 3 (Beijing: Renmin chubanshe, 1993), pp. 315–321.
14 Deng Xiaoping, 'Jianchi shehui zhuyi, fangzhi heping yanbian' ('Uphold Socialism, Prevent Peaceful Evolution'), *Deng Xiaoping wenxuan,* Vol. 3 (Beijing: Renmin chubanshe, 1993), pp. 344–346.
15 Christopher Hughes, 'Nationalism in Chinese Cyberspace', *Cambridge Review of International Affairs*, Spring/Summer 2000, vol. 13, no. 2, pp. 195–209.
16 Johnston, pp. 27–28.
17 Deng Shichao, 'Zhongguo-dongmeng ziyou maoyi qu dui dongnanya huaren zhengzhi de yingxiang shixi' ('Preliminary Analysis of the Impact of the China–ASEAN Free Trade Area on the Overseas Chinese in Southeast Asia'), *Dongya yanjiu* (*Southeast Asian Studies*), 2003:3, pp. 64–68.
18 Jürgen Haacke, 'China's Diplomacy Toward ASEAN After the Asian Crisis', *Asian Perspective* 26:4, 2002: 13–52.
19 Johnston, p. 34.
20 'Guoji xingxi he jingji wenti', *Deng Xiaoping wenxuan*, Vol. 3, pp. 353–356.
21 Qiao Mu, 'Duojihua qushi bu hui gaibian' ('The Trend Towards Multipolarity Cannot Change'), *Dangdai yatai* (*Contemporary Asia Pacific*), 2002:6, p. 12.
22 'Joint Statement by the PRC and the Russian Federation', *Beijing Review*, Vol. 39, No. 20, May 13–19, pp 6–8, 1996.
23 Joint Declaration of the Heads of State/Government of the Association of Southeast Asian Nations and the People's Republic of China (8 October 2003, Bali). Online. URL at: http://www.aseansec.org/15265.htm (consulted 30 June 2004).

24 Qiao Mu, p. 12.
25 Denny Roy, 'China's Reaction to American Predominance', *Survival* 45:3 (Autumn 2003), pp. 57–78.
26 Chu Shulong and Wang Zaibang, 'Guanyu guoji xingshi he wo dui wai zhanlue ruogan da wenti si kao' ('Thoughts on Major Problems Related to the International Situation and Our Foreign Strategy'), *Xiandai guoji guanxi* (*Contemporary International Relations*), 1999, no. 8, pp. 1–3. Yan Xuetong, 'Guoji huanjing ji waijiao sikao' ('Considerations on the International Environment and Foreign Relations'), *Xiandai guoji guanxi*, 1999:8, p. 11.
27 Johnston, p. 33.
28 Chu Shulong and Wang Zaibang, pp. 1–3. Qiao Mu (op. cit.).
29 Qiao Mu, pp. 12–13.
30 Chu Shulong and Wang Zaibang, p. 6. Yan Xuetong, p. 11.
31 Chu Shulong and Wang Zaibang, p. 5.
32 Deng Xiaoping, 'Zai jun wei kuoda huiyi shang de jiang hua' ('Talk to the Central Military Commission'), *Deng Xiaoping wenxuan*, Vol. 3, pp. 126–129.
33 Chu and Wang, p. 6.
34 Yan Xuetong, p. 11
35 Chu Shulong and Wang Zaibang, p. 6.
36 Qiao Mu, pp. 10–13.
37 Deng Shichao, 'Zhongguo-dongmeng ziyou maoyi qu dui dongnanya huaren zhengzhi de yingxiang shixi' ('Preliminary Analysis of the Impact of the China–ASEAN Free Trade Area on the Overseas Chinese in Southeast Asia'), *Dongya yanjiu* (*Southeast Asian Studies*), 2003:3, p. 65.
38 'Report of the Regional Meeting for Asia of the World Conference on Human Rights, Bangkok, 29 March–2 April 1993' (United Nations General Assembly, A/CONF.157/ASRM/8, 7 April 1993).
39 Qiao Mu, p. 12.
40 Lu Zhongwei (ed.), *Fei chuantong anquan lun* (*On Non-Traditional Security*), (Beijing: Shishi chubanshe), 2003, p. 56.
41 For a Chinese analysis of India's growing influence and intentions in Southeast Asia see Lu Guangsheng, 'Shixi 21 shiji chu yindu de dongnanya zhanlue', *Nanyang wenti yanjiu* (*Southeast Asian Affairs*), 2003:1, pp. 38–44.
42 Reinhardt Drifte, *Japan's Security Relations with China Since 1989* (London: Routledge, 2003), p. 36.
43 Alagappa, 'Systemic Change, Security and Governance in the Asia Pacific', in Chang Heng Chee (ed.), *The New Asia-Pacific Order* (Singapore: Institute for Southeast Asian Studies, 1997), pp. 70–72, cited in Drifte, p. 36.
44 Lu, p. 57.
45 Johnston, p. 40. It might be the case that Johnston is able to draw his conclusion regarding the lack of positive reception of the New Security Concept only because he fails to address Southeast Asia, an oversight that recurs with most of the points he discusses in his article.
46 Johnston, p. 38.
47 *ASEAN China Foreign Ministers' Informal Meeting Joint Press Release,* 21 June 2004, Qingdao, China. Online: URL at: http://www.aseansec.org/16167.htm. Consulted 30 June 2004.
48 Joint Declaration of the Heads of State/Government of the Association of Southeast Asian Nations and the People's Republic of China (8 October 2003, Bali). Online: URL at http://www.aseansec.org/15265.htm (consulted 30 June 2004).
49 Assistant Secretary of State James Kelly described China's policy towards ASEAN as 'challenging the status quo aggressively' in testimony to the House Committee on

International Relations, 2 June 2004. Online: URL at http://wwwc.house.gov/international_relations/108/kel060204.htm (consulted 4 July 2004).

50 Haacke, p. 36.

51 Leifer, 'The ASEAN peace process: a category mistake', *The Pacific Review*, 12:1 (1999), p. 34.

52 Johnston, p. 56.

53 'Full Text of Jiang Zemin's Report at 16th Party Congress', Online: URL at www:16congress.org.cn/English/features/49007.htm

54 Christopher R. Hughes, 'ICTs and International Security', in Christopher R. Hughes and Gudrun Wacker (eds), *China and the Internet: Politics of the Digital Leap Forward* (New York: RoutledgeCurzon, 2003), p. 141.

55 Chu Shulong and Wang Zaibang, p. 4; Yan Xuetong, pp. 7–11.

56 Qiao Mu, p. 13.

57 Xu Xhixin, 'Pulimakefu duojihua waijiao pingxi' ('Critical Analysis of Primakov's Multipolar Diplomacy'), *Dong ou zhongya yanjiu* (*Eastern Europe and Central Asian Research*), 2002:1, pp. 33–37.

58 Cui Xinjie, 'Lingtu zhengduan de zhanlue sixiang yu shijian' ('Thought and Practice on Territorial Disputes') in Gong Li (ed.) *Deng Xiaoping de waijiao sixiang yu shijian* (*Deng Xiaoping's Foreign Policy Thinking and Practice*), Heilongjiang jiaoyu chubanshe, 1996, p. 256.

59 Leifer (1999), p. 38.

60 Leifer (1996), p. 48.

9 Michael Leifer and the security of Southeast Asia's maritime thoroughfares[1]

Alan Chong

A distinct feature of the political region of Southeast Asia is its maritime entrails. With the exception of Laos, the other nine states comprising ASEAN possess coastal boundaries. Historically, since pre-modern times, access to trade and culture has been seaborne. The study of the empires of Srivijaya, Majapahit, Melaka, and Aceh has also confronted scholars with the task of interpreting maritime territoriality as a substitute for control of land. The coming of modernity with the advent of Portuguese, Dutch, British, Spanish, French, and subsequently, Soviet and US power continued to underline the importance of the naval bases of imperial control. In this regard, it is not surprising that this chapter contemplates Michael Leifer's contribution to the parameters of a *Southeast Asian* notion of maritime security. In retrospect, it might also be said that the foregoing exegesis substantiates more fully Barry Buzan's prescient comment that Leifer's detailed monograph on the Malacca Straits problematic signaled a shift in scholarship on maritime issues from one dominated by global naval supremacy and generic law of the sea studies, "towards the community of regional specialists."[2]

A survey of existing literature concerning the subject of maritime security at the time of writing did not supply the present work with any consensual definition of exactly what it is to be secured for or against. Traditional approaches to strategic studies would invoke the naval discourses of generating force projection assets for the twin roles of advancing conquest and policing trade routes vital for the politico-economic vitality of empire. Names like Corbett, Mahan, and their ancient predecessor, Thucydides, would be likely to grace the syllabi of courses on both peacetime global defense and prospective war-fighting. Maritime security would in this sense be fixated with attaining military supremacy across the oceans, the possibilities of implementing or fending off blockades, the doctrinal implications of naval support and interdiction for land campaigns, and the balance of power sustained by possession of capital ships and aircraft carriers.[3] Invariably, maritime security pertained only to national security or alliance security. While national partisanship in the employment of seaborne military power persisted, naval strategy began to evolve in the post-Cold War era into more multilateral *and* pacific roles. Some scholars believed that naval confidence and security-building measures were a logical extrapolation of the

European Cold War experience into postures of common verifiable security in every region of the world.[4] Others posited that United Nations peacekeeping operations in the 1990s established a new role for navies in an era of decentered threats to national security. Naval forces were now tasked to support relief operations in and adjacent to humanitarian disaster zones, and where applicable, explicit UN peace-enforcement activities.[5] The latter was actualized in the genocidal turn of events attending to the break-up of the Yugoslav federation; in the restoration of order in Haiti and Somalia; as well as in the recovery of Kuwaiti independence in 1991 following Saddam Hussein's unprovoked invasion of the oil-rich sheikhdom the year before. Naval power operating under UN mandates temporarily suspended, in principle, national loyalties for the higher goal of maintaining general peace and order under the rubric of global security. It was also developmental security that the UN was called to intervene for in cases like Somalia and East Timor. In these cases, military force was called upon to fulfill law-and-order missions where navies were quite marginal, or at best supplementary, in sustaining a fragile peace. From naval peacekeeping to the prevention of terrorism of the *Al Qaeda* variety, the activating momentum lay in the September 11, 2001 terrorist attacks on New York and Washington D.C. This is where the multilateral employment of naval force takes on yet more quasi-civilian roles such as patrolling against piracy and its potential conjunction with terrorist actions.

Leifer's contribution, as this chapter will suggest, transcends these mainstream obsessions with maritime security by arguing for a *local politics of the maritime thoroughfares*. To account for this, the analysis will begin with a summary of the sources of Leifer's thinking on the international relations of Southeast Asia. Thereafter, it will be possible to contextualize the salient features of his maritime pronouncements. Finally the conclusion will attempt to take stock of a *Leiferesque* approach to maritime security and its relevance to Southeast Asia's geopolitical insecurities in the wake of the post-September 11, 2001 "War on Terror". It will be evident that there will be one thread of continuity throughout, chiefly that Leifer intended to comprehend Southeast Asia as a distinct security region with unavoidable intrusions by external powers.

Leifer's reading of Southeast Asian geopolitics

To Michael Leifer, the evolution of the international relations of Southeast Asia begins with the facts of transiting from a "colonial international system" to the wider anarchical international society conceived by the writings of Hedley Bull and Martin Wight. In this English School usage, international society is understood to refer to an association of states which may be institutionalized or non-institutionalized, conscious of common interests and values, and bound by an agreed code of conduct that did not necessarily privilege equality.[6] In this regard, the advent of Western colonialism from the 1500s onwards had refocused local potentates' external affairs toward their respective imperial metropoles. Formal colonies, as well as other quasi-sovereign dependent territories such as those entities accepting colonial residents and protectorates, were in a subordinate relationship defined by local political isolation within Southeast Asia and exclusive "alien control" from their respective Western metropoles.[7] Imperial relationships were inherently intra-systemic. After anticolonial agitation succeeded in remapping local colonial authorities into sovereign Southeast Asian nation-states, the postcolonial milieu translated into an encounter with neighboring novices in foreign relations as well as a plethora of Small and Great Powers constituting an anarchical international society.

Based on these premises, Leifer went on to describe the foreign relations of the new states of Southeast Asia as "strange and novel."[8] He further elaborated that "following the departure of the colonial powers, new states were created which derived in territorial form from past political considerations and administrative convenience and not necessarily from any viable conception of nation."[9] Against this set of realities, the new states had to secure the trappings of a conventional Westphalian state: territorial demarcation, domestic sovereign legitimacy, external legitimacy and bonding their populations for material development. On land, the Thai–Cambodian, Viet–Cambodian, Thai–Burman border disputes, as well as the Indonesian–Malaysian disputes on Kalimantan, were symptomatic of the reworking of colonial legacies. On water, most of the boundary disputes were extensions of those about land frontiers; these invariably were intensified over adjacent straits (Malacca and Singapore Straits), fishing grounds (Gulf of Thailand and South China Sea), island ownership (Spratlys, Macclesfield Bank, Pratas Islands, Pedra Branca, Ligitan, and Sipadan) and access to undersea minerals (coastal waters, Natunas, and Spratlys). Not surprisingly, Leifer's monographs in 1972 and 1974 devoted considerable attention to the politics of development in Third World conditions within the region. Foreign policy and security strategies of the new states issued from the parameters set by their aspirations to become modern, sovereign, and proprietary over geography.

This developmental agenda could not be reconciled conveniently with the dominant Cold War considerations enforced by superpower involvement worldwide. Even the former colonial metropoles were inducted into the straitjacket of the bipolar contest. The United States, USSR, China, Britain, France, and the Netherlands interpreted much of the developmental conflicts of Southeast Asia into their wider international priorities. This necessarily complicated both the domestic and intra-regional politics of the new states which could never realistically entertain the prospect of being insulated in a discrete regional international society. Writing in 1974, Leifer predicted that regional order would remain "elusive and subjective" depending on two developments: first, whether major external powers would "tolerate and help sustain" local pacific settlements of disputes; and second, whether the postcolonial states could "show themselves capable of overcoming an internal debility which has been their striking common characteristic since independence."[10] These two worlds would collide, and occasionally coexist peacefully, in the maritime spaces of Southeast Asia where mercantile lifelines and military threats transit.

On-shore politics as the source of maritime security controversies

Bearing in mind his insider knowledge of Southeast Asian politics, it is not surprising that Leifer has consistently maintained that the sources of the interruption of seaborne commerce and energy supplies are "more likely to occur from events on-shore rather than off-shore."[11] In further support of this position, he pointed out from the vantage point of 1983, that the Arab oil boycott of 1973, the politically motivated Iranian decision to curtail oil exports in 1979, and the Iran–Iraq war that commenced in 1980, posed altogether more severe threats to worldwide economic interdependence than the actual possibilities of maritime interdiction by hostile vessels and aircraft.[12] This underlying premise is reflected in the entire gamut of Leifer's analyses of sovereign claims in the Malacca Straits, the South China Sea island disputes, and the security of sea-lanes in and around ASEAN.

The Straits of Malacca

The Straits of Malacca, and its adjoining Straits of Singapore, have generated no small amount of rival claims of sovereignty ever since its littoral states gained independence from their respective colonial masters. According to Leifer's reading of history, the coming of Westphalian statehood did not transform overnight Indonesian, Malaysian and Singaporean attitudes about maritime boundaries into proprietary ones. There have been rich historical precedents. The ancient Malay empire of Srivijaya had based itself at Palembang on what is now the Indonesian island of Sumatra, the greater part of whose coast bordered the Straits of Malacca. It greatness was derived from the tolls it collected from the shipping that sailed within its naval reach and to the ports it controlled. It was also a strategic trading location lying midway as a geographical chokepoint between the Indian Ocean territories and China. Srivijaya's decline was attributed to predatory attacks by the Chola Empire based in what is now Sri Lanka and southern India, competition from another island kingdom based in Java, and a natural enemy in the form of sedimentation all along its eastern coast bordering the Malacca Straits. This combination of geoeconomic and geopolitical rivalry was to remain a perennial feature of that waterway well into the twentieth century. Srivijaya's successor empires in the form of Majapahit and Melaka (Malacca) reprised the similar pattern of attempting to base imperial prosperity upon control of the Straits from a proximate port city. The coming of the Portuguese in the early sixteenth century also followed the earlier pattern of imperial maneuvers around the Straits and adjacent waterways. The mercantile and military plenipotentiaries of the Portuguese did not seek to occupy large hinterlands. They seized the port of Malacca as part of a formation of strategic trading centers ringing the Indian Ocean, the Straits of Malacca, what is now Celebes Sea, as well as Macau in southern China. With their maneuverable fleets of men-of-war, they established patrols along the transoceanic equivalent of the "Silk Route" connecting Asia and Europe. With such an established pattern, the Dutch, the British and the French hardly needed any leap in strategic thinking to displace the Portuguese in their turn by either capturing Portuguese possessions or establishing rival ports in the vicinity for markets and naval projection. Leifer has also noted that the 1824 Anglo-Dutch Treaty represented the high point of European attempts to attain peaceful coexistence between their rival empires by utilizing the Straits of Malacca as a *de facto* boundary demarcating the Dutch East Indies from the British possessions in and around the Malay Peninsula.[13] As early as 1944, impatient anticolonial mentalities fostered under Japanese auspices on both sides of the Straits considered the possibility of uniting a greater Malay–Indonesian fatherland across the waters that had divided them under erstwhile European domination.

In 1957, seven years after independence from the Dutch, the Republic of Indonesia lost no time in arguing for the legal assertion of sovereignty over the Straits of Malacca on the wider principle of it being an "archipelagic state". This came on the eve of the 1958 UN Conference on the Law of the Sea in Geneva. The basis of such a claim was that baselines drawn from the extremities of the Indonesian archipelago would encompass waterways with a status that would be almost on par with that of landed sovereignty. Leifer's understanding of Indonesia suggests that behind the posturing of legalism lay a postcolonial state's attempt to come to terms with keeping imperial potentialities at bay on its proximate waterways. Indonesian, and subsequently Malaysian, foreign policy identity had called for the explicit manifestation of the nationalistic notion of "*tanah air*", or "our land and sea".[14] Furthermore Indonesian elites feared the return of extraterritorial aggrandizement from the sea with memories of Dutch occupation in earlier centuries, as well as more recently in 1946-50, still fresh. The Cold War heightened Indonesian suspicions of seaborne political subversion since the rebellions on Sumatra in the 1950s were fomented by sympathizers in neighboring Malaya and Singapore, as well as the American CIA. Leifer had also observed that the nascent Indonesian Republic suffered the effects of the Dutch naval blockade in the struggle for independence. During a connected dispute with the Netherlands in 1960 over the status of West New Guinea, Indonesian military weakness was underlined by the fact that the Dutch deployed their aircraft carrier *Karel Doorman* in the vicinity. Furthermore, during Jakarta's *Konfrontasi* campaign against Malaysia, the British amassed a sizable naval deterrent in nearby Singapore. In September 1964, the Royal Navy dispatched the aircraft carrier *Victorious* through the Lombok Strait in an ostensible exercise of gunboat diplomacy.[15] The identification of Indonesian nationalism with the general Third World demand for politico-economic redress played into the defensiveness with which the claims of the Malacca Straits were pursued. The prime contention between Jakarta, Singapore, the Western maritime powers, and the Soviet Union lay in the Indonesian claim to the power to grant rights for innocent transit to military and civilian vessels of any nationality from the position of prior Indonesian sovereignty over all Straits defined within the archipelago. In spite of the abrupt change of regime in 1965-66 when President Sukarno was removed from office through a military coup headed by General Suharto, Jakarta's position on the Straits remained steadfast. Between 1970 and 1972, Indonesian officials marshaled the support of the Asian-African Legal Consultative Committee, as well as likeminded archipelagic states such as the Philippines and Fiji to lobby for the acceptance of its interpretation of the projected international law of the sea. By November 1971, the three littoral states of Indonesia, Malaysia, and Singapore had reached an agreement on the status of the Straits. This represented a victory for the Indonesians, and in tandem the Malaysians, on the issue of sovereignty but on the basis of mutually ensuring navigational safety in the waterway. This came in the wake of a series of near-accidents involving Japanese merchant shipping in the waterway which in turn triggered official Japanese concern. There was, however, an important clause of exception, placed at the insistence of Singapore, which merely "took note" of the positions of Jakarta and Kuala Lumpur in relation to the question of the international status of the Straits.

Before one delves into the politics behind the Singapore position, it is useful to note briefly Kuala Lumpur's belated official collusion with the Indonesian position on archipelagic status. The rapprochement with Indonesia began with the fall of the Sukarno Government in the wake of the 1965 coup. Against this background there revived elements of the vision of cultural and political brotherhood first raised formally in the closing days of the Japanese Occupation of both territories. The formation of the Association of Southeast Asian Nations (ASEAN) in 1967 reinforced the pattern of diplomatic fraternity between Kuala Lumpur and Jakarta. Leifer's writings drew attention to the fact that in that same year, with the signature of a bilateral "Security Arrangement" for joint counter-insurgency operations along their common border in northern Borneo, both countries effected the beginnings of a security community between themselves. The two countries also shared a solemn interpretation of those parts of the ASEAN preamble which stressed that its member states owed themselves a primary responsibility to ensure their political stability, and that other dimensions of national security were free from external interference.[16] Not surprisingly, ASEAN's clause that foreign bases within the organization's territories were temporary and subject to continued local concurrence led up to the Indonesian–Malaysian common front in pushing for Kuala Lumpur's proposal for a Zone of Peace, Freedom and Neutrality in Southeast Asia. In 1969 and 1970, both countries moved speedily to conclude two maritime border demarcation treaties covering both the Straits of Malacca and the South China Sea. In this regard both countries had officially and symmetrically claimed a 12-mile maritime boundary extending from their coasts into the center of the Straits of Malacca, effectively dividing the waterway between their respective sovereignties. Over the next five years, Kuala Lumpur's position was further vindicated by the occurrence of a series of navigational accidents including the grounding of the Japanese oil tanker *Showa Maru* which produced a two-mile oil slick in the waterway. Leifer's conclusion in his 1978 book is worth repeating here with its historical implication of Srivijaya, Majapahit and Melaka stamped over it:

> In the context of Indonesian-Malaysian enténte such intentions point to a measure of historical continuity in the straits area at a time when its political environment had been changed fundamentally by the extension to Southeast Asia of the European nation-state model.[17]

The Republic of Singapore, being dependent upon the sustenance of uninterrupted shipping traffic through the Straits of Malacca, Singapore, and on to the South China Sea and the Pacific, understandably tempered its acquiescence to the new solidarity between its two larger littoral neighbors. Singapore also had to factor in its reliance upon Japanese shipping concerns in the waterway since its Japanese-built petrochemical industry depended in turn on Japanese access via the most proximate routes to Singapore waters. A sensible strategy would have been for the Republic to have aligned obstinately to the positions of the major maritime powers insisting upon unqualified respect for the right of innocent transit through the Straits. Yet the recurrence of navigational accidents since the 1960s, and hence safety issues as well, have ensured a degree of concession on Singapore's part to the need for trilateral coordination with Jakarta and Kuala Lumpur over the Straits. Hence the 1971 agreement, and subsequently those of 1973 and 1977, gradually amounted to a deepening of Singaporean collaboration with Indonesia and Malaysia on technical issues exemplified by the monitoring of vessel traffic separation in the Straits. All these developments came conveniently upon the heels of Premier Lee Kuan Yew's reconciliation with President Suharto following the hanging in 1968 of two Indonesian marines captured in connection with the *Konfrontasi* campaign of the Sukarno era. This pattern of "regional solutions to regional politics" has once again reared its head over recent attempts to secure the Straits from piracy and *Al Qaeda*-inspired terrorism.[18] In order to encourage his Malaysian and Indonesian counterparts to agree to the implementation of joint air patrols to supplement naval patrols, Singaporean Foreign Minister George Yeo publicly explained that "there is discomfort when the Strait of Malacca and Singapore Strait are loosely described as 'international straits'. They are not." He noted that the UN Convention on the Law of the Sea (UNCLOS) described them as 'straits used for international navigation.'[19]

Island disputes in the South China Sea

Like the imbroglio over the Straits of Malacca, the international disputes over the possession of islands in the South China Sea were identified by Leifer as an extension of postcolonial territorial adjustments derived from the vagaries of treaties drawn up by the colonial powers. Second, but no less important, is the availability of sea-bed mineral resources in and around the islands for national exploitation. These resources include oil and gas deposits whose extraction had already been activated by Indonesia, Malaysia, the Philippines, Vietnam, China, and to a limited extent, Brunei, since the early 1990s. This was often achieved through the granting of concessions to private Western energy companies for exploration and extraction. Joint ventures with the respective national oil corporations have also been pursued where possible. In Leifer's view, these overlapping issues have always constituted sufficient reasons for the respective disputants to assert their sovereignty and mineral access through acts of force where expedient.[20] China's flagrant application of gunboat diplomacy in 1974 to consolidate acquisition of the Paracel Islands, and again in 1988 over parts of the Spratlys, supports such an assessment. In both cases, the victim of China's actions was Vietnam. In the 1990s, the Philippines also bore the brunt of Chinese aggrandizement. Brunei also encountered similar treatment from the Malaysian navy over oil prospecting in the southernmost parts of the Spratlys. Indonesia too felt menaced by China's claims stretching southward to the maritime vicinity of the gas-rich Natunas Islands which Indonesian companies are already exploiting.

The legal sources of these overlapping claims lie with both the facts of geography and the vagaries of UNCLOS drawn up after much international acrimony in 1982. It allowed coastal states to extend their sovereignty over natural resources on the seabed and in its subsoil in a maritime area 200 nautical miles from the littoral state's coast. At the same time the Convention declares that "rocks which cannot sustain human habitation or economic life of their own shall have no exclusive economic zone or continental shelf."[22] This constitutes the legal and political controversy surrounding the implementation of the "Exclusive Economic Zone" for the claimants of the Spratlys, the Paracels, and even potentially the Indonesian-owned Natunas. There are also other intramural island disputes within ASEAN, such as the Singapore–Malaysia diplomatic contestation over Pedra Branca and the Philippine claim to the Malaysian state of Sabah and its adjacent islands. The Malaysian–Indonesian dispute over Ligitan and Sipadan was exemplarily concluded in December 2002 through a legal judgment by the International Court of Justice, to which both governments have officially deferred to. That the latter case was resolved was due to the coincidence of political goodwill on both sides. For Leifer, such local disputes engage wider maritime security attention only when unilateral acts of sovereignty invoking the UNCLOS become construed as real and imagined obstructions to freedom of navigation by third party vessels.[21]

The wider issue of sea-lane security

Michael Leifer's third maritime concern was with the amorphous and overlapping notion of sea-lane security. In plain terms, this referred to the ability of both military and non-military vessels to freely transit through the maritime arteries of Southeast Asia. One threat would be the collective failure by both littoral states and the international community to tackle navigational concerns in narrow and shallow passages. Another salient threat would be the possibility of interdiction or attack by hostile naval and air forces upon traffic in these lanes. This understanding overlaps in large measure with the preceding summaries of the Malacca Straits and South China Sea disputes, but with a difference. The latter two disputes primarily concern struggles for the assertion of national control over sea space, and for land space adjacent to sea spaces. Sea-lane security issues stem partly from collateral disruption arising from ongoing territorial disputes, and partly from the offensive naval capabilities of third parties that are either uninvolved in local territorial disputes except in monitoring roles, or are involved on grounds of extra-regional security considerations.[23] During the Cold War, the latter notion of sea-lane security applied to superpower naval rivalry in and around Southeast Asia. Some secondary threats were also identified by Leifer in terms of piracy against commercial shipping resulting once again in collateral danger to navigational safety in the various waterways.

In his two main articles addressing sea-lane security, Leifer was unmistakably conscious in refining his concern through updates of the condition of Southeast Asia's "international society". He devoted as much space to local disputes over maritime jurisdiction as he did to the roles of regional and extra-regional great powers. At various times, the naval interests of the Soviet Union, the United States, and China were discussed under separate subheadings from the angle of threat to regional maritime order. In 1983, using typical Cold War lenses, Leifer analyzed the prospects of the Soviet predation on sea-lanes in the following manner:

> One possible way in which Soviet naval power might pose a threat to the security of sea-lanes in South-east Asia would be through an attempt to deny surface deployment to its principal adversary, for example in maritime narrows such as the Straits of Malacca and Singapore. Indeed charges that it is the intention of the Soviet Union to command and control these straits have issued with some regularity from Beijing.[24]

At the same time, Leifer noted that in spite of rivalry with the United States, the two had collaborated in upholding a "liberal regime of passage" at UNCLOS. Hence the Soviet menace ought to be placed in perspective:

> As a major maritime power with global naval and commercial interests it would be virtually impossible for the Soviet Union to adopt an isolated discriminate position of denial in respect of any one set of straits used extensively for international navigation, without incalculable repercussions affecting other such straits through which she might wish to deploy.[25]

Implicit in Leifer's perspective on sea-lane security is a clear appreciation of the dilemma of reciprocity within a regional commons as manifested by the network of Southeast Asian waterways. Not surprisingly Leifer's 1991 survey on regional security in East Asia and its relationship with the maritime regime constituted by UNCLOS adopted a similar tone of analysis. China had replaced the Soviet Union as the most prospective violator of strategic tranquility in East Asian seas. But Leifer weighed his conclusions unmistakably upon benign balancing by the United States:

> Any coastal state, including China, would be more likely to be deterred from engaging in any naval action disruptive of maritime order if the regional balance of power were so constituted that the opportunity costs of such action would be conspicuously evident. It is for this reason that the role of the United States remains critical, however much regional states might prefer to manage their security environment themselves… The record of the use of force in East Asia to assert maritime claims indicates that it is most likely to occur when the regional balance is in flux and countervailing power can be discounted. Regional security would seem to require that such countervailing power, if it cannot be generated locally on a cooperative basis, should be available from an acceptable external source for which there is only one candidate.[26]

This piece of policy analysis, verging upon prescription, is worth quoting at length as a defining illustration of Leifer's approach to sea-lane security. Realist balancing has been widely criticized for its vagaries and conservatism in analyzing reality, but in the context of the maritime thoroughfares trafficked by vessels flying the flags of an ensemble of local and extra-regional powers, it is from a perspective of insurance against future mischief that such measures enjoy the most purchase. In sum, in exploring Leifer's readings of disputes over the Straits of Malacca, the islands in the South China Sea, and his analysis of sea-lane security, one is essentially grappling with an understanding of what constitutes the operation of an interstate maritime society derived from inevitable land-based interdependence.

Southeast Asia as a maritime society tolerant of limited contestation

As Yuen Foong Khong's contribution to this volume has also argued, Leifer's analytical vocabulary has revealed traces of his intellectual embrace of the English School notion of an "international society". This chapter's earlier portions have amplified this argument in relation to his early monographs on Southeast Asian statehood and their international relations. This is a pertinent angle to adopt if one is to further substantiate a *Leiferesque* approach to Southeast Asia's, and even East Asia's, maritime security. In retrospect, it is perhaps a matter of regret for present scholarship that Leifer did not devote more than two or three articles, and a monograph, to a definitive outline of an East Asian maritime security hypothesis. It is this conjectural gap that this subsection endeavors to fill.

Based on the preceding treatments of the local on-shore politics corresponding to disputes over major waterways and islands, it can be observed that Leifer always warned his readers against the temptation of jumping to conclusions derived from worst case scenarios.[27] Maritime security ought never to be construed as a zero sum game since it operates upon facts of geography, interdependence, and its links to on-shore politics. There are obviously a finite number of deep water passages within regional waters for both military and civilian use. A serious campaign of military interdiction could easily exacerbate the suspicions and antagonisms of coastal states and previously neutral extra-regional powers, thereby precipitating complications to the initiator's naval objectives. Furthermore, the relative military power projection capabilities of the major extra-regional powers would give one another pause. In support of such an interpretation, Leifer has frequently cited that rare partnership between the United States and the USSR over the implementation of UNCLOS and the Malacca Straits dispute. The triggering of a devastating external power intervention in the event of a local disputant's attempt at creating a *fait accompli* in the course of asserting local claims could conversely also muddle the latter's ambition to be the local hegemon on the waterways. Typifying English School assumptions, Leifer has always insisted that statesmen and military chiefs at their respective helms of *raison d'état* possess sufficient rationality to pull back from all-out war.

Hedley Bull has pointed out that peace in international society translates largely as the absence of war.[28] In the post-1965 maritime scenario, Leifer would understand Indonesian and Malaysian reticence in actually enforcing sovereign inspections of third party vessels making innocent passage through the Malacca and Singapore Straits. Both these claimants could understand that Cold War conditions meant that the US Navy's navigational access to vital chokepoints had to be preserved, even if unannounced, because they deterred Soviet–Vietnamese designs in the region. Additionally, China's attempts at gunboat diplomacy *vis-à-vis* Vietnam and the Philippines over the Spratly and Paracel Islands could be explained as a measure of controlled escalation akin to the moves of a seasoned gambler. Similarly, Soviet Cold War behavior was not indiscriminately antagonistic toward the US naval presence in the Indian Ocean and South China Sea. Moscow played the same chessboard and was always aware that unhealthy precedents could backfire upon its ambitions across time. Additionally, Japan, by virtue of its special defense relationship with Washington, would see to it that the United States heeded its counsel of open access for oil tankers transporting its energy supplies from the Middle East through the Straits of Malacca and the South China Sea. As noted in Leifer's monograph on the Malacca Straits, Japan had fleshed out its willingness to secure navigational safety in the waterway as early as 1968 by fully funding the Malacca Straits Council which involves Japan and the three Southeast Asian littoral states in maintaining navigational safety through lighthouses and buoys. The earlier quotation from Leifer's assessment of sea-lane security has also suggested that, in principle, a multiplicity of big fishes in the proverbial Southeast Asian pond helpfully complicates straightforward cost-free military aggrandizement by all. By November 2002, even China signaled some acceptance of such logic by co-signing with rival claimants to the Spratlys, a Declaration on the Conduct of Parties in the South China Sea, pledging joint explorations for oil and gas in the islands in consultation with all signatories. In 2004 alone, this code of conduct was tested on two serious occasions.[29] From May to August, China protested Vietnam's inauguration of plans to upgrade the tourism infrastructure, including airport-building, on its occupied portions of the islands. In September, the Philippines and China reached a bilateral agreement to seek joint exploration of oil in their parts of the archipelago, arousing, in the process, the diplomatic ire of Vietnam and expressions of concern from other claimants. Vietnam, China, and the Philippines did not resort to gunboat solutions but limited their remonstrations to diplomacy By March 2005, the Philippines, China and Vietnam signed a landmark tripartite agreement to survey potential oil and gas deposits among the islands. A Philippine oil company spokesman described the agreement as a purely "commercial transaction that has no reference to political claims or territorial rights."[30]. In this way, however reluctantly, both littoral states and extra-regional powers restrain their military rivalry and pay more than lip service to common security in Southeast Asian maritime matters. This is further vindicated by the "doubletalk" issuing from Kuala Lumpur and Jakarta over Washington's offers of assisting littoral state navies in preventive naval patrols against piracy and terrorism under the recently floated Regional Maritime Security Initiative.[31] Joint Indonesian–Malaysian–Singaporean naval patrols were enacted in large measure to dilute public temptations for US naval unilateralism, while preserving local sovereignties over the Malacca Straits as allowed under UNCLOS.

What is the Leiferesque approach to maritime security in Southeast Asia?

It is evident from the preceding venture that there are grounds for positing a Leiferesque approach. In doing so, one is necessarily cautious about retrospectively labeling Leifer a theorist, a label he has manifestly avoided in his career. Yet Leifer has never been averse to the indulgence of his colleagues and students in the construction of theory. He has always been most concerned with being realistic, and reasonably correct, insofar as trend analyses and policy prescriptions need to be to make them readable. Being a social scientist and a friend of Southeast Asia, his commentaries have always embedded nuggets of advice for those who cared to reflect upon them.

This chapter has unabashedly made a case for reflecting on these nuances and extrapolated them as a Leiferesque approach to regional maritime security characterized by two features. First, maritime security ought to be analyzed from the angle of on-shore politics casting its footprint on off-shore issues. The contestations over ownership of the Malacca Straits, the islands in the South China Sea, and sea-lane security all stem from land-based considerations of sovereignty and other factors of power mobilization. It is therefore not surprising to find Malaysian maritime analysts arguing that the seaborne version of a war on terror in the Malacca Straits is a partial misnomer: pirates are economically driven by land-based poverty, criminal extravagances and their potential for making common cause with ideological extremists; hence the gravity of counter-terrorism should be grounded in on-shore poverty alleviation, as well as effective policing against criminal rackets and terrorist planning.[32] Both Indonesian and Malaysian officials have frequently reiterated in recent years that in spite of the totalizing discourse of a global war on maritime terror, theirs still involves a struggle for recovering overdue sovereignty over coastal spaces.[33] The second feature is Leifer's emphasis on inscribing a template of international society on any analytical canvas of maritime security. As it has been argued, Southeast Asian waters are an indelible thoroughfare of commerce and military traffic. Both littoral states and extra-regional powers have come to recognize, either by word or by deed, a common interdependence upon access to geographical passages. In short, a maritime society tolerant of limited contestation will always be a retarding factor against the prospect of cataclysmic naval outcomes in the region. Michael Leifer should in the final analysis be read as either a partial liberal institutionalist or a chameleon realist of the English School.

Notes

1 The author wishes to thank Ralf Emmers and Joseph Liow for the invitation to contribute this chapter. In the course of preparation, invaluable research assistance was also rendered by Mr Ma Shaohua to whom I owe special gratitude.
2 Barry Buzan, "Review: Regionalization of the Law of the Sea; Malacca, Singapore and Indonesia," *Pacific Affairs* vol. 53 no. 1, 1980, 177.
3 Refer for instance to H. H. Herwig, "The Future of Sea Power," in K. Neilson and E.J. Errington (eds) *Navies and Global Defense: Theories and Strategy*, Westport, CT: Praeger, 1995, pp. 209–219.
4 A. Mack (ed.) *A Peaceful Ocean? Maritime Security in the Pacific in the Post-Cold War Era*, St. Leonards: Allen and Unwin in association with the Peace Research Centre, Australian National University and the Institute of Strategic and International Studies, Malaysia, 1993.
5 M. Pugh, J. Ginifer and E. Grove, "Sea Power, Security and Peacekeeping after the Cold War," in M. Pugh (ed.) *Maritime Security and Peacekeeping: A Framework for United Nations Operations*, Manchester: Manchester University Press, 1994, pp. 10–31.
6 In Ch. 3 of this volume, Khong Yuen Foong provides a detailed study of Leifer's received influence from his English School colleagues.
7 Michael Leifer, *The Foreign Relations of the New States* (Studies in Contemporary Southeast Asia), Camberwell, Victoria: Longman, 1974, p. 4.
8 Ibid., p. 26.

9 Leifer, *Dilemmas of Statehood in Southeast Asia*, Singapore: Asia Pacific Press, 1972, p. 8.
10 Ibid., p. 109.
11 Leifer, "The Security of Sea-lanes in South-East Asia," *Survival*, 25, 1983, 23.
12 Ibid.
13 Leifer, *International Straits of the World: Malacca, Singapore and Indonesia*, The Netherlands: Sijthoff and Noordhoff, 1978, pp. 9–10.
14 Michael Leifer and Dolliver Nelson, "Conflict of Interest in the Straits of Malacca," *International Affairs* vol. 49, no. 2, 1973, 191.
15 Leifer, *International Straits of the World*, p. 16.
16 Ibid., pp. 28–30.
17 Ibid., p. 31.
18 "Malaysia Urges Asian Nations to Protect Strategic Waterways," *Agence France Presse* 4 October 2004.
19 Quoted in Bhagyashree Garekar, "S'pore–KL Talks on Air Patrols", *Straits Times (Singapore)* 30 July 2005.
20 Leifer, "The Maritime Regime and Regional Security in East Asia," *The Pacific Review* vol. 4, no. 2, 1991, 128–131.
21 Article 121 of UNCLOS 1982 cited in ibid., p. 128.
22 Ibid., p. 129.
23 Leifer, "Security of Sea-lanes in South-East Asia," p. 16.
24 Ibid., p. 21.
25 Ibid., p. 21.
26 Leifer, "Maritime Security Regime," p. 135.
27 See for instance Leifer, "Security of Sea-Lanes in South-East Asia," pp. 21–23; *Dilemmas of Statehood*, p. 150; "Expanding Horizons in Southeast Asia?," *Southeast Asian Affairs 1994*, Singapore: ISEAS, 1994, pp. 3–21.
28 Hedley Bull, *The Anarchical Society: A Study of Order in World Politics*, London: Macmillan, 1977, p. 18.
29 Mark J. Valencia, "China's Push for Offshore Oil: A Chance for Joint Deals," *Straits Times* (Singapore) 25 September 2004.
30 "Update: Philippines, Vietnam, China in Spratlys Survey Deal", *Dow Jones International News*, 14 March 2005.
31 "Stay out of Straits, KL Tells Foreign Powers," *Straits Times (Singapore)* 11 October 2004.
32 Mak Joon Num, "Malacca Straits Safety: Take the Fight to the Pirates," *Straits Times* (Singapore) 3 July 2004. A point acknowledged by two recent works on maritime security in the post-September 11 mode: Michael Richardson, *A Time Bomb for Global Trade: Maritime-Related Terrorism in an Age of Weapons of Mass Destruction*, Singapore: ISEAS, 2004; Graham Gerard Ong, *"Ships can be Dangerous too": Coupling Piracy and Maritime Terrorism in Southeast Asia's Maritime Security Framework*, ISEAS Working Paper: International Politics and Security Issues Series No. 1, Singapore: ISEAS, 2004.
33 "Indonesia Must Define Continental Shelves Soon: Government Official," *Asia Pulse* 14 July 2004.

10 Singapore's strategic outlook and defence policy

Tim Huxley

From 1965 onwards, Michael Leifer's research and writing on Southeast Asian politics and international relations often touched on Singapore, particularly in terms of the city-state's relationship with its immediate neighbours, Malaysia and Indonesia, its role within ASEAN, and its interest in maritime security. However, though he contributed a chapter on Singapore's foreign policy to an edited volume in 1989,[1] his analysis of the city-state's international outlook and policies was only fully developed in his last book, *Singapore's foreign policy: coping with vulnerability*, published in 2000 shortly before his death.[2] This book was the first substantial study of Singapore's foreign policy to be published.

Security perceptions and policies, in the broadest sense, were central to Leifer's examination of Singapore: his book revolved around the central theme of the republic's vulnerability as a geographically and demographically small state, populated mainly by ethnic Chinese, sandwiched between two much larger neighbours. For historical and cultural reasons, relations with these neighbours (particularly Malaysia) have been characterized by deeply embedded structural tensions. As Leifer says, 35 years after separation from Malaysia, the same overriding concern evident in 1965 still governed Singapore's foreign policy: 'that every effort should be made to keep the fortunes of the Republic out of the play of solely regional forces that cannot be fully trusted'.[3]

According to Leifer, this guiding principle moulded a special type of balance of power or distribution of power approach in Singapore's foreign policy.[4] This involved not only striving to keep the United States militarily involved in Southeast Asia and building up the Singapore Armed Forces (SAF) as a deterrent, but also entering into multilateral security dialogue with the aim of 'engaging the interest of extra-regional states in its environment and in its independence'. Unfortunately for Singapore, the regional economic downturn since the late 1990s and its social and political repercussions have significantly exacerbated tensions with neighbours, in some respects returning the city-state to the 'dire circumstances' of the mid-1960s.[5] However, because of its economic progress, its highly developed defence capability, and its wide political and economic links beyond its immediate locale, by the time of Leifer's final analysis, Singapore was much better equipped to 'cope with vulnerability' than it was in 1965.

This chapter examines the military underpinnings of Singapore's balance of power strategy, in terms of both the development of the republic's own military capability and doctrine of deterrence, and its international defence relations. It seeks to explain why Singapore should have engaged, in Michael Leifer's words, 'in defence provision well beyond that of any regional neighbour'.[6]

Deterrence through total defence

Officially, 'Singapore's defence philosophy is not built on the premise of an existing external threat',[7] but rather on maintaining and developing a deterrent capability aimed at preventing threats from arising. Singapore's 'deterrence strategy' is operationalized through Total Defence (TD), a concept first enunciated in 1984 to 'unite all sectors of society – government, business and the people – in the defence of the country'.[8] According to the government, Military Defence is only one of TD's five components, the others being Psychological Defence, Social Defence, Economic Defence, and Civil Defence.[9]

Military defence

Though the government claims all elements of Total Defence are essential, Military Defence provides the core of Singapore's deterrent and its capacity to defeat aggressors if deterrence fails. Key elements of Singapore's military defence policy include high defence spending, universal military service, operational readiness, technological superiority over potential adversaries, developing integrated and balanced forces, and defence diplomacy. Even before the acute concerns over terrorism which arose during 2001, the Ministry of Defence (Mindef) emphasized the importance of working with other government departments to develop defences against 'non-traditional threats' including terrorism, cyber-attacks and chemical warfare.[10]

While Singapore's defence spending has increased substantially since the 1960s, the government has been wary of provoking a Southeast Asian arms race. For this reason, and also to ensure that building up the SAF did not damage the economy, shortly after independence the government capped defence spending at 6 per cent of GDP.[11] Rapid economic growth during the 1990s meant that military expenditure was generally contained at 4–5 per cent of GDP. Sustained high defence spending has funded continuous improvements to military capabilities, through procuring increasingly sophisticated equipment, building extensive infrastructure, large-scale overseas training, and generously remunerating the SAF's professional core personnel.

Conscripts and reservists, respectively NSFs (National Servicemen Full-Time) and NSmen (National Servicemen) in SAF parlance, constitute the great majority of military personnel. While the SAF might have found sufficient professional personnel for its air and naval components, given Singapore's small population and its usually dynamic economic conditions it would have been impossible to develop an army significantly larger than the brigade-strength force inherited from Malaysia in 1965 without compulsory military service. Following two years of full-time national service, NSMen complete a 13-year training cycle, with the result that almost 300,000 'operationally ready' reservists are available. Operational readiness is critically important in view of Singapore's lack of geographical strategic depth: active and reservist units' readiness for war is evaluated regularly. Mobilization can bring the SAF to a war footing in approximately six hours, and selected reservist units, together with civilian resources needed by the SAF, are mobilized frequently.[12]

Technology is used as a force multiplier to compensate for lack of strategic depth and reliance on conscripts and reservists. Equipment is continually enhanced, through procuring new systems from overseas and by upgrading hardware locally, with local defence industry and government defence scientists playing vital parts. Local industry and Mindef agencies have also developed a range of indigenous defence equipment. Serious attention is paid to exploiting new information and communications technologies to give the SAF a 'strategic edge' in command, control, communications and intelligence.[13] Mindef has tried to ensure that development of the SAF's various branches proceeds synergistically. Since the 1990s, the Integrated Warfare doctrine has provided a framework for integrating the three services' capabilities.

Singapore's threat environment

Having governed Singapore since 1959, even by Southeast Asian standards the People's Action Party (PAP) has enjoyed an exceptionally lengthy tenure. Party leaders' strategic outlook has dominated defence policy and strategy. PAP ministers have repeatedly expressed concern over the city-state's innate vulnerabilities and weaknesses.[14] Assessing these 'constraints' in 1987, then-Prime Minister Lee Kuan Yew asserted that Singapore 'cannot count on springing back on our feet if we are knocked off balance' and that Singapore is 'peculiarly vulnerable'.[15]

Structural vulnerabilities

Unique geographical and demographic factors confer distinct economic advantages on Singapore. The island's location astride important trade routes at Southeast Asia's geographical centre allowed it to develop its entrepôt role during the colonial period, when it became a vital commercial link between Southeast Asia and the wider world. Since separation from Malaysia, the absence of natural resources has forced the government to develop a more diversified economy based on manufacturing and services as well as entrepôt trade. At the same time, Singapore has not had to contend with the problem of an impoverished rural population. Singapore's highly urbanized population, composed predominantly of the descendants of ethnic Chinese immigrants, has provided an energetic workforce as well as financial and trading links with Chinese communities elsewhere in the region.

However, these same factors carry strategic disadvantages. Singapore is a city-state with a resident population of only 3.4 million sandwiched between much more populous neighbours – Malaysia (population 23 million) and Indonesia (220 million). Small population size has promoted a sense of vulnerability. Incidents such as Iraq's invasion of Kuwait have heightened the Singapore government's concern over the inherent insecurity of small statehood.[16]

The lack of natural resources and the continuing importance of entrepôt commerce – Singapore's annual international trade is three times as large as its GDP – have enforced extreme dependency on the outside world. Singapore still relies on Malaysia for much of its water; virtually all fuel and most food is imported. Moreover, Singapore is surrounded by the territorial waters of Indonesia and Malaysia: the city-state has no access to the high seas, on which it depends for 85 per cent of its trade, other than through neighbours' waters.[17] Serious disruption of Singapore's physical links with the outside world would threaten not just its economic well-being: its very national survival would be jeopardized. Moreover, a significant decline in new investment by foreign multinational companies in manufacturing because of loss of confidence in the republic's security would seriously damage its economy. Foreign confidence is also key to the continuing success of Singapore's increasingly important financial and banking sector.

Singapore's extremely small land area means that it utterly lacks territorial strategic depth: it cannot yield territory to an aggressor with the expectation of later regaining it. Its population and its civilian and military infrastructure are highly concentrated and vulnerable to physical attack, further weakening its overall strategic position.

Singapore's location in a geopolitically and ethnically complex, and potentially unstable, region has accentuated its government's external security concerns. Its population is 77 per cent Chinese in a region where this ethnic group has traditionally been distrusted and often persecuted, exacerbating Singapore's sense of vulnerability. Singapore's ethnic and religious make-up, which includes a 14 per cent Malay Muslim minority, affects its security in another, related sense. Malaysia and Indonesia both have Muslim majorities and Chinese minorities, and the spread of Malaysia's 1969 race riots to Singapore demonstrated the linkage between developments in these neighbouring countries and communal relations within Singapore. Though increasing prosperity has helped to subdue communal tensions in all three states, altered economic or political circumstances could still destabilize relations between ethnic Chinese and indigenous communities.

Singapore and the regional balance of power

Because of these vulnerabilities, Singapore has always been less reserved than its ASEAN partners in acknowledging the importance of balance of power mechanisms for maintaining national and regional security. Indeed, an appreciation that its interests are best served by preventing the regional dominance of any power 'which might in consequence be able to challenge its independence' has been a fundamental foreign policy aim since the late 1960s.[18] As Lee Kuan Yew said in 1966, it was vital for Singapore to have 'overwhelming power' on its side.[19] This balance of power approach has operated at two levels, with Singapore endeavouring not only to prevent Indonesia and Malaysia from dominating its immediate locale but also to forestall any 'adverse change in the overall regional balance'.[20] Singapore's horizons for maintaining a favourable overall regional balance of power were originally essentially restricted to Southeast Asia but, recognizing the increasing power and assertiveness of China and potentially of Japan, its interest expanded during the 1990s to subsume wider East Asia. Because of Singapore's limited diplomatic influence and military capacity, it has based its balance of power strategy at the grand regional level principally on borrowing political and military strength from extra-regional powers.[21] However, at the sub-regional level, it has relied far more on its own resources.

In contrast to Indonesia and Malaysia, which have argued for a regional security system managed by regional states, Singapore's leaders – remembering their island's subjugation by the Japanese during the Second World War as well as Indonesia's aggressive policy of Confrontation against Malaysia (then including Singapore) during the 1960s, and ever-conscious of their city-state's inherent vulnerabilities – have feared that such a policy would open the way for larger Asian states to dominate smaller ones.[22] Soon after independence Singapore made clear its support for a regional status quo based on a multipolar balance of power, and has subsequently sought to develop mutually valuable relations with a wide range of powers. Since the late 1960s Singapore's leaders – and particularly Lee Kuan Yew – have repeatedly expressed anxiety that the declining military presence and involvement of the Western powers (pre-eminently the United States) in Southeast Asia and, since the 1990s, East Asia as a whole endangers regional stability by providing opportunities for other large powers to assert themselves, potentially threatening Singapore's freedom.

From Singapore's viewpoint, the late 1960s and 1970s brought potentially adverse changes to Southeast Asia's political and military configuration. President Nixon's 1969 Guam Doctrine heralded a reduced direct US commitment to regional security. The 1972 Paris Peace Agreement led to the withdrawal of US combat forces from South Vietnam, and ultimately to communist victories there and in Cambodia in 1975. Vietnam was united under a communist regime, as was Laos. US air force units were finally withdrawn from Thailand in 1976. Singapore had lent both rhetorical and material support for the US war effort in Indochina since 1967, but these developments – which threatened to increase the regional influence of China and the Soviet Union – provoked the city-state into a more active role in regional balance of power politics. Most importantly, whereas Singapore's support for ASEAN had initially been lukewarm, from 1975 it began to appreciate that the Association might be useful for expressing solidarity among Southeast Asia's non-communist states in the region's new circumstances.[23] Throughout the 1980s Singapore took a leading role in maintaining ASEAN's opposition to Vietnam's domination of Cambodia.

Singapore and the major powers

These developments led Singapore to see the United States' role as vital in an emerging quadrilateral balance of external influences on Southeast Asian security, also involving China, the USSR and Japan. During the late 1970s and 1980s Singapore sought to strengthen military cooperation with Washington to help delay the attenuation of the United States' regional security role. Despite frictions over issues ranging from trade relations and human rights to the supply of military equipment, the foundations for close bilateral strategic relations were established.

The Cold War's end left Singapore's belief in the continuing importance of the United States' regional security role undiminished. Singapore's leaders have repeatedly emphasized the importance for East Asian regional security of a stable triangular relationship between the United States, China and Japan.[24] Singapore has viewed a continuing substantial US military presence in East Asia as a vital constraint not only on China's regional behaviour but also on the potential remilitarization of Japan's foreign policy.[25] Whereas Singapore had previously had little opportunity to promote rather than merely encourage the United States' regional security engagement,[26] by 1990 the prospect of US naval and air forces withdrawing from the Philippines (and hence from Southeast Asia) allowed the republic tangibly to facilitate Washington's continued military presence by expanding access for American ships and aircraft. Subsequently, Singapore-US security relations have developed into a quasi-alliance.

However, Singapore's positive outlook on the United States' regional role has not implied that it would support future strategies aimed at 'containing' China. Indeed, during the Taiwan Straits crisis in early 1996, Lee Kuan Yew encouraged Washington as well as Beijing to act with restraint. Lee stressed his great concern that US efforts to contain China might eventually divide East Asian states into antagonistic camps according to their attitude towards the People's Republic.[27] Such a development would place Singapore in a particularly uncomfortable position. Despite its generally pro-Western stance, for domestic political reasons it is extremely unlikely that Singapore could ever overtly take the side of the United States and Taiwan in a future conflict with China. Particularly since the profit motive replaced communism as the guiding ideology of the People's Republic, it is difficult for most Singaporean politicians, officials, business people and opinion-formers to conceive of China as a threat. While Washington may view defence relations with Singapore primarily in terms of their contribution to balancing China, Singapore's government sees their utility more in terms of maintaining regional stability in general terms, while also bolstering the island's security in the face of more local security concerns.

The Five Power Defence Arrangements

Though the United States has played a hugely more important part than other Western states in Singapore's balance of power thinking since the late 1960s, the republic has also supported intensified security cooperation under the aegis of the Five Power Defence Arrangements (FPDA), established in 1971 with Singapore, Malaysia, the United Kingdom, Australia and New Zealand as members. The initial underlying rationale for the Arrangements was that the defence of Malaysia and Singapore remained indivisible, and that they still faced certain common potential threats – most importantly, a possible revival of Indonesian adventurism or a major escalation in the Malayan Communist Party's campaign of violence against both governments. While the nature of the threats they face has changed, this notion of the indivisibility of the defence of Malaysia and Singapore has persisted.

Part of the FPDA's significance for Singapore is undoubtedly its contribution – minor but not insignificant – to maintaining a favourable overall regional balance of power. Singapore has valued institutionalized security cooperation with the UK and Australia (and also until the breach in Anzus during the mid-1980s, New Zealand) partly because their close alliances with Washington provided an indirect security link to the United States.[28] The FPDA has also been important for Singapore in the sense of providing a context for sustaining bilateral defence relations with its three extra-regional members. However, the FPDA has also served more localized purposes for Singapore by providing a neutral forum for continued defence cooperation and security-related confidence building with Malaysia despite repeated strains in bilateral relations, and by providing a potential counterweight to any revival of Indonesian adventurism.

In two main senses, Singapore's own growing military capability has facilitated efforts to encourage a favourable regional balance of power. In the first place, Singapore's evident ability to share the regional defence burden strengthens its hand when attempting to persuade extra-regional powers to maintain their regional security roles. Without possessing fairly sophisticated capabilities, it would be difficult to engage the United States or the extra-regional FPDA powers in militarily significant cooperation. Second, the availability of high-grade local military infrastructure – particularly air bases and naval dockyards – which has been developed primarily for the SAF, allows Singapore to accommodate visiting US and incidentally Australian, New Zealand and British forces without the need for any significant expenditure on fixed facilities by friendly powers. At the same time, Singapore is able credibly to claim that it does not host foreign military bases, thereby placating neighbouring Indonesia and Malaysia.

Sub-regional tensions

The conflicts in Indochina and the Soviet–Vietnamese alliance formed important elements of the regional strategic backdrop against which the SAF was developed between the late 1960s and the late 1980s. However, the potential danger from immediate sub-regional neighbours was probably a more important driver of Singapore's military build-up even during the Cold War.

During the 1990s, some observers argued that Singapore and its neighbours, Malaysia and Indonesia, constituted an increasingly cohesive sub-regional community, drawn together not only by economic complementarities but also by common security interests, particularly in the maritime sphere. Some saw the emergence of a distinct and potentially divisive interest group within ASEAN,[29] or alternatively viewed the three states as the incipient driving force – 'a provisionally emerging regional security core' – within a still cohesive ASEAN.[30] However, these analyses underestimated tensions between these states and the potential for conflict between them. The concept of a 'Malay archipelago complex', including the three states together with Brunei, and characterized as much by competition and latent conflict as by cooperation, was closer to reality.[31] Within this often tense sub-regional environment, Singapore has used conventional diplomacy and economic instruments to manage relations with Malaysia and Indonesia, but military deterrence has also played a central – if obscured – role.

The continuing expansion of Singapore's defence effort during the 1990s provided clear evidence that concern over external communist threats was not the only important influence on its security policies. In 1991, defence minister Yeo Ning Hong emphasized that despite the end of the Cold War Singapore would not reduce defence spending or shorten the period of conscription.[32] Far from cutting military expenditure, between 1990 and 1998 Singapore approximately doubled defence spending in real terms. While Singapore's phenomenal economic growth meant that its government could well afford to spend more on defence and it was logical to do this because of regional strategic uncertainty, the scale of the increased spending suggested more tangible security concerns. The subsequent maintenance of Singapore's defence effort despite tough economic conditions since the late 1990s has served to underline this point.

Singapore's perennially unstable relationships with immediate neighbours indicate clearly the sub-regional locus of its most pressing external security concerns. The city-state's neuralgic relations with Malaysia and Indonesia derive to a considerable extent from ethnic factors. Partly to reduce the potential for conflict with its neighbours, after 1965 Singapore's government asserted a multiracial national identity, and avoided close political identification with either the People's Republic of China (PRC) or Taiwan. Participation in ASEAN, which Singapore joined in 1967 as one of five founding member-states, and efforts to build mutually profitable links with Indonesia and Malaysia have also been key to efforts to cement the republic's Southeast Asian identity. However, Singapore has not been able to mitigate entirely the sub-regional complications accruing from its perceived Chineseness. Though Malaysia and to a lesser extent Indonesia have also prospered, widespread jealousy of the wealth of many ethnic Chinese in the region has sometimes translated into resentment of Singapore's outstanding economic success. Moreover, the strengthening of Singapore's Chinese identity during the 1990s, resulting from renewed domestic emphasis on Chinese language and culture, as well as closer relations with the PRC since the establishment of diplomatic relations in 1990, have tended to heighten negative regional perceptions of Singapore.

Singapore's determination since 1965 to defend and assert its national sovereignty, deriving originally from the PAP leadership's experience of union with Malaysia in 1963-65 and Indonesia's simultaneous attempt to assert sub-regional hegemony, has also complicated relations with Indonesia and Malaysia. In the early years after separation, relations with Kuala Lumpur remained cool, as Singapore resisted Malaysian pressure on a collection of relatively minor issues. Singapore's execution in 1968 of two Indonesian marines convicted of terrorist offences soured relations with Jakarta. Moreover, Singapore was unnerved by the warmth of the initial rapprochement between Kuala Lumpur and Jakarta in the aftermath of Confrontation. In 1971 Singapore, sensitive to threats to its seaborne trade and its role as a regional shipping centre, refused to acquiesce in Indonesia's and Malaysia's joint challenge to the traditional legal status of the Straits of Malacca and Singapore.[33] These and other tensions help to explain Singapore's attempts during the late 1960s and early 1970s to develop 'a range of countervailing external relationships'[34] in order to balance its continuing economic dependence on, and political and strategic vulnerability within, its immediate region. Following the collapse of anti-communist forces in Indochina, from the mid-1970s Singapore devoted greater energy towards developing cooperative relations with Malaysia and Indonesia, but it has consistently demonstrated unwillingness to compromise on issues affecting its sovereign prerogative or economic interests. Singapore's difficult relations with Malaysia and Indonesia have reinforced its distrust of regional security formulas resting on the exclusion of extra-regional powers; indeed, its sub-regional security concerns have contributed to its support for both the United States' engagement and the FPDA.

There can be little doubt that Singapore has developed its military capabilities in large part to deter Malaysia and Indonesia from interfering with its vital interests. Since the late 1980s, backbench PAP Members of Parliament and local newspaper columnists have sometimes highlighted sub-regional threats to Singapore's security, particularly from Malaysia. However, Singapore's government believes that 'to name an enemy is to make an enemy', recognizing that Singapore cannot afford to live in a permanent state of hostility with its larger neighbours on which it depends for a good part of its long-term economic prosperity as well as day-to-day necessities. Open hostility would also imperil Singapore's domestic communal relations and adversely affect foreign investment.

Although Lee Kuan Yew claimed in his 1987 SAF Day speech that his government did 'not consider our neighbours in South-east Asia to be threats', he did indicate a concern with 'irrational and extremist forces' in Southeast Asia.[35] From Singapore's viewpoint, the worst-case sub-regional scenario has been that an ultra-nationalist or fundamentalist Muslim regime might take power in Malaysia or Indonesia, and that Singapore could find itself the victim of a neighbour's aggressive foreign policy aimed at overturning the sub-regional political status quo. A variation on this theme is fear that domestic political instability and violence in either neighbour, particularly if this involved conflict between Muslim indigenes and ethnic Chinese, could spread to Singapore.

However, even relatively stable Indonesian and Malaysian governments have sometimes complicated life for Singapore. A crucial explanation for Singapore's often uncomfortable relations with its neighbours, and particularly Malaysia, is the link between domestic politics and foreign policy in these countries. Singapore has often found itself an easy target for criticism by Malaysian – and since 1997 Indonesian – politicians seeking a scapegoat for domestic social, political and economic problems. Notably, the most serious downturns in Singapore's sub-regional bilateral relationships have occurred during economic recessions and accompanying political turmoil in the republic's neighbours.

Malaysia: the most likely adversary?

Since 1965, Singapore and Malaysia have generally avoided policies or actions which might seriously jeopardize the other's political or social stability. Simultaneously, they have cooperated on a wide range of mutual interests, and common membership of ASEAN has helped mitigate bilateral tensions. Bilateral economic relations have remained important for both sides: trade between Singapore and Malaysia has remained substantial, as has Singaporean investment in Malaysia. Malaysia continues to supply Singapore with more than half of its water, as well as much of its food. Personal connections between the two states remain strong.

Singapore and Malaysia have also cooperated on security. Links between the two states' internal security organizations have endured. Malaysia's Marine Police and Singapore's Police Coast Guard have collaborated against piracy and illegal immigration. Malaysia's and Singapore's armed forces exercise together through the FPDA. At times there has also been bilateral military cooperation outside the FPDA. Singapore has stressed its recognition of the continuing indivisibility of the two states' defence.[36]

However, while the two states have remained highly interdependent, relations have simultaneously been characterized by considerable tension and mutual distrust: this is the most sensitive and unstable relationship between any pair of ASEAN members. Stresses and strains over a wide variety of issues became more pronounced from the time of Israeli President Herzog's visit to Singapore in 1986. Between then and Dr Mahathir Mohamad's retirement from Malaysia's premiership in late 2003, bilateral disagreements became almost routine, occasionally triggering unofficial calls in Malaysia for Singapore's water supply to be cut off, and even partial military mobilization by Singapore.

The accession of a new prime minister in Malaysia has brought high hopes that outstanding bilateral problems will be resolved, ushering in a new era of stable and mutually beneficial bilateral relations. However, even resolution of all outstanding disputes would not necessarily bring long-term harmony. The nub of the matter is that the particular bilateral contentions are symptoms rather than causes of structural tensions which have been embedded in the bilateral relationship since 1965 due to the two states' ethnic compositions and their governments' divergent political visions. Domestic political change in either or both states could improve relations (if political styles converged through the rise of more liberal leaderships on both sides of the Causeway, for example), but alternatively it could further complicate it (if, for instance, a more assertively Islamic or nationalist government came to power in Malaysia). In the meantime, Singapore's government has maintained an upbeat rhetorical stance while continuing to prepare for the worst.[37]

Indonesia: a secondary concern

Although Singapore's relations with Jakarta during the 1980s and 1990s involved wide-ranging collaboration, including close links between the SAF and the Indonesian armed forces (ABRI), Indonesia has never ceased to be a security concern for the city-state, and the SAF's deterrent capabilities have been developed with Indonesia in mind as well as Malaysia.

During the late 1960s and early 1970s it was commonplace for observers to portray Singapore as 'a Chinese nut in a Malay nutcracker'. The new state's political relations with both Indonesia and Malaysia were less than comfortable, while after Confrontation there appeared to be a fraternal coziness in relations between Singapore's two immediate neighbours. By the end of the 1980s, however, there had been a fundamental realignment in the triangular relationship. Relations between Indonesia and Singapore warmed considerably, while a gulf developed between Indonesia and Malaysia. This realignment was manifested mainly in political and economic terms, but it also had strategic overtones.

Despite their apparent warmth, uneasiness persisted beneath the surface of Singapore–Indonesia relations during the 1990s. Singapore was acutely aware that it falls within the geopolitical zone sometimes referred to as *Asean kecil* (small ASEAN), which senior Indonesian officers see as vital for Indonesia's security. This security concept's essence is that no hostile outside power should be allowed a physical presence within 1500 km of Jakarta. While this might be reassuring for Singapore in the unlikely event of a threat to itself from a major power, it is also worrying in the sense that a future Indonesian regime might view its security interests in its sub-regional 'buffer zone' as justifying interference with Singapore's political or economic freedom of action.

By the mid-1990s Singapore's government was anxious over Indonesia's likely political trajectory and its implications for bilateral relations and the regional security environment, as it became increasingly evident that no clear succession to Suharto had been planned. A long-standing Singapore government fear was that the succession could bring to power a radical leadership which might destabilize bilateral relations.[38]

The 1997 economic crisis brought dramatic political changes and deteriorating relations with Jakarta sooner than expected. Suharto's ouster heralded a new and essentially unwelcome era, in which Singapore's interests have not been accommodated as easily as they had been under the New Order. Indonesia's economic and political crisis during 1998-9 seriously undermined ties, and relations during B. J. Habibie's presidency from May 1998 were tense. The formation of the Abdurrahman Wahid–Megawati Sukarnoputri government in October 1999 allowed a thaw. Nevertheless, Indonesia's continuing domestic instability, and particularly the rise of Islamist politics, stoked Singapore's fears, and even provoked concern that Indonesia might disintegrate. There was a growing perception in Singapore that its sub-regional geopolitics had returned full circle to the situation of the late 1960s, in which the city-state was sandwiched between two unstable, potentially threatening neighbours.[39]

Singapore's strategy

Official statements emphasize Singapore's 'non-directional deterrence'. This, however, belies the fact that the interaction of Singapore's innate vulnerabilities, historical experiences and contemporary relations with neighbours have generated national military strategy reflecting acute concerns over fairly precise threats.

Singapore's complex, often strained relations with its immediate neighbours have provided its defence strategy's core rationale: the maintenance of a sub-regional balance of power in maritime Southeast Asia based on deterrence by Singapore's national military capabilities. In some circumstances, regional or extra-regional associates might supplement national resources, but the government has always viewed self-reliance as the *sine qua non* of Singapore's defence, calculating that no external assistance could be expected if Singapore failed to demonstrate the willingness and ability to defend itself.[40] In the early years of independence, the government sometimes conveyed the impression that the SAF's essential role was to provide token resistance until Singapore's friends came to the rescue. But during the 1970s, particularly in view of the scaling down of FPDA partners' military presence in Singapore and the SAF's concurrent build-up, increasingly it became both necessary and realistic to think in terms of self-reliant defence.

Singapore's strategy evolves

While the SAF's capabilities remained rudimentary, defensively-oriented and based on an infantry-dominated army, Singapore used the analogy of a 'poisonous shrimp' (small, but indigestible to predators) to describe its strategy. The idea was that any aggressor would find that the costs of attempting to invade Singapore outweighed any conceivable benefits. How the SAF would defend Singapore was never specified precisely, though the assumption was presumably that Singapore-based UK, Australian and New Zealand forces would support its resistance to direct military intervention (whether this came from Malaysia, Indonesia or other sources).

The 'poisonous shrimp' concept remained Singapore's *declaratory* strategy even during the 1980s. However, with the encouragement of Israeli military advisers, as defence funding increased rapidly during the late 1960s and early 1970s the SAF's organization, training, doctrine and equipment inventory were developed to support the only strategy which made sense if Singapore, with its peculiar geo-strategic vulnerabilities, was to base its deterrent on national military resources: strategic pre-emption of potential adversaries (primarily Malaysia). It was not until 1984, though, that it was officially acknowledged that Singapore's core strategy had evolved. According to Brigadier-General Lee Hsien Loong, then Chief of Staff (General Staff), the 'poisonous shrimp' strategy was deficient in that it offered Singapore merely a choice of 'suicide or surrender' as it implied that the SAF would fight an unwinnable war on its own territory. In Lee's view, the city-state needed a strategy conveying the message 'I may not completely destroy you but you will have to pay a high price for trying to subdue me, and you may still not succeed.'[41]

Though official statements have never referred explicitly to the SAF's offensive capabilities, let alone to its pre-emptive strategy, by the 1990s they were emphasizing the SAF's need to achieve a 'swift and decisive victory' over aggressors.[42] In 1997, Minister of State for Defence Matthias Yao spoke of the need to give any aggressor a 'knock-out punch in round one'.[43] But he did not admit that Singapore might throw the first punch.

Singapore's geopolitical circumstances and the nature of its armed forces' equipment, organization and training indicate heavy emphasis on the offensive as part of a pre-emptive deterrent strategy, but over time this strategy has become more sophisticated and flexible. Since the 1980s, the 'hardening' of air bases and C3 (command, control and communications) sites, construction of an underground ammunition depot, and exercises using highways as auxiliary runways or under simulated biological and chemical warfare conditions, have indicated the SAF's intent to develop sufficient resilience to absorb an aggressor's first strike. The growth of Singapore's civil defence capability has supported this objective. These developments have significantly widened Singapore's crisis options, by reducing the compulsion to strike first. This could be beneficial in two ways. First, it would allow a margin of error in assessing an adversary's intentions: if the adversary struck first, it need not imply total disaster. Secondly, Singapore could decide to absorb the first wave of an enemy's offensive to gain political advantage: its subsequent counter-attack would more clearly constitute self-defence. It is hard to imagine that any regional adversary could feel sufficiently confident to strike first, though, in view of Singapore's obvious preparations to hit back, hard.

However, the greater sophistication of Singapore's strategic posture during the 1980s and 1990s – and particularly the new emphasis on civil defence – may also have reflected fears that the SAF might otherwise have been unable to deter certain types of threats. For example, Mindef developed plans from the late 1970s for contingencies which might have arisen from the presence of Soviet forces in Vietnam or from wider conflict between the rival superpower-led coalitions.[44]

By the early 1980s, Singapore's growing military capabilities enabled it to contemplate limited power projection in the wider Southeast Asian region as well as deterrence through pre-emption within its immediate sub-region. Mindef prepared contingency plans for deploying SAF ground forces and probably also strike aircraft, possibly in conjunction with Malaysian and Indonesian contingents, to help defend Thailand in case of a large-scale Vietnamese incursion from Cambodia. There has also been a significant maritime dimension to the SAF's power projection capability. Securing Singapore's vital maritime trade in the event of a regional conflict would require the navy to protect not only Singapore-registered and -owned vessels but also other merchant ships serving Singapore, probably in close collaboration with the navies of regional and extra-regional allies and associates.

War with Malaysia?

While the SAF is evidently sufficiently flexible in terms of its organization, equipment and doctrine to be useful in a wide variety of national security contingencies, its capabilities have been refined with specific contingencies in mind: these envisage above all the possibility of war with or in Malaysia, though Singapore's defence planners have undoubtedly also considered possible conflicts with or in Indonesia. Such contingencies have been played out repeatedly in SAF staff college exercises since the late 1960s.

The central assumption of Singapore's strategic thinking is that deploying forces in peninsular Malaysia, with or without the Malaysian government's acquiescence, might be necessary to forestall a repeat of the Japanese offensive of 1942, which had demonstrated the extreme difficulty of defending Singapore once an enemy controlled the landward hinterland. During the late 1960s and 1970s Singapore's defence planners considered the scenario of an upsurge in the MCP's insurgency overwhelming Malaysia's security forces, which would then require assistance to prevent a communist takeover.[45] In the 1980s, thought was given to helping to defend Malaysia against Vietnamese aggression.

Always more credible from the Singapore government's viewpoint, though, were scenarios in which conflict *with* Malaysia would be triggered by political instability there leading to widespread communal violence or interference with Singapore's vital water supply from Johor. In such circumstances, Singapore's government might judge direct military intervention in the Malaysian peninsula to be necessary in order to protect fleeing ethnic Chinese refugees or to secure control over the water pumping stations.[46]

Political objectives of Singapore's strategy

Assuming that Singapore's offensive and possibly pre-emptive strategy would be militarily successful (by no means a foregone conclusion) raises the question of what *political* outcome Singapore would hope for. Long-term occupation of Malaysian territory would be hazardous not only because of a predictable international outcry (though this might be muted if Singapore did not strike first), but also because the likelihood of protracted resistance from remnants of the Malaysian armed forces supported by the Malay population in the occupied territory. Relations with Indonesia, the West and Japan would, at best, have been complicated. The confidence of local and foreign investors in Singapore's economy might be seriously damaged. There would probably be a hostile reaction among Singapore's own Malays. By throwing the SAF into action against Malaysia, Singapore might transform itself into the 'Israel' of Southeast Asia.

The key to understanding Singapore's strategy, though, is that the SAF's capability to inflict severe damage on Malaysia is not intended to be used. The capability is a deterrent – a regional 'doomsday machine' intended to force neighbouring states to treat the city-state with a degree of respect and caution which might otherwise be absent. Indeed, the nature of Singapore's strategy and the dangers implicit in pushing too hard on issues of vital interest to Singapore are apparently well understood in Malaysian government circles. Malaysian cabinet members have sometimes signalled their recognition of the danger of conflict. In 1992, Malaysia's foreign minister stressed that the alternative to settling the dispute with Singapore over Pedra Branca using diplomacy was war, which Malaysia did not want.[47] In 1998, after announcing a ban on Singapore's military aircraft from using Malaysian airspace, the defence minister declared that 'Malaysia would not easily go to war with Singapore'.[48] Moreover, Malaysia's government has ensured that Singapore's water pumping stations and pipelines in Johor are not physically interfered with, despite calls by Malay nationalist and Muslim organizations in both 1986 and 1998 for the supply to be cut off.

The Singapore–Malaysia military balance

In March 1978 Goh Keng Swee, then Singapore's deputy prime minister and defence minister, argued that the republic did not want to arm itself 'to the teeth' for fear of starting 'an arms race in our part of the world'.[49] And because of its concern not to transform potential military adversaries into real ones, Singapore has never expressed publicly its concerns over the developing conventional warfare capabilities of the Malaysian Armed Forces (MAF). Nevertheless, between the late 1980s and mid-1990s, it appeared that the MAF's expanding conventional capabilities might considerably undermine Singapore's existing military superiority. Malaysian equipment purchases during the 1990s – including F/A-18 strike aircraft, various ground-based air defence systems, and Eryx anti-tank missiles – certainly complicated Singapore's planning. Moreover, in contrast to the SAF's almost total lack of operational experience, during the 1990s Malaysia's army improved its combat readiness through deploying units on international peacekeeping operations in Cambodia, Somalia and Bosnia.

If Singapore had not taken these developments seriously in planning its own defence posture, its deterrent might eventually have lost credibility. But it was never likely that Singapore's leadership would allow this to happen. During the 1990s, the 'SAF 2000' force modernization focused on maintaining and enhancing the SAF's technological advantages, particularly by developing advanced C3, ISR (intelligence, surveillance and reconnaissance) and ILS (integrated logistic support) capabilities in order for Singapore's military to benefit from the RMA (Revolution in Military Affairs) that was crucially influencing Western military thinking. At the start of the present decade, Singapore's defence establishment began considering broader issues related to military modernization, and participation in the RMA is now presented as one component of a thoroughgoing process of military transformation aimed at creating a '3G' (third generation) SAF. Senior Mindef officials and SAF officers see such transformation as imperative if the SAF is to develop its operational flexibility in an 'uncertain and complex security landscape', make the most of a limited defence budget as equipment costs escalate, compensate for a demographic shift that will reduce personnel strength, and exploit the RMA as fully as possible. Simultaneously, many of the SAF's equipment procurement programmes – such as Amraam air-to-air missiles, new combat aircraft, and submarines – have apparently been aimed at blunting the likely impact of the MAF's modernization. While the SAF still suffers from important weaknesses in relation to its Malaysian counterpart, the differential impact of the recession of the late 1990s (which led to major cuts in Malaysian defence spending) only highlighted the continuing credibility of Singapore's deterrent.

New Indonesian scenarios

During the 1990s Indonesia's growing prosperity, technological capacity and aspirations to develop well-equipped, modern armed forces capable of projecting power meant that Singapore could not dismiss its giant southern neighbour's long-term military potential. However, major cuts in ABRI funding because of the recession which gripped Indonesia from 1997 forced the cancellation of important equipment contracts, and the bilateral military balance has continued to strongly favour Singapore, despite the tentative revival of Indonesia's military procurement since 2003.

Nevertheless, since 1997 Singapore's security environment to the south has been less predictable than at any time since the 1960s. Indeed the Indonesian archipelago could generate a variety of unconventional and low-intensity, but nevertheless serious, threats. Some of these threats – such as environmental problems caused by the burning of Indonesian forests – are not amenable to military solutions. Others, though, could involve the SAF: possibilities include a major exodus of persecuted minority groups as refugees, large-scale migration in search of economic opportunities or even food if Indonesia's economy enters a new recession, and extensive piracy. Since the revelations in late 2001 regarding a region-wide Islamist conspiracy to overthrow the existing political order in Muslim-populated Southeast Asia, Indonesian-based terrorism has also emerged as a serious concern for Singapore.

The nearby Riau islands (the closest of which, Batam, is only 20 km away) potentially present serious challenges to Singapore's security. The islands could become jumping-off points for refugees and illegal immigrants or bases for pirates preying on commercial shipping entering and leaving Singapore as well as for terrorists. Taken together with the post-1998 record of ethnic clashes and industrial disputes in Riau, these considerations suggest the potential for a 'complex emergency' in the islands to Singapore's south, which might in extreme circumstances require some form of military intervention. By the late 1990s, potential military operations to the south came to figure more prominently in Singapore's strategic thinking, vindicating the emphasis earlier in the decade on building up the SAF's maritime, amphibious and rapid deployment capabilities.

* * *

Without the deterrent provided by the SAF, Singapore would have been at the mercy of its neighbours, and particularly Malaysia, to a far greater extent. It would have been a 'political football' subject to kicking whenever its neighbours' domestic problems indicated a scapegoat might be useful; its own political, economic and social stability would have been seriously endangered. It would be difficult to over-state the extent to which strong defences have provided necessary reassurance not only to Singapore's population but also to local and foreign investors that they can continue to prosper in security.

Since the late 1980s, Singapore's government has striven to reduce the city-state's vulnerabilities. For example, it has attempted to lessen dependence on Malaysian water by seeking alternative supplies from Indonesia and by investing in desalination plants.[50] It has also tried to increase national food security by securing guarantees of emergency rice supplies from Thailand, while planning to increase local production of fish and vegetables.[51] Moreover, since the 1990s, there has appeared to be genuine interest in constructing a new, less conflictual pattern of relations with Malaysia.

Singapore also realizes that military power is not an appropriate instrument for dealing with all challenges to its interests. Its military capabilities are only marginally relevant to threats deriving from regional environmental degradation (the SAF might help reduce marine pollution by policing regional waters, but can do little to prevent the air pollution caused by Indonesian forest fires) and of no use when fighting for the open international trade regime which is crucial for Singapore's well-being. Recognizing the reality of regional and global interdependence, during the 1990s Singapore's foreign policy has made greater use of the city-state's 'soft power' based on its economic and ideational strengths, and has engaged more fully in the activities of the UN and other international institutions. The government has stressed the importance of regional confidence-building mechanisms, notably the ASEAN Regional Forum and the Shangri-La Dialogue. Nevertheless, the political and security-related fallout from the regional recession of the late 1990s underlined the persistent significance of unpredictable sub-regional relations to Singapore's security, and the continued perceived relevance of military means to managing such concerns.[52]

Notes

1 Michael Leifer, 'The conduct of foreign policy', in Kernial Singh Sandhu and Paul Wheatley (eds), *Management of success. The moulding of modern Singapore* (Singapore: Institute of Southeast Asian Studies, 1989).
2 Michael Leifer, *Singapore's foreign policy. Coping with vulnerability* (London: Routledge, 2000).
3 Ibid., p. 161.
4 Ibid., p. 26.
5 Ibid., p. 155.
6 Foreword to Tim Huxley, *Defending the lion city. The armed forces of Singapore* (St Leonards: Allen & Unwin, 2000), p. v.
7 *Defence of Singapore 1994–95* (Singapore: Ministry of Defence, 1994), p. 5.
8 Ibid.
9 Ibid., pp. 13–16.
10 *Defending Singapore in the 21st century*, p. 13.
11 Interview with Defence Minister Lee Boon Yang, *Defense News*, 5–11 December 1994, p. 38.
12 Tim Huxley and David Boey, 'Singapore's army – boosting capabilities', *Jane's Intelligence Review*, April 1996, pp. 174–5; David Boey, 'Singapore: a fragile nation toughens up', *Jane's Intelligence Review*, July 1996, pp. 318–19.
13 'Information technology. Giving the SAF a strategic edge', *Pioneer*, March 1990, pp. 14–17.
14 For a typical exposition of Singapore's vulnerabilities, see interview with Dr Yeo Ning Hong, second minister for defence, in Southeast Asia supplement, *International Defense Review*, December 1986, p. 10.
15 Speech by Prime Minister Lee Kuan Yew, *Straits Times*, 3 July 1987.
16 See comments by Prime Minister Goh Chok Tong, 'Singapore must not be another Kuwait', *Straits Times*, 13 August 1990; Defence Minister Yeo Ning Hong, 'Nation's security depends on strong defence: Dr Yeo', *Singapore Bulletin*, April 1991, p. 1.

17 Cdre Teo Chee Hean, 'Maritime powers in South-East Asia', *Pointer*, vol. 17, no. 4 (October–December 1991), p. 54.
18 Michael Leifer, *Dictionary of the modern politics of South-East Asia* (London: Routledge, 1995), p. 30.
19 Quoted in Chan Heng Chee, *Singapore: the politics of survival, 1965–1967* (Singapore: Oxford University Press, 1971), p. 45.
20 Leifer, 'The conduct of foreign policy', p. 968.
21 Wu Yuan-li, 'Planning security for a small nation: lessons from Singapore', *Pacific Community*, vol. 3, no. 4 (July 1972), p. 662.
22 Obaid Ul Haq, 'Foreign policy', in Jon S. T. Quah, Chan Heng Chee and Seah Chee Meow (eds), *Government and politics of Singapore* (Singapore: Oxford University Press, 1987), p. 290.
23 Leifer, 'The conduct of foreign policy', pp. 973–4.
24 See, for example, the interview with Defence Minister Lee Boon Yang, *Asian Defence Journal*, July 1995, p. 6.
25 Interview with Defence Minister Tony Tan, 'Attracting, keeping the best as SAF regulars a key concern', *Straits Times*, 1 February 1996.
26 Leifer, 'The conduct of foreign policy', p. 978.
27 Interview with Senior Minister Lee Kuan Yew, *Straits Times*, 9 June 1996.
28 Leifer, 'The conduct of foreign policy', p. 971.
29 Sheldon W. Simon, 'The regionalization of defence in Southeast Asia', *Pacific Review*, vol. 5, no. 2 (1992), pp. 112–14; Richard Stubbs, 'Subregional security cooperation in ASEAN: military and economic imperatives and political obstacles', *Asian Survey*, vol. 32 (1992), pp. 397–410.
30 Donald K. Emmerson, 'Indonesia, Malaysia, Singapore: a regional security core?', in Richard Ellings and Sheldon W. Simon (eds), *Southeast Asian security in the new millennium* (Armonk, NY: M.E. Sharpe, 1996), p. 86.
31 N. Ganesan, 'Taking stock of post-Cold War developments in Asean', *Security Dialogue*, vol. 25 (1994), pp. 458–60.
32 'NS period and defence budget will not be cut', *Singapore Bulletin*, January 1992, pp. 1, 8.
33 Leifer, *Dictionary of the modern politics of South-East Asia*, pp. 147–8.
34 Leifer, 'The conduct of foreign policy', p. 969.
35 Speech by Prime Minister Lee Kuan Yew, 'Why Singapore is ready to pay a high premium for security', *Straits Times*, 3 July 1987.
36 See, for example, interview with Lieutenant-General Winston Choo, Singapore's Chief of Defence Force, in *Asian Defence Journal*, March 1989, p. 47.
37 For a more detailed assessment of Singapore–Malaysia relations, see Huxley, *Defending the lion city*, pp. 44–50.
38 Interviews, Singapore, July–August 1996.
39 For more detail on Singapore-Indonesia relations, see Huxley, *Defending the lion city*, pp. 50–5.
40 See Lee Kuan Yew's 1967 comments on this theme, cited in Alex Josey, *Lee Kuan Yew. The crucial years* (Singapore: Times Books International, 1980), p. 376; and subsequent remarks by Rear Admiral Teo Chee Hean, second defence minister, in 'Singaporeans should be willing to fight to keep country's independence', *Pioneer*, December 1997, p. 11.
41 'A conversation with BG Lee Hsien Loong', *Asean Forecast*, vol. 4, no. 10 (October 1984), p. 164, cited in Bilveer Singh, 'A small state's quest for security. Operationalizing deterrence in Singapore's strategic thinking' in Ban Kah Choon, Anne Pakir and Tong Chee Kiong (eds), *Imagining Singapore* (Singapore: Times Academic Press, 1992), p. 123.
42 See, for example, *Defence of Singapore 1994–95*, p. 17.

43 Statement by Mathias Yao, Minister of State for Defence, at the Singapore Combat Engineers' 30th anniversary parade-cum-commissioning of the Combat Engineer Tractor, Mindef Internet Webservice, 11 April 1997.
44 Chin Kin Wah, 'Singapore: threat perceptions and defence spending in a city-state', in Chin Kin Wah (ed), *Defence spending in Southeast Asia* (Singapore: Institute of Southeast Asian Studies, 1987), pp. 199–200.
45 'Australia, Singapore prepare to defend Malaysia', *Canberra Times*, 10 May 1977.
46 For a more detailed scenario for war with Malaysia, see Huxley, *Defending the lion city*, pp. 58–62.
47 Andrew Tan, *Problems and issues in Malaysia–Singapore relations*. Working Paper no. 314 (Canberra: Strategic and Defence Studies Centre, Australian National University, 1997), p. 15.
48 *Straits Times*, 4 November 1998.
49 *Parliamentary Debates Singapore*, vol. 37, no. 9 (14 March 1978), cols. 770–1.
50 'Three water plants by 2011', *Straits Times Weekly Edition*, 9 May 1998.
51 'Rice pact with Thailand soon', *Singapore Bulletin*, April 1999, p. 3; 'Move to boost fish and vegetable supply', *Singapore Bulletin*, September 1999, p. 16.
52 See speeches by Deputy Prime Minister and Defence Minister Tony Tan, Mindef Internet Webservice, 1 July 1999 and 28 July 1999.

11 Michael Leifer on Cambodia and the Third Indochina Conflict

Ang Cheng Guan

This chapter attempts to review Professor Michael Leifer's contribution to the study of Cambodia and the Third Indochina Conflict from the perspective of an international historian of contemporary Southeast Asia. As a student of that subject, I have long benefited from Leifer's writings. Although he is not considered a historian, his writings bear elements of the historian's preference – sensitivity to the particularity of circumstance[1] and the narrative/process-tracing as a more satisfactory approach to explain outcomes than covering laws.[2] Leifer's writings also display the best practices of contemporary (and) international history. Contemporary history remains a controversial sub-field of history which Jonathan Haslam described as 'the most contentious and problematic history of all'.[3] International history, on the other hand, is a new field with an old pedigree,[4] and is very much in vogue, especially since the end of the Cold War. The range of works in diplomatic or international history is enormous and it has long since moved beyond the recounting of what one clerk said to another or focusing only on the domestic bases of foreign policy. One of the most difficult tasks of the international historian is to balance the knowledge of everything that happened in and around a certain sequence of events and the knowledge of everything relevant that happened outside that particular sequence of events that affects the interpretation of it.

The opening of the once secret communist archives has enabled historians to construct a fuller picture of the Cold War period which until its end had been largely shaped by the reading of primary documents declassified regularly by the non-communist Western governments, particularly the United States and Britain. In the past decade, there has been a proliferation of scholarly writings on various aspects of the Cold War which relate to Eastern Europe, the former Soviet Union, and to a lesser extent communist China and Northeast Asia. In contrast, the general consensus is that the literature of the Cold War in Southeast Asia, (with the possible exception of Indochina and the Vietnam War) bucks this trend.[5] One major obstacle faced by historians working on the Cold War years in Southeast Asia is the unavailability of primary documents. Notwithstanding the end of the Cold War, there is no indication that Southeast Asian governments are considering making documents of the Cold War years accessible to scholars in the near future.

In an article published in a recent issue of *International Security* David C. King observed that because Europe was so important for such a long period of time, international relations scholarship has focused on explaining the European experience; concepts, theories and experiences were all derived from the European experience. However, the Eurocentric ideas were not universal and could not accurately explain the Asian experience.[6] The value of Leifer's contribution is thus in his study of Southeast Asia and the Cold War. They are indeed highly polished first drafts of history. Many years from now when historians are able to write the International History of Southeast Asia, I am confident that they will find Leifer's writings useful signposts.

Leifer's writings (on Cambodia) are set within the framework of what is often described as the English School of International Relations in which the principal focus is 'order' and which is based on the belief that states, and in this case Cambodia, are constantly searching for 'some measures of regularity in their international activities' by creating 'stable mechanisms of habits and practices that ensure survival'. To Leifer, the Third Indochina conflict was a disagreement on the fundamental principles on which state interaction occurs and as such is seen as an 'essential dispute' in which reconciliation (and through that the re-establishment of 'order') could only be achieved through the application of the triple 'institutions' of balance of power, diplomacy and international law. This was the organizational theme of Michael Leifer's Cambodia story.[7]

But to borrow a phrase from Stanley Hoffman writing in a different context, Leifer did not begin (as Kenneth Waltz did, for example) his study of international relations with the requirement of method, that is, by laying down a very interesting and rigorous notion of theory. This quality put Leifer closer to the historian than the international relations specialist that he is known to be. As Alan Sked (of LSE's equally well-known International History Department) put it, historians tend to simply ignore the philosophical and theoretical issues which underlie the so-called 'paradigmatic debate' that so often obsesses their international relations colleagues.[8] Leifer's writings tend to be empirical/descriptive. As King, Keohane and Verba reminded us, 'we cannot construct meaningful, causal explanations without good description; description, in turn, loses most of its interest unless linked to some causal relationships. Description often comes first; it is hard to develop explanations before we know something about the world and what needs to be explained on the basis of what characteristics.'[9] Yuen Foong Khong offered an explanation as to why empiricism reigned in discussions of Southeast Asia during the Cold War. According to Khong, during the Cold War, the defining theoretical parameters – bipolarity and its effects – appeared fixed; and therefore analytical attention seemed more usefully directed at describing the manoeuvres of the relevant players in the bipolar game.[10]

This is perhaps an appropriate point (before launching into the subject of Cambodia and the Third Indochina Conflict proper) to explain briefly why Michael Leifer wrote in the way he did. In his formative years as a research student at the LSE in the mid-1950s, Leifer was very much influenced by his doctoral supervisor Elie Kedourie (who was a political historian of the Middle East). He described the experience of being supervised by Kedourie as 'awesome, daunting and highly rewarding', 'rich, formative and long-lasting'. In his words, it was from Kedourie that he

> learned at first-hand the values that should inform the life of an academic community. It was from him also that that I acquired a fuller understanding of the activity of politics and what might be expected of those who indulged in it. I like to think that such an understanding gleaned from tutorial conversations has stood me in good stead during my own academic career in interpreting a regional field of study different from that which originally brought me under Elie's intellectual influence.'[11]

Unfortunately, Leifer's 'personal note' on Elie Kedourie is very brief and therefore in order to gain a deeper understanding of Leifer's writing style and approach, we need to know a little more about his intellectual mentor, Elie Kedourie, which in turn leads us to the ideas of Michael Oakeshott. Kedourie was well known as an 'Oakeshottian'. For Kedourie, history was a chronological narrative of the actions of key individuals within a particular context or set of circumstances. Chronology is the structure. History is about events – not structures, forces or laws. Kedourie's writings are essentially non-judgemental historical accounts eschewing moral appraisal, preferring to let actions and thoughts be judged on their own terms.[12] These 'Kedourie' characteristics would also be the trademark of Michael Leifer's writings, as will be described below.

Leifer's early writings on Cambodia

Cambodia is a natural and logical point from which to embark on a review of Michael Leifer's writings. In his assessment of the state of Southeast Asian studies in the region, Harry J. Benda, the first Director of the Institute of Southeast Asia Studies (ISEAS) in 1969 noted that the Southeast Asian region had expended very little research effort in the study of Cambodia.[13] Leifer was one of the few who helped fill the scholarly lacuna. His very first articles published after he obtained his doctorate (in 1959) were on Cambodia. He published 'Cambodia and Her Neighbours' in the Winter 1961–62 issue of *Pacific Affairs*.[14] In the 1960s, he was also a regular contributor to *Asian Survey*[15] on Cambodian affairs which culminated in his first book published in 1967 entitled *Cambodia: The Search for Security*,[16] which is a significant early contribution to the historiography of modern Cambodia. Leifer's scholarship significantly advanced the study of the international history of Southeast Asia during the Cold

War years, and helped bring valuable perspective to the Vietnam (Indochina) War and the Vietnamese invasion of Cambodia.

Although *Cambodia: The Search for Security* is the only full-length study of Cambodia that Leifer wrote, the subtitle of the book would remain the organizing theme/focus of many of his subsequent writings, principally articles and book chapters, on Cambodia until the 1990s. Cambodia also served as a major platform for Leifer to widen his scholarship into the international relations of the Asia Pacific, for which he is remembered as a pioneer.

Cambodia: The Search for Security attempts to describe and explain the problems of external security faced by the newly independent state of Cambodia (which achieved its independence from the French in November 1953 and had it formally confirmed by the Geneva Conference of July 1954) and how the country managed its security through its foreign policy. Leifer's first book possessed three qualities which would become trademark features of much of his subsequent writings (and which by no coincidence were also the characteristics of Elie Kedourie's well-known doctoral thesis 'England and the Middle East'. One, the style of writing is crisp, concise and in places even elegant. Leifer's writings are never dull or dry. One finds hardly any jargon in his text and he could put across complex issues simply and clearly. In explaining Cambodia's foreign policy, Leifer was able to integrate and weave the internal imperatives, the external geopolitical factors as well as the peculiarities of the country's principal protagonist, Sihanouk, into an organic and very readable narrative. Two, Leifer had a good grasp of the chronology of events. He never allowed the chronology, which he adhered to very closely, to suffocate his narrative. Rather, because of his sensitivity to chronology, he was able to contextualize his analysis, identify core issues, develop a feel for the illuminating detail, the subtle twists and turns and the 'watersheds'. Three, Leifer's writings had an element of 'objectivity' which some might choose to call his 'academic detachment'. *Cambodia: The Search for Security* is first and last an attempt to describe and explain. The author rarely if ever imposes his own stance on the reader, preferring to let the events and the protagonists speak for themselves. And on the occasions where he inserts a personal opinion, which is always very well-considered and measured, the reader is fully aware of the author's intrusion and he usually left that to the end. This is a refreshing quality considering that a large proportion of the writings during and about the Cold War period had the tendency to be partisan and ideological.

To illustrate the above, allow me to highlight how Leifer described and explained how Sihanouk arrived at the conclusion that 'neutrality' was the solution for Cambodia's security problems and how the policy failed him, which is a major theme of the book. It was Max Weber who articulated that the social scientist should respect and empathize with the meanings which political actors gave to their actions, as well as being aware of (and highlighting) the frequent disconnection between the actors' intentions and the results. Leifer drew attention to the fact that independent Cambodia faced a security problem that had been in abeyance during the colonial period. The two traditional antagonists were

Thailand and South Vietnam. Sihanouk anticipated that an independent South Vietnam would be an uneasy neighbour and that a reunified Vietnam controlled from Hanoi would bring about the resurgence of traditional Vietnamese–Cambodian enmity. Furthermore, these two traditional antagonists had powerful patrons. Thailand and South Vietnam were closely associated with the United States whereas North Vietnam was aligned with the Soviet Union and more significantly China. Sihanouk was keenly aware of and interested in the growing influence of China displayed at the 1954 Geneva Conference. Then, Beijing had shown that it was prepared to sponsor a settlement in Indochina that gave limited gains for the communists in Vietnam and Laos but not in Cambodia. But Sihanouk was not confident that Vietnamese communist subversive activities (in which SEATO guarantee would be of little efficacy) would not recur in Cambodia in the future. But any commitment of foreign troops in Cambodia would create a different set of problems as was seen in the public protests during Dulles's February 1955 visit to Phnom Penh to discuss US military aid to Cambodia. Sihanouk had to avoid being too closely associated with the so-called imperialist countries (which he needed to court) and antagonizing his domestic opposition as a consequence as well as upsetting Beijing which had so far shown its ability to restrain Cambodia's external enemies. Apparently, it was the Indian government which introduced Sihanouk to the 'neutrality' way out of his conundrum following a visit by Indian Prime Minister Nehru in November 1955. Sihanouk gradually learned to exploit the Cold War confrontation to the advantage of Cambodia. He sought to use the opposing powers to establish a political equilibrium that he thought would safeguard Cambodia's territorial and national integrity. Here, Leifer quoted Sihanouk to good effect: 'Our neutrality has been imposed on us by necessity. A glance at a map of our part of the world will show that we are wedged in between two medium-sized nations of the Western bloc and only thinly screened by Laos from the scrutiny of two countries of the Eastern bloc, North Vietnam and the vast People's Republic of China. What choice have we but to try to maintain an equal balance between the "blocs"?'

Cambodia's policy of neutrality was not solely the result of external circumstances. There was also a domestic angle to it as Leifer revealed. Despite having won overwhelmingly in the 1955 general election, Sihanouk realized that there remained a hard core within the country that continued to oppose his authority and that he would have to act prudently to avoid providing them with opportunities to enhance their political position. One sure way of ensuring his position and silencing his critics who might accuse him of compromising Cambodia's sovereignty was to demonstrate that Cambodia's newly won independence was real. All policies have their ups and downs. In this case, while Sihanouk's neutrality policy reactivated the traditional antagonisms with Cambodia's neighbours, it also consolidated national unity against the external threats more than any other issue could.[17]

Sihanouk's policy of neutrality appeared to have worked reasonably well until mid-1961. Leifer noted from about August 1961, 'the beginnings of a modification of neutrality from a policy founded on equal balance to a policy that sought to respond to a transformation of that balance in favour of one side'. The Laotian crisis, and the related growing conflict in Vietnam brought about this change of attitude which Leifer described as a likely watershed in the development of Cambodian foreign policy. Sihanouk became increasingly concerned with the growth of political divisions in Cambodia, especially of a generational kind which could generate internecine conflict like that which was taking place in Laos. Sihanouk feared that the internal divisions within Cambodia, if left uncurbed, would only provide opportunities for external intervention. This was especially worrisome to Sihanouk as Cambodia bordered Laos on the north and he had expected Laos to become communist in the not very distant future.[18]

Sihanouk had initially decided to seek insulation and protection through great power guarantees. He apparently hoped that such guarantees would produce a balance of political forces that would automatically ensure Cambodia's territorial integrity. The 1962 Laotian settlement had demonstrated that such a desirable balance no longer existed.[19] To Sihanouk, there could either be a neutral or a pro-Communist Thailand, to which China might give free rein at Cambodia's expense, or a reunited Vietnam under the control of the regime in Hanoi. In both scenarios, Cambodia needed Beijing for protection against the traditional threats coming from Thailand and Vietnam. Thus, Sihanouk increasingly regarded the accommodation of China as a necessary posture as he believed China was certain to dominate Asia in the future.[20]

Another change took place around mid-1966 when it seemed that Sihanouk's concern about the possible extension of the Vietnam War into Cambodia was becoming more important than his regard for communist sensibilities. Unfortunately, Leifer was unable to elaborate on this change as his study ended in 1966.[21]

Cambodia: The Search for Security remains to date one of the most, if not the most comprehensive and nuanced account of Cambodia's foreign policy in the early post-independence years (up to about 1966). In his conclusion and writing from the vantage point of 1966, Leifer made the prescient observation that Cambodia's political future seemed to be linked inextricably with the Vietnam conflict. According to Leifer, any settlement satisfying Cambodia's minimum security needs would have to wait until there was a resolution of the Vietnam question. The challenge for Cambodia was to remain detached and intact until a more permanent arrangement for the peaceful and independent existence of the states of Indochina was decided by the powers concerned.[22]

The 1970 coup

Leifer did not neglect to remind his readers that Sihanouk had his flaws. He was a very sensitive man and often saw insults where none existed.[23] Also, Sihanouk had the tendency to merge his personal ambitions with national imperatives although, to be fair, he managed to maintain a clear order of priorities of which the security of Cambodia was his principal objective.[24] There was, however, little Phnom Penh could do of its own accord to safeguard its own security. Cambodia was, as Leifer described it, 'very much a prisoner of unfortunate circumstances'. Sihanouk must be credited for keeping Cambodia independent and stable while much of Indochina was in turmoil. Sihanouk was the guiding hand in Cambodian foreign policy. He provided the inspiration and dynamic spirit for the conduct of his country's foreign relations. Leifer's description of Sihanouk again reflects the influence of Elie Kedourie. As Alan Beattie so eloquently explained,

> Kedourie's writing contain also detailed consideration of the circumstances, character and thoughts of particular individuals. This is not 'biography' (in the sense of an attempt to reduce thoughts to upbringing or social location), but rather a desire to specify the circumstances to which individuals were responding, the stock of ideas available to them, the use they made of the responses. These vignettes are thus both an exercise in revealing the relationship between thought and circumstance and a reaffirmation of the difficulty and danger of abstract generalization.[25]

Thus the coup which ousted Sihanouk in March 1970 was one of the most important turning points in contemporary Cambodian history, and its ramifications were felt right up to the 1990s. It is therefore worthwhile to re-visit Leifer's treatment of this episode. An article by Leifer, 'Rebellion or Subversion in Cambodia?' in the February 1969 issue of *Current History* is most useful for an understanding of the situation in Cambodia prior to the coup. Of course, neither Leifer not anybody else predicted the March 1970 coup. But that was not the intention of the article, which attempted to answer the question whether the process of insurgency which Cambodia was then experiencing was a product of internal circumstances or outside intervention. To Leifer, in order to answer that question, it was necessary 'to put the chronology of relevant events to critical analysis'. Leifer's concluding observation about a year before the coup is worth citing in full:

> At this point of time, Cambodia is by no means aflame. The government gives the appearance of being in control, while the basis of effective rebel support would appear to be restricted. The rebels have an ability to create conditions of insecurity, but their prospect of success will depend (discounting external factors) not only on the exploitation of genuine grievance but also on an ability to identify with the nationalist cause for which Prince Sihanouk has been the most ardent and passionate advocate. This would seem unlikely. The political practice of Sihanouk, in any case, is not beyond question, and he may fail to appreciate the relationship between social change and popular expectations and demands and the sense of

> frustration of those educated young men who oppose his personal style of government.[26]

Reiterating the observation he made as early as 1968,[27] Leifer explained the March 1970 coup in his book *Dilemmas of Statehood in Southeast Asia.*[28] A special problem was that the institutional base created by Sihanouk in 1955 (the Sangkum) had not progressed beyond being a vehicle for personal rule which served also to contain the disruptive clash of political forces. It had not served as an instrument for fostering an integrative process of participation in political life because of Sihanouk's monopoly position. Although Sihanouk was aware of the innate weakness of the political system that he created, he did not take any substantive action. Discontent among urban youth linked with economic grievance and personal frustration, rural unrest and the long-standing irritation of the Cambodian political elite all focused on the political order personified in Sihanouk. Here we have an example of one of Leifer's most memorable lines: his observation that 'those who deposed Sihanouk replaced him with power but not legitimacy. And they were to discover early on that the 'de-Stalinization' of a man revered for so long by so many is not easily accomplished.'

But the immediate problem of legitimacy was overshadowed by the ongoing Vietnam War. The ousting of Sihanouk not only left a domestic political vacuum, but also 'disturbed a wide politico-military equilibrium which the Cambodian Government did not have the resources to restore'. Leifer reminded his readers that the strength of Sihanouk's political leadership was that both domestically and internationally it sustained a viable and peaceful political order.

The 1970 coup or putsch had been the subject of a bitter debate since it took place and many commentators maintained that the United States (particularly Henry Kissinger, US National Security Adviser), was responsible for it. In the 1990s, declassified US secret cables showed that the US government was not behind the coup although, after it took place, the needs of the Vietnam War dictated that they support Lon Nol.[29] The final reference to this pivotal period of modern Cambodian history is Leifer's 'The International Dimension of the Cambodian Conflict' published in the October 1975 issue of *International Affairs*. Published about five years after the coup, Leifer's account of who was responsible, brief as it may be, shows his careful handling of evidence and remains one of the most balanced that I have read. He wrote,

> Without accepting at face value the accusation by Prince Sihanouk that the CIA master-minded his overthrow, there is evidence which not only indicates prior plotting by General Lon Nol but also contingency planning which took into account the probable hostile reaction of the Vietnamese communist for whom Cambodia had become a major military facility… Whether this indication of prior planning by Lon Nol involved a connection with some branch of the American intelligence 'community' is not as important in the context of this article as the probability that Lon Nol, either acting alone or

with Sirik Matak, his principal government deputy, had a clear awareness that the removal of Sihanouk would be more than just a domestic affair.

The objective of this particular article was to examine the international/external factors which came into play as a direct consequence of March 1970 coup. With the ousting of Sihanouk, Cambodia finally became directly involved in the Vietnam and (perhaps the more appropriately term) Indochina War. The article covers the period from the March 1970 coup to the fall of Phnom Penh in April 1975 and it takes in the roles and interests of the US, China, the Soviet Union, Vietnam and ASEAN during those years. Leifer's article provides a useful historical context/background for the next period of Cambodia's tragic history.

In 'The International Dimension of the Cambodian Conflict', Leifer noted that 'with the fall of Phnom Penh, Cambodia was deliberately sealed off from conventional international dealings. All diplomatic missions were closed and foreign personnel excluded.' And as prescient as he always was, he made the observation that 'Taken together with more tangible evidence, it is possible to suggest that Cambodia may be a less than compliant neighbour of the Vietnamese communists and that a significant international consequence arising from the change of government in Phnom Penh has been to underline tensions amongst communist states in Asia.'

Leifer's later writings on Cambodia

One of the most significant turning points in the history of Cambodia and in the international politics of the region is the Vietnamese invasion of Cambodia in December 1978. Five years after 'The International Dimension of the Cambodian Conflict', Leifer returned to write on Cambodia again, beginning with his contributions to the January 1980 and 1981 issues of *Asian Survey*.[30] He was then 47 and by the time he had finished writing on Cambodia in 1993, he was 60 years of age. Many are perhaps more familiar with his writings on Cambodia during and on this period (1980–93).

Reflecting on the Cambodian situation one year after the Vietnamese invasion, Leifer noted that the 'tormented country of Kampuchea assumed an international political significance of a kind once associated with Vietnam'. The initiatives to convene an international conference to resolve the Kampuchea problem failed principally because the key parties to the conflict were not in favour. The fighting continued in the final months of 1979, and its course over the dry season into 1980 would demonstrate whether or not there was a viable military option within Kampuchea that with a modicum of external assistance could resist the complete imposition of a Vietnamese ordained political order in Indochina. The answer to that question, Leifer correctly believed, would be central to any further attempt to promote a political settlement in a country that was described once as an oasis of peace in Southeast Asia.

By 1980, it was clear that the nature of the protracted conflict within and over Kampuchea has made it most unlikely that there could be any form of political settlement unless there was a decisive change in the battlefield one way or another. The Khmer Rouge represented the only viable direct military challenge to Vietnamese dominance but they were an unacceptable political alternative for ASEAN members and their Western sympathizers. But the fact was that any resistance to Vietnam's design in Indochina required 'the bloody instrument of the Khmer Rouge'.

Leifer gave a talk to the Asia Society on 10 November 1982 (which was subsequently published in the June 1983 of the British journal *Asian Affairs*) where he described and explained the crux of the Third Indochina Conflict. At issue, he explained, was the question of the political identity and external affiliations of Cambodia/Kampuchea which was made more complicated by the fact that it was not an exclusively inter-Communist affair. The lecture also described the developments of the conflict as it entered its fourth dry season. This lecture was one of his most illuminating expositions on the balance or, as Leifer put it, more accurately the *distribution* of power within the peninsula and beyond in Southeast Asia. It is one of the best pieces I have read on the Third Indochina War – all the key issues concisely and succinctly laid out. Leifer's prognosis was that the interlocking pattern of conflict in Indochina made the early prospect of a political settlement seem unlikely. An ideal settlement would take the form of the reconstitution of the government of Kampuchea in such a manner that it would be acceptable to Vietnam and to China and Thailand. To pose a solution in these terms is to beg the question because one has done no more than identify the central and, so far, insuperable problem.

Leifer's next two essays, essentially made the same points. He also made at least two contributions to 'The 5th Column' of the *Far Eastern Economic Review* on the Cambodian issue.[31] His last substantial piece on the Cambodian conflict was published in *Conflict Studies* in May 1989, where he related the developments from the end of 1987 to early 1989.[32] Neither side has been able to impose a military solution or concede a political one, either from exhaustion or pressure from an external patron. Leifer hit the nail on its head when he noted that unless Sino-Vietnamese relations were repaired, the final phase of the Cambodian conflict would remain incomplete.

On 17 January 1990, Leifer gave a second talk on Cambodia at the Asia Society (which was subsequently published in the June 1990 issue of *Asian Affairs*) where he again emphasized the issue of Sino-Vietnamese relations. This was his second update on Cambodia to the Asia Society, eight years after his first in 1982. Notably, he did not express confidence that a resolution was in sight. But as he pointed out, as with so many contemporary political issues, the pace of events is such that no sooner have you written a line than you have to revise it. Indeed, events and developments were happening at a furious pace during the late 1980s and it would take many more years before historians could piece the jigsaw together. The Soviet Union had completely withdrawn from Afghanistan by

February 1989. The Chinese and the Vietnamese had their first meeting at the vice-ministerial level, the first in nine years, in January 1989. This was followed by the Sino-Soviet Summit (15–18 May 1989), the first since 1959. An International Conference on Cambodia in Paris was convened from 30 July until 30 August 1989. Vietnamese troops were completely withdrawn from Cambodia by 26 September 1989, a process that began in January 1989. The Berlin Wall fell on 10 November 1989, heralding the collapse of communism in Eastern Europe.

A few months after Leifer gave his Asia Society talk, a second round of vice-ministerial talks between China and Vietnam too place from 8 until 10 May 1990, which was followed by a secret meeting between the Chinese and Vietnamese at Chengdu in September 1990. Meanwhile, a Cambodian Summit was convened in Tokyo from 4 until 6 June 1990 where the idea of a Supreme National Council (SNC) was mooted, and this was formalized at the Second Informal meeting on Cambodia in Jakarta on 9 September 1990. The SNC had its inaugural meeting in Bangkok (17–19 September 1990) but made no headway in reaching a political settlement. Then in the third quarter of 1991, there were three meetings of the SNC in quick succession – June, July and August 1991. A coup took place in Moscow in August. In July, August and September, Le Duc Anh (who was the general who oversaw the Vietnamese invasion of Cambodia in 1978), Vice-Deputy Foreign Minister Nguyen Duy Nien and Foreign Minister Nguyen Manh Cam made separate visits to China. On 23 October 1991, the Third Indochina Conflict came to an end at the International Conference on Cambodia in Paris. By the end of the year, the Soviet Union was history. Leifer concluded his story of the Third Indochina Conflict in 'The Indochina Problem'.[33]

Conclusion

By way of conclusion, Michael Leifer reminds me of some aspects of Thucydides as well as of Isaiah Berlin's fox. When Thucydides chose to write the history of the Peloponnesian War, the war was still ongoing. The same held true for Leifer with regard to the Cambodian conflict. Like Thucydides, 'his research was among people, not among papers', to borrow a phrase from the noted translator of Thucydides, Rex Warner.[34] Thucydides, though not unaware of the use of documents (often considered the foundation of modern historical writing) made very limited use of them. One also finds it hard to verify the reliability of his informants because often they are not named. This was also true of Leifer. As Yuen Foong Khong so elegantly put it, Leifer 'wore his learning lightly and while realizing the unattributable quotes are far from definitive, he was more than happy to allow time to prove their veracity'.[35] In this respect, I must confess that I find Kenton J. Clymer more satisfactory reading. But Clymer had the advantage of time and even then he laments that many documents remain classified.[36] Historians should, however, be careful not to over-emphasize the utility of documents. Yuen Foong Khong reminded us of Leifer's 'prodigious propensity for field work' and his privileged access to his LSE students turned top civil servants and even ministers. The combination of Leifer's findings garnered from his fieldwork and the documentary evidence (when they are made available) would certainly help the historian tell a more accurate story.

Michael Leifer has often been described as a 'realist'. In my view, like Thucydides, Leifer's 'realist' perspective is what appeals at least to the student of international/diplomatic history. Robert Kaplan reminded us that

> our much-vaunted foreign-policy idealism is mainly confined to the media and academia, and particularly to the intellectual journals of opinion. Those who sit behind the important desks at the National Security Council, the Departments of Defense and State, and the Pentagon are usually realists...Even the rare administrations that were associated with foreign-policy idealism converted to realism sooner or later... Realists almost always run foreign policy; idealists, I have found, attend academic conferences and write books and articles form the sidelines.[37]

Realism, in Kaplan's words, is 'in part the ability to see the truth behind moral pretensions'. This is clearly shown in Leifer's chapter 'Vietnam's Intervention in Kampuchea'.[38]

I wish Leifer had said more about Cambodia, perhaps delving a little deeper into some aspects. His writings traversed the region's complex history and Cambodia was but one of his many subjects in his Southeast Asian journey. It is also perhaps worth making the observation that a large proportion were written before the 1990s when computer use was rare, which makes his research and writings all the more commendable. Having said all that, most significantly, to me, Leifer always gave due regard to the facts insofar as they are known and always tried to give all sides of the contemporary arguments. I found this especially worthy of emulation.

Notes

1 Alan Beattie, 'Elie Kedourie's Philosophical History' in Sylvia Kedourie (ed.), *Elie Kedourie, CBE, 1926–1992: History, Philosophy, Politics* (London: Frank Cass, 1998), p. 117.

2 See Paul W. Schroeder, 'Review Article: The Function of Encyclopaedic Knowledge' in *The International History Review,* XXV, 4, December 2003, pp. 877–885.

3 Jonathan Haslam, 'The Cold War as History' in *Annual Review of Political Science*, 2003, Volume 6, pp. 77–98.

4 Zara Steiner, 'On Writing International History: Chaps, Maps and Much More' in *International Affairs*, Volume 73, Number 4, 1997, pp. 531–546.

5 Robert J. McMahon, 'The Cold War in Asia: The Elusive Synthesis' in Michael J. Hogan (ed.), *America in the World: The Historiography of American Foreign Relations since 1941* (New York: Cambridge University Press, 1995), pp. 501–535; Richard Mason, 'Origins of the Cold War in Southeast Asia: A Survey of Post-revisionist Interpretations', unpublished paper presented at the Conference on Southeast Asian Historiography since 1945, 30 July–1 August 1999, Penang, Malaysia.

6 David C. King, 'Getting Asian Wrong: The Need for New Analytical Frameworks' in *International Security*, Volume 27, Number 4 (Spring 2003), pp. 57–85.

7 See Liselotte Odgaard, *Maritime Security between China and Southeast Asia: Conflict and Cooperation in the Making of Regional Order* (Burlington, VT: Ashgate, 2002), Chapter 2: 'The English School and the Study of Order'; Barry Buzan, 'The English School: An Underexploited Resource in IR' in *Review of International Studies*, Volume 27, 2001, pp. 471–488.

8 Alan Sked, 'The Study of International Relations: A Historian's View' in *Millennium: Journal of International Studies,* Volume 16, Number 2, pp. 251–262 (1987).

9 Gary King, Robert O. Keohane and Sidney Verba, *Designing Social Enquiry: Scientific Inference in Qualitative Research* (Princeton, NJ: Princeton University Press, 1994), Chapter 2.

10 Khong Yuen Foong, 'Making Bricks Without Straw in the Asia Pacific?' in *The Pacific Review*, Volume 10, Number 2, 1997.

11 Michael Leifer, 'A Personal Note' in Sylvia Kedourie (ed.), *Elie Kedourie, CBE, FBA, 1926–1992: History, Philosophy, Politics* (London: Frank Cass, 1998), pp. 29–30.

12 Alan Beattie, 'Elie Kedourie's Philosophical History', in Kedourie (ed.), *Elie Kedourie*, pp. 109–131.

13 Harry J. Benda, *Research in Southeast Asian Studies in Singapore*, Institute of Southeast Asian Studies Singapore Occasional Paper Number 1, March 1970 (first published in *Journal of the South Seas Society*, Volume XXIV (1969)).

14 Michael Leifer, 'Cambodia and Her Neighbours' in *Pacific Affairs*, Volume XXXIV, Number 4 (Winter 1961–62).

15 The first issue of *Asian Survey* was published in March 1961. Its main purpose is 'to provide insights into current developments in Asia – to concern itself as much with the topical foreground as with the background of contemporary affairs'. See Michael Leifer, 'The Cambodian Opposition' in *Asian Survey*, Volume 2, Number 2 (April 1962); 'The Cambodian Elections', Volume 2, Number 7 (September 1962); 'Cambodia: In Search of Neutrality', Volume 3, Number 1 (January 1963); 'Cambodia: The Politics of Accommodation', Volume 4, Number 1 (January 1964); 'Cambodia: The Limits of Diplomacy', Volume 7, Number 1 (January 1967).

16 Michael Leifer, *Cambodia: The Search for Security* (London: Praeger, 1967).

17 The above is summarized from Leifer, *Cambodia: The Search for Security*, pp. 17–19, 60–61, 65, 70–79.

18 Ibid., pp. 127–131.

19 Ibid., p. 134.

20 Ibid., p. 142.

21 Ibid., p. 183.

22 Ibid., p. 185.

23 Ibid., p. 76.

24 Ibid., p. 19.

25 Beattie,'Kedourie's Philosophical History', p.121.

26 Michael Leifer, 'Rebellion or Subversion in Cambodia?' in *Current History*, February 1969, p.113.

27 Michael Leifer, 'The Failure of Political Institutionalisation in Cambodia' in *Modern Asian Studies*, Volume 2, Number 2, 1968.

28 Michael Leifer, *Dilemmas of Statehood in Southeast Asia* (Singapore: Asia Pacific Press, 1972), pp. 77–78.

29 'Coup Questions: Secret Cables Rebut Theory that US Ousted Cambodia's Sihanouk in 1970' in *Far Eastern Economic Review*, 13 January 1994, pp. 30–31.

30 Michael Leifer, 'Kampuchea 1979: From Dry Season to Dry Season' in *Asian Survey*, Volume XX, Number 1, January 1980 and 'Kampuchea in 1980: The Politics of Attrition' in *Asian Survey*, Volume XXI, Number 1, January 1981.

31 Michael Leifer,'Obstacles to a Political Settlement in Indochina' in *Pacific Affairs*, Volume 59, Number 4, Winter 1985–86 and a slightly revised version 'Obstacles to peace in Southeast Asia' in Hiroshi Matsumoto and Noordin Sopiee (eds), *Into the Pacific Era: Southeast Asia and Its Place in the Pacific* (Malaysia: Institute of Strategic and International Studies, 1986). Michael Leifer, 'ASEAN under Stress over Cambodia' in *Far Eastern Economic Review*, 14 June 1984, p. 34 and 'The Road to Phnom Penh is Blocked by Moscow' in *Far Eastern Economic Review*, 25 December 1986, p. 30.
32 Michael Leifer, 'Cambodian Conflict – the Final Phase' in *Conflict Studies*, Number 221, May 1989.
33 Michael Leifer, 'The Indochina Problem' in T.B. Miller and James Walter (eds), *Asia-Pacific Security After the Cold War* (Sydney: Allen and Unwin, 1993).
34 Thucydides, *The Peloponnesian War* (Harmondsworth: Penguin Books, 1954), p. 20.
35 I wish to thank Professor Khong for sharing with me the draft version of his paper 'The Elusiveness of Regional Order: Leifer, the English School, and Southeast Asia' which was written for this conference.
36 Kenton J. Clymer, 'The Perils of Neutrality: The Break in US–Cambodian Relations, 1965' in *Diplomatic History*, Volume 23, Number 4, Fall 1999, pp. 609–631; Kenton Clymer, 'Jimmy Carter, Human Rights, and Cambodia' in *Diplomatic History*, Volume 27, Number 2, April 2003, pp. 245–278.
37 Robert Kaplan, *The Coming Anarchy: Shattering the Dreams of the Post Cold War* (New York: First Vintage Books Edition, 2001), pp. 138–139.
38 Michael Leifer, 'Vietnam's Intervention in Kampuchea: The Rights of State v. the Rights of People' in Ian Forbes (ed.), *Political Theory, International Relations and the Ethics of Intervention* (London: Macmillan, 1993).

12 Domestic security priorities, "balance of interests" and Indonesia's management of regional order[1]

Leonard C. Sebastian

Indonesia uses diplomacy as a means of establishing cooperative regional interrelationships to create a favourable regional environment to ensure its security well-being, thereby ameliorating or diminishing perceived security concerns without the use of force which in turn reduces the causes of insecurity and augments Indonesia's national security. Similarly Indonesia's use of preventive diplomacy in the management of regional order not only plays a critical role in dealing with issues that have moved, or might otherwise move, into the sphere of military conflict but significantly embellishes its claim to regional leadership.[2]

Michael Leifer's significant contribution to the understanding of Indonesian foreign policy is a product of his meticulous application of sound area studies techniques to the craft of international relations. Throughout his seminal book *Indonesia's Foreign Policy*[3] he constantly reminds readers that the determinants of foreign policy could only be ascertained through a comprehension of Indonesia's history, its formative historical experiences, traditions, political culture, the nature of domestic political processes, and the perceptions of its leaders. Indeed Leifer's analysis of Indonesian foreign policy, with its emphasis on Indonesia's domestic political conditions manifested through deeply entrenched historical antipathy against certain extra-regional powers, contrasts significantly with the approach-driven analysis that is commonplace in the study of international relations. Coincidently, it has now become fashionable in mainstream international relations theory, whether realist or constructivist, to acknowledge that foreign policy behavior is not necessarily conditioned by systemic pressures, and greater emphasis is now being placed on the role of intervening domestic variables. Research in the 1990s seemingly placed greater importance on the state adjusting and appraising transformations in the international arena on the basis of its own unique political circumstances or structures.[4] Studies also indicate that rather than balancing against threats, the majority of states have chosen to bandwagon against them.[5] Recent research in the field of neo-classical realism contends that systemic factors do not necessarily condition states to balance against threats, but rather states are more susceptible to "underbalancing behavior, which includes buck-passing, distancing, hiding, waiting, appeasement, bandwagoning, and ineffective half measures" and such actions are conditioned by "the domestic political process."[6] Social constructivism as a research program has paid more attention to the domestic realm due to the fact that so many of their key variables—discourses, identities, institutions, and norms—would not only have greater explanatory value but indeed are more evident at the national level. A start has been made but surely much more could be done to mature constructivism as a research program through a better appreciation and theorization of domestic politics.[7] Yet interestingly, the perspectives of Michael Leifer all those years ago were unique and insightful in demonstrating this nexus between foreign policy and domestic politics, and in *Indonesia's Foreign Policy* he made his point emphatically by stating that foreign policy with all its concomitant linkages with domestic policy were "never truly separate in any state, became interlocked in symbiotic embrace."[8]

The bases of Indonesian foreign policy

Indonesia as a political entity did not exist until the archipelago's administrative and territorial consolidation by Dutch colonial authorities in the early years of the twentieth century.[9] Empires of different importance had existed previously in the same area and had exercised suzerainty or varying measures of control over interposing waters. Since its independence as a state, Indonesia with its successive governments had never taken its boundaries for granted owing to a sense of vulnerability compromised by the porous nature of a penetrable archipelago, primordial strife simmering below the surface, and also the historical experience of foreign intervention involving the use of sea power.

The relative defenselessness of Indonesian governments against external forces with appropriate capability to penetrate the soft exterior of the archipelago amplified this sense of vulnerability. Maritime capability, a decisive element in any external challenge within the archipelago, was shown during the pre-colonial period by the Chola Tamil raids on Srivijaya in the eleventh century and the Mongol punitive expedition to Java at the end of the thirteenth century. Subsequently, a superior Dutch naval power had overcome that of the Portuguese, while the actual process of consolidation of Dutch control through the archipelago depended, in part, on the protection of dominant British naval power. The effective use of naval *force majeure* by the Japanese in World War Two was another example of the vulnerability of the archipelago. Indonesia's geographic configuration, combined with social diversity, had the propensity to encourage centrifugal political tendencies. During the Sukarno era, regional rebellions broke out in Maluku, Aceh, Sumatra, and Sulawesi. Indonesia's weakness is further aggravated by discrepancies in its geo-strategic capabilities. It lacks significant air and maritime capabilities to effectively defend the archipelago.[10]

Despite immense material improvements during the Suharto era, little has altered in Indonesia's circumstances and Leifer's *Indonesia's Foreign Policy* neatly captured the main tenets of Indonesia's quest for external security which have remained unaltered since independence, namely security in the sense of state survival and territorial integrity.[11]

> The experience of upholding independence in both domestic and international dimensions generated an abiding concern for the integrity of a state beset by social diversity and physical fragmentation. That concern was reinforced by a conviction about the country's attractiveness to external interests because of its bountiful natural resources and important strategic location. A common and consistent theme of Indonesia's foreign policy has been the need to overcome an intrinsic vulnerability.[12]

In order to protect the integrity of the state and overcome intrinsic vulnerability, successive policy-makers have shown little interest in federalism and an aversion toward foreign enclaves, which might be used as stepping stones for interference by outside powers. Thus maximizing autonomy in the political and military sense had been viewed merely as a supporting, secondary objective.

Paradoxically, as Leifer again points out, "the continuous sense of vulnerability has been combined with an equally continuous sense of regional entitlement based on pride in revolutionary achievement, size of population, land and maritime dimensions, natural resources and strategic location produced the conviction that Indonesia was entitled to play a leading role in the management of regional order within Southeast Asia".[13] This sense of entitlement has been reflected in the foreign policy of Indonesia under both Sukarno and Suharto who aspired to regional leadership and ultimately, to world leadership of the Non-Aligned Movement. But these aspirations have seldom motivated attempts at territorial aggrandizement. Nevertheless, the West Irian campaign, *Konfrontasi*, and the invasion of East Timor in 1975 demonstrate that Indonesia was willing to take military action across its borders when it felt its own security was potentially endangered. Hence, in areas of external security, where security concerns cannot be resolved diplomatically and reach a level where the situation becomes a direct threat to national security, military actions to achieve security take precedence. Although regime change and *reformasi* in 1998 has brought changes in foreign policy, they were less in aspirations and goals than in priorities and above all, in idiom and style. Like Suharto, Megawati has exhibited cautious pragmatism, and while Wahid was erratic, and Habibie politically weak, none would disavow Sukarno's strategic perspectives, regional ambitions, and archipelagic doctrine (*Wawasan Nusantara*).[14]

The "regionalization" of national resilience

The sense of geographical and historical vulnerability, the result of Indonesia's multiplicity of ethnic, cultural, and linguistic traditions, its lack of a united and unifying history as a single political entity, and its huge size and archipelagic nature have conspired to make the building of a modern, cohesive nation-state from Sabang to Merauke a formidable task indeed. These inherent difficulties have been exacerbated, moreover, by a long history of external pressures and interventions by foreign powers at the expense of Indonesian unity, with outside forces often exploiting Indonesia's diversity in order to gain a strategic foothold inside the country, along the lines of locating and striking at a chain's weakest link. Or at least such is the historical perspective in Jakarta, which is perhaps understandable in light of Indonesia's actual experience to date, not only the periods of Dutch (and British) colonialism and the Japanese occupation during World War II, but also the various intrigues and machinations of the United States, the former Soviet Union, and China that have characterized the post-war era in Southeast Asia. These beliefs and experiences gave rise to an Indonesian brand of nationalism which manifested itself in the "independent and active" (*Bebas dan Aktif*) foreign policy promulgated by the country's first Vice-President Mohammad Hatta in September 1948. Such an approach to foreign policy allowed Indonesia significant scope to adapt policies necessary to secure its national interests while being free from constraints arising from alignments with external powers.

This view in Indonesia that the world is basically a hostile, uncertain, and unsafe place is a theme emphasized throughout Weinstein's study entitled *Indonesian Foreign Policy and Dilemma of Dependence.*[15] What has evolved into an obsession with national security is the result of a common perception that Indonesia, as a new country and a developing country, is always *vulnerable* to practices of divide and rule carried out by stronger foreign powers bent on exploiting and/or subjugating Indonesia for their own selfish interests. This, together with the continuing fear of dismemberment of the Indonesian nation, and the resulting emphasis on unity, rapid economic development and economic nationalism, political stability and the absolute sanctity of national borders, is shown for example in its articulation of the *Wawasan Nusantara* concept and the importance Indonesia attached to the Law of the Sea as the means to secure the "archipelago principle." In giving recognition to Indonesia's archipelagic state concept, the Law of the Sea recognizes the key element of Indonesian national outlook. This concept of territorial and national unity which regards Indonesia as an inseparable union of land and water (*tanah-air* or homeland) was first mooted in 1957. More importantly the extension of territorial seas to 12 nautical miles and the concept of archipelagic sea lanes passage has given Indonesia greater control over the exploitation, use, and security of her archipelagic waters.

It was within this same context of safeguarding national self-determination, national security, and territorial integrity that Indonesia made the decision to invade East Timor in 1975 and forcibly integrate the territory into the Republic as Indonesia's 27th province. Indeed, virtually the same justification, and the same vocabulary, had been employed by two very different Indonesian governments during the 1960s as Sukarno, and after him Suharto, were ultimately successful in realizing Jakarta's long-standing claim to the much larger and strategically more important area of Irian Jaya. As Michael Leifer explains, "both the East Timor and the Irian Jaya acquisitions, although viewed by some as representing expansionistic tendencies on Indonesia's part, actually had much more to do with a widespread and historically-based Indonesian perception of the innate vulnerability of the Republic, especially to any conjuncture between dissension and external interference."[16] Leifer continues:

> The so-called act of free choice (on Irian Jaya) conducted in 1969 did not permit an authentic expression of self-determination. It was conducted in a sober manner without the public display characteristic of the Sukarno era, but the priority of ensuring the integrity of the archipelago and of the Jakarta administration over the controversial issues of East Timor served to confirm a strong attachment to a strategic perspective which existed before the internal transfer of power in March 1966. Indeed, a sense of strategic imperative overrode deference to the conventions of the international system.[17]

This last point is particularly crucial in terms of understanding Indonesia's approach to external security for it reaffirms the extent to which Indonesia is prepared to do whatever it deems necessary to safeguard its most basic concerns—in this case the security and territorial integrity of the nation itself—even at the risk of doing damage to the conduct of its foreign policy in less immediate and crucial areas. There is no doubt that the East Timor takeover had created additional complications and difficulties in Indonesia's relations with its major Western trading partners and aid donors.

Equally important, the Timor invasion served to revive (in some sectors, at least) the unfortunate spectrum of an Indonesia bent on further expansionism or at least on asserting its primacy and dominance as the largest and most populous state in the region. As a result of a concern in Indonesia that these suspicions and fears persist among Indonesia's neighbors, the Indonesian response since 1975 has been to greatly expand bilateral contacts as well as to step up regional diplomacy. These moves would benefit Indonesia in two ways. First, they would provide a platform to build understanding and appreciation of Indonesia's positions on Irian Jaya and East Timor. Second, they would bring to the forefront an effective non-military approach to resolving this perennial problem of territorial vulnerability without raising the specter of Indonesian expansionism.

With the tensions in the Southeast Asian region increasing following the Vietnamese invasion of Kampuchea (Cambodia), there was an effort to broaden the Doctrine of National Resilience to a concept of Regional Resilience. The fundamental reason for the need of a strong national and regional resilience is due to the fact that political stability is indivisible among the ASEAN states. Political instability in any one state would have repercussions for all other states since such political instability often spills over the state's boundary. Hence, the

Declaration of ASEAN Concord signed by the five heads of government in 1976 stated that:

> The stability of each member state and of the ASEAN region is an essential contribution to international peace and security. Each member resolves to eliminate threats posed by subversion to its stability, thus strengthening national and ASEAN resilience.[18]

The main concern was, of course, internal instabilities with external implications, that is, communist subversion (supported either by the People's Republic of China or the Soviet Union) and radical Islamist extremism (supported by certain Middle East countries). The history of post-independence Indonesia is rife with incidences which indicate that internal instabilities often provide the incentive for external intervention which in turn would aggravate the situation. The lack of credible defense force to serve as a deterrent for external intervention has led to the need to develop effective non-military strategies to ensure, first, that Indonesia's national integrity is not compromised, and second, that a favorable regional security environment is maintained. Hence, the next part of this chapter focuses, first, on the conceptual foundations of diplomacy and, second, onthe critical role diplomacy plays in the national security of Indonesia.

The external dimension of national security

National security has been a major foreign policy concern of the New Order Regime. The preponderance of national security concerns has been highlighted in an implicit adherence to a "concentric circles" approach to international relations as emphasized by a Foreign Ministry official quoted by Gordon Hein:

> Indonesia views international relations in terms of concentric circles, beginning with the nation itself—meaning independence, national unity, national security and the national interest—and then extending out to include ASEAN, then the rest of Southeast Asia, and then Asia as a whole and the other developing and other Islamic countries and finally global matters. Our pragmatic approach is such that we always look to safeguard the one before reaching out to the next.[19]

As suggested by the above quotation, the external dimension of national security begins with certain unchanging principles and highest priority tasks and geographic areas and then proceeds—gradually and as changing capabilities, interests, and circumstances allow—to "reach out" to involve greater numbers of issues and countries more geographically distant from Indonesia and of less immediate concern to Indonesia's basic security and well-being. Utilizing this culturally rooted Javanese "*mandala*" approach, namely, the idea that the immediate outer rings (in a series of radiating rings of security) must be secured if the center (the Indonesian state) was to be secure;[20] the "concentric circles" concept was effectively crafted by the late General Benny Murdani, in the 1980s as Indonesia's grand strategy aimed at creating a *cordon sanitaire* around the country. According to Murdani:

> In order to prevent an enemy from easily reaching the regional borders of the country, defense planners conjured up the existence of a "cordon sanitaire" surrounding the territory of the sovereign state. The "cordon sanitaire" mentioned were of several kinds and shapes, beginning with countries which were under foreign domination, up to those linked by regional cooperation in politics or economics; all of them were intended both for security and to obtain a longer reaction time to prepare a counterattack in facing an enemy invasion.[21]

With these considerations, strategic planning during Murdani's tenure as Armed Forces Commander saw the development of a three-tiered security zone with ASEAN as an area of vital security interest, followed by the rest of Southeast Asia, including Australia and Papua New Guinea, as the area of prime security interest and anything outside it, especially in West Asia, the Indian Ocean region, and the area to the east of the Pacific Ocean, as the area of strategic security interest.[22] These ideas have been refined succinctly in the 1995 Defence White Paper:

> In a geostrategic context, Indonesia's basic defense and security strategy is one providing for layered security. The deepest layer is domestic security, followed by sub-regional (ASEAN) security, regional (South East Asia) security and security of neighboring regions, in that order. This strategy is also called defense-in-depth.[23]

In its very essence, this "concentric circles" approach has meant that Indonesian foreign policy must first and foremost serve the nation itself: national unity, national security, and the national interest.[24] For Indonesia, then, the starting point, the primary concern, the "innermost circle" within the concentric circles approach to external security policy-making, has always been the state itself. And even ahead of the state's material well-being and development, there is the state's very existence, its unity and territorial integrity, and its security. These security principles continue today to guide perceptions on Indonesian national security[25] and largely explain why the Republic has invested much stock in regional diplomacy. Indeed, it could be argued that ASEAN itself—its current successes, its future viability, even its very existence—has always been inexorably bound to two significant factors pertinent to Indonesia. First, it provides the platform for continuing bilateral and multilateral dialogue with its northern neighbors (particularly Malaysia, Singapore, and Thailand), thereby ensuring that a peaceful and relatively autonomous regional order develops in

Southeast Asia sufficiently guaranteeing Indonesian security. Second, its membership of and commitment to ASEAN, while providing Indonesia with a role commensurate with its position as the largest and most populous state in the region, also helps ameliorate the suspicions and fears among its neighbors with respect to possible Indonesian expansionism. This sentiment was expressed lucidly by a leading Indonesian journalist quoted by Gordon Hein:

> To a great extent ASEAN is Suharto's creation. It came about because Indonesia under the New Order abandoned the "Crush Malaysia" campaign and ceased being aggressive. Suharto did not want, and still does not want other countries to fear Indonesian expansionism. ASEAN is a way to ensure that it does not happen again.[26]

Hence by curtailing its previously aggressive approach to attaining security in its northern approaches in favor of being a good regional neighbor, Indonesia has maintained that its national interest does indeed continue to be best served within the framework of ASEAN. In keeping with this theme, the next section attempts to highlight how Indonesia utilizes regional diplomacy in a quest to attain a conducive regional environment capable of meeting its external security needs.

The search for a durable regional order

The idea that maintaining national regional security is the fundamental right and responsibility of the countries of the region themselves, acting separately and in concert with one another, has long been a hallmark of Indonesian external security policy. It derives from a perception that all external powers, however seemingly benign, will in fact seek to dominate smaller and weaker states for their own interests to the extent that these states are vulnerable and divided among themselves. To safeguard their long-term stability and their independence, then, the states of Southeast Asia must ensure that they are full and active participants in all decisions affecting the region, rather than merely witnessing the manipulation of events by competing external powers or passively accepting the imposition of some kind of regional structure that does not reflect the aspirations and the initiative of the Southeast Asian states themselves.

In the early 1960s, Sukarno used precisely this line of reasoning to help justify his opposition to the formation of Malaysia, charging specifically that Indonesia, as the "leading" nation in the region, had not been properly consulted by Great Britain before it undertook a major unilateral action that was bound to effect the regional environment, and hence the vital security interests, of the Republic. As an alternative to what was seen as a great power imposition, Sukarno instead sought an approach that would make the future of Malaysia a matter of regional negotiations, based on what Leifer calls the Indonesian "prescription for regional order which excluded a role for outside states."[27] Sukarno was not entirely unsuccessful in this endeavor. Indeed, in the "Manila Accord" of 1963, the government of Malaya and the Philippines went on record as accepting the basic Indonesian conception of regional self-reliance without alliances to foreign patrons. Specifically, the third article of the Accord states: "The Ministers were of one mind that the three countries share a primary responsibility for the maintenance of the stability and security of the area from subversion in any form or manifestation in order to preserve their respective national identities."[28] And later that year, a joint statement by the three heads of government—Sukarno, Tunku Abdul Rahman, and President Macapagal—went even further in seeming to embrace the Indonesian point of view:

> The countries of Southeast Asia share a primary responsibility of the region and ensuring their peaceful and progressive national development... They are determined to ensure their stability and security from external interference in any form and manifestation in order to preserve their national identities in accordance with the ideals and aspirations of their peoples... All foreign bases are temporary.[29]

As Leifer has noted, the establishment of ASEAN truly marked:

> Indonesia's assumption of a primary role in promoting a system of regional order "involving" a refusal in principle to accept the need for the role of an external power to fill any so-called power vacuum created within Southeast Asia by the retreat of colonialism. Indeed, the concept of regional power vacuum was alien to a strategic perspective which spanned the administration of Sukarno and Suharto.[30]

And it is thus with total legitimacy that Suharto could report to the MPR (Majlis Permusyawaratan Rakyat or People's Consultative Assembly) that officially named him full President in March of 1968 that ASEAN had been created "at Indonesia's initiative."[31]

An argument can be made that politically vulnerable states could find regional arrangements useful for coping with their domestic challenges and countering common threats to regime survival. Their common vulnerabilities arising from similar ideological outlooks and domestic political predicaments can provide the basis for unity in dealing with the regional security environment. Shared perception of a common internal enemy can also provide a strong impetus for regional cooperative arrangements, in addition to coordination on measures to ensure internal security. Thus, while alliances of weak powers generally have proven ineffectual in coping with aggression, security cooperation among vulnerable states against threats to domestic and regime security may fare better. Not only do such threats constitute the most pressing security problems of Developing World countries, but dealing with them does not require significant military capabilities and in fact can be pursued through non-military means.

Regional cooperation in Southeast Asia was seen as an essential response to the threat posed by communist advances in Indochina, a security concern against which the US policy of military confrontation was not an entirely credible answer. These developments brought about a greater convergence in the security perspectives of the four other ASEAN states with that of Indonesia. From the outset, Indonesia had stressed that the close and dependent security ties of regional countries with external powers carried with it the risk of aggravating great-power rivalry in Southeast Asia.

Furthermore, mutualities between Indonesia and other ASEAN countries in their domestic security concerns served to strengthen regional cooperation. Similarities in regime values among the ASEAN countries were the basis for the notion of a common enemy, "seen to feed and depend for its success on a cluster of social conditions that are essentially the same in the various countries."[32] The ASEAN regimes all shared three major dilemmas during the 1970s: "the reconciliation of economic growth with equity, national integration and ethnic pluralism, and political stability and participation."[33] There was a general consensus among ASEAN policymakers that instability resulting from their failure to resolve these dilemmas could be the most serious threats to the political and security order in ASEAN. In this sense, the ASEAN countries' calculation of the mix of security concerns to regional security was weighted heavily toward domestic challenges, even as the external situation for the ASEAN states deteriorated with the intensification of the Sino-Soviet rivalry and the US debacle in Indochina.

It is in this context that the Indonesian concept of national and regional "resilience" advanced by the New Order regime was adopted as something of an ASEAN motto by the other members of the group, highlighting the importance of domestic order and regime stability as an objective of the regional agenda. According to Irvine, the concept of national resilience is an "inward-looking concept, based on the proposition that national security lies not in military alliances or under the military umbrella of a great power, but in self-reliance deriving from domestic factors such as economic and social development, political stability and a sense of nationalism."[34] In this context, the Indonesian concept of regional resilience is the sum total of national resilience in individual ASEAN states, that is:

> If each member nation can accomplish an overall national development and overcome internal threats, regional resilience can result much in the same way as a chain derives its overall strength from the strength of its constituent parts.[35]

Hence, in the Indonesian perception, every ASEAN country should strive toward its own national resilience. The collective resilience of all the ASEAN countries would constitute regional resilience which in turn would have a positive impact on the national stability of the respective ASEAN members. Hence, due to the vulnerable nature of the archipelago, the stability of Southeast Asia is deemed important to Indonesia's own stability. As such, regional resilience forms the ideological basis of forward defense in Indonesian security thinking.

The incorporation of the Indonesian conception of regional autonomy and self-reliance into the official body of ASEAN policy was taken a step further with the adoption of the "Kuala Lumpur Declaration" of 17 November 1971, which pledged "necessary efforts to secure the recognition of, and respect for, Southeast Asia as a 'Zone of Peace, Freedom and Neutrality,' free from any form or measure of interference by outside powers."[36] This declaration in support of the "ZOPFAN" ideal was a direct result of Indonesian lobbying that had in turn been prompted by a Malaysian call for the "neutralization" of Southeast Asia. Specifically, Prime Minister Tun Abdul Razak had put forward the idea of a Southeast Asia whose neutrality would be guaranteed by the great powers most concerned with the area, namely, China, the Soviet Union, and the United States. For Indonesia, the notion that Southeast Asian neutrality should be achieved and maintained through a deliberate balancing process controlled by conflicting external powers ran completely against its own conception of regional security as resting on genuine, self-reliant cooperation of the states in the region themselves regardless of ideology. After all, according to Indonesia's then Foreign Minister Adam Malik, ASEAN represented

> the growing determination of the nations of this region to take charge of their own future, to work out problems of their development, stability and security together. It signifies the rejection by those countries of the assumption that the fate of Southeast Asia is going to be determined by outside powers...37
> Neutralization that is the product of 'one-way' benevolence on the part of the big powers, at this stage, would perhaps prove as brittle and unstable as the inter-relationship between the big powers themselves... It is only through developing among ourselves an area of internal cohesion and stability based on indigenous sociopolitical and economic strength that we can ever hope to assist in the early stabilization of a new equilibrium in the region that could not be the exclusive 'diktat' of the major powers. However dominant the influence of these powers may be, I think there is and there should be a scope for an indigenous Southeast Asian component in the new, emerging power balance in the region. In fact, I am convinced that unless the big powers acknowledge and the Southeast Asian nations assume a greater and more direct responsibility in the maintenance of security in the areas, no lasting stability can ever be achieved... To this end, therefore, the nations of Southeast Asia should consciously work towards the day when security in their own region will be the primary responsibility of the Southeast Asian nations themselves. Not through big power alignments, not through the buildup of contending military posts or military arsenals but through strengthening the state of our respective national endurance, through effective regional cooperation and through cooperation with other states

> sharing this basic view on world affairs... It is here that the importance of such an organization as ASEAN comes to the fore.[38]

It is this vision of an autonomous, cooperative regional order in Southeast Asia, transcending ideology and excluding great power interference, that Indonesia continues to uphold, not just as an abstract, idealized vision demanding occasional lip-service but as a concrete, if long-term, goal of actual external security policy. Like the principles of nonalignment and the need to maintain an "independent and active" foreign policy, the commitment to the ultimate establishment of a "Zone of Peace, Freedom and Neutrality" in Southeast Asia is genuine and deeply felt across the full spectrum of elite political opinion in Indonesia.

It is within this context that the very real ambivalence felt for the United States and its role in regional affairs becomes understandable. It is not just that the US is considered less than totally reliable or that Indonesia, as a country proud of its history of nationalism, independence, and nonalignment, does not want shared anti-Communist ideology and economic necessity to result in too close a bilateral relationship with the United States; it is also that, in the Indonesian conception of regional order, the intrusion of *any* external power into the region on behalf of a particular country or countries tends to reduce regional autonomy and, hence, can endanger stability. Existing tensions are exacerbated, other external forces tend to enter to provide countervailing power, and overall national and regional autonomy is ultimately sacrificed in favor of a rigidly polarized system where "vertical" ties between individual regional states and external powers become more important than the "horizontal" ties among the regional states themselves. These "vertical" ties between stronger external powers and weaker regional states, moreover, inevitably involve some form of domination and dependence, so it comes to be in the interests of all the external powers to continue this polarized regional system. The "losers" in this bleak scenario are thus the countries of the region themselves, who end up not only divided but dependent as well, prevented from mobilizing their own common interests on behalf of true regional peace and cooperation. It is this scenario that the ZOPFAN ideals were supposed to mitigate against, and it is this scenario that, in the view of many Indonesians, has unfortunately come to pass in Southeast Asia.

The "balance of interests"

It is important to note that while the commitment to non-alignment as a principle runs absolutely across the board among the Indonesian political elite, Indonesia, has in fact, long accepted a fairly broad interpretation of non-alignment—one that makes allowances for special circumstances and for the specific needs and ideological predilections of individual regimes on pretty much a live-and-let-live basis, its own deeply felt anti-communism notwithstanding. For example, in the wake of communist victories in Indochina, Indonesia was trapped between its principled commitments to non-alignment and regional accommodation, on the one hand, and the pragmatic necessity of maintaining strong military links to an anti-communist superpower on the other.[39] Hence, while Indonesians voice support for the idea that non-alignment as a principle should transcend ideology, they are pragmatic in asserting that each country has the right to choose its own form of government and follow its own developmental path, in accordance with its particular national priorities, cultural background, and historical evolution.

This approach was aptly demonstrated during the debates within ASEAN circles in the late 1980s which accompanied the Singapore offer to host some US naval facilities to make it easier for the Philippines to continue to host the US bases.[40] From the public record, both the official and unofficial reactions in Jakarta to news of the Singapore offer were more reserved and less colored than the controversial mixture of domestic politics that characterized debate in Malaysia. Similarly, at the Kuala Lumpur Conference in 1971, Malaysia recommended the adoption of a policy seeking the agreement of the great powers not to intervene in Southeast Asia, in return for ASEAN declaring itself to be formally neutral in international affairs. Singaporean and Thai objections were significant factors in the dilution of the concept of neutralization to ZOPFAN. Indonesia's strong opposition to the Malaysian proposal arose from the scheme's tacit assumption that ASEAN remained dependent on the acquiescence of the great powers to secure regional stability. Indonesia sought to achieve the same objective, but on the basis of the internal and autonomous strength of ASEAN members themselves.[41] As a compromise, Jakarta supported a more vague, though less offensive, concept of ZOPFAN.

This conciliatory approach to ZOPFAN is the result of another principle inherent in Indonesian external security policy, namely, the "balance of interests" concept. According to the 1995 Defence White Paper:

> The basic premise followed in implementing Indonesia's defense and security strategy is not balance of power but balance of interests. This premise encourages the cultivation of international dialogue among nations maintaining regional peace.[42]

It is for the very need to "balance the interests" of the ASEAN countries that Indonesia did not adopt an overtly hostile posture toward the Singapore decision of providing the United States with military facilities in the Republic. Indeed, Jakarta saw it as part of Singapore's attempt, in line with Indonesia's thinking of engaging the US in the region and part of the exercise of "balancing the interests" of the great powers in the region, especially at a time when the US was having difficulties with its bases in the Philippines.

The principle of "balance of interests" was also at work when Indonesia acceded to the Australia–Indonesia Agreement on Maintaining Security. In signing the agreement, Indonesia was able to put aside some of the doctrinaire perceptions that were inherent in the Non-Aligned Movement during the Cold

War years.[43] Australia is firmly allied to the United States and also a member of the Five-Power Defence Arrangement. At one time, these factors would have placed Australia beyond the pale so far as a leading non-aligned nation like Indonesia is concerned. But times have changed. Indonesia now has a more mature, hard-nosed appreciation of its strategic circumstances. It recognizes the changing equilibrium of power in Asia and believes that it is not in Indonesia's interest to see an emerging great power dominate Asia, and certainly not Southeast Asia. There seems to be a tacit realization in Jakarta that ASEAN thinking on security cannot deal adequately with the long-term challenges a country like Indonesia faces in securing its maritime environment. In part, this is due to the end of the comfortable certainties of the Cold War. In 1995, China's more aggressive posture on the South China Sea generated alarm in Jakarta, particularly when Beijing declined to say whether it still held a traditional claim in the area of Indonesia's biggest off-shore natural gas deposit near the Natuna Islands.

While some progress has been made toward building dialogue and a sense of trust in the ASEAN Regional Forum, multilateral security, while a laudable goal, is cumbersome and requires a sustained period of time to prove its worth. Hence the need for Indonesia to buttress its security requirements by incorporating both bilateral and multilateral instruments. The key, for Jakarta, is the need for neighbors to have structures for consultation.

Proponents of ZOPFAN may feel that Indonesia has compromised its non-aligned stance and, therefore, Indonesian foreign policy lacks consistency. This argument, though, misses the point. The key from the Indonesian perspective is who determines regional order. Will it be the countries of the region or the great powers? This has been a constant theme in Indonesian foreign policy and was highlighted in the earlier discussion on Indonesian approaches to the resolution of the Cambodian crises. With the great powers of the region—China, Japan, Russia, and the United States—temporarily constrained just now or engaged in a period of introspection or passivity, the opportunity has presented itself for medium-sized countries like Indonesia to shape the development of the region by molding the institutions, processes, and methods of resolving problems which will form the pattern of the next period of international relations in Southeast Asia and the wider Asia-Pacific region. Jakarta's pro-active approach to regional security reflects this trend, and foreign policy will continue to be subordinated to "an inherent duality driven by circumstances and an innate sense of pragmatism."[44]

At present, the Indonesian understanding of ZOPFAN differs from that expressed in the past. There is ZOPFAN as excluding great power military presence and there is ZOPFAN with limited goals, namely, the maintenance of strategic equilibrium. The approach to ZOPFAN has always varied between these two concepts—exclusion and equilibrium. The current Indonesian approach emphasizing the need to maintain a strategic equilibrium was stressed by then Vice-President Try Sutrisno:

> In the new environment that affects regional and global security today, the concept and approach of ZOPFAN is still valid. As a flexible blueprint designed to create peace and security in this part of the world, ZOPFAN is still open to refinement and adjustment to the changing needs that exist in our rapidly changing regional and global environment. There is a need for a commonly agreed stance for greater mutual restraint among the countries of the Asia Pacific region. This includes the major powers from the region. On the contrary, it would encourage prompt measures to lead them to constructive engagement. ZOPFAN is not designed to solely create freedom and neutrality to serve the needs of the sub-region. Rather it is designed to lead to a system of relations between the countries of the sub-region and countries that lie outside the region. It aspires to mutually beneficial relations within the sub-region and between the sub-region and the rest of the world.[45]

In sum, starting from the premise that big-power competition and influence in Southeast Asia will be a fact of the region's—and therefore of Indonesia's—political life for some time to come (especially in light of ASEAN's difficulties in defining its desired regional "neutralization"), Indonesia has assessed that certain security advantages are seen to lie in highly variegated but carefully supervised forms of big-power "access" to the region. Thus, ideally, a pattern of "fuzzy", yet for that reason perhaps effective, counterbalances would be created, allowing each major power a political or commercial investment, or even indirect strategic stake in the region, but not a decisive one, so that caution will not control confidence in strategic decision-making. The underlying policy rationale is for Indonesia to be "permeable" and non-threatening to outside influences, yet "resilient" enough and efficient enough in her national "territorial management" so that development can proceed with political stability.

The "balance of interests" strategy is also at work with regard to the issue of the religious versus the secular nature of the Indonesian state[46] which has been a source of continual controversy since the earliest days of the nationalist movement. Indonesia has avoided giving an Islamic tenor to its foreign policy, at least partly because it faces a carry-over effect of Islamic identification and mobilization into the realm of domestic politics with negative ramifications for security, stability, and even the question of national identity itself. This has meant that the basic goal of foreign policy is to do the absolute minimum necessary to meet Indonesia's perceived obligations as a member of the Islamic world and therefore placate Islamic political sentiment domestically. This has allowed Indonesia to focus its foreign policy on issues that it regards as more vital to the interests of the nation, while simultaneously avoiding any kind of "Islamic" orientation in its outlook and behavior that might carry over into domestic political life with potential negative implications for continued national stability. As Michael Leifer has suggested, "a prime consideration has been to prevent international issues being used or exploited either to advance demands presented by Muslim groups or to enhance the political standing of Islam per se within the Republic."[47] It is at least partly because of domestic political concerns, then—concerns that get to the heart of political power and national identity in Indonesia—that "Islam has never exercised a perceptible influence on the international outlook of the Indonesian state; nor has it enjoyed a place in the formal rhetoric of Indonesia's foreign policy."[48] The terrorist attacks on the World Trade Center and the Pentagon on September 11, 2001 however, created a predicament for the Indonesian government. Once the United States retaliated by conducting a military campaign to neutralize Al Qaeda's operational capabilities in Afghanistan, hard-line Muslim groups demonstrated vociferously and placed tremendous pressure on President Megawati to condemn US actions. Despite a jittery start, the government was able to placate Muslim sentiments and dissipate large-scale demonstrations by criticizing the normative aspects of the US military campaign without attacking the United States directly.[49] As Sukma correctly contends, the Indonesian government's response to the US-led War on Terror was in fact proof of Indonesia's consistency in not having an overtly Islamic dimension to its foreign policy as long as it was not "contradictory and detrimental to Islamic interests":[50]

> Islam has entered Indonesian foreign policy only in form rather than substance. That peculiarity in the relationship between Islam and foreign policy reflects constraints imposed on foreign policy by the primary consideration of domestic priorities and the interests of the state and the regime. In more specific terms, such constraints stem from the dilemma of state identity and also the condition of internal weakness.[51]

In international affairs, this approach has meant that Indonesia meticulously avoids having an explicit Islamic cast to its foreign policy. As the country with the greatest number of Muslims on earth, for example, Indonesia participates in the Islamic Conference Organization; but it steadfastly refuses to become a full member of the organization on the principle that while Indonesia is an Islamic country, it is not an Islamic state. Similarly, it has been careful always to avoid couching its diplomatic support for Palestinian self-determination in any but the most secular of vocabularies, while its overall profile in Middle Eastern political affairs has been decidedly and deliberately low profile.[52]

Conclusion

National security has been a major foreign policy concern for Indonesia. Throughout the course of its post-independence history, regional and extra-regional factors have impacted on domestic security concerns. As Suharto has articulated:

> Our concept of security is inward looking, namely to establish an orderly, peaceful and stable condition within each individual territory, free from any subversive elements and infiltrations, wherever from their origins might be (sic).[53]

Concern thus was centered on the potential for hostile foreign—especially Communist—powers to encourage destabilizing domestic political movements. This perspective was at the heart of the concept of *Ketahanan Nasional*. A fundamental component of the security dimension to Indonesian foreign policy, the concept of national resilience, emphasizes the need for economic progress, political stability and a high national morale to guard against such a threat.[54]

For Indonesian strategists, national security can and does touch all important aspects of national life, such is the level of concern that Indonesia is not yet firmly established as a cohesive, unified, and stable nation. The concerns regarding the continuing fear of dismemberment of the Indonesian nation and the resulting emphasis on unity, rapid economic development and nationalism, political stability and the absolute sanctity of borders plus fears over the compromising of its independence by the intrusion of external powers reveal an Indonesia that is still plagued by some basic uncertainties and insecurities.

A preoccupation with national security and national integrity remains an enduring aspect of Indonesia's foreign policy during the both the Wahid and Megawati administrations. To ensure that potential breakaway provinces are denied international support, President Wahid had traveled extensively to seek reassurances that countries would respect Indonesia's territorial integrity. The East Timor experience of 1999 has resulted in a foreign policy strategy that seeks to ensure that there is no support for independence movements in Aceh and Papua and that it can prevent foreign intervention in the strife-torn region of Maluku.

The realization that Indonesia's national security concerns cannot be resolved solely by utilizing the military option has resulted in the use of bilateral as well as multilateral diplomatic initiatives to resolve its anxieties regarding its vulnerability. But as Michael Leifer has described so well, these feelings of vulnerability are paradoxically mixed with a notion of what he calls "regional entitlement,"[55] that is, that by virtue of its size, population, natural resources, strategic geopolitical position, rich cultural traditions, and historical legacy, Indonesia is "entitled" to play a significant role in shaping not only its own destiny but also that of Southeast Asia as a whole. This idea is easily extrapolated, moreover, to mean that Indonesia, as the largest and "most important" country in the region, has the right and the responsibility to take the lead in forging a viable long-term regional order, one that will help to preserve Indonesia's own security and that is in keeping with the view that Indonesia should be an independent and active subject, rather than merely a passive object, in international affairs.[56]

Being as yet unable to realize such aspirations and unwilling to permit any extra-regional power to achieve dominance in Southeast Asia, Indonesia has continued to focus prominently on the regional dimensions of its security policy.

In the Indonesian view, self-interested external powers will succeed in making their divisive and domineering inroads into a given region only to the extent that the region is itself lacking in unity, strength, and resilience. And it is only through concerted, cooperative action by the states of the region themselves that external powers can be effectively excluded from the region and true security established and safeguarded for the long term. In giving a regional dimension to its security policy, Indonesia, in essence, has involved the application of the concept of national resilience at a region-wide level. In other words, the national resilience of each member state of ASEAN is held to be integral to the security of the region as a whole. This much was incorporated by ASEAN into its Declaration of Concord.[57]

Certainly the "concentric circles" approach to external security is not so rigid as to require that Indonesia succeed in establishing a regional order of perfect harmony in Southeast Asia before turning its attention to other, broader concerns. Indeed, Indonesia has in fact become gradually more active, more assertive across the full range of bilateral, multilateral, and global issues and organizations. The emphasis on regionalism allows Indonesia to operate at a level of diplomacy that is appropriate both for its needs—as a nation still emphasizing security and development—and for its aspirations—as an emerging, middle-power nation seeking a broader international role commensurate with its achievements to date. The utilization of a step-by-step approach in external security policy is seen as beginning with certain unchanging principles and highest priority tasks and geographic areas and then proceeding—gradually and as changing capabilities, interests, and circumstances allow—to "reach out" to involve greater numbers of issues and countries more geographically distant from Indonesia and of less immediate concern to Indonesia's basic security and well-being.

Notes

1 Professor Michael Leifer was one of the external examiners for my doctoral dissertation awarded by the Australian National University. For close to a year, in 1995–96, he was my colleague at the Institute of Southeast Asian Studies (ISEAS). His room was next to mine and my abiding memory of him is his daily visits to seek my assistance whenever he had trouble with his computer. Apparently he rarely used a computer at LSE. Regardless of his plight he would always have time for a chat and an encouraging word. Through personal conversation and my observation of his performance in seminars I became an admirer of the extraordinary sweep of Michael Leifer's mind, the unity of method and substance and the unity of coherence which was the most striking attribute of his work. An irreplaceable loss, his death has deprived the field of Southeast Asian International Relations of one of its most original and incisive contributors.

2 The qualities of the Republic of Indonesia, the world's fourth most populous country, the largest democracy in the Muslim world, and geo-strategically, Southeast Asia's most significant state give it the attributes of a "pivotal state". According to the authors of an influential study, a "pivotal state" is a "geo-strategically important state to the United States and its allies" and its importance is attributed to its ability not only to "determine the success or failure of its region but also significantly affect international

stability." See Robert Chase, Emily Hill and Paul Kennedy eds., *The Pivotal States: A New Framework for US Policy in the Developing World* (New York: W.W. Norton, 1999): pp. 6, 9.

3 Michael Leifer, *Indonesia's Foreign Policy* (London: Allen & Unwin, 1983).

4 See for example, Jack L. Snyder, *Myths of Empire: Domestic Politics and International Ambition* (Ithaca, NY: Cornell University Press, 1991) and Thomas J. Christensen, *Useful Adversaries: Grand Strategy, Domestic Mobilization and Sino-American conflict, 1947–1958* (Princeton, NJ: Princeton University Press, 1996).

5 See Paul Schroeder, "Historical Reality vs. Neo-realist Theory," *International Security*, Vol. 19, no. 1 (Summer 1994): pp. 72–107.

6 Randall L. Schweller, "Unanswered Threats: A Neoclassical Realist Theory of Underbalancing," *International Security,* Vol. 29, no. 2 (Fall 2004): p. 166.

7 For useful examples, see Ted Hopf, *Social Construction of International Politics: Identities and Foreign Policies, Moscow, 1955 and 1999* (Ithaca, NY: Cornell University Press, 2002); Jeffrey T. Checkel, "The Constructivist Turn in International Relations Theory," *World Politics*, Vol. 50, no. 2 (February 1998): pp. 324–348; and Andrew Cortell and James Davis, "Understanding the Domestic Impact of International Norms: A Research Agenda," *International Studies Review*, Vol. 2, issue 1 (Spring 2000): pp. 65–90.

8 Leifer, *Indonesia's Foreign Policy*, p. 37.

9 Indonesia is the most extensive archipelago in the world, comprising over 13,000 islands that straddle the equator and stretch for over 4,800 km in a southwesterly direction from south of the Indian sub-continent to north of Australia. The Indonesian sea area is four times larger than its land area which is about 1.9 million sq. km. The sea area is about 7.9 million sq. km. (including the EEZ, Exclusive Economic Zone) constituting about 81 per cent of the total area of the country.

10 Indonesia's physical structure and location have also nurtured two contradictory perspectives. As an island-nation with as much territorial water as territorial land, it is sometimes viewed as open, porous, and vulnerable. On the other hand, it could also be viewed as surrounded by a "great moat" that provides protection. Its strategic location in the middle of several major sea arteries forces the country into the mainstream of international politics even if it should prefer to remain aloof. See Robert O. Tilman, *Southeast Asia and the Enemy Beyond* (Boulder, CO: Westview Press, 1987), p. 40.

11 See "Every domestic issue has a foreign policy aspect," *Jakarta Post*, 8 November 2004.

12 Leifer, *Indonesia's Foreign Policy*, p. 173.

13 Ibid., p. 173.

14 The principle argued by Indonesia since the 1958 Convention on the Law of the Sea, that an archipelago nation is entitled to claim all waters between its islands as internal waters was upheld by the United Nations International Convention on the Law of the Sea in 1982 though the Sunda and Lombok straits are recognized as international waters. On 21 March 1980, Indonesia claimed a 200 km Exclusive Economic Zone (EEZ) around its outer perimeter and this was formalized by law in 1983. For useful early perspectives on the *Wawasan Nusantara* concept see Michael Leifer and Dolliver Nelson, "Conflict of Interest in the Straits of Malacca," *International Affairs*, Vol. 49, no. 2 (April 1973): pp. 190–203. A more detailed treatment of the subject can be found in Leifer, *Indonesia's Foreign Policy*, o p. 143–147.

15 Franklin B. Weinstein, *Indonesian Foreign Policy and the Dilemma of Dependence* (Ithaca, NY: Cornell University Press, 1976), p. 128.

16 Leifer, *Indonesia's Foreign Policy*, p. 174.

17 Ibid.

18 *10 Years ASEAN* (Jakarta: ASEAN Secretariat, 1978), p. 111.

19 Quoted from Gordon Robert Hein "Suharto's Foreign Policy and Second-generation Nationalism in Indonesia" (Ph.D dissertation, University of California, Berkeley, 1986), p. 368.
20 Anthony Milner, James Cotton, Pauline Kerr, and Tsutomu Kikuchi, eds, "Perceiving National Security: A Report on East Asia and Australia," *Australian Journal of International Affairs*, 47, no. 2 (October 1993), p. 224.
21 Benny Moerdani, *Upholding the Unity and Unitary of the Nation: Vision and Views of General of the Army (Ret) L.B. Moerdani 1988–1991* (Jakarta: Yayasan Kejuangan Panglima Besar Sudirman, 1993), p. 187.
22 Ibid., p. 25.
23 See *The Policy of The State Defence and Security of the Republic of Indonesia* (Jakarta: Ministry of Defence and Security, 1995), pp. 16–17.
24 Variants of the concentric circle model are also highlighted in Dewi Fortuna Anwar, *Indonesia in ASEAN: Foreign Policy and Regionalism* (New York/Singapore: St Martin's Press/Institute of Southeast Asian Studies, 1994) and in Anthony L. Smith, *Strategic Centrality: Indonesia's Changing Role in ASEAN* Pacific Strategic papers, no. 10 (Singapore: Institute of Southeast Asian Studies, 2000).
25 "Defend Pancasila, ABRI told," *Jakarta Post*, 24 January 1994.
26 Hein, "Suharto's Foreign Policy", p. 374.
27 Leifer, *Indonesia's Foreign Policy*, p. 86.
28 Cited in ibid., p. 86.
29 Cited in ibid., p. 121.
30 Ibid., pp. 119–120.
31 Ibid., p. 122.
32 Arfin Jorgensen-Dahl, *Regional Organization and Order in Southeast Asia* (London: Macmillan, 1982), p. 102.
33 Kusuma Snitwongse, "Internal Problems of ASEAN states: The Dilemmas of Nation-building," in T.B. Millar, ed., *International Security in the Southeast Asia and Southwest Pacific Regions* (St. Lucia, Qld: University of Queensland Press, 1983), p. 144.
34 David Irvine, "Making Haste Slowly: ASEAN from 1975," in Allison Broinowski, ed., *Understanding ASEAN* (London: Macmillan, 1982), p. 40.
35 Jusuf Wanandi, "Security Issues in the ASEAN Region," in Karl D. Jackson and M. Hadi Soesastro, eds., *ASEAN Security and Economic Development* (Berkeley, CA: University of California Press, 1984), p. 305.
36 Leifer, *Indonesia's Foreign Policy*, p. 83.
37 Adam Malik, "Indonesia's Foreign Policy," *The Indonesian Quarterly* 1, no. 1 (October 1972), cited in ibid., p. 142.
38 Quoted in *Far Eastern Economic Review* 25 September 1971, cited in ibid., pp. 148–149.
39 Sukarno was, of course, charged by some with having abandoned strict principles of non-alignment by developing good relations with communist countries at the expense of relations with the West, while Suharto has been similarly criticized for Indonesia's close economic ties with advanced capitalist countries.
40 For a useful summary of the various debates in ASEAN capitals over the Singapore offer to host US (military) facilities, see Philip Methven, *The Five Power Defence Arrangements and Military Cooperation Among the ASEAN states: Incompatible Models for Security in Southeast Asia*, Canberra Papers on Strategy and Defence no. 92 (Canberra: Strategic and Defence Studies Centre, Research School of Pacific Studies, The Australian National University, 1992), pp. 69–91.
41 Peter Polomka, "Indonesia's Future and South-East Asia," *Adelphi Papers*, no. 104 (Spring 1974), p. 26.
42 See, *The Policy of The State Defence and Security of the Republic of Indonesia*, p. 17.

43 For a useful perspective of the various interpretations of Indonesia's *bebas-aktif* foreign policy stance, see Rizal Sukma, "Indonesia's *Bebas-Aktif* Foreign Policy and the 'Security Agreement' with Australia," *Australian Journal of International Affairs*, Vol 51, no. 2 (July 1997): pp. 231–241.

44 Michael R.J. Vatikiotis, "A Giant Treads Carefully: Indonesia's Foreign Policy in the 1990s," in Robert S. Ross, ed., *East Asia in Transition: Toward a New Regional Order* (New York/Singapore: M.E. Sharpe/Institute of Southeast Asian Studies, 1995), p. 216.

45 Try Sutrisno, "Strategic Dynamics and Security in the Asia Pacific Region." Keynote address at the Seminar on "Regional Security in the Asia Pacific Toward 2001," Canberra, 22 September 1994, pp. 20–21.

46 The tension between the religious and secular nature of the Indonesian state has been described as Indonesia's "dual identity dilemma" in Rizal Sukma, *Islam in Indonesian Foreign Policy* (London: RoutledgeCurzon, 2003).

47 Michael Leifer, "The Islamic Factor in Indonesia's Foreign Policy: A Case of Functional Ambiguity," in Adeed Dawisha, ed., *Islam in Foreign Policy* (Cambridge: Cambridge University Press, 1983), p. 148. Other useful studies include Michael Leifer, "The Peace Dividend: Israel's Changing Relationship with South-East Asia," *Institute of Jewish Affairs Research Reports*, no. 1 (February 1994); and Leo Suryadinata, "Islam and Suharto's Foreign Policy," *Asian Survey*, XXXV, no. 3 (March 1995), pp. 291–303.

48 Leifer, "The Islamic Factor in Indonesia's Foreign Policy," p. 148.

49 For a discussion on the subject, see, Leonard C. Sebastian, "Indonesian State responses to September 11, the Bali Bombings and the War in Iraq: Sowing the Seeds for an Accommodationist Islamic Framework?" *Cambridge Review of International Affairs*, Vol. 16, no. 3 (October 2003): pp. 429–445; and Sukma, *Islam in Indonesian Foreign Policy*, Chapter 7.

50 Sukma, *Islam in Indonesian Foreign Policy*, p. 142.

51 Ibid., p. 140.

52 Leifer, "The Islamic Factor in Indonesia's Foreign Policy," pp. 144–159. This is essentially the theme of Leifer's article.

53 Leifer, *Indonesia's Foreign Policy*, p. 161.

54 Justus M. Van der Kroef, "Indonesia: Strategic Perceptions and Foreign Policy," *Asian Affairs* (New York) 2, no. 3 (January–February 1975), p. 164.

55 Leifer, *Indonesia's Foreign Policy*, pp. 75–105 and 142–182.

56 This idea that Indonesia must become an active *subject,* not merely the passive object in international relations, and should strive to carry out it own role, and implement its own national vision, in regional and world affairs is stated in Ide Anak Agung Gde Agung, *Twenty Years of Indonesian Foreign Policy: 1945–1965* (The Hague: Mouton, 1973), pp. 25–28.

57 Leifer, *Indonesia's Foreign Policy*, pp. 161–162.

13 Michael Leifer's reflections on the foreign policy of Singapore

Chin Kin Wah

Introduction

My first encounter with Michael Leifer took place in less than auspicious circumstances when I was an undergraduate at the LSE's Department of International Relations. He had reported me "missing" from his tutorials in International Institutions to which I had been assigned by the Registry at the start of my second year. Some background to this episode is necessary here. The year before (1969), Leifer had joined the LSE after six years as Lecturer in Politics at Hull's Centre for Southeast Asian Studies and the prevailing prejudice, which passed off as conventional wisdom among senior students in the IR Department was that LSE had acquired a very good Southeast Asianist but not one who was particularly known for his contribution to "general" IR or theory building. At the time Southeast Asia was an even more peripheral academic interest at the LSE—the general advice from senior students to those who wanted to be area specialists in Southeast Asia was that they should gravitate towards "the other place" off Russell Square. Thus it was that when I found myself assigned to Leifer's tutorial for International Institutions my instinctive reaction was to gravitate towards "the other class" led by a neo-functionalist.[1] My recalcitrance was compounded by my failure to inform Leifer of the self-arranged switch—hence the letter from the Registry. Subsequently when I did run into him for the first time at the lift landing in the basement of the East Building, I found myself being profusely apologetic to which his response was, "Don't be perturbed, Mr Chin. Don't be perturbed!"

It is a tribute to the achievements of Michael Leifer that over the years the IR Department at the LSE became a Mecca for graduate students including many from Southeast Asia, who sought academic mentorship in their studies on and research into the international relations of this fascinating region. But the episode that I have just recounted keeps resurfacing in my mind whenever I hear exchanges on the place and extent of theoretical content in his works on Southeast Asia.

Those who follow his writings invariably catch the strong flavor of an underlying realism but as a colleague at the LSE observed, his was "a unique blend of realism and humanity that denies simple categorization… (It was) impossible to pigeon-hole (him) as left or right, realist or international institutionalist… He was his own man and respected for it."[2] Another colleague also noted that he did not reject the "realist" label although his concerns were much broader.[3]

Whatever might be said about his theoretical underpinnings, his lack of theoretical pretension and dislike for "theoretical" faddishness was manifestly clear. What Leifer said at a National University of Singapore inter-faculty seminar on "International Conflicts and their Resolution with Special Reference to the Kampuchean Problem" was revealing of his realist orientations. The protracted Kampuchean conflict was then entering its ninth year with no resolution in sight, but among liberal academic circles in the region it was already becoming fashionable to talk of "the peace process." The chairman of that seminar had wondered aloud whether any of the theories of communication and conflict resolution such as those identified with John Burton might have relevance to the resolution of the Kampuchean (Cambodian) problem. Leifer's quick response was as realist as it was instructive:

> The Chairman in his opening remarks mentioned the name of John Burton who has been identified with a theory of conflict which maintains that if only contending parties could be brought together under an appropriate aegis then they would overcome their misunderstanding of one another. Moreover, once they did come to understand each other under the mediation of an impartial intermediary then political light would dawn and conflict resolution would take place. Burton's theory of conflict tends to overlook the possibility that some combatants may understand each other only too well. Indeed, the better they get to know each other, the more they may come to be confirmed in what divides them with conflict resolution arising only from attrition. Such is the situation in the conflict over Kampuchea."[4]

Leifer's disdain for intellectual faddishness was again brought home to me years later in November 1995 at an ISEAS (Institute of Southeast Asian Studies) – SWP (Stiftung Wissenschaft und Politik) conference in Singapore on "Strategic Concepts and Strategic Culture in East Asia and Europe" at which references were liberally made to regional "security discourses" which might be revealing of the strategic culture of the region. His remark to me on the sidelines of the conference was equally revealing, "Mention discourses and I feel like reaching for my revolver!"[5] The remark might have sounded like a repudiation of constructivism, and indeed his realist perspectives on ASEAN have been sharply contrasted with the constructivist treatment of the region.[6] But Leifer also appeared to have reflected a certain constructivist thinking long before the arrival of constructivist theorizing. In *Dilemmas of Statehood in Southeast Asia*, published in 1972, he had noted in reference to what was essentially a discursive element that it was "only in recent years (that) political leaders of some (Southeast Asian) states (have) begun to *think constructively* [my emphasis] in regional terms."[7] Yet, he chose in this book to "focus on the *reality* [my emphasis] of political life both within and between the states of Southeast Asia" in reaction to the "tendency to romanticize the Asian condition, certainly in the rhetoric (read "discourses") of some leaders."[8] In the then prevailing context of intra-regional discord and external power interventions, when regional identification was in its infancy, realism provided a more viable lever of understanding to the attempts at regional association. In later years as the region transited the Cold War, Leifer related with facility ideas of realism to those of neo-liberal institutionalism in his pioneering work on the ASEAN Regional Forum—if only to bear out his own balance-of-power premises.[9]

Leifer's method remained largely grounded in diplomatic history. As he put it in the preface of *Dilemmas of Statehood in Southeast Asia*, "the focus is on particular problems; the method is to draw heavily on substantive examples which have an illustrative function." Such an approach had a special appeal to one not given to operating in tight theoretical frameworks.

I recall the three anecdotes from my interactions with Leifer over the years to highlight three things about him. First, despite the ambivalence of some students toward him in his early days at the LSE, Leifer could, if he wanted, relate the empirical to the theoretical with ease. Indeed a theoretical assumption, even if mostly un-stated upfront, underlay most of his analysis of the Southeast Asian region. Second his lack of theoretical pretensions was matched by a disdain for intellectual faddishness. Third, he could think in constructivist terms although realism remained largely the major signature tone of his many pieces on the foreign policies of Southeast Asian states. Others in this volume have exhaustively addressed the theoretical aspects of Leifer's work. I touch on his theoretical underpinnings largely as a point of entry to his reflections on Singapore's foreign policy, which the rest of this chapter will focus on.

Realist Leifer and realistic Singapore

Leifer did not publish a stand-alone volume on Singapore's foreign policy until the year 2000—it was to be his last book.[10] But Singapore, and not just its foreign policy, had featured in many of his writings that spanned an academic career of well over 30 years during which he had watched Singapore grow up, so to speak—from its entry into and subsequent turbulent history as a semi-autonomous component state in the new Malaysian federation, to its attainment of national sovereignty in 1965 when it acquired formal competence to articulate and chart its own foreign policy course, to its maturing as a player of acknowledged status, in the global diplomatic arena. By Leifer's own revelation, Singapore was his first "port of call" when, as a young academic teaching at the University of Adelaide, he began to develop an interest in Southeast Asia. There is a sense of his having come full circle when I recall his final public appearance in Singapore on 6 January 2001 at a forum that was intended to be a local launching of his first and, as it turned out, last book on Singapore's foreign policy.[11]

One can surmise the reasons for his attraction to Singapore as an area of academic enquiry. It would seem that the realist academic inclinations of Leifer particularly suited his enquiry into the foreign policy of this unique city-state whose leaders (Lee Kuan Yew in particular) were, and continue to be, known for being tough-minded and realistic. Lee Kuan Yew, the acknowledged founding father of independent Singapore and its first Prime Minister (from 1959 when the island was given a limited form of self government to 1990 when he relinquished the position to Goh Chok Tong, becoming in turn Senior Minister in the Cabinet), is given the last word in *Singapore's Foreign Policy*. In what Leifer describes as an epigraphic statement that captures the essence of Singapore's foreign policy practice, Lee says, "In an imperfect world, we have to search for the best accommodation possible. And no accommodation is permanent. If it lasts long enough for progress to be made until the next set of arrangements can be put in place, let us be grateful for it."[12] This is as realistic a statement as it is pragmatic.

In his contribution to a massive tome on the molding of modern Singapore published by ISEAS in 1989, Leifer had cited Lee Kuan Yew's son, BG Lee Hsien Loong (the third Prime Minister of Singapore since 12 August 2004), who saw the world of states as sharing many of the characteristics of the world of beasts, to underscore Singapore's realist worldview.[13] The point received further emphasis in this same chapter when Leifer observed pointedly that it was the philosopher Thomas Hobbes who "has provided the accepted paradigm for the nature of international relations with which Singapore has to contend." He recalls a speech by S. Dhanabalan in 1981 in which the former Singapore Foreign Minister had likened international relations to a Hobbesian state of nature wherein a prime value was placed on order without which "the life of states would be like that of men in the state of nature: 'nasty, brutish and short'."[14]

This realist worldview of Singapore is also reflected in the way the republic approaches the management of its foreign policy—an approach strongly reflective of balance-of-power thinking, albeit not necessarily in the narrow classical usage. As Leifer sees it, such thinking is not expressed in "crude mechanical terms based solely on responding and adjusting to indices of military strength through changing alignments in the promiscuous manner of eighteenth-century Europe" (i.e. in terms of re-dressing an unfavorable distribution of power[15]) but rather on a reading of whether a hegemon is likely to be benign (or the least objectionable among the great powers) or malign in the context of Singapore's interest.[16] Singapore's concern has not been to counter or seek countervailing balance against "each and every potential or actual hegemon" but rather to take an accurate read of its potentials to damage Singapore's interest. Its view of the US as an essentially benign hegemon in the light of Singapore's self interest has led "all governments of Singapore from shortly after independence to view the USA as a protecting and not a menacing power."[17] Such a view has been sustained post-Cold War, post-9/11, and post-Iraq war. BG Lee Hsien Loong has stressed often enough the need for the US to stay engaged in the region and remain "a major element in the power balance of Asia" given that it is the only country that can realistically balance China.[18]

Over a quarter of a century earlier Leifer had drawn attention to a comment by Singapore's first Foreign Minister, S. Rajaratnam, about the smaller powers not being able to escape the gravitational pull of the great powers although "they can, by intelligent calculation about the right distances and the correct velocity, orbit without being destroyed and even with profit to themselves."[19] To the extent that the United States is perceived to be benign, its gravitational pull is deemed beneficial. As another former Foreign Minister (currently Deputy Prime Minister and Minister of Law) S. Jayakumar puts it, in the post-9/11 world the US is the "only one with the capability to lead" the global struggle against terrorism.[20] In keeping close to the US orbit in this struggle Singapore evinces more of a "bandwagoning" with the US against threats rather than a specific state.[21]

In summation, the realist worldview of Singapore is reflected in the way the republic approaches the management of its foreign policy—an approach underlined by a certain balance-of-power thinking. The flexible manner in which Leifer applies the balance of power concept—sometimes to depict a particular world view, sometimes to refer to a prevailing condition in the pattern of international relations, sometimes to depict a particular kind of policy which should be better described as bandwagoning with a benign hegemon to balance against threats—seems to mirror the way Singapore's foreign policy makers themselves apply the concept in their foreign policy rhetoric.

Asserting sovereign rights and national interests

Singapore's realist outlook is also manifested in its consistent assertions of sovereign rights and national interest. Several instances in its foreign policy—the tough stand taken over the hanging of the two Indonesian marines in 1968 despite Suharto's intervention on their behalf; opposition to Vietnam's invasion and occupation of Cambodia (the principle of non-interference being repeatedly invoked to uphold the shield of sovereignty notwithstanding the moral repugnance inspired by the Khmer Rouge regime which Vietnamese power subsequently deposed); the stand taken over its invitation of Israel's President Chaim Herzog in 1986 despite diplomatic protests from Brunei, Malaysia and Indonesia[22]; the caning of American teenager Michael Fay in 1994 despite the personal intervention of then president Bill Clinton; its backing of the US-led war in Iraq despite signs of some domestic unease especially among its Muslim constituents[23]—serve as useful reminders of Singapore's hard headedness. More recently strong critical reactions from China's Foreign Ministry to then Deputy Prime Minister Lee Hsien Loong's visit to Taiwan shortly before he became prime minister again elicited Singapore's assertion of sovereign rights and independent action in the face of external great power pressure. As BG Lee subsequently explained, "Singapore's relations with China are based on equality and mutual respect. Singapore is a good friend of China. But to call off the trip at China's request would have undermined our right to make independent decisions, and damaged our international standing. As a small country, this is a vital consideration in our dealings with all countries."[24] In the case of its backing of the US in the Iraq war, Jayakumar responded to those who questioned the wisdom of its policy (at a time when WMDs, one of Washington's declared causes of war against Iraq had not been found and where intervention by force had not been mandated by the UN) by asserting that the protection of national interests lay at the heart of the matter.[25]

Given the strong realist underpinnings in Singapore's foreign policy one could well assume that moral considerations, although pertinent, are mostly subordinated to national interests or are not regarded as a high foreign policy objective. Indeed such key words as "Morality," "Ethics," "Norms," "Human Rights," and "Democracy" are conspicuously absent in the index of Leifer's *Singapore's Foreign Policy*. This is not a reflection on his personal values, which were marked by a strong humanism. It is a reflection rather of his detachment that personal values did not get in the way of his observations and judgment about Singapore's foreign policy.

The unique character of realism in Singapore's foreign policy also predisposes it toward an easier relationship with some regimes than with others. As Leifer notes in the context of Singapore–US relations, "Singapore's governments have found it easier to strike up a better working relationship with Republican administrations in Washington…The difficulty with Democratic administrations has followed from their tendency to place greater emphasis on the moral dimension of foreign policy."[26] He refers to past instances in which US championing of human rights issues and its notions of good governance had impinged on the asserted sovereignty of Singapore, resulting in a clash of political cultures between them.

The domestic structure of Singapore's foreign policy making has also fitted nicely into the realist state-centric "billiard-ball model" of international relations. Leifer has noted the strong domestic base from which Singapore's foreign policy is conducted. Such a dimension has its importance in governing the management of relations with the PRC especially at a time in regional relations when it was prudent not to be perceived as a "third China." Such "firm authority of government has meant that domestic political considerations have not impinged on policy to the same extent as in may other post-colonial states."[27] For post-colonial Singapore there has been little room for public debate and input into the foreign policy making process. In the years between 1968 and 1981 when the PAP dominated parliament with no opposition in sight it was even easier to discourage public questioning and debate on sensitive foreign policy and defense issues.

Finally it could be said that the innate vulnerability and "siege mentality" of Singapore rooted in the unique circumstances of its geographic location, physical size and ethnic composition of its population and the fragility of an emerging, new state held certain parallels with Israel[28]—a country which had a special resonance to Leifer as a Jew and had in its antecedent (the issue of Palestine) inspired his doctorial dissertation at the LSE. How Singapore has chosen to address certain aspects of this vulnerability through development and strengthening of its defense capability and widening as well as deepening of its international defense networking is the subject of another chapter in this volume. My focus here is on how Leifer has reflected on the exceptional quality of Singapore and its foreign policy.

Singapore's "exceptionalism"

Singapore's attainment of international stature and status of a developed state with commendable skill despite initial fears for its own viability as a sovereign nation is part of the success story of what Leifer calls "an exceptional state."[29] Leifer did not intend his last book to be a tribute to Singapore, although it reads like one. However his fondness for his subject matter, warts and all, is quite unmistakable. There is a generosity of spirit in his footnotes that give recognition to the growing corpus of works (largely Singaporean but with many Western contributions too) on various aspects of Singapore's foreign and defense policies. That this island state once described by a former Indonesian president as an inconsequential "little red dot" could have attracted so much academic attention is in itself a statement of Singapore's "exceptionalism." But more importantly his usage of the "exceptional" label serves to encapsulate many of the defining features and fundamentals of Singapore's foreign policy.

To Leifer, Singapore's exceptionalism lies not only in its size, location, economic success despite obvious natural resource constraints, and subsequent international reputation and status; it was apparent even from the time when Singapore was just a state within the Malaysian Federation. Not only did its Head of Government continue to be designated Prime Minister, it also manifested a tendency to conduct its own foreign relations and to highlight the shortcomings of Kuala Lumpur's foreign policy.[30] Singapore's engagement in such exercises of diplomacy at a historical juncture when it did not have the constitutional competence to do so has been discussed in much greater detail in an earlier work by Peter Boyce.[31] Leifer, however, in his edited volume of David Marshall's *Letters from Mao's China*, published in 1996, reminds us of an even earlier exercise in diplomacy by the first Chief Minister of pre-independence Singapore. That engagement by David Marshall took place soon after he had resigned from that position in 1956 when the Chinese People's Institute of Foreign Affairs invited him to lead a delegation of observers from Malaya and Singapore to visit China. Although Marshall found it politically expedient to go as an "adviser" to the delegation he was received as a foreign dignitary and met with senior figures in China including Premier Zhou Enlai.

Interestingly for students of foreign policy, the visit, as Leifer points out, provided the Chinese government an opportunity to elucidate its position *vis-à-*

vis the Overseas Chinese issue and allay fears concerning their links with Mainland China. Just as interesting was the occasion that the visit provided for Marshall to intervene successfully on behalf of small communities of Jews stranded in China, a number of whom were technically Soviet citizens, to obtain the necessary exit visas to enable them to resettle in Israel. This episode in Leifer's words "reveals David Marshall's abiding sense of Jewish identity underpinned by powerful humanistic qualities."[32] In these comments, one could sense that Leifer was also holding a mirror to himself. Indeed the empathy that Leifer showed for his subject was reflected in the enthusiasm and speed that he applied to the completion of the work while on attachment as a Distinguished Visiting Fellow at the Institute of Southeast Asian Studies, Singapore.[33]

The exceptional quality of Singapore as a state can be summed up by reference to the circumstances of its acquisition of independent statehood; in its foreign policy culture rooted in siege and insecurity; in its consistently held realist international outlook; in its ability to cope with and mitigate its innate vulnerability and in the way it excelled in the culture of competitiveness. It can also be said that having to live on edge in a regional environment that could not be taken for granted was a manifestation of that exceptionalism as well as a driving force for Singapore's economic success. One is reminded of a remark by Singapore's second Prime Minister and now Senior Minister, Goh Chok Tong, that if Singapore could just weigh anchor and relocate itself to the vicinity of, say, Hawaii, it might assuredly enjoy a more sanguine regional ambience though not necessarily a domestic economic vitality.

Some paradoxical elements

Among Leifer's list of the exceptional is that small core of political elites who laid the foundations of Singapore's foreign policy, identified its fundamentals, and sustained and defended its objectives over time. Foremost among them is Lee Kuan Yew who, as the design of the soft cover edition of *Singapore's Foreign Policy* aptly suggests, continues to cast a long shadow over Singapore's foreign policy.[34] That influence, as Leifer points out, is both an asset and at times a factor that complicated the management of relations with nearest neighbor Malaysia and elsewhere in the region where the sharpness of his *obiter dicta* was not always appreciated. Indeed, the Lee factor is one of a long list of paradoxes that also mark the exceptionalism of Singapore's foreign policy.

There are other seemingly paradoxical elements noted by Leifer:

1 Singapore attempts to drive and yet suffers the region (in other words it needs the region and it does not.) Its prosperity is derived in part from its regional location and yet the same region gives cause for Singapore to want to transcend it.

2 There is a "contradiction between a declared initial intent of being friends with all, and especially close neighbors, and a prickliness in the way in which those relations are handled in practice."
3 For a small state like Singapore, its domestic and foreign policies are inextricably mixed, yet foreign policy making remains largely the preserve of a small elite. It remains a moot question whether growing openness and the evolving democratization process will also open up the space for the civil society engagement in the foreign policy realm.
4 Singapore repudiates the use of force in the conduct of foreign policy but embraces the utility of force for deterrent purposes. Nevertheless growing confidence in its own defense capabilities has also strengthened its willingness to participate in wider confidence building and defense diplomacy and as well as cooperative security.
5 Realism (or its practice of a balance of power policy) is the dominant foreign policy paradigm but it does not exclude liberal internationalism in economic policy or in cooperative security arrangements. Leifer himself has observed that Singapore has become "more of a regional partner because of an ability to identify a juncture between self-interest and common interests."[35]
6 Despite its rhetoric of independence and sovereignty, Singapore had chosen in an act of economic pragmatism to embrace multinational corporations at a time when it was fashionable for dependency theorists to target them negatively.

The successful management of these paradoxes calls not only for diplomatic adroitness but also for a pragmatic (i.e. non-ideological, non-doctrinaire) mindset. Pragmatism is often implied in Leifer's analysis of Singapore's diplomatic success, but it is not a word often encountered in *Singapore's Foreign Policy* although the last words given to Lee Kuan Yew in Leifer's book (referred to earlier in this chapter) serve well to underline the pragmatism in Singapore's foreign policy practice. "Pragmatism" appears only twice—both times in a section which discusses Singapore's relations with China where the need for pragmatism was particularly important in the early days of China's opening up to the outside world, and when the historical baggage of relations with Southeast Asia, as well as the shadow of Taiwan over Singapore's relations with Beijing, had to be seriously reckoned with. But in an earlier work Leifer had written about how pragmatism "became a declared virtue from necessity when the island became a sovereign state by default."[36] Citing a 1985 speech by BG Lee Hsien Loong then newly inducted into politics from the military, Leifer remarked that the pragmatic ideal that BG Lee endorsed (namely formulating policies on a purely rational basis and abjuring doctrinaire approaches) "has run like a continuous vein through the collective outlook of Government in Singapore."[37]

One may add that Singaporean pragmatism also makes it possible for an otherwise idealistically inclined practitioner of diplomacy to be reconciled with the hard headed realist world view of the dominant policy makers. A seasoned and internationally respected practitioner of Singapore's diplomacy, Tommy Koh considers himself a "practical (or pragmatic) Idealist—one who is neither a Realist (seeing national interest as the exclusive basis for foreign policy) nor Moralist (seeing moral values as the primary determinant of foreign policy)." As a "practical Idealist" he recognizes the possibility that a government would encounter conflicts between its national interest and fidelity to law and morality. In such a case it might "feel compelled to subordinate considerations of law and morality to its national interest."[38]

If pragmatism serves to qualify idealism, it can also blunt the sharp edges of realism. As pointed out earlier in this chapter, the realism behind Singapore's foreign policy practice does not necessarily exclude elements of liberal internationalism, or multilateral cooperative security practices where these can serve Singapore's national interest. This is borne out in Leifer's observation of the manner in which Singapore provided a lead in ASEAN toward the creation of the ARF, which in his view "marked an exception to conventional balance of power practice."[39] The idea of working together with the US and Japan to ensure a stable arrangement of independent states (both Communist and non-Communist) in Southeast Asia had been publicly mooted by Lee Kuan Yew in 1980. The post-Cold War environment of the early 1990s in the Asia Pacific provided that opportunity for ASEAN to engage the United States, Japan, and China within a multilateral cooperative security framework to promote regional stability. In Leifer's account, the 1992 Fourth ASEAN summit in Singapore and the subsequent rotation of the ASEAN Standing Committee chairmanship to Singapore presented opportunities for the republic to set the stage for the promotion of this kind of multilateral security cooperation.[40] Whatever might be said about the liberal neo-functionalist assumptions (namely "an incremental linear process of dialogue can produce a qualitative improvement in political relationships"[41]) of the ARF, Leifer's realism led him to conclude in his seminal work on the ARF that the prior existence of a favorable balance of power had been crucial to the successful launching and maintenance of the multilateral forum.[42] That Singapore was able to give substance to the underlying liberal assumptions of the ARF is perhaps a reflection of its "pragmatic realism" notwithstanding its baggage of historical experiences.

Structural tensions in relations with neighbors

Historical baggage is relevant in understanding Singapore's relations with Malaysia—but the key phrase, which underlies the attempt to make sense of that complex but critical relationship, is "structural tension" which the reader will encounter repeatedly in *Singapore's Foreign Policy*. Such structural tensions attest to the complex web of interpenetrating domestic influences which add an extra dimension of sensitivities to inter-state relations. Do "structural tensions" point to a persisting somber reality in cross-Singapore Straits relations that will persist beyond generational leadership change, and even self-sufficiency in water supply on the Singapore side? The transition of political leadership in Malaysia from Mahathir Mohamed to Abdullah Ahmad Badawi resulted very quickly in an improvement in the atmospherics of Malaysia–Singapore relations. There remain nevertheless very substantial issues to be resolved—the question of the price of water to be supplied to Singapore in the long term, the relocation of Customs, Immigration and Quarantine facilities in Singapore, withdrawal of central provident funds by peninsula Malaysian workers on their departure from Singapore, development of Malayan Railway land in Singapore, replacement of the existing causeway by a bridge, to name but a few.

While relations with post-Suharto Indonesia are not as structurally rooted, the tensions that have emerged are grounded in Indonesia's domestic vicissitudes over which Singapore has little control. This in turn highlights a policy problem and a policy nightmare for Singapore. The problem (which underlines yet another paradox for Singapore) is how to uphold a sacred principle of non-intervention in the domestic affairs of other states while registering the need to express concern over domestic developments of neighbors, which impinge on the well-being of Singapore itself. The nightmare is that shifting domestic fortunes in its two nearest neighbors might reaffirm the encirclement complex in the city-state. And here former Indonesian President Abdurrahman Wahid's widely circulated fit-of pique comments at the Indonesian Embassy in November 2000 about *inter alia,* Singapore's disdain of its Malay neighborhood, and his suggestion of a Malaysia–Indonesia collusion to turn off the taps on Singapore fed precisely into this kind of encirclement psyche.

Some lacunae in analysis

For Singapore, going global, international defense networking, and the pursuit of an active foreign economic policy serve to transcend what Leifer calls the "tyranny of geography."[43] Leifer, however, does not squarely address the form of new generation challenges on the foreign policy front as Singapore's economy matures, as it widens its global diplomatic reach, as domestic expectations and even values change with changing demographics and rising educational levels, and as neighbors recover their competitiveness.

Leifer's works on Singapore give scant treatment to foreign economic policy or political economy aspects of foreign policy making—in particular the resort to bilateral free-trade trade pacts with Australia and New Zealand, Canada, the United States, Jordan, Japan, Korea, India (and others in various stages of discussion) and the implications and impact, including political ramifications (if any) on the regional backyard, namely ASEAN. If such initiatives—which carry political-strategic implications—are intended to transcend the limitations of Singapore's own region, how will it strike a balance between driving the region by way of commitment to economic multilaterialism such as AFTA (the ASEAN Free Trade Area) and more recently, to accelerated ASEAN economic integration (through the proposed ASEAN Economic Community) and its reinforcing of bilateral trade deals which in a way is an acknowledgement of the lack of mileage achieved through multilateral negotiating frameworks such as the WTO and APEC? The emergence of East Asian regionalism and the rise of China will also have to be related to the need for continued strategic and economic engagement of the United States. These were nascent trends at the time when *Singapore's Foreign Policy* was being completed.

India today would also have deserved more than the gloss over it receives—described in *Singapore's Foreign Policy* as "diplomatically distant" and serving as a mere contrasting footnote to the importance of China, which gets the largest section in a chapter on the major powers. Nevertheless Leifer acknowledged Singapore's role in promoting India as a dialogue partner of ASEAN and in supporting its membership in the ARF although he did not consider these developments as having an ameliorating impact on Singapore's own sense of vulnerability *vis-à-vis* its immediate regional environment. However, as India re-orientates its international outlook and attitudes toward the Southeast Asian region and extends its strategic reach, it will be an increasing reminder to ASEAN of its strategic presence on its western flank. Indeed the world post-9/11 has witnessed dramatic reorientations of Indian policy toward the United States and China while the war against international terrorism has given India a lever for security cooperation not only with the United States but also with some ASEAN states. Leifer in fact had anticipated the lengthening shadow of India over the ASEAN region. In a 1994 interview with *The Star* newspaper, he spoke of the Indian economy as one

> which has often been underestimated and which at least in certain sectors could be quite significant…You have a population of 800 million plus, probably a quarter of that is in the modern sector. There you have tremendous intellectual achievements. For example the attainment in the sciences is quite remarkable. Given the way in which the Government of Narasimha Rao has completely changed economic doctrines, I think one must not discard India.[44]

Currently, Singapore in its perennial search for economic opportunities abroad has caught another round of the "Indian fever" after the initial reaching out to India during the early 1990s. Indeed Singapore has never until now had to face the concurrent rise of China and India. India not only affords Singapore an opportunity to diversify its economic risks *vis-à-vis* China but also some prospects of mitigating a future over-dependence on China.

If there is a seeming neglect of India in the subsequent book on Singapore's foreign policy, it is perhaps an intended statement of the comparatively greater significance of East Asia to Singapore. The economic pull of a more vibrant Northeast Asia, despite an economically stagnant Japan, on Singapore and its impact in turn on the Southeast Asian environment would call for deeper exploration today, especially since we have come increasingly to recognize the importance of factoring in economics in any security and foreign policy evaluations. Singapore's economic entry into China and its hoped-for "in-sourcing" strategy of creating a large external economy (whereby in the China case, overseas investments would also drive the domestic Singapore economy) is transforming the traditional notion of space and will increasingly strengthen Singapore's stake in the internal stability of China itself—a significant transformation from the early Cold War years when China was readily perceived as a threat to the domestic stability of regional states including Singapore.

Plugging into and tapping the benefits of globalization will open up new vulnerabilities to "soft security" threats as the East Asian economic crisis of the late 1990s bore out. The SARS epidemic was also a reminder of the downside of globalization to the most globalized and open economy in the region. A whole host of non-traditional security concerns (in particular international terrorism) are crowding into the security agenda of Singapore—a phenomenon which Leifer did not quite capture in his final work.[45]

Just as important is the fact that globalization will transform Singapore's society in as much as the importation of foreign talent will impact upon critical sectors of society and the economy and even on security. Globalization will also impact on the way we have traditionally looked at the assumptions of national sovereignty. Increasingly, the study of Singapore's foreign policy will have to include an assessment of the interactions between foreign policy and domestic political processes. After all, foreign policy is ultimately about the welfare and sense of well-being of a people.

Conclusion: Coming full circle

The saga of how "exceptional" Singapore copes with its vulnerability (which is not to be equated with insecurity or sense of external threat to its territorial integrity) is one that Leifer has sought to illuminate in his various writings on the republic's foreign policy. Speaking at the launching in Singapore of his final book, he observed with reference to the ending of the Cold War which removed one "ASEAN glue" and the devastating aftermath of the 1997 economic crisis on Singapore's neighbors particularly Indonesia, that "now, the region is regressing toward the uncertain landscape in which Singapore became independent. There is a quality of political déjà vu about Singapore in the first years of the twenty-first century." While this did not mean a return to 1965, "there is a certain disconcerting 'full circle' quality with the return of regional factors, which are beyond the control of Singapore."[46] In the post-9/11 era and particularly after the Bali bombings of October 2002 and the revelation of the Jemaah Islamiah plots to destabilize the region, including Singapore, the specter of international terrorism which finds conjuncture with militant Muslim groups in Singapore's hinterland hangs heavily over the planners of Singapore's homeland security. The threat is not from a state actor but from a trans-border regional terrorist network with possible linkages to Al Qaeda.

On a more upbeat note Leifer observes that Singapore's exceptional economic development gives it a capacity to manage "better than most in addressing acute regional economic adversity. Such development has enabled the island state to cope with vulnerability in a way unanticipated at independence."[47] But in starker tones he concludes, "Singapore copes with vulnerability by trying to be extraordinary in the way in which its achievements are projected and perceived well beyond its little pond. In the process, nothing is taken for granted and nothing is guaranteed."[48] Are there any lessons that others could learn from Singapore's experience? Leifer's answer is more circumspect. He has written in the preface of his book that because of the unique character of Singapore's circumstances, it "does not necessarily follow that there are clear lessons to be learned by other states from its conduct of foreign relations."[49]

Notes

1 Leifer was by no means a-theoretical. Indeed his chapter in an edited book on functionalism published in 1975 showed that he was well acquainted with David Mitrany's functionalist thinking. Taking into account the historical experience of Southeast Asia and the needs of the state as perceived by the various governments of the region, Leifer saw little prospect for functionalism in so far as it was conceived by Mitrany as "a way of limiting authority to specific activity and hopefully in the process to break away from the traditional link between authority and defined territory." (See "The Limits of Functionalist Endeavour: the Experiences of South-East Asia," in A.J.R. Groom and Paul Taylor (eds) *Functionalism: Theory and Practice in International Relations*, New York: Crane, Russak, 1975, p. 283.)

2 Adam Roberts, "Obituary: Professor Michael Leifer," *The Independent*, 9 April 2001.

3 Michael Yahuda, "Professor Michael Leifer: Analysing the Politics of Southeast Asia over Thirty Years," *The Times,* 28 March 2001.

4 Michael Leifer, "Conflict over Kampuchea: The Issues at Stake," speech delivered at an inter-faculty seminar on "International Conflicts and their Resolution with special reference to the Kampuchean problem," National University of Singapore, 1988, unpublished.

5 The remark sounded like a paraphrase of the opening line in Nicholas J. Rengger's chapter, "Culture, Society, and Order in World Politics" included in a volume of essays entitled *Dilemmas of World Politics: International Issues in a Changing World,* edited by John Baylis and N.J. Rengger (Oxford University Press, 1992, p. 85). Rengger himself was paraphrasing a remark on culture attributed to an infamous character from German history. Rengger wrote, "Culture is one of those terms that often prompts people (especially international relations scholars) to reach for their revolvers."

6 See e.g. Sorpong Peou, "Realism and Constructivism in Southeast Asian Security Studies Today: A Review Essay," *Pacific Review*, Vol. 15 (1), 2002, pp. 119–138.

7 Michael Leifer, *Dilemmas of Statehood in Southeast Asia*, Singapore: Asia Pacific Press, 1972, p. x.

8 Ibid., p.152.

9 Michael Leifer, *The ASEAN Regional Forum: Extending ASEAN's Model of Regional Security*, Adelphi Paper 302, Oxford University Press for IISS, 1996. It can be argued that a pre-disposition not to challenge the post-Cold War balance-of-power situation in the Asia-Pacific did make it possible for an ARF-type cooperative security venture to

emerge. Leifer indeed relates to the ARF in more realistic terms—seeing it as "a modest contribution to a viable balance or distribution power within the Asia-Pacific by other than traditional means" (p. 59). He had in an earlier op ed piece expressed the view that "the very attempt to lock China (a rising power) into a network of constraining multilateral arrangements (exemplified by the ARF) underpinned hopefully by a sustained and viable American presence would seem to serve the purpose of the balance of power by means other than alliance." (Michael Leifer, "Truth about Balance of Power," *ISEAS Trends* No. 64, in *Business Times*, 30-31 December, 1995.) While expressing unease over the premium that Leifer placed on the existence of a stable balance of power as a pre-requisite for a successful ARF, Yuen Foong Khong nevertheless acknowledged his "strong theoretical argument, minus the jargon." Despite his strong realist emphasis on the balance of power, Leifer was not oblivious to the non-power variables (economic dynamism, the role of culture, norms and identities) in his analysis of the ARF. (Yuen Foong Khong, "Making Bricks without Straw in the Asia Pacific?" *Pacific Review*, Vol. 10 No. 2 (1997), p. 295.)

10 Michael Leifer, *Singapore's Foreign Policy: Coping with Vulnerability*, London: Routledge, 2000.

11 For a reconstruction of that forum by Chin Kin Wah and Simon Tay, see "Coping with Vulnerability: Singapore's Foreign Policy in the 21st Century," *Singapore Institute of International Affairs Reader,* Vol. 1 No. 1, July 2001, pp. 45-58.

12 *Singapore's Foreign Policy,* p. 162.

13 Michael Leifer, "The Conduct of Foreign Policy," in Kernial Singh Sandhu and Paul Wheatley (eds.) *Management of Success: The Moulding of Modern Singapore*, Singapore: Institute of Southeast Asian Studies, 1969, p. 965.

14 Ibid., p. 968.

15 Such considerations may well operate, however, in the development of Singapore's defense force structure with a view on the assets and capabilities of neighboring countries.

16 *Singapore's Foreign Policy*, pp. 98–99.

17 Ibid., p. 99.

18 *Straits Times*, 13 November 2002, p. A6.

19 Michael Leifer, *The Foreign Relations of the New States*, Camberwell: Longman Australia, 1974, p. 102.

20 *Straits Times*, 12 March 2004, p. H7.

21 "Bandwagoning" as a means of balancing against threats is a concept often attributed to Stephen Walt's *The Origins of Alliance Formation,* Ithaca, NY: Cornell University Press, 1987.

22 For his commentary on the impact of the Herzog visit on Singapore's relations with Malaysia, see Michael Leifer, "Israel's President in Singapore: political catalysis and transnational politics," *Pacific Review,* Vol. 1 No. 4 (1988), pp. 341–353.

23 During the 1991 Gulf War Singapore Muslims expressed their discomfort over the loss of Muslim lives and this in turn led to questions being raised about their sense of loyalty. In the run up to the Iraq war four Muslim groups issued a joint statement appealing to the government to "oppose, or at least abstain from supporting any collective attacks on Iraq." (*Straits Times,* 5 September 2002).

24 Q & A with DPM Lee on his visit to Taiwan, Ministry of Foreign Affairs, Singapore, 21 September 2004. (http://app.mfa.gov.sg/sections/press/report_press.asp?3943). In a subsequent National Day Rally speech as prime minister, Lee Hsien Loong concluded his lengthy comment on Singapore-China relations with a reassertion of Singapore's national interest: "(F)rom time to time, issues will arise. The big powers have their own interests and will exercise their influence to get their way. We may be old friends, but when our interests diverge—or even when our approaches to the same problem

differ—they have to put theirs first, and so must we. This is a reality of the compelling pressures of national interest." (*Straits Times*, 23 August 2004, p. 14.)
25 *Straits Times,* 12 March 2004, p. H7.
26 *Singapore's Foreign Policy*, p. 106.
27 Leifer, "The Conduct of Foreign Policy," p. 966.
28 An island state located in the middle of a predominantly Malay–Muslim Sea (neighborhood), Singapore has at times been described as a second Israel.
29 The notion of "exceptionalism" associated with the unique qualities of Singapore was developed by Leifer in an earlier work, "Singapore in Regional and Global Context: Sustaining Exceptionalism," in Arun Mahizhnan and Lee Tsao Yuan (eds), *Singapore: re-engineering success*, Oxford: Oxford University Press, 1998, pp. 19-30.
30 Michael Leifer, *Singapore's Foreign Policy*, p. 29.
31 Peter Boyce, "Policy without Authority: Singapore's External Affairs Power," *Journal of Southeast Asian History,* Vol. 6, No. 2, September 1965, pp. 87-103.
32 *Letters from Mao's China by David Marshall*, edited with an introduction by Michael Leifer, Singapore Heritage Society, 1996, p. 3.
33 According to the ISEAS Librarian, who was curator of the Marshall letters and had been instrumental in persuading Leifer to undertake the project, the latter confidently agreed to "do it in two weeks" after reviewing the file of 57 letters. And he was on time, "delivering the manuscript complete with his introduction. He would see me everyday, sometimes more than once a day, as the editing work progressed." (Ch'ng Kim See, "A Personal Tribute to Michael Leifer" [Unpublished], Singapore: ISEAS Library, 2004.)
34 As Leifer puts it, Lee on relinquishing the prime ministership, continues to leave his mark on Singapore's foreign policy practice "partly through imposing his own experience of political impermanence…He has also left his mark through combining cerebral and outspoken combative qualities." (*Singapore's Foreign Policy*, pp. 7–8.)
35 Ibid., p. 974.
36 Leifer, "The Conduct of Foreign Policy," p. 268.
37 Ibid., p. 967.
38 Tommy Koh, *The Quest for World Order; perspectives of a pragmatic idealist*, edited with an introduction by Amitav Acharya, Singapore: Times Academic Press for Institute of Policy Studies, Singapore, 1988, p. 7. Koh was described by his editor as "something of an iconoclast within the Singapore government, sometimes holding views that are different from mainstream official thinking." (Ibid., p. xx.)
39 *Singapore's Foreign Policy*, p. 134.
40 For this account see iIbid., pp. 132–136.
41 Leifer, *The ASEAN Regional Forum*, p. 59.
42 See ibid., p. 57.
43 Ibid., p. 39.
44 *The Star*, 12 February 1994.
45 It is noteworthy that while non-alignment appears in the index, non-traditional security is conspicuous by its total absence.
46 *SIIA Reader*, pp. 47–48.
47 *Singapore's Foreign Policy*, p. 155.
48 Ibid., p. 162.
49 Ibid., p. xiii.

14 The domestic sources of regional order in Michael Leifer's analysis of Southeast Asia

James Cotton

Other contributors to this book have dealt in some detail with Michael Leifer's use of various analytic tools – and especially with his understanding of 'order' – in his work on Southeast Asia. In the interests of developing the most comprehensive depiction of his contribution to scholarship, this chapter adopts a complementary approach. However regional order is understood, for it to be genuinely *regional* the states of Southeast Asia must be actors. They must themselves be active participants in the generation of order, or it will be imposed upon them or (depending on the definition of 'order' that is adopted) it may appear by default. The consideration of this issue can only proceed from the analysis of domestic dynamics. The focus for this chapter will thus be on Michael Leifer's writings regarding how the resources, capabilities and understandings of the world available to the states of Southeast Asia have been brought to bear on their practice of regional and foreign policy. The discussion that follows deals, first, with Michael Leifer's last appearance in the classroom. As with much of his work, his remarks on that occasion dealt extensively with these themes which were evidently a preoccupation up to his final days. It then passes to a consideration of some of the formative intellectual influences upon his approach before considering in more detail his work on the nations of Southeast Asia and especially on Indonesia.

Michael Leifer's final seminar

I had the privilege – a great privilege but a great sadness as well – to attend Michael Leifer's last seminar at the LSE. Fittingly it was on the subject of Indonesia's foreign policy. As ever it was delivered without notes but with a confidence and command that I could only envy. For a time I suspended all belief and the scholar I saw before me was energetic, compelling, and at the height of his powers.

His portrait of Indonesian policy was painted using bold strokes but with occasional asides of detail. He took Indonesia's foreign policy since independence as constituting almost a single process. In many respects this was and is an unconventional view, as many authorities insist upon discerning a major break in continuity between the era of Sukarno and the New Order. In advancing this argument I recognized him to be building upon the remarkably prescient remarks, found in his *Indonesia's Foreign Policy*, where this continuity was foreshadowed. There he says:

> Indonesia's foreign policy, as it emerged after the internal transfer of power [of 1965], reinstated a former course rather than pursuing a novel one… The rhetoric of Sukarno was repudiated and membership in an anti-imperialist axis revoked, but an underlying continuity was maintained because the new political leadership, although fervently anti-communist, had given up neither opposition to membership of military alliances nor an aspiration to a pre-eminent role in regional affairs. That continuity was qualified in a novel form by a progressive economic association with industrialized capitalist states which was, in effect, an alignment.[1]

In 1983 Michael Leifer was able to suggest that both Indonesian regimes, though proclaiming non-alignment, had in fact rendered themselves dependent upon external powers in pursuit of their ends. In 2001 he was able to develop the parallel further. Both alignment strategies had failed, and the legacy of this failure would leave the nation prostrate in both instances.

The first phase of Indonesia's foreign policy was expressed in the ideals of Bandung. The country would avoid entanglements with the dominant power blocs of the early Cold War period and concentrate instead upon the liberation of its people from toil and shortage. However, Sukarno squandered the national estate in grandiose projects and military adventures, the latter requiring for their realization that very alignment with external powers he had initially sought to avoid. With Indonesia a member, by 1965, of the Beijing–Pyongyang–Phnom Penh–Jakarta axis of the NEFOS (the New Emerging Forces[2]) and having walked out of the United Nations, its position as a critic of almost all the institutions of world politics was stridently proclaimed. This position, however, was not sustainable. Sukarno was undone by the consequences of the commitment to confrontation with Malaysia along with his increasing reliance upon the Indonesian Communist Party (PKI). The former made the military key players, the latter stimulated first their apprehension and then their opposition. Sukarno's fall and the bloodletting that followed sundered the relationship with Beijing though it was not until 1966 that the policy of *konfrontasi* was concluded, and diplomatic relations between Jakarta and Kuala Lumpur were not formalized until 1967.

Sukarno's failures produced a legacy of unrest and shortage. The new regime realized there was little time to build a popular constituency. To achieve this objective, Suharto set his course by a different standard. Aspiring to be known as *bapak pembangunan*, 'the father of development' (a title actually granted to the president by the national parliament) Suharto opened the country to foreign investment and fostered linkages with global business. Initially it seemed that

Suharto was pursuing that domestic focus neglected by his predecessor, though he later ignored economic fundamentals in favour of personal and family enrichment. However, early in his long years in office, foreign policy again proved the weak element in the presidential strategy. His commitment to an ill-considered and brutal venture in East Timor constituted thereafter a perennial drain on resources, while forcing a dependence on the United States for armaments. It is noteworthy that on this occasion Michael Leifer adopted a much more critical assessment of the deleterious character of the invasion than is in evidence in his published work, no doubt reflecting the impact of the events of 1999. The Timor venture soiled the reputation of the country in the non-aligned movement, the chief tenet of which was of course anti-colonialism. Suharto was thus denied his ambition, despite Indonesia's size and historical role, to become the senior statesman of the Third World. With the military discharging also a central political role, and their activities in Timor ensuring that the military sector remained a high priority, Suharto's domestic strategy prevented the emergence of an independent civil society, a free media, or the rule of law. For all its apparent progress in development, Indonesia thus lacked the institutions that would protect the positive economic achievements of the New Order and also permit an orderly transition to the next regime.

Meanwhile, Indonesia's ambition to exercise a leading regional role was realized through the formation of ASEAN. But with Indonesia as the key country of the association, the Timor issue also undermined its claims that it adhered to the principle of non-intervention and the pacific resolution of disputes, and accordingly that it aspired to the achievement of a 'Zone of Peace, Freedom and Neutrality' in the region. ASEAN's principles were further compromised by the enlargement of the group to incorporate Myanmar/Burma. On the one hand this associated ASEAN ever afterwards with a regime that has become a watchword for the neglect of human rights and the denial of democracy. On the other, Jakarta favoured Myanmar's membership partly on the grounds that in this state also the military played a major and independent role in the political order and thus the Burmese were, to an extent, ideological soul mates. In the process, ASEAN's image as a liberalizing regional force was damaged.

The final act in the Suharto drama was the consequence of the growing cupidity of the first family and the absence of a mechanism for orderly political succession. The regional financial crisis was the product of the withdrawal of investor confidence in Indonesia which Suharto's unanimous 're-election' in 1998 and his acceptance of an IMF rescue package did nothing to reverse. This in turn was the response to squabbling and disunity among Suharto's ministers, cronies and advisers, and the perception, at home and abroad, that national goals were being sacrificed in the interests of enriching Suharto's offspring. Disorder spread across the archipelago. The currency collapse left the country so weakened that it had no choice in 1999 but to follow the directions of international financiers, their sentiments reinforced by the remarks of the US president himself, and accept the humiliation of an Australian-led intervention in East Timor.

In short, under both its long-term presidents, Indonesia's great potential was not realized. The permanent improvement in the lot of the ordinary people that the nation's great reserve of natural resources might have delivered was not achieved. And in each administration, though for different reasons, the poor management of external entanglements weakened the ruling regime. Michael Leifer concludes his book on Indonesia with a quotation from some remarks made by Suharto in 1969: 'We shall only be able to play an effective role if we ourselves are possessed of a great national vitality', observing that these sentiments were 'likely to remain valid for the rest of the twentieth century'.[3] And so the situation remains more than 20 years later, with the Megawati and Wahid presidencies generally assessed as missed opportunities.

If 1998–99 was a major watershed in Indonesia's external policies, the impact of September 11 may yet prove similarly momentous. For so many reasons it is a matter of profound regret that Michael Leifer did not live to write about the impact of September 11 on Indonesia and on Southeast Asia. With his knowledge of the Middle East and Islam as well as his long acquaintance with Indonesia and its elites, he would have been able to make an especially well-informed contribution. And it is an issue where domestic dynamics have been especially determining. There are some hints of what he might have had to say in the several references he makes to the controversy stirred in 1986 when Israeli President Chaim Herzog visited Singapore.[4] He represents this episode as an indicator that elites in Indonesia and especially in Malaysia had yet to take the city-state's independence seriously. Yet the subtext of this episode was surely that it indicated that Malay and Muslim solidarity was a current that ran very deep in the region and was indeed also, as he argued, an issue manipulated by the then rulers of Malaysia. In this instance it counted for more than the ASEAN principles of non-interference and respect for sovereignty and also for more than the economic and other forces that bound Malaysia and Singapore to a common fate. If, in current circumstances, Indonesia and the other members of ASEAN are to develop a common and effective policy to counter terrorism, domestic (and regional) political dynamics might not suffice to drive it. Engagement with external powers would be crucial, a view to be extrapolated from his belief that for regional organizations to make a significant impact (as was the case in the Kampuchea/Cambodia issue) their interests must intersect with those of the major powers.

The LSE and Elie Kedourie

Michael Leifer's extensive knowledge of Indonesia was the fruit of many field trips, and also of his growing connections with those of his former students who ascended the ranks of the intellectual elite within Indonesian society. But he brought to this subject a philosophical sensibility which he never discussed explicitly in his writings and which is brought to bear so artfully that it is often only glimpsed. It derived, in large measure, from some aspects of his initial training. Michael Leifer spent the better part of his career at the LSE first as student and then as teacher, in the latter guise conducting courses in the Department of International Relations not only on his geographical specialization but also mainstream courses on international society. Given the fact that the LSE, according to some versions of the story, was the original home of 'The English School',[5] it might be concluded that he was a member, albeit especially focused on Southeast Asian rather than global affairs. Most analysts of this 'School', however, do not regard his writings as falling within its ambit, a judgment which is supported by the fact that the history of the development of the discipline at the LSE makes sparse – though inevitably respectful – references to his contributions.[6] This is not, of course, to dispute the proposition that his usage of the idea of 'order' bears the influence of such colleagues as Martin Wight and Hedley Bull.

It should be emphasized that Michael Leifer was a doctoral student not in the Department of International Relations but in the Department of Government, where his supervisor was Elie Kedourie.[7] Not only was Kedourie a distinguished Middle Eastern scholar, he also possessed a deep knowledge of political theory. While there is no single key to understanding Kedourie's approach, he deeply distrusted nationalism and published an extremely influential work on the subject. Nationalism, according to his view, was an example of that ideological turn in political thinking that had been made possible by the French Revolution as that revolution was contemplated through the lens of German rationalist and romantic philosophy. Flawed as a political doctrine, its application to the circumstances of the Middle East on the part of the British in their attempts to construct modern regimes led to disaster.[8] Though this position was developed especially in connection with the Middle East, Kedourie held the view that as a general rule regimes organized according to nationalist criteria were, on that ground alone, no more or less acceptable that any others. What mattered was regime performance: 'The only criterion capable of public defense is whether the new rulers are less corrupt and grasping, or more just and merciful, or whether there is no change at all, but the corruption, the greed, and the tyranny merely find victims other than those of the departed rulers'.[9]

There is a strong echo of Kedourie in Michael Leifer's assessment of nationalism. As might be expected, this influence can be detected in the text of the latter's first substantial work, his (unpublished) doctoral thesis. The subject of this thesis was British policy on the Palestine issue in the period immediately prior to the end of the British mandate. In the prevailing conditions of the post-war Middle East, on the view of Foreign Secretary Ernest Bevin, Britain required the support of what was taken to be a coherent Arab nationalist movement. Thus it was decided in London that 'to alienate the Arabs over Palestine would be to court disaster in the entire region'.[10] However, though the thesis notes the fundamental ideological divisions that existed within the Labour tradition (and thus within the post-war Labour government) regarding the character of nationalism, there are suggestions that by proceeding as though that was a single Arab interest the British made some contribution to bringing about the appearance of one. Thus Michael Leifer refers to 'British sponsored pan-Arabism', and also to the British predilection, when in doubt, to 'conciliate Arab Nationalism'.[11] In the event, as executed principally by Bevin, British policy was spectacularly unsuccessful, in effect abandoning the Jewish population of the territory to a military contest with Arab forces while also exhibiting a studied inconsistency in its practical expression of tacit support for the latter. In this aspect of its argument, the thesis would seem thus to sustain Kedourie's scepticism regarding the practicality and baleful consequences of any policy that takes nationalist claims seriously.

Though the focus of his work then shifted to Southeast Asia, Michael Leifer retained the critical view of nationalism that he had originally acquired while researching on the Middle East under Kedourie's direction. Thus, on the former region, he wrote more than thirty years ago: 'Nationalism as a force triumphed to varying degrees [in Southeast Asia] in the propitious circumstances following the Second World War. But if it was intimately associated with the transfer of power it did not automatically guarantee structural consolidation in the new state. National independence did not mean the negation of politics which arose out of deep-seated conflicts of interest among elite groups and their followers'.[12] In short, a regime established on the basis of nationalist credentials was not necessarily any better or worse than a regime formed on an alternative basis. What mattered was the relationship between rulers and ruled. And despite their nationalist credentials, both of Indonesia's long-term rulers neglected that relationship.

The fertility of Kedourie's approach is measured by its influence on more than one generation of scholars associated with the LSE. It is noteworthy that in the case study on China by Christopher Hughes in this collection a similar dynamic is postulated.[13] Nationalism in contemporary China is a 'resource' for the rulers – it neither identifies an improved form of governance nor contributes, except in an illusory way, to resolving the existing 'contradictions' (to use the Marxist term advisedly) between rulers and ruled. Its limitations are clearly manifest in the contemporaneous use by the regime of the concept of 'multi-lateralism' as a means to defuse the otherwise unrealizable demands of a populace in whom nationalist sentiments have been deliberately inculcated. The latter implies that China can use a variety of fora to build coalitions and win supporters for its positions, principally in its contest with the United States. Nationalist claims therefore have to be muted to achieve nationalist ends. This approach is quite consistent with Marxist logic, but is self-evidently a merely formulaic resolution of a tension which does not derive from nationalism but from the realities of power in the PRC.

The fate of Cambodia

Cambodia was for Michael Leifer an enduring interest, and derived initially, as he related the story, from his assuming responsibilities, when he joined the Adelaide University Politics Department of W.G.K. Duncan at the beginning of his career, for the supervision of a Cambodian graduate student. He returned to the issue many times, considering both the domestic dimensions of the country's ensnarement in the widening Indochina conflict and also the impact especially on the diplomatic approach adopted by ASEAN as a result of Vietnam's expulsion of the Khmer Rouge regime. The chapter in this collection by Ang Cheng Guan presents as careful and insightful a reading of Michael Leifer's *oeuvre* on this topic as has yet been written, being by no means restricted to his analysis of the 'Third Indochina Conflict'.[14]

The threats posed to Cambodia's stability, and ultimately its survival, derived principally from its geo-political predicament. With some success, Sihanouk had combined traditional appeals and the office of the monarchy to win a measure of political legitimacy. Cambodia also had the good fortune to possess a relatively homogeneous ethnic population. However, Sihanouk felt compelled to remind his countrymen of the predatory intentions of their neighbours in order to present the policy of neutrality, and himself as its consummate practitioner, as essential for the nation's survival.[15] In taking this course, Sihanouk long sought to balance the conflicting forces that were brought to bear on his fragile realm. The military junta that replaced him lacked legitimacy, and its policies inescapably drew the state even further into the Vietnam conflict. Neither this regime nor its Khmer Rouge nor its 'Democratic Kampuchea' successors permitted a manageable equilibrium to emerge among Cambodia's neighbours and would-be patrons.

Ang writes of the analysis developed by Michael Leifer in 1983:

> The interlocking pattern of conflict in Indochina makes the early prospect of a political settlement unlikely. An ideal settlement would take the form of the reconstitution of the government of Kampuchea in such a manner that it would be acceptable to Vietnam and to China and Thailand. To pose a solution in these terms is to beg the question because one has done no more than identify the central and, so far, insuperable problem.[16]

But the problem, namely Sino-Vietnamese alienation, was at that point indeed insuperable. Only a combination of military exhaustion and the emerging dynamics of the post-Cold War security environment opened the way for a settlement, and Michael Leifer's writings from that time onwards traced the gradual movement of the diplomatic pieces to the *denouement* engineered by UNTAC (United Nations Transitional Authority in Cambodia).

In considering this body of work, Ang is right to suggest that Michael Leifer felt no need to proceed from an explicitly stated methodology, and his description of his approach as akin to the 'narrative/process-tracing' of international history is especially well-chosen. I believe, however, a little more can be said regarding the intellectual basis of Leifer's scholarship. Here at least a further point can be made about an additional silence in that work. The Cambodia volume was published in the United States in 1967 by Praeger, then a major social science and area studies publisher. But it was decidedly different from many of the works on such subjects that appeared under this imprint. Ang correctly identifies a major intellectual context of much writing on East Asian international relations through this period as the Cold War narrative, the very dominance of which (as Yuen Foong Khong has effectively argued[17]) encouraged a form of empiricism in this field. It should be recalled, however, that there was at least one further context. The 1960s saw a surging tide of work on political development and its preconditions. Almond, Coleman, Pye, Verba, and others all sought to theorize development, and very little US analysis of Southeast Asia did not pay at least some attention to the arguments in question. Development was the end-point of the current political processes at work in Southeast Asia, and development would lay the basis for the creation of a democratic political order. Michael Leifer was undoubtedly aware of these intellectual trends. He encountered them first hand at Cornell (where indeed he wrote the first draft of *The Foreign Relations of the New States*) and his familiarity is demonstrated by very occasional references to works of this genre. Why is their influence on his work so slight?

Here again, perhaps, there are parallels with the views of Kedourie, whose position on nationalism has already been noted. Just as Kedourie regarded nationalism as a false panacea for the troubles of the non-European world, he was sceptical (again in his published works principally in connection with the Middle East) of the capacity of non-Western societies to adapt the fundamentals of liberal democracy to their own social dynamics. His last book, published posthumously, contains a chapter on the illusory nature of any democratic project in Iraq which, though composed at the time of the first Gulf War, could have been written yesterday.[18] Michael Leifer, it can be suggested, adopted similar assumptions in his analysis of Southeast Asia. This is not to claim that he was a mere echo of Kedourie, just as Kedourie hardly originated this approach (which, in this instance, derived largely from Michael Oakeshott),[19] but rather that all were consummate practitioners of an enduring and recognizable style of political analysis.

The detachment – in most cases it would be correct to label it the objectivity – of Michael Leifer's many works on the region may thus be better understood. He no more expected Cambodia to become a democracy than he believed that ASEAN would transform itself into a Southeast Asian version of the European Union. These views liberated his work from the false teleologies almost as much in evidence in security analysis now as was the case in the 1970s.

This is not say that he regarded authority relations in Southeast Asia as unchanging or not open to improvement. He was intensely aware that neither appeals to primordial or cultural values, nor the adoption of modern symbols nor even the manipulation of external issues were sufficient to engender an active sense of nationhood. When states faced challenges from without, or were beset by deep-rooted religious or cultural conflicts, national loyalties could be elusive or simply unattainable. Indeed these themes are central to his *Dilemmas of Statehood in Southeast Asia* which in some respects is a pessimistic assessment of Southeast Asia's future. He was adamant, however, that it was only by attending to the economic and social betterment of the population that modern states could be constructed in the region.

Singapore and survival

From Cambodia, Michael Leifer turned to Singapore. Despite the extensive influence of the British, the city-state was as much a test of the adaptability of Western notions of governance to the circumstances of an Asian political system. It is far from accidental that the relationship between rulers and ruled is a major preoccupation also of Michael Leifer's work on Singapore. His first commentary on Singapore dates from the earliest years of the city-state's independence.[20] It was a subject he returned to repeatedly, and was the focus of his last book. Throughout these various commentaries he recognizes the pre-eminent contribution of Lee Kuan Yew whose intelligence and determination he undoubtedly respected. Given his extensive knowledge of the various political systems of Southeast Asia, Michael Leifer had a rare appreciation of just how much potential there was for state instability and incapacity in the region. He therefore found much to admire in the city-state's infrastructure, public facilities, and vibrancy. As early as 1972 he commented that, in the context of the region, Singapore was 'in a class of its own' in regard to the 'effective performance' of its government.[21] He also accepted to a degree the main proposition of Lee's foreign policy. This was that for geo-political as well as ethnic reasons, as a sovereign state Singapore was uniquely vulnerable. In the interests of survival its human as much as its physical resources therefore required the most careful management, and this in turn necessitated limitations on political association and expression. Domestic and external policies were therefore very much more closely bound together than was the norm in the society of states.

Yet Michael Leifer was well aware of important contradictions and inconsistencies as the Singaporean political project unfolded. Lee was not as prescient as he liked to pretend, or as his 'meritocratic' rhetoric required his government to be. Policies regarding such fundamentals as births, language, immigration and citizenship fluctuated widely. Such policy shifts had important external as well as domestic consequences. Here we return to the logic of the observation made in 1986 regarding the regional perception of the limitations to Singapore's sovereign status. What was a domestic matter for Malaysia or, *a fortiori*, for Indonesia was almost inescapably an issue with 'foreign policy' ramifications for the city-state. Thus, when Lee decided to direct the creation of a particular 'Chinese' identity to unite what was then a heterogeneous community by emphasizing the teaching of *putonghua* and Confucian ethics, this undoubtedly increased the divide between the city-state and its immediate neighbours. There were also inconsistencies in Lee's style. A leader who was not averse to lecturing audiences in the western world about the need for circumspection in dealing with the sensibilities of Asian peoples and leaders could be brutally frank or even dismissive in his assessment of the region. Among other examples of the latter, Michael Leifer cites Lee's expression of his doubts regarding Vice-President B J Habibie's qualifications for high office which later proved a major impediment to relations with Indonesia when Habibie succeeded Suharto.[22]

In a short essay which probes the rationale behind the relentless pursuit of improvement in the city-state, Michael Leifer contends that there is a flavour of Nietzsche in Lee's approach.[23] Its practice amounts to nothing less than a 'triumph of the will' over obstacles that would be too great for ordinary individuals. I believe there is something of an oblique message in this suggestion. It should be seen in the context of an earlier discussion of the doubtful legitimacy of many of the regimes in the region. In this company, Michael Leifer regards Singapore as exceptional, and he postulates that Lee's effective government would in time produce 'a viable framework ... for a consolidated polity'.[24] There is thus the suggestion that authoritarian means will eventually prove unnecessary. Necessary or superfluous, the politics of will were still essential to the Singapore of 20 years later.

Michael Leifer's assessment of this phenomenon is revealing. He was an intensely ethical individual, demanding the highest standards of himself and also of those who would shape the lives of others. In accounting for Lee's calculations he might well have referred to Confucius instead of Nietzsche. At one stage in his career Lee indeed suggested that his strategy was Confucian in character, and the particular features of the city-state's governance that are the subject of the article in question have a Confucian ring, including the notion that in Singaporean democracy the people are held to account by the rulers according to the latter's exacting standards rather than themselves being the arbiters and sources of policy. In this respect there might appear to be some parallels between Confucius and Nietzsche. The Confucian *junzi* in monopolizing government office cleaved to a moral outlook unintelligible to the common man. Nietzsche believed that the deeds of the *übermenschen* moved history forward, but he also held that their standards, such as they were, they set for themselves and in so doing conventional morality was overturned. By contrast, the Confucian *junzi* never lost sight of the prescription that the first responsibility of government was to attend to the material needs of the population and that no governing regime would prosper without the trust of its people. Michael Leifer may have been suggesting that in Lee's outlook there was more of a Nietzschean detachment than a Confucian attention to building and maintaining trust.

These and other writings of Michael Leifer on Singapore are also revealing for what they do not say. He was always measured in his assessment of the strengths and weaknesses of the Singaporean project, a topic regarding which partisanship and passion often occlude analysis. In particular, he was never especially concerned to take the Singaporean regime to task for its democratic failings since, while he was well aware of them, he did not consider such an approach to be especially enlightening, given the gulf that still separated Singaporean society from the Western social environment that had engendered the practice of liberal democracy.

Indonesian foreign policy

Having clarified some of the assumptions implicit in Michael Leifer's scholarly work, this chapter returns to the analysis of Indonesia to consider the foundations that were laid for that final seminar. As has been noted, his earliest writing on Southeast Asia was concerned with Cambodia and with Singapore. Both were and are states whose impact on regional order has been severely limited, though the rulers of the latter have strained mightily to overcome their geographical and other constraints. From individual states he moved to develop a synthetic account of the Southeast Asian region, writing in the early 1970s books on the development of nationhood and on the practice of foreign policy. Both books contained chapters on regional association, the focus of which was ASEAN, its antecedents and its prospects. Indonesia, as the core regional state, already looms large in these books, and thus his next major project was almost inevitably on the foreign policy of the archipelagic state, a work published in 1983.

His writing on Indonesia is factually extremely dense, yet the story line is never obscured by the detail. And it again appears to follow from his work on Cambodia and Singapore. Both of these states were consumers rather than producers of regional order. For the term 'regional order' to have any coherent meaning, it would need to consist in something more than the mere manifestation, in a particular geographical location, of a wider or global balance. It should be recalled that when Michael Leifer's first three books were written the Indochina war was raging. As he later noted, 'When Indonesia helped to form ASEAN in August 1967, the regional environment was dominated by the scale of US military intervention in Indochina'.[25] Michael Leifer was one of very few analysts who were attempting to see beyond this particular episode of the Cold War to the possible shape of the era beyond. If distinctive regional arrangements were ever to emerge, the success or failure of ASEAN would be crucial, and the major player in any of these developments would be Indonesia. Indonesia's foreign policy thus merited the closest attention, and this project resulted in what was possibly Michael Leifer's best individual work.

His depiction in that book of the manifest failings of Sukarno's leadership once he had assumed direct control of the government in 1959 is consistent with the treatment of that theme in his last seminar. Though he notes the more sober and realistic goals of the New Order, and he underlines Suharto's preparedness to set aside grand visions for the nation's international status in the interests of domestic economic development, the depiction of the practice of foreign policy is highly critical. Thus, regarding for example the Jakarta conference on Cambodia, convened by Suharto in 1970, Michael Leifer's judgment is dismissive:

> As a diplomatic occasion, the Jakarta Conference was depicted within Indonesia as the most important undertaking of its kind since the Bandung gathering in April 1955. As an exercise in the projection of influence within South-East Asia, it was virtually a non-event; even the US government displayed only a tepid interest... [A]part from its being so evidently a gathering of supporters of the political *status quo* after the fall of Sihanouk, the conference had no bearing whatsoever on the cruel course of events in Cambodia itself... All in all, it was a sobering experience for a government which had insisted on incorporating its prescription for regional order in the founding document of ASEAN.[26]

From the vantage point of the early 1980s, Michael Leifer concluded that the policies of the Suharto administration were to be understood in terms of 'both a spectre and a vision'.[27] The former was the continuance of great power interference in the region, the latter was the construction of the most comprehensive forms of cooperation across Southeast Asia. To that point, efforts to avoid the first and promote the second had largely proved ineffectual.

In many respects Michael Leifer's book on ASEAN is an extension of the project begun with his account of Cambodia under Sihanouk and continued through the analysis of Indonesian foreign policy. The focus of the work, however, is much less on domestic issues, and as it deals mostly with ASEAN's grappling with the Kampuchea/Cambodia issue it will not be considered in detail here. It is noteworthy, nevertheless, that the assessment of the group is somewhat more positive. After a halting beginning, the ASEAN states had been forced by the Vietnamese invasion of Cambodia to focus their collective energies in order to confront a material threat to their interests. This effort was at least a partial success. Thus Michael Leifer expresses the view that by 1982 'ASEAN had made its mark over Kampuchea as a diplomatic community'.[28] This achievement should not be overstated. The crisis was not a consequence of any actions taken by the member states, and their cooperation, which undoubtedly contributed to the eventual resolution of the problem, led to nothing more positive than the *status quo ante*, albeit a development that opened the way to Vietnam's later ASEAN membership. In short, this was less a positive than a reactive initiative. While Southeast Asia had come some way since the 1970 Jakarta conference, its collective capacity for generating regional order was still modest. In some respects, the strong reservations Michael Leifer later expressed regarding the potential for the ASEAN Regional Forum as an agent of regional order were rooted in his assessment of the limitations of ASEAN.[29]

ASEAN norms as a source of regional order: a category mistake

'We shall only be able to play an effective role if we ourselves are possessed of a great national vitality.' This quotation appears twice in *Indonesia's Foreign Policy* (where indeed it occurs in the book's concluding sentence) and also in *The Foreign Relations of the New States*.[30] Michael Leifer apparently regarded these sentiments as so important that he quoted them again in his much later piece on Indonesian nationalism.[31] What deeper meaning did he discern in this remark? In *Dilemmas of Statehood in Southeast Asia* he suggests that the Indonesian democracy of the 1950s collapsed because it was 'deficient in terms of its socio-political underpinning',[32] by which he meant that there was no generally acknowledged framework of beliefs and loyalties existent for the country as a whole within which there could be an orderly contest between competing political forces and programmes. His discussion in that text shows that he believed that such a framework would only be erected when the mass of ordinary citizens felt that the operations of the political realm had a positive impact upon their lives. It would not be produced through the proclamation of false panaceas or by appealing to sectional religious identities.

In a lecture delivered at the National University of Singapore in 1987 on the subject of ASEAN he noted that in attempting to develop norms of regional association there was something of a contest, in Southeast Asia, between what he termed 'the visionary and practical conceptions of regional order'.[33] In his conclusion he suggests that in the working out of this contest there is not 'adequate attention being paid to the commonplace'.[34] Though often sought out by policy practitioners, Michael Leifer generally eschewed practical advice, but here he seems to be proposing that ASEAN focus more on real and practical problems than on grandiose conceptions. To take a concrete example, in our own discussions at the beginning of 2001 on the 'haze' problem that beset Southeast Asia in 1997-98 (and that was in evidence again in 2004) he was in agreement that ASEAN was much more efficient at producing declarations and agreements than at addressing the root causes of what threatened to become an environmental and economic disaster.[35] This was so because the latter would require, at the very least, disagreeable sentiments to be expressed regarding Indonesia's internal governance.

It is rare for an academic author to speak directly to his audience regarding his intentions. With a writer as understated and analytical as Michael Leifer it could be expected that the analysis would be the exclusive source of the voice. This is generally true of his writings, yet there is an important exception to this rule, in the form of a 'Postscript' to his 1972 study, *Dilemmas of Statehood in Southeast Asia*. Having noted that the work contains a good deal of criticism of a part of the world where the author 'is not domiciled' his analysis might thus be regarded as 'presumptuous'. While not rejecting such a reaction, Michael Leifer offers the following comments:

> Nonetheless, there can be no doubt that the peoples of Southeast Asia face a great number of serious problems which they need to tackle in a forthright way. In this respect, there has been a tendency to romanticize the Asian condition, certainly in the rhetoric of some leaders. It is with this tendency to delude in mind that this book has been written, in the hope that whether from conviction or anger the Asian audience, for whom it is in part intended, will be critical not only of its contents but also of their own societies.[36]

These sentiments are utterly consistent with the rejection of rationalist doctrines characteristic of Kedourie and Oakeshott.[37] The nations of Southeast Asia confront many practical problems. Doctrines such as nationalism, or indeed inflated notions of regionalism, will not help with their resolution. In practice they may actually do real harm, absorbing energies in chimerical programmes or serving to deflect the criticism that might otherwise be the due of ineffective or corrupt rulers. On this view, real politics is a constant attending to practical issues through the reconciliation – always impermanent – of conflicting interests within a structure of rules for such reconciliation. Michael Leifer's statement is a plea for normal politics in a region still too much influenced by visions of grander but poorly founded projects.

If it is accepted that the philosophical basis of Michael Leifer's work is to be found in the ideas of Kedourie and Oakeshott, then there are major implications for his understanding of 'order'. These implications, moreover, sustain the position proposed at the beginning of this chapter that attention to the domestic dimension is fundamental to an understanding of this issue. Kedourie and Oakeshott had little time for international politics as an intellectual project, though Kedourie had originally been a student of Martin Wight (perhaps the most influential British writer on the subject, and certainly the most learned). Not only did Kedourie enjoy cordial relations with his former teacher after joining the LSE staff, but after Wight's untimely death he delivered a lecture paying tribute both to the extraordinary range of his knowledge and to his inspirational teaching style.[38] However, as Terry Nardin has shown, Oakeshott's ideas can be made to inform a remarkably coherent understanding of 'the society of states'.[39] ASEAN, from the Oakeshott perspective, is a species of 'purposive' organization. Its constituents, however, are states, and in so far as states exist to pursue the notion of politics defined above – in short, to the extent that their proceedings are governed by the rule of law – they cannot be wholly devoted to a external purpose or programme with any more than merely rhetorical content. And it should be noted that most ASEAN member states aspire to this character, though there are still some examples in the region of ideological or military regimes (and one or two to which the term 'quasi-state' might apply).[40] It follows from this position that either ASEAN is an organization conforming to norms possessed only of rhetorical force or it is an organization incapable of reconciling its programme with the fundamental character of its constituent elements. Whichever alternative is the case, the notion of an ASEAN 'regional order' is incoherent. While there is no specific evidence that Michael Leifer explicitly reasoned thus – and as an analyst of concrete developments he was not required to do so – it can be understood why he preferred to characterize ASEAN as a 'diplomatic community' rather than as an organization bound by specific norms. For diplomacy is a tool that serves the interests of states rather than subordinates those interests to any wider purpose or conception of order.

Notes

1 *Indonesia's Foreign Policy* (London: Allen & Unwin/RIIA, 1983), 110–11. Unless otherwise indicated, all references in this chapter are to works authored by Michael Leifer.
2 'New Emerging Forces', in *Dictionary of the Modern Politics of South-East Asia* (London: Routledge, 1995), 186.
3 *Indonesia's Foreign Policy*, 181.
4 'Israel's President in Singapore: Political Catalysis and Transnational Politics', *The Pacific Review* vol 1 (1988), no 4, 341–52; c.f. *Singapore's Foreign Policy: coping with vulnerability* (London: Routledge, 2000), 91–4. The former essay was written on the invitation of the present author while acting as guest editor for this number of *The Pacific Review*. Michael Leifer was a member of the original editorial board.
5 Tim Dunne, *Inventing International Society: A History of the English School* (New York: St.Martin's Press/St. Antony's College, 1998).
6 Brian Porter, 'A Brief History Continued, 1972–2002', in Harry Bauer and Elisabetta Brighi eds, *International Relations at LSE. A History of 75 Years* (London: Millennium Publishing, 2003), 39–40.
7 'A Personal Note', in Sylvia Kedourie ed., *Elie Kedourie 1926–1992. History, Philosophy, Politics* (London: Frank Cass, 1998), 29–30. See more generally, Michael Leifer, *Zionism and Palestine in British opinion and policy, 1945–1949* (London: LSE unpublished PhD thesis, 1959). The present author took Kedourie's course at the LSE in 1972–73. Over a lunch in January 2001 at the LSE with Michael Yahuda, Christopher Hughes and myself, each of us having discussed Kedourie's influence on our lives, Michael Leifer remarked, 'He is the reason we are all here'.
8 Elie Kedourie, *The Chatham House Version and other Middle-Eastern Studies* (London: Weidenfeld & Nicolson, 1970).
9 Elie Kedourie, *Nationalism* 3rd edition (London: Hutchinson, 1966), 140. See also, 'Introduction', Elie Kedourie ed. and intro., *Nationalism in Asia and Africa* (London: Weidenfeld and Nicolson, 1971), 1–152.
10 *Zionism and Palestine in British Opinion and Policy, 1945–1949,* 265a.
11 *Zionism and Palestine in British Opinion and Policy, 1945–1949,* 267, 274.
12 *Dilemmas of Statehood in Southeast Asia* (Singapore: Asia Pacific Press, 1972), 27.
13 Christopher R. Hughes, 'Nationalism, Multipolarity and Multilateralism in Chinese Foreign Policy: Implications for Southeast Asia', IDSS–LSE Conference paper, May 2004.
14 Ang Cheng Guan, 'Michael Leifer on "Cambodia and the Third IndoChina Conflict"', IDSS–LSE Conference paper, May 2004.
15 *Cambodia: the Search for Security* (New York: Praeger, 1967), 84–106; *The Foreign Relations of the New States* (Camberwell: Longman Australia, 1974), 50–3; *Dilemmas of Statehood in Southeast Asia*, 109–10.
16 Ang Cheng Guan, 'Michael Leifer on "Cambodia and the Third IndoChina Conflict"', IDSS–LSE Conference paper, May 2004, 12.

17 Khong Yuen Foong, 'The Pre-requisites of Regional Order: Leifer, the English School, and Southeast Asia', IDSS–LSE Conference paper, May 2004.
18 Elie Kedourie, *Democracy and Arab Political Culture* 2nd edition (London: Frank Cass, 1994), 25–36.
19 See Elie Kedourie, 'Michael Oakeshott: A Colleague's View' and Alan Beattie, 'Elie Kedourie's Philosophical History', in Sylvia Kedourie ed., *Elie Kedourie 1926–1992. History, Philosophy, Politics* (London: Frank Cass, 1998), 5–7, 109–31. The present author attended Oakeshott's seminar in 1972–73.
20 'Communal Violence in Singapore', *Asian Survey* vol 4 (1964), no 10, 1115–21.
21 *Dilemmas of Statehood in Southeast Asia*, 112.
22 *Singapore's Foreign Policy*, 142.
23 'Triumph of the Will', *Far Eastern Economic Review* 15 November 1990, 27.
24 *Dilemmas of Statehood in Southeast Asia,* 112.
25 *Indonesia's Foreign Policy*, 130.
26 *Indonesia's Foreign Policy*, 135.
27 *Indonesia's Foreign Policy*, 170.
28 *ASEAN and the Security of South-East Asia* (London: Routledge, 1989), 119.
29 *The ASEAN Regional Forum*, Adelphi Paper 302 (London: Oxford University Press, 1996).
30 *Indonesia's Foreign Policy*, 112, 181; *The Foreign Relations of the New States,* 103.
31 'The Changing Temper of Indonesian Nationalism', in *Asian Nationalism* (London: Routledge, 1999), 168.
32 *Dilemmas of Statehood in Southeast Asia*, 100.
33 *ASEAN's Search for Regional Order* (Singapore: National University of Singapore, Faculty of Arts and Social Sciences Lecture 12, 1987), 20.
34 *ASEAN's Search for Regional Order*, 21.
35 James Cotton, 'ASEAN and the Southeast Asian "Haze": Challenging the Prevailing Modes of Regional Engagement', *Pacific Affairs* vol 72 (1999), no 2, 331–51.
36 *Dilemmas of Statehood in Southeast Asia*, 150.
37 Michael Oakeshott, *Rationalism in Politics and Other Essays* (London: Methuen, 1962), 1–36.
38 Elie Kedourie, 'Religion and Politics: Arnold Toynbee and Martin Wight' (Fourth Martin Wight Memorial Lecture), *British Journal of International Studies* vol 5 (1979), April, 6–14.
39 Terry Nardin, *Law, Morality and the Relations of States* (Princeton, NJ: Princeton University Press, 1983).
40 Robert H. Jackson, *Quasi-States: Sovereignty, International Relations and the Third World* (Cambridge: Cambridge University Press, 1990).

15 Michael Leifer's contribution to Southeast Asian studies

Michael Yahuda

Michael Leifer was a friend and colleague for nearly forty years and we enjoyed some thirty years together as close colleagues at the London School of Economics. I knew him perhaps too well to be able to encapsulate his thinking and writing within any of the particular schools of International Relations to which it has become fashionable to assign scholars. Moreover, I am not really a specialist on Southeast Asia as my main field of interest centres more on China. Indeed most of what I know about Southeast Asia I learned from him. Nevertheless having sat by side with Michael as we ran together a postgraduate course, 'The International Politics of the Asia-Pacific', as an option for the International Relations Master's degree, I had many opportunities to hear and see first hand his presentations on the subject and his criticisms of the presentations of others. One of the highlights of our course was the Spring Term Seminar in which every year leading scholars and practitioners would give talks to our postgraduate students on contemporary developments in the region. These provided occasions to see Michael at his best, as he would engage visiting speakers in challenging some of their deeper assumptions and analytical approaches. He would do so always with a glint in his eye and he knew when to be gentle, say with a student who was on the point of completing his or her PhD thesis, and when to be tough, say with a leading authority on the subject. It is that close association with Michael Leifer that gives me the temerity to speak on his contribution to the field of Southeast Studies.

Although Michael Leifer was the most dispassionate of scholars, who rarely allowed his personal experience to enter into his framework of analysis or to intrude into his writings, his intellectual understanding of the subject was deeply informed by his personal history. I should perhaps make it clear that although Michael was diffident about injecting a personal note into his scholarly writings, he was a man of forthright views and he gave full rein to these in his many writings. But the clue to the origins, depth and intellectual coherence of his thinking, I submit, is to be found in his personal history.

Michael Leifer was born into a Jewish family in the East End of London. His father was a cabinet-maker. The young Michael was an accomplished musician and taught the violin to help pay for his Bar Mitzva and he even performed for the London School Boys Symphony Orchestra. The love of music stayed with him throughout his life and, more importantly for our purposes, so did his Jewishness that was inculcated from an early age. Later in life as a busy scholar and the senior academic administrator at the LSE, Michael found the time to play a leading role in his local synagogue in southwest London. In fact Michael came into Southeast Asian Studies almost by accident. His PhD thesis, which was supervised by the late great Middle East scholar and writer on nationalism, Elie Kedourie, was entitled, 'Zionism and Palestine in British opinion and policy, 1945–1949.' After being awarded his PhD in 1959, Michael found his first academic job, on the recommendation of Kedourie, at the University of Adelaide in South Australia. At that time there was little interest in Adelaide in the Middle East and with the encouragement of Professor Duncan, Michael shifted his attention to Southeast Asia, 'Australia's near north'. It was his supervision of a Cambodian student that first drew Michael's attention to that country, on which he subsequently published his first book.[1] By this time he had returned to England, where from 1963 he was a lecturer at the Centre for South East Asian Studies at the University of Hull, from which he moved to the LSE in 1969.

Several important points should be noted from this brief personal history:

- At that time in the 1960s Michael Leifer was in an unusual position as an academic specialist on Southeast Asia who had no previous experience in the colonial civil service or in any of the Western armies that had been stationed there. Nor did his interest arise from being married to a Southeast Asian. He and his wife, Frances, had been teenagers together in East London. Nor did Michael have an attachment to any particular Asian country either through his parents or from having lived there for any time. Unlike many who were drawn to the region because of their opposition to the Vietnam War, Michael Leifer had no political axe to grind. In other words, it was his dispassionate quality that was highly distinctive at that time and that has remained with him ever since.
- His Jewishness had a huge impact on the values that Michael Leifer brought to bear in his many writings. It combined a deep humanitarianism with a tough-mindedness that allowed no room for sentimentality. Like all the major religions, Judaism contains within it much that is diverse and contentious and yet it stresses law, due authority, reasoned argument and charity. It provided Michael Leifer not only with a code of values that was marked by a deep personal integrity, but also with a basis for empathy with the great religions of Southeast Asia and the different ways in which they veered from the strictly orthodox interpretations. Michael's Jewishness also sensitized him to the vulnerabilities and challenges to survival of which most Southeast Asian peoples are conscious in one form or another.
- Michael Leifer's thesis provided him with many insights into the problems of de-colonization, the struggles for independence, the development of national identities, the difficulties of reconciling competing ethnic groups

and the complexities of the relationship between these more local politics and the interests of the greater powers. All of these were evident in the struggles that led to the independence of Israel and they read like a list of the key issues faced by the nascent states of Southeast Asia. No wonder that Michael Leifer's first book possesses the intellectual maturity and sureness of touch that would normally be associated with a far more established writer.

Security and the balance of power

Michael Leifer is often regarded as an adherent of the Realist School. In Martin Wight's terms these are the hard men of International Relations who deal with blood and guns. This is the school that is associated with German *realpolitik* which places the determinism of power and survival at the heart of the subject and which therefore focuses exclusively upon the state as the irreducible unit of military power and more specifically on the great powers whose relations determine the character of any given era. I think, however, that such a labelling does Michael Leifer a grave disservice.

To be sure, Michael Leifer was very much concerned with the problems of security and survival of states in Southeast Asia and no amount of pious liberalism about the significance of trade or economic interdependence and institutionalism could address the very real problems of Southeast Asia. Michael Leifer was always a close student of the balance of power, but more in the sense of the distribution of power than as some kind of mechanism that operates almost independently of human will – as suggested by Kenneth Waltz's neo-realism.[2] Perhaps it is worth citing Leifer's view on the balance of power at greater length:

> Although it is possible to identify the patterns of major regional relationships, the term balance of power as a generalization to explain that pattern is less than precise. As an indication of the condition of the relationship between states, it means the distribution of power. But the problems of introducing precision into an assessment of such a distribution are legion if only because quantitative indices are not sufficient on their own and do not lend themselves to necessary comparison. Balance of power as an actual policy of states has been clearer in terms of a common goal which has been to deny the emergence of any undue dominance or hegemony. Traditionally the instrument of the balance has been war because in the last resort it was the only means available with which to preserve the independence of states. The advent of nuclear weapons, however, has transformed the classical positive relationship between war and policy. And in East Asia, three of the four principal powers possess such weapons if to a differing degree.[3]

It will be seen that balance of power is understood here in the classical sense associated with Hedley Bull [4] and the reference to 'order' in the title of the essay from which the above quotation is drawn, is suggestive that Leifer could be placed among the adherents of the 'English School'. However, unlike those, who have sought to address the guidelines shaping international politics as a whole, Leifer has confined himself to Southeast Asia and has eschewed on the whole considerations as to the extent to which international relations correspond to some kind of society. Thus Leifer's use of the term 'order', which is one of the central concepts of the English School, especially as exemplified by Hedley Bull, is significantly different and distinctive. For him it is not sufficient that states should conduct their relations with due regard to the norms of international society. In Leifer's view 'order' – at least in its regional manifestation – should encompass more than an observation of common international rules about sovereignty, non-interference, etc., to be based on a regional balance of power that is congruent with the balance between the relevant external great powers so as to include a shared common perception of external threat and agreement about how these should be met.

Interestingly, once when being told that he was regarded as a Realist, Michael Leifer responded with a wry comment that he has been called 'worse names'. He regarded the Realist School as intellectually rich, incorporating a wide variety of writers and views that bore little resemblance to the caricature that is frequently encountered in International Relations literature on theory.

If there is a common thread that runs through Michael Leifer's very extensive writings it is his concern with the security problems of the smaller and lesser states of Southeast Asia. To be sure, he was ever alert to the way they have been affected by the changing relations between the external great powers. But the main emphasis has been on the lesser powers. His writings also displayed extraordinary sensitivity to the ways in which domestic sources of vulnerability interact with external security issues. Much of his scholarly effort was devoted to showing both the strengths and the limitations of Southeast Asian attempts to develop regional institutions, notably ASEAN and the ASEAN Regional Forum, to enhance their security through the management of conflict avoidance. Unlike the determinism often associated with Realism, Leifer's approach highlighted the importance of leadership and the wide scope for the exercise of choice. He did not engage in ananalysis of the balance of power in global terms nor did he confine himself to focusing on relations between the great powers. Rather his concerns were to examine how small or medium states in the region could survive in the context of competition between the great powers and how regional bodies could enhance the security of member states. It is therefore typical and illustrative of his approach that Leifer's first and last books should be focused on the problems of cultivating independence by the relatively small and vulnerable states of Cambodia and Singapore, respectively.[5]

Thus in the 1960s and 1970s Leifer's works focused principally upon the problems experienced in the aftermath of independence and how the establishment of new patterns of governance amid ethnic, cultural and social divergences affected and were affected by foreign relations. These are perhaps best illustrated in his *Dilemmas of Statehood* (1972) and *The Foreign Relations of New States* (1974). These were followed by studies that examined some of the problems bequeathed from the colonial era especially with regard to competing claims to territorial bounds on land and at sea. These may be seen, for example, from his monograph, *The Philippine Claim to Sabah* (1968), his various articles on the separation of Singapore from Malaysia, and his studies of the management of the Straits of Malacca, *Malacca, Singapore and Indonesia* (1978). The last drew Michael Leifer into a careful study of the emergence of the Law of the Sea Convention of 1982 and its impact on Southeast Asia.

With the recovery of the Southeast Asian states from the immediate problems following independence, Leifer's attention shifted to studying the evolving character of the region's main multilateral institution, ASEAN. Far from dismissing its effectiveness from a Realist perspective, Michael Leifer recognized early on its distinctive contribution as a mechanism for the management of conflict avoidance. But he contested attempts by other scholars to impose upon it theoretical constructs derived from other experiences of regionalism, notably that of Europe. At the same time he was not persuaded by the often overblown rhetoric of some of its leaders. It was an approach that he famously applied to the ASEAN Regional Forum too. Despite criticisms that he was too conservative and doubting, Leifer's monograph, *The ASEAN Regional Forum: Extending ASEAN's Model of Regional Security* (1996) has stood the test of time. Nevertheless Michael Leifer saw virtue in the enterprise as attested by his active participation in the Council for Security Cooperation in the Asia-Pacific (CSCAP), which served as a second-track diplomacy instrument for the ARF. Leifer served for two years as one of the co-chairmen of the EU team membership until his untimely death.

However, even as the ASEAN states prospered in the 1990s and developed new multilateral institutions, Michael Leifer never lost sight of their underlying fragility. That is perhaps why he attached more importance to the significance of good governance in the provision of domestic security, sound infrastructure and the delivery of economic performance than he did to the appearance of formal democratic institutions. And it was with a heavy heart that he delivered his last public presentation (to his beloved LSE seminar on the international politics of the Asia Pacific in early 2000) on the domestic turbulence in Indonesia that undermined its leadership role in ASEAN.

The significance of leadership and choice

From the outset Michael Leifer paid considerable attention to the role of leaders and the significance of the choices they could make. In part this stemmed from the relative weakness of the institutions in the new states (or states with entirely new political systems), but it also reflected his appreciation of the long-term implications of particular strategies chosen by Southeast Asian leaders and of their capacity to work together. For example, in an analysis of ASEAN's contribution to the security of the region, Leifer observed, 'the benefits from membership for promoting political stability have been mixed and have depended on qualities of leadership displayed unevenly within the Association'.[6]

Michael Leifer's first and last books may be seen as commentaries upon the international identities and strategies for survival chartered by the respective leaders, Prince Sihanouk of Cambodia (in the mid-1960s) and the then Senior Minister Lee Kuan Yew of Singapore, who had guided his island country since its forced separation from Malaysia in 1965. Although the strategies of neutrality of Cambodia at that point and of an assertive foreign policy by Singapore were arguably a product of circumstances, Leifer shows how in both cases these strategies were indelibly shaped by the personalities and domestic political choices made by both men.

Similarly, in his masterly unravelling of the furore raised by the visit of the Israeli President Herzog to Singapore in 1986, Michael Leifer shows how the responses of Dr Mahathir of Malaysia and Singapore's Lee Kuan Yew were both intensely personal, while raising major institutional implications for ASEAN. For Dr Mahathir it was a personal affront for Lee to have invited Israel's head of state when his political position in Malaysia had led him to emphasize the Islamic dimensions of his country (and his domestic Malay constituency) by declaring his solidarity with the Palestinian Arabs and his denunciation of what he saw as Jewish control of the international media. For his part, Lee Kuan Yew saw much in common between his country and the embattled state of Israel and considered that it was unpardonable of Mahathir to break the ASEAN norm of non-interference by claiming the right to say who could visit the sovereign state of Singapore.[7]

Perhaps it was his sensitivity to the importance of leaders (and those who advise them) that gave Michael Leifer unparalleled access to them in Southeast Asia. Doubtless that played a part, but it was also his unique intellectual qualities and his dispassionate perspectives that made them value his counsel. In any event Michael Leifer was able to use this vast network of associations to ensure that his analysis was always well informed and directed to the key issues of the region. It is a tribute to his integrity that he never betrayed the confidentiality of his sources, nor allowed them to distort his judgement. Indeed on more than one occasion a book or an article of his was banned for a time from one of the ASEAN countries. Interestingly, after the passage of a certain time the said country would quietly relent. Michael Leifer, to my knowledge, never recanted.

Teacher

If Michael Leifer's qualities as a researcher and writer will remain readily available to students of Southeast Asia, only his students will be able to recall his qualities as a teacher. He was a demanding teacher who gave of the highest quality himself and sought no less from his students. The result was that he was able to draw more quality out of students than many thought they had. All felt enriched by him and by the high standards he set.

This was particularly true of his supervision of research students. On more than one occasion Michael Leifer told me how rewarding he found the experience of beginning with a student who knew less than he and who was still finding his or her way in the theoretical intricacies attendant upon the subject, and who at the end of several years had mastered the theory and knew more about the particularities of the topic than even Leifer himself. Michael Leifer found the process of supervision itself to be the most pleasurable part of being a university teacher. Both he and the student learned from it and he had the unique enjoyment of seeing someone flourish and mature intellectually through their work together.

Michael Leifer's former students are now to be found in leading positions in government, business and academia throughout Southeast Asia. They are perhaps his most abiding contribution to Southeast Asian studies and more broadly to the future of Southeast Asia itself. He certainly cherished and nourished the relationship he had built up with them over the years.

Conclusion

Michael Leifer was my closest colleague at the London School of Economics and we had much in common. We were both Jews, who had strong, but not uncritical feelings about Israel and were both students of the international politics of East Asia – he of Southeast Asia and I of China. Neither of us had familial, personal or ideological ties to the region of our study. He once did me the honor of saying that 'we shared the same prejudices.' But be that is it may, I regarded Michael as my mentor. He had deep historical knowledge of his region, especially of its encounter with the West and the aftermath. His disciplined intellectual approach that always sought to explain contemporary developments within the framework of International Relations theory, without seeking to employ such theory as a straitjacket was a model that few could emulate. Nor did he seek to use developments in Southeast Asia as 'case studies' for the 'proof' of one theory or another. His was both the modest and the more daunting challenge of seeking to explain his subject in terms that could allow for generalizations and for general understanding. Indeed another facet of his contribution that should have been mentioned is his broadcasting. He always made himself available to the BBC World Service and other networks and was always able to place the latest news within a lucid and clear intellectual framework that reached beyond the specialist to the general listener.

Southeast Asia has lost one of its most sympathetic and knowledgeable friends, who precisely because of his incisive and often critical approach has influenced several generations of students and practitioners alike.

Notes

1 Michael Leifer, *Cambodia: The Search for Security* (London: Pall Mall Press and New York: Praeger, 1967).
2 Kenneth N. Waltz, *Theory of International Politics* (Reading, MA: Addison-Wesley, 1979).
3 Michael Leifer, 'The Balance of Power and Regional Order' in his (ed.), *The Balance of Power in East Asia* (Basingstoke: Macmillan, 1986), p. 145.
4 See his *The Anarchical Society, A Study of Order in International Politics* (London: Macmillan, 1977), chapter 5, pp. 101–126.
5 See note 1 for Cambodia. Michael Leifer's last book was *Singapore's Foreign Policy: Coping with Vulnerability* (London: Routledge, 2000).
6 Michael Leifer, *ASEAN and the Security of Southeast Asia* (London: Routledge, 1989), p. 151
7 Michael Leifer, 'Israel's President in Singapore: Political Catalysis and Transnational Politics' *Pacific Review*, vol. 1, no. 4 (1988), pp. 341–353.

Index

Note: ASEAN as an entry on its own has not been indexed as a main entry as it appears throughout the text